Living the Science of Mind

Living the Science of Mind

Ernest Holmes

DeVorss & Company, Publishers

ISBN: 0-87516-627-X
Library of Congress Catalog Number: 90-84240
Ninth Printing, 2000

DeVorss & Company, Publisher
P.O. Box 550
Marina del Rey, CA 90294-0550

For more information,
please visit our website: **www.devorss.com**

Printed in The United States of America

Contents

A Word from the Publisher

THE ESSAYS collected in this book have been drawn, with two exceptions, from Ernest Holmes' 48-lesson *Home Study Course in the Science of Mind* (subsequently titled, *Change Your Thinking, Change Your Life*), which was first issued in 1939 as an alternative to the study of the Science of Mind at a Religious Science center or church, and which took on these essays in 1953. Since the course has been available only from the Religious Science organization in Los Angeles as advertised in its magazine, *Science of Mind*, the essays have quite understandably been overlooked by many others besides those who took their instruction with a teacher or minister.

Ranging in length from a single page to several pages, these self-contained pieces stand wholly on their own, without the necessity of being read consecutively, having originally been keyed somewhat loosely to the study-course lessons they accompanied. For the lessons themselves, the reader should turn to the six volumes of *Change Your Thinking, Change Your Life*. However, for the text of some of Ernest Holmes' most important writings, he need go no further than this book.

The essays gathered here stand in unique relationship to the body of Holmes' work, which spans approximately forty years. Serving as in-depth commentary on the many topics of his textbook, *The Science of Mind*, these pieces together make a companion volume to the textbook that nothing else in the corpus of Holmes' writings, with the possible exception of his *How to Use the Science of Mind*, quite does. Using the Topics & Pages table provided on p. xi, the user of this book should be able to locate subjects directly related to any part of the teaching portion of the textbook (i.e. pp. 25–422 of *The Science of Mind*).

A word about several of the essays is in order. Two of them are taken, with the kind permission of the estate of Ernest Holmes and the United Church of Religious Science, from the long-out-of-print anthology *Mind Remakes Your World* (1941), edited by Ernest Holmes and Maude Allison Lathem. These are "The New Thought Movement" (p. 64), which is all but a dated portion of the introduction to the volume, and "Science of Mind" (p. 7), which was Holmes' contribution to the body of the anthology. The essay "A Brief History of New Thought" (p. 58) is given in its entirety except for several consecutive paragraphs on mysticism that bear no clear relation to the essay and that may have been accidentally interpolated, especially since the paragraph immediately following them takes up precisely where the text before them leaves off. However, because of their inherent interest, we have printed them as an essay in their own right with the title "What the Mystics Have Taught" (p. 56), borrowed from the title of the relevant chapter (20) in *The Science of Mind*.

As for the unused material from the six-volume study course, besides the lesson material keyed to the *Science of Mind* textbook, we have omitted the serial commentaries on Thomas Troward's *Bible Mystery, Bible Meaning* and on Ralph Waldo Emerson's essays "History" and "Spiritual Laws"; the keys to metaphysical charts appearing in the textbook; all but one of the treatment-meditations given separately from the essays (the sole exception being too exemplary to omit; see p. 434); poetry; and all but one of the longer pieces that have since been issued separately as booklets (the exception being "What We Believe" [p. 83], an important document a somewhat fuller statement of which appears in the booklet *What Religious Science Teaches*).

In compiling these essays the effort was made to group them topically instead of adhering to the more random order in which they appear in the six volumes. While such an arrangement is necessarily somewhat subjective, it is hoped that the present ordering will nonetheless be of help to the reader. The compilation roughly corresponds to the following topical outline:

Topics & Pages

Publication of this book makes widely available, for the first time, some of the maturest and most interesting, personal, and helpful of Ernest Holmes' writings, covering a broad range of topics. As such, it should prove to be a sure guide to the Truth student and a rare companion to, as well as commentary on, Holmes' masterpiece, *The Science of Mind.*

ARTHUR VERGARA
Editor

Science of Mind Communications has a large selection of additional books on subjects related to Living the Science of Mind. *Write to:*

SCIENCE OF MIND
POST OFFICE BOX 75127
LOS ANGELES, CA 90075

Living the Science of Mind

What Is the Science of Mind?

THE SCIENCE of Mind is an outgrowth of the spiritual faith which people have had throughout the ages. Before science was conceived, the Presence of God was felt. Before ever mental actions or reactions were analyzed, history was filled with instances of men and women who had experienced God.

The Science of Mind is comparatively new, but the mental experience of the Invisible Universe is as old as the history of man. It is new in that for the first time in history we have put together all findings which contribute to the establishment of man's relationship with the Universe, to the end that he may be able to apply his spiritual understanding to the everyday problems of human life.

This science necessarily starts with the proposition that we are living in a Spiritual Universe whose sole government is one of Harmony, and that the use of right ideas is the enforcement of its Law.

The Science of Mind is built on the theory that there is One Infinite Mind which of necessity includes all that is, whether it be the intelligence in man, the life in the animal, or the invisible Presence which is God. In it we learn to have a spiritual sense of things. This spiritual sense of things is what is meant by the Consciousness of Christ. To be able to discern the spiritual idea back of its physical symbol is to use the mind that Jesus used.

The Science of Mind is intensely practical because it teaches us how to use the Mind Principle for definite purposes, such as helping those who are sick, impoverished, or unhappy. Each one of us should learn to become a practitioner of this science, a demonstrator of its Principle, a conscious user of its Power. Power already exists, but the existence of Power is of no particular value to us until we use it. We must not only be conscious of Power, but we must be actively conscious of it. This is one of the first lessons we learn in the Science of Mind.

This science is more than mental; it is also spiritual, since we live in a Spiritual Universe. The Science of Mind declares the

Truth about this Spiritual Universe and it also declares the Truth about false belief, considering everything which is opposed to Good as an accumulation of human thought, the collective negative suggestion of the race.

Wrong conditions are resolved into false beliefs, and through the use of right ideas a transformation of thought takes place. We learn to build our ideas upon an affirmative rather than a negative factor. To state the Truth and deny or disregard that which in belief is opposed to it, is to prove that the Principle of the Science of Mind is actual.

The ever-increasing thousands of persons who are daily proving this Principle add to our conviction that we are dealing with the most intense reality the human mind has ever conceived. The practice of this science is the application of a definite technique, the law of right thought, of true spiritual understanding.

It is necessary that you have a complete conviction that there is such a Principle and that you understand the scientific use and application of it. Conscious knowledge alone gives you the conscious control of the laws of nature. The advance in any science always corresponds to the conscious use made of the laws of nature. There could be no advance in science without such conscious use of nature's laws.

It would be unwise to approach the Science of Mind with superstition. You must approach it with understanding. Above all, you must approach it with the definite intention in mind of making conscious use of its Principle. You must come to realize that Mind exists as a Principle in the Universe, just as electricity exists as a principle.

Once you understand this it will not be difficult to see that thought is the tool of Mind, that right ideas enforce the Law of Mind; nor will it be difficult to see that physical objects are fundamentally spiritual in their nature, that an objective fact is but a symbol of a subjective or an invisible cause. It certainly follows that if you are to make practical use of the Science of Mind you must be able to convert things into thoughts, and by changing the stream of consciousness produce a corresponding change in an objective situation, whether this be used for helping those who are sick, or to meet any other need.

2

The question naturally arises whether man has a right to use his thought for whatever purpose he wills. The more sincere one is, the more likely he is to ask this question. Strangely enough, he would not ask this relative to any other science but would feel that all laws exist to be used, and any sane person would naturally desire to benefit himself and others through the use of nature's laws. Why should any exception be made to the greatest of all laws—the Law of Mind in Action—and the enforcement of this Law through right ideas?

One of our fundamental propositions is that God is all there is. When you say God is all there is, that includes everything, all possibility and all action, for Spirit is the invisible essence and substance of all form. It is impossible to separate the highest use of this science from the most exalted conception of an immanent Spirit, a transcendent Spirit, an available Spirit.

Perhaps one might at first have an aversion to the idea of using spiritual power for material purposes, but in the Science of Mind we discover that there are no final material purposes; that whether life exists in an objective or a subjective state, whether it is visible or invisible, all is Spirit; that Spirit or Intelligence, plus what It does, constitutes the entire Universe, including man.

The Science of Mind reveals that every man is a potential Christ. Every man has inherent God-Power within him. And how could this God-Power be used other than through his thought? Since it would be impossible for a man to act as an intelligent being unless he could first think, the very idea of man supposes a center of consciousness, a center of thought activity. The Science of Mind reveals that this center of God-activity within each one is a complete and unique manifestation of the Parent Mind; that the Power of God does actually exist in man.

It is a basic proposition in our philosophy that we live in a Mental or Spiritual Universe and that things can be resolved into thoughts. This is the foundation upon which all scientific practice must be established, and when you are able to establish this premise in your own thought, you at once find yourself equipped with an instrument through which you can change your environment.

The Science of Mind does not deny the physical universe. The objective universe is the Body of God. That Body includes our physical being. In reality every idea of our physical being is a Divine idea.

The misconception of the Spiritual Universe causes our universe to appear separated from good, and in fact we experience this separation. But that which is a fact in experience is not necessarily true in principle. Bondage cannot be conceived by the Divine, and yet we all know that bondage is a part of man's experience.

In trying to seek a solution for this enigma we must either conclude that there is an ultimate good and an ultimate evil in the universe, or we must conclude that there is but one Ultimate, which is Good, and that this Ultimate by Its very nature and by our very nature is compelled to appear to each one of us in the form of our belief. If you can accept this proposition it will be easy enough for you to see how it is that false belief binds humanity.

If that which binds is false belief and not the Truth, then you will see why Jesus told us that a knowledge of the Truth would produce freedom. He did not mean that knowledge of the Truth creates freedom, but that knowledge of the Truth makes us free by aligning us with that which was never bound.

If we accept the foregoing conclusions as true it follows that the Divine Creative Principle is already perfect, having neither confusion nor chaos within It. It was, is, and will remain exactly perfect. Our individual universe shall be redeemed from its bondage in such degree as we become actively conscious of the Truth of our being. We must use the Law as a Law of Liberty, else we shall be using It as a law of bondage.

The Science of Mind provides us with a definite technique for the use of this Law and teaches how each one can use It in freeing himself and demonstrating to his complete satisfaction that right ideas, correctly used, can and must produce right conditions.

So far, science, revelation, and philosophy have arrived at no conclusion which could disturb this proposition, and every day the physical sciences are more completely proving that the physical universe in which we live is more like a *gigantic thought* than anything else. Now if the physical universe, or the cosmos as a whole, is more like a gigantic thought than anything else, it follows that our immediate world is a part of this thought.

How amazed we all should be if we awoke some fine morning, not only with the absolute conviction that this is so, but also with the inner insight which would enable us to see exactly what it means. Then we too should be able to say to the paralyzed man, "Stretch forth thine hand!" But before we can do this we must see the principle of freedom instead of the belief in a paralysis of this principle.

The Science of Mind is a reinterpretation of the Universe by a process of thought which Jesus used. We learn that there is one body, the body of right ideas. Jesus sensed this Body of God, which includes man's body, as a perfect, harmonious unit, and he realized that the evil which binds man is not a principle within itself nor a thing of itself, and most certainly not a person, but merely a false system of thought. He understood that his knowledge of good annihilated that which denied good. This fundamental fact he clearly brought out in his teaching; the Truth known is followed by the Truth demonstrated.

The Science of Mind does not necessarily create a new religion or sect, for it may be added to any spiritual system of thought since it is a complement to all. The person who already has the greatest spiritual faith will make the most active demonstrator of Truth. The person who naturally has a spiritual insight or who has already trained himself to have spiritual insight will more quickly sense the truths which the Science of Mind portrays. He will more quickly lay hold of its technique and more perfectly demonstrate for himself and others that the Invisible is the cause of the visible.

For every science there must be a technique or a way of proving its truth. Science of itself is a knowledge of laws and principles and systematic arrangement. And the technique of any science is the way in which we use this knowledge of laws and principles.

Applying this rule (which is common to all sciences) to the Science of Mind, it naturally follows that if there is such a principle as Universal Mind, and if It does work according to the Law of Cause and Effect, and if thought, self-contemplation, or self-knowingness is that which stimulates Its action, then correct thinking can and must produce objective or visible results.

We must lay even more stress on the *use* of the Science of Mind than we do on seeking to establish its Principle. As a matter of fact its Principle is self-evident; its use is exactly what we make it. And the first thing that any student of this science should do is determine to make daily use of it. In this, as in all other things, we should be practical. Too much study of any principle without making conscious use of it will lead to mere theorizing, and I am sure we all wish practical results.

You are ready to use the Principle governing the Science of Mind the very moment you accept the fact that there is such a principle and that it does operate through your thought. But this seems to be the place where many fall down. They talk so much about the Principle and use It so little. They permit themselves to become confused by the introduction of contradictory ideas. They spend too much time in merely philosophizing, theorizing, speculating, until finally they live in a world of wistful wishing, of daydreams.

You must come to see that the Science of Mind is an actual Principle to be definitely used; that no matter how much Good may exist in the Universe, only as much Good can come to you as you can conceive. Above all things, determine now to use this science. Do not say, "I expect to have understanding enough within a year to use it." Seize upon whatever facts present themselves to your mind today, begin to use such truth as you grasp, and you will become an effective practitioner.

Science of Mind

LET US approach the Science of Mind and Spiritual Psychology with its vast possibilities, without fear; in true humility, happily, willing to accept, eager to experiment.

There is nothing supernatural in metaphysical laws. That which today appears supernatural, after it has become thoroughly understood, will be found to be spontaneously natural. We know that faith has worked miracles in the lives of men in all ages, and to those who follow different religious convictions, its wonder-working power has produced amazing results.

We know that the prayer of faith has healed the sick. Naturally, we ask ourselves how such results are brought about. If we were to ask the average person who teaches the principles of Spiritual Mind Power, no doubt we should receive an answer similar to the following: "We believe in God as the Infinite Spirit permeating everything. We believe that there is a Law of Mind which responds to our thought, faith and conviction. We believe that the universe in which we live is a Spiritual System and that the Kingdom of Good is ours and is present with us now." Such declarations as these, meaningful as they are, are statements of one's conviction, but a declaration of faith in certain principles is quite different from the conscious use of such principles. It is not enough for an electrician to say he believes in electricity, that he believes it to be an ever-present reality or energy, or that it can run all the machinery in the world; it is necessary for him to apply his understanding of electricity for the definite purpose of producing light, heat and motive power.

Too many people in our field mistake a declaration of belief in Spirit for an effective mental treatment. No greater mistake can be made. We must not only believe that God, or Divine Reality, is all Power; we must use our belief in a definite way. This is what constitutes correct mental practice. Man's thought is creative because his thought is God-power flowing through his individualized will and imagination.

A spiritual treatment, to be effective, must be spoken from

a consciousness which knows itself to be the presence, the power and the activity of God. This Spiritual Power can and will heal, accomplish, demonstrate, answer prayer. It not only will but It must, for this is Its nature.

Spiritual Power is of no particular value to us until we use It. We must not only be conscious of this Power, we must be *actively* conscious of It. This is one of the first lessons we learn in spiritual science. It is written that Jesus, standing before the tomb of Lazarus, said, ''Father I thank Thee that Thou hast heard me. And I knew that Thou hearest me always.'' Afterwards he gave the command, ''Lazarus come forth.'' Jesus first *recognized* the Power, ''Father I thank Thee that Thou hast heard me''; next he consciously *unified* himself with It, ''And I knew that Thou hearest me always.'' Following this, he made a declaration, an affirmation, a command; he told Lazarus to come forth. This was *conscious acceptance.* We could not find a better method for our own mental use of spiritual thought power. Since the whole process of a spiritual treatment is an activity of thought, it follows that the one thinking must consciously be aware that his treatment will be effective.

Although we are surrounded by Divine Intelligence, Love and Wisdom, we may lack an actual higher guidance because we lack the higher acceptance of such guidance. Daily we should state that we are guided and directed into right action; we should know that there is an Intelligence which goes before us and makes perfect, plain and immediate our way. Divine Guidance is as definite a Principle in the universe as is the law of attraction and repulsion, but the use of Divine Guidance is what we make it. Its use is through the activity of right ideas. Our acknowledgment of good becomes the good which we acknowledge—''His word runneth very swiftly.''

The greater the conviction, the more power our word will have. We should act as though we already have dominion over evil. We should declare the truth by stating that there is nothing to be afraid of; Good is omnipotent. Good instantly, effectively and permanently destroys both fear and the effect of fear. The Freedom of God is our freedom; the Power of God is our power; the Presence of God is in us now. The Mind of God is our mind and the Joy of God is our joy.

Spiritual mind treating is not daydreaming, and it is more than meditation. *Meditation is for the purpose of inbreathing the Essence of Reality; treatment is for the purpose of using this Essence in definite constructive ways.*

Because the Spirit is personal to each, then each individual-izes God and no two persons are alike. Thus God as Infinite Person is not only real to each one of us, but real in a unique sense. Treatment should be filled with an atmosphere of this Reality. We should make statements similar to this: "Because God is infinite in His capacity to know, there is a Mind within me that knows exactly what I should do today. Realizing that the Spirit with me is God; being conscious of the Divine Presence as the sustaining Principle of my life; I let that Mind be in me which was also in Christ Jesus. This Mind guides me today in my every decision. I declare the same guidance for all people."

Our true inheritance is self-sufficiency, perfection, peace and wholeness. This certainly includes abundance, self-expression and happiness. The Will of God and the Nature of God are identical, since God could have no will opposed to His nature. Hence, if God is wholeness, peace and joy, then the Divine Will for all is wholeness, peace and joy. The Will of God is always toward the more abundant life. We have misdirected the energy which is already for us, hence the importance of re-educating the mind to a more direct perception of its relationship to God.

The Science of Mind deals with a Principle in Nature which acts like other principles. If we wish to use this Principle as a science, rather than to use It merely in a hit-and-miss method, we must make a scientific approach to, and a conscious use of, spiritual power. We need not go outside ourselves to do this.

The Principle of Truth, of Mind and Spirit, or whatever term one wishes to designate It by, is the Actor, the Doer—"Be still and know that I am God." The Creative Principle acts upon thought. We should call upon this inner Intelligence, in belief and in confidence, knowing that It will respond to us.

God as Spirit is the Divine Presence, while the Principle of this science is the Law of Cause and Effect. The Divine Knower operates through mechanical Law. This Law is Mind in action. When you give a treatment you should feel that all the power there is in the universe is flowing into your word. Believe that Truth swings instantly into manifestation through your conviction, for this is the power of your treatment. Be simple and direct.

This has nothing to do with will power, mental concentration or suggestion. There is that within each one of us which is conscious of its unity with Good, with all the Power there is. Upon this Power, Presence and Light we must depend with complete confidence. Thus faith passes into experience with scientific certainty. Faith is the most dynamic power known.

Effective treatment must be independent of any existing circumstances, for the Divine Creative Spirit knows no circumstances; It is the Creator of them. Here is the crux of the whole matter. This is why we are told never to count our enemies but to "Look unto me and be ye saved."

When you say "There is One Life and this Life is God," you have made an abstract statement about a Universal Principle, but when you add, "This Life is my life now," you have consciously connected this Principle with your own experience. In giving treatments one should use the words and thoughts which convey the desired meaning to his own mind. Treatment should be simple, unlabored, calm, and designed only to convince the thought of the one who gives it. All treatment is self-treatment. The manifestation of the treatment is in the Law of Cause and Effect.

It is impossible to divorce a true concept of God from the most powerful mental treatment, merely because God, or the Creative First Cause, constitutes our entire being in Reality. The act of self-knowing, which takes place in our thought, is in Reality the One Mind recognizing Itself. The action of this Mind, through our thought, creates our experience. Spiritual mind treatment is an active thing, but its activity is a mental and spiritual recognition either in the form of spoken words or of a deep inner realization of the truth, applied for some particular purpose.

10

The Power that creates exists before we use It. However, It can give us only that which we mentally take, and often our unbelief becomes our acceptance, our fear a misplaced faith. We bind ourselves by the very power which could as quickly free us. We should increase our receptivity and have a greater faith, if we wish to experience a larger degree of livingness. Our bowl of acceptance must be held up so that the outpouring of Spirit may be measured into our individual experience. It is self-evident that the Creative Spirit must express Itself in the terms of the instrument through which It flows. So far as we are concerned, this instrument is faith, belief, acceptance. We should lift our thought upon the cross of Unity and here, where the winds of God blow free, accept the Divine Givingness and the Divine Forgiveness, which are eternal in the nature of Reality.

All treatment is for the purpose of stimulating an interior awareness. If we are treating for physical or financial betterment for ourselves, or for someone else, inwardly we should become aware that the good we desire is now manifest. All of Spirit is wherever we center our thought. Truth in Its entirety is forever with us, ever available. Spiritual Power awaits our recognition, and Divine Guidance our consent. The Spirit flows through us as an outlet for Its own self-expression.

To dwell upon lack is to create it. To think of disease is to perpetuate it. To remain unhappy is to attract more unhappiness. Deliberately we must turn from that which hurts. The Law of Mind exists in a formless state and can only take the form for us which our thought gives It. When we think within ourselves, we think upon It; when we direct our thought, we are directing It. It is in this way that our word becomes the law unto that thing whereunto it is spoken. We should sense this Power which is at the point of our word, while being careful to realize that we need not put power into our word, for as a matter of fact, we really take it out. This is not concentration; it is conscious belief definitely directed.

The particular form of mental procedure in this practice is unimportant; the all-important factor is whether or not one believes in, and understands, the spiritual nature of things. We must believe that love, goodness, truth and beauty are at the

11

center of everything, therefore at the center of the person, the condition or situation which we designate in our treatment. We must believe that Love is God, infinite, eternal and ever present. We cannot escape Love. We exist in Love and are One with It. We live by, through and in It. It motivates our entire thought, purpose, plan and action. Everything we see, we see with the eyes of Love. Everything we hear, we hear with the ears of Love. We see God everywhere; wherever we look we see Him, wherever we go we find Him.

The process of reasoning which one uses in a mental treatment must establish his thought upon a spiritual basis, enthrone him in a Kingdom of Good and give him dominion over evil. Thoughts and things are not separated; they are identical. When the practitioner uses the word "elimination" he must believe that something is being eliminated; when he uses the words "right action" he must believe that the entire right action of the universe is centered, through that word, upon the object which he designates, or for the purpose which he has in mind. In this way, business is an activity of consciousness and the business of Mind is never inactive. Man's business is God's business and God's business is man's business, which is the business of life.

We do not deny the physical universe; we affirm that it is *Mind in form*. The physical body exists that the soul may function on this plane. Body is not an unreality; quite the reverse. It is a divine and perfect reality when rightly understood.

We are compelled to think of Spirit either as apart from us or within us. If apart from us, there is no way to find It. If within us, there is no escaping the divine fact. *Unfoldment and not search is what we need.* Unless mind healing becomes spiritual, it degenerates into the process of exchanging one negative idea for another. How can we expect any result to rise higher than its cause? Hence, all true mind healing is spiritual; it rests upon a deep inner realization of the Divine Goodness.

The Creative Principle can operate for us only by operating through our belief; hence we limit It to such belief. *We must know that the body of God, the body of our patient and the body of our affairs are one and the same thing.*

The winning or losing of what we call a demonstration lies entirely in one's state of thought or consciousness, in whether or not he is able to perceive more good than evil. For since the Divine Spirit and Law is the only Actor, the true Saviour, the All in All, It has no opposition, no competition, no otherness. A consciousness of God should run through our entire treatment. Thus we may say, "I baptize all people in the essence of love; I pour the spirit of joy upon all occasions; I throw mental peace around every form. There is that within me which proclaims 'Behold, I make all things new.'"

Our work rests entirely upon demonstration. If the thought is not manifesting rightly in our experience, we should work until it does. We should have a deep realization of the Divine Presence, and out of the spiritual power generated in this realization speak our word with complete conviction. When we give a treatment we must believe, for this is the power of the treatment.

The following is a suggested outline for treatment. There is no magic in any particular words. Words are effective only in so far as they stimulate a corresponding recognition of their meaning in the mind of the one who uses them.

TREATMENT FOR HEALTH AND PROSPERITY

This word is the Presence, Power and Activity of the Infinite Mind in me. Therefore It is the law unto the condition or the person for whom It is spoken. It is perfect in Its action and permanent in Its manifestation.

Infinite Intelligence governs, guides, directs, sustains and animates my life (if treating for someone else mention his name). *The Infinite Mind knows no mistake. It is never discouraged. This Mind is my Mind now. All belief in fear, discouragement, disappointment or failure is erased from my consciousness.*

I am forever supplied with every good thing, forever happy, radiant, well and complete. This word establishes the law of wholeness and harmony throughout my entire being and in everything I do, say or think (or the person for whom or the condition for which I am working). *My life represents that which knows no limitation, is forever manifesting complete joy and freedom through me.*

Spirit daily provides me with everything necessary to my happiness, to my wholeness, and to my complete self-expression. I represent the Principle of Divine Activity which never tires, which is birthless, changeless and deathless. I know that the Infinite Intelligence which sustains all things, and the Perfect Law which holds everything in its proper place, governs my life and action (or his life and action).

My whole being responds to joy, to peace, to truth and to abundance. Only that which is good can enter my experience. (At this point one may definitely state that the particular good he seeks is now accomplished.) *I know that as a result of this word, happiness, health and prosperity immediately spring into action and manifest through me* (or through him). *I know that the action of Spirit in me* (or him) *is always complete, perfect and enduring.*

Every organ, action and function of my physical being represents this Divine and Perfect Life, manifesting within me. I am aware of my Partnership with the Infinite and I know that everything which I do shall prosper.

(Enter into a silent realization and acceptance of what you have said.)

It is done. I accept. I believe. I know.

Science, Superstition, and Common Sense

IT SEEMS as though we were born to be superstitious, because we all inherit the legacy of the entire race mind. Freud, the first man to chart the unconscious, said that neurotic thought patterns will repeat themselves with monotonous regularity throughout life unless they are changed. He was referring to what he called the unconscious and what we call the subjective state of our thought.

While there has been a great deal of controversy about Freud's life and teaching, one thing is certain: It would be impossible to write an adequate book on psychology today without its being profoundly influenced by his discoveries. We are not concerned with his philosophy of life from a spiritual viewpoint, but only with the scientific discoveries that he undoubtedly made and which caused psychological research to be recharted to conform to new patterns.

When Freud said that we are prone to repeat morbid thought patterns he was right. But Jung, his able contemporary, added to this the thought that we are subject to the influence of what he called the collective unconscious, which means the sum total of all human emotions from time immemorial.

There was a time when theology taught that there was a devil, a hell, a limbo, a purgatory, and a paradise. Because ages on end believed this, it created a pattern in the collective unconscious which influenced everyone. They were born with this idea, and as a matter of fact this theory has never yet been entirely cleared up. There are countless thousands who still adhere to this superstition.

At one time it was thought that it would be impossible to cultivate the desert and waste places, and make them productive. The thought was that it was unnatural, and so it could not be done. But some person had the courage to go ahead and make the attempt, and he was successful because he was complying with the laws of nature.

Common sense and science must be applied to religious and spiritual things as to everything else, for we can no longer monotonously repeat "Thus saith the Lord" because of certain proclamations of some of the early prophets. We must analyze their statements to see whether they are speaking from Divine patterns or from the inertia of human thought patterns which they had unconsciously inherited.

True religion, true science, and true common sense should go hand in hand, together with that other subtle something which is the essence of feeling—that which is beyond words.

It is not always easy in a world of confusion, superstition, and unbelief to maintain an independent position in one's own thought, a position based on the plain common sense that Jesus had, that Life cannot produce death, that the Universe holds nothing against us, that the gift of Heaven is eternally made but still must be received. Science is helping us to receive this gift. All the comforts and the good that have come to modern life through science are not contradictions of nature, but rather they are affirmations of the limitless resources of Life.

The very fact that two blades of grass can be made to grow where only one grew is an affirmation that the Universe Itself did not limit the growth; it waited for someone to perceive its possibility. Poverty will one day be wiped from the face of the earth, not because God will some day decide that He is ready to change conditions, but because man, cooperating with God, with nature, and with law, will proclaim an abundance that already existed.

War will cease, not when God decides this for us, but when enough people know that it is no longer desirable, and steadfastly maintain their position. From communion with Spirit man will come to perceive the deeper Reality, the broader sharing in human experience.

So disease will one day be wiped from the face of the earth, as science, sense, and the philosophy of Spiritual Truth take the place of ignorance, superstition, fear, and confusion.

You are a forerunner in this field, breaking down barriers of race consciousness, the accumulated effects of misconceptions, and the morbid fears of the universe in which we live. When science, common sense, and a right philosophy combine, the half-gods will have to go.

There is no point in waiting for this consummation in human affairs, for we cannot change the thought of the whole world overnight. But, fortunately, we can change our reactions to it, and build a strong and impregnable barrier in our own consciousness against everything that denies the Supreme Good.

In actual practice we should daily say: *I am not bound by the superstitions of the race. I no longer fear God or the Universe in which I live. I have implicit confidence in the Supreme Good, and I permit It to flow through me and to bless everything I contact.*

Little by little there will be added to our own unconscious or subjective reactions a new body of thought, which ultimately will be projected and expanded into the Universal Mind. We shall not only be freeing ourselves but we shall be helping to free the whole human race from the bondage of fear, ignorance, superstition, and thoughts based on what the past has brought forth. The past is dead.

Thinking Affirmatively

THERE IS a Power for Good in the Universe greater than you are, and you can use It. We all believe this. The question is: Why do we not use It more effectively? If all things are possible to faith, why do we not have more faith? If affirmative prayers are answered, why do we not always pray affirmatively? Let us try to figure out just how we can more effectively cooperate with the Law of Mind in Action.

First, let us begin with the thought that we are all united with an Invisible Force which is creative, and that we are already One with a Universal Mind which can do anything.

Next, let us consider that we are centers within this Mind, and that the sum total of all our thoughts is either silently attracting Good to us or repelling It from us.

And third, let us know that we can change our thinking and, in so doing, cause the Law of Good to act affirmatively for us instead of negatively.

Let us start with the first proposition. We are surrounded by a Creative Mind which reacts to our thought. This is the basis of all faith and all effective prayer. This is why Jesus told us that when we pray we should believe we already have what we desire. When Jesus said that it is done unto us as we believe, he implied that there is a Power that can, will, and must react to us. But this Power has no choice other than to react to us in the way we think. This Power acts as a Law operating on our beliefs. This is why Jesus said that it is done unto us *as* we believe.

Until the time of Jesus, it had been believed that God *might* help us, that there were concessions He would make if we pleased Him, or if we performed certain rites or ceremonials. Jesus changed these suppositions into certainties. He said simply and directly that there is a Power that operates on your belief, the way you believe. Therefore, he added, be sure that you believe that you already have what you desire and then the Law of Good will bring it to you. But even the Law of Good, which is All-powerful, can bring you only as much good as you accept. This accepting is an act of your own mind; it is an act of faith.

18

No one else before Jesus had made such a claim. Only within the last hundred years, or less, have people come to realize that he was talking about a Spiritual Principle in which we all are rooted, which operates on our faith, our conviction, and our acceptance.

It is the very simplicity of his claim that causes us to overlook its deep and dynamic meaning. Jesus was really saying this: You are surrounded by a Mind, a Power, an Intelligence, or a Principle that receives the impress of your thought and acts upon it exactly as you think. Your thought is like an image held in front of a mirror. Thought itself is a Law, reflecting back to you what you think.

Now we come to our second concept: We are thinking and active centers in this Mind, and the sum total of all our thoughts is either silently attracting Good to us or repelling It from us. This shows the part we are to play in our use of the Power greater than we are. It is the sum total of all our thinking that we must consider. And in doing this one of the first things we learn is that about 90 percent of our thinking is unconscious.

Psychologists now tell us that 8 percent of our accidents are unconsciously invited; that at least 75 percent of our diseases are unconsciously created; that our success or failure in life is largely unconscious, and, of course, our happiness or our misery is almost entirely so.

You see, scientific investigation verifies what you and I are talking about. Most of our thinking is unconscious. Here is where habit patterns of thought are laid down from infancy. It should be our purpose to find out what these thought patterns are and, when they are unhappy or morbid or filled with fear, to change them so that the natural, normal flow of the Life Force Itself shall be resumed.

So we come to our third idea: We can change our thinking and in so doing cause the Law of Mind to act affirmatively for us instead of negatively. Jesus gave us the perfect technique for doing this.

He told us that when our faith is in the Good it will obliterate evil; that is, Good and evil are not equal powers. Good always overcomes evil. The affirmative attitude will always

19

overcome the negative. This is why we are now told to accentuate the positive and forget the negative. Just keep on thinking about peace and let confusion go. Affirm the Good and forget the evil. This is a sound teaching.

So Jesus told us that when we pray we should become quiet, enter the closet of the self, close the door of the senses, and here make known our requests. But when we do this we should be certain that we accept the answer, and then we shall get it. *When ye pray, believe that ye receive . . . and ye shall have. . . .*

This whole idea is so simple that it often eludes us. We are surrounded by a Creative Mind which reacts to our thinking. The sum total of all our thinking decides what is going to happen to us. We can change our thinking and cause the very Law that limited us to bring us freedom. What more could we ask? What more could be given than this?

The Bible says, *If ye know these things, happy are ye if ye do them* (John 13:17). So let us proceed to the doing.

Going back to our first statement that we are surrounded by a Mind Principle which acts creatively on our thinking, let us make this the basis of our belief. Whether we call this Mind Principle Spirit, God, or Law makes no difference. The only thing that matters is whether we accept this Self-Operating Power around us, a Power which actually can and will do whatever ought to be done for us if we believe in It. And do we accept the fact that the sum total of our thinking decides what is going to happen to us?

Our first proposition is one of faith. We must believe. It is natural to have faith and to believe, but when we find that we lack these qualities we now know what to do about it, because belief and faith are mental attitudes. So we practice affirmative prayer daily, by saying: "I do have faith; I do have conviction; I do believe; I do know and understand that there is a Power greater than I am; I do realize that I can use It; there is nothing in me that can doubt, deny, or limit this Power; my whole being accepts It, both consciously and unconsciously." Thus we are preparing our minds to pray affirmatively, which means to pray effectively.

If there is a Principle of Mind that reacts to our thinking or to our belief, it naturally follows that if we say, "It cannot," then It cannot because we do not let It. If we say, "It won't," then It won't because we do not permit It. And if we limit It to a little good, It cannot give us a greater good. The Power Itself is Absolute; the way we use It is relative.

We can practice believing because thoughts are things, and when we say, "I believe," and "There is no doubt in me," we do two things: we affirm our belief and by so doing build a positive acceptance in the mind; and at the same time we reject our doubts by denying them. This is the way thought works. Realizing that 90 percent of our thinking is unconscious, we should daily affirm that there is nothing in us that denies the good we affirm; that every experience we have ever had which denies that good is wiped out of mind and memory as a negative force; that we are forgiven our mistakes and encouraged to go on and do better.

We are now ready to entertain our third basic concept and see if we cannot actually bring ourselves to believe that we possess the good we desire even though we do not see any possible way for it to happen. This also can be reduced to a simple method. You can say to yourself, "I do accept this good. I do believe my prayer is answered. I do affirm the presence of love, friendship, happiness, prosperity, health, peace—whatever the need may be—and nothing in me denies, rejects, or refutes it. I do accept it."

You will find that, after you have done this for a while, there will come a gradual acceptance of your affirmation. And you will learn that, as the subjective reactions of your thought build up an affirmative attitude, things will begin to change in your environment. It may take a little time, but you now have courage, knowing that you are dealing with a definite Principle and that It cannot fail.

We are all surrounded by a certain amount of skepticism and doubt, and perhaps many people think what we believe is all nonsense. This should not disturb us in the least. We are to know that we are working independently with God and the great Law of Good. Whether we are working for ourselves or our family or our friends or the whole world, every affirmative spiritual statement we make will have some Power. An invisible Law of Good will be acting upon it.

You have no one to prove this to but yourself. But if you do prove it to yourself, no doubt your friends will begin to ask you what it is all about. You have no authority for what you do other than the authority of what happens when you do it.

We have nothing to give to the world unless we have first proved it. The blind cannot lead the blind. But alone with Truth, one man can pass from weakness into strength, from fear into faith, from defeat into success, and even while he is still living, from a state of continual death into a realization of everlasting life.

Let God Do It

IN THE Colorado Rockies there is a beautiful valley from which many fountains gush forth. Each fountain is different, more water comes from some than from others, but there is only one body of water at a deep, subterranean level which flows through each one of them.

Each fountain is supplied from this body of water, and the water that gushes through each has a pressure within itself that causes it to flow upward with an irresistible force. This may be likened to our own Spiritual Natures. We as individuals each have our own thoughts, feelings, hopes, aspirations, and desires, and each is directly and intimately connected with the one Divine Life, Energy, and Power.

Each of us is a fountain of Life. There is a God-pressure back of each one of us, a Life-force seeking outlet through our thoughts and acts. There are many fountains, many individuals, but only one God-pressure back of all.

One of the most remarkable sayings of Jesus was that he of himself could do nothing: . . . *the Father that dwelleth in me, he doeth the works.* Could we not say of each fountain up there in the Rockies that the fountain of itself could do nothing because it is merely an outlet for the pressure back of it?

Let us personalize these fountains and give to each the power to block the flow of water through it. One fountain might say: "Well, I don't know whether there is water enough. I am not quite certain that I am an outlet for this great ocean of water. I am not even certain that I believe there is enough pressure in it to keep on flowing—perhaps it will stop tomorrow." Another fountain might say: "I am so confused over everything, I am so uncertain about everything, that I have come to the point where I really don't know what's going to happen." And another fountain might be so filled with fear and distrust that it would block its own channel. While still another might get jealous of the other fountains and gradually come to hate them.

Let us make believe that these mental attitudes of the fountains could actually stop the flow of water through them. Would that not be about the way all of us are at times? We become so frustrated with our little thoughts and fears and doubts that it makes it impossible for us to let God flow through us with the joy of life. Our problem is not with God, who is the River of Life. It is not with the Divine Pressure that seeks to express Itself through us. Our trouble is with ourselves.

Each one of us is an inlet to the Divine, but because we are individuals we can inhibit Its flow, we can block It or squeeze It down to a small volume or even stop It; or, by opening up all the channels of faith and conviction and hope, we can increase Its flow. When the natural joy of life is unblocked it will flow freely through us and we shall become whole and happy. But doubt, fear, uncertainty, anxiety, and a sense of insecurity can so congest our mental life that nothing Good can get through.

We are born with a natural desire to express life. But almost from birth certain factors have entered our experiences which have tended to congest the flow, until finally it has almost stopped. We are trying to be fountains all on our own, not realizing that each one is rooted in God; that there is a Power greater than we are, a pressure against our lives from a Divine Source which is Self-Acting.

When Jesus said that a Power greater than he was operating through him, he knew exactly what he was talking about. And because he kept the passageway of his own thought clear, this Power was able to work through him.

Jesus never made any complicated statements. His words were simple and direct. He said there is a Fountain of Life from which your life is drawn, and if you will unstop everything in your mind that congests this Fountain you will be whole. This was the foundation of his teaching—clear your mind of everything that doubts the existence of God; live as though Love were the great Reality; bless and curse not, and then accept and let.

Let us use another illustration from nature and think of a great body of water up in the mountains. It is our desire to use this body of water to irrigate the valleys. We have learned that by a natural pressure within itself, which we call gravitational force, this water will flow from the high mountaintops down into the valley. But we have met with certain obstructions—there are hills and perhaps mountains in the way.

In the early days when they brought water down into Rome they built long channels around the mountainside. This was done with terrific labor. And then there came a time when someone discovered that water, by its own pressure, will reach its own level. They discovered that if they would connect a pipe with the high level they could run water down through the valleys and up over other mountains and hills, and, provided they never tried to make the water go higher than its source, they could deliver it anywhere and in complete volume.

But there is something else we should remember about bringing water down from the high mountaintops: No matter how large the source, the flow to any particular spot is limited to the size of the pipe through which it flows. If it is a one-inch pipe we shall have a one-inch flow of water; if it is a ten-inch pipe we shall be able to deliver a ten-inch flow wherever we want to use it. But in no instance do we force the water down. We neither push it nor pull it nor draw it. It furnishes its own pressure.

But suppose some day we go out to open the headgate through which the water flows and no water comes. What do we do then? Do we sit down and bemoan our fate? Do we lament and beat our breast and say, "Woe is me!" Do we say, "Perhaps God doesn't want us to have water today"? Or do we question whether or not the water is withholding itself from us? We do none of these things. We realize that somewhere the pipe is blocked, and so we follow it back and discover that sand has gotten into it, or mud or silt. We clean out the debris and at once the flow resumes.

The flow did not stop of itself; it was stopped because something got in its way. But we were able to remove the obstruction. We did this definitely and deliberately. We knew what we were doing and how to do it. We were complying with a natural law, and when we let the law have its way, everything was all right.

This is pretty much what happens in our lives when they are

25

unhappy and incomplete—somewhere we have stopped the flow. The water is still up there in the mountains, the pipe is in place, but somewhere something has gotten into this pipe that does not belong there. So we turn on the faucet and nothing happens.

Well, there is no use sitting around bemoaning our fate. It is time for us to do something about it. It is time for us to follow the pipeline of our own existence back to its Source, to find out what blocks it and to loose it, to free it, that the flow may resume. It is time for us to let God do it.

But before God can do it we must clear our minds of everything that hinders His doing; we must keep the pipeline open and let the Water of Life flow down into our living. And remembering that everything in our thinking that is unlike our highest concept of Good will clog the pipes, we must look to ourselves and be honest. If we find anything in our thinking that denies Life, let us clear it away. We can stop being afraid if we want to. We can stop having resentments. We can at once stop all unkindness, winnow out every doubt, and gain faith through the simple practice of learning to believe. Here is where faith and patience and the will to try and keep on trying must be used.

One can say to oneself every day, "I am a fountain of Life, and the living waters of God flow through me." One can say to oneself, "I will express joy today. I will be happy. I will bring gladness and enthusiasm into every experience of my life. I will maintain a quiet confidence and peace and a sense of serenity. And I will be glad for the achievement of others and rejoice in their success." One can learn to love people if one wishes to.

It is this kind of thinking that irrigates the dry places of life and brings laughter and joy into everything we do. It can bring health and freedom in place of sickness and bondage. It can bring abundance and prosperity where there might have been impoverishment.

But there is one thing that we must remember. It is not enough to know that the pipeline of our existence begins way up there in the high mountaintops into which the hand of God is pouring the Eternal Waters of Life, for this is our inlet to the Divine. This inlet is forever established. We have to be certain that we are an outlet to It. And it is only as the other end of the pipe is kept open that the water flows.

This is why Jesus told us that we must forgive if we would be forgiven; we must love if we would be loved; we must make others happy if we would be happy ourselves; we must give if we would receive.

Sometimes we hug our little good too closely to ourselves, — YES not being willing to cast it on the four winds of heaven lest it will not return. But Jesus said the very act of giving will at the same time bring to us a receiving—*good measure, pressed down, and shaken together, and running over*, he called it. It is the one who gives the most who gets the most. And so let us learn to draw the Divine Substance down into our own lives, and as freely as It has been given to us, let us give It to others. Thus alone shall we be made whole.

What Is Religion?

RELIGION MEANS our attitude toward God. This attitude is based on our concept of the relationship which exists between God the Universal Spirit and man the individual spirit. If we believe that God is some far-off Divine Being from whom we are isolated, we shall give up in despair or our entire endeavor will be in seeking a reconciliation and reunion with this Divine Being.

We are compelled to think of the Spirit as either apart from us or within us, and if God is apart from us rather than a part of us, our search will be to reunite ourselves with this Divine Source of our being. Moreover, in our search we shall be laboring under the difficulty imposed by not knowing where to go or how to get there. But if we can conceive of the Divine Being as already existing within us, no search is necessary. Instead of a search there is an unfoldment.

Again, if we conceive of the Divine Being as separated from us, any communication must be across the void which separates us. From this viewpoint prayers, petitions, or attempts at communication with the Infinite must bridge some gap, cross some chasm, travel in some unknown direction with no certainty that they will reach their goal. Communion with the Infinite is possible only on the supposition that the Infinite is Omnipresent and, if Omnipresent, at the center of our own being.

All religions are attempts to interpret man's relationship with this indwelling and overarching Infinite, with a Spirit which fills all nature, all time, and all space with Its Presence. The purer the religion, the more completely has it approached an attitude of Unity, a complete Oneness between God and man. Jesus boldly declared, *He that hath seen me hath seen the Father.* The purer the form of the religion, the more perfectly has it presented the idea of an indwelling Presence which directly responds to man's thoughts.

The recognition that the Spirit thinks through our thought and expresses Itself through our act must necessarily create an intimacy which makes Divine communion more real and more beneficial than would any concept based on the thought of God as separate from our lives.

A true religious concept is an indispensable aid in spiritual mind healing. The mental practitioner has a better chance of success when he believes in the indwelling Spirit, when he believes that God's work is already accomplished and perfect even though it is eternally unfolding. Moreover, his words will have more power when he believes that they are power, and he endows them with power in such degree as he senses the Divine Presence back of them.

This inner testimony of the soul is real and valid. Who could deny the artist the privilege of appreciating beauty? We all know that as a result of his sense of beauty he creates the beautiful, which is the object of art. We know that some artistic productions surpass others, and we recognize that back of them is a deep impression, a subjective feeling. We have not weighed or measured the reality which the artist contemplates, and yet we have evidence of it in his work.

The mental science practitioner whose mind is filled with spiritual awareness will speak a more powerful word than the one who rests his claim solely on the Law of Cause and Effect. The practitioner whose thought reaches the highest spiritual level will demonstrate that his word has the greatest power. The fact that the Law of Mind knows only how to obey and has no purpose of Its own to execute demonstrates the proposition that a higher altitude of thought will find a corresponding higher level of manifestation, just as water will reach its own level by its own weight. It is in this sense that a true religious perspective is necessary to effective mental practice.

The Law, being a Doer and not a Knower, never acts of Itself; It merely reacts. The Word of Spirit is the enforcement of this Law. How can we expect a result to rise higher than its cause? It is self-evident that there is a coordinating Spirit, and this coordinating Spirit must have within Itself a prototype or a perfect idea of every form.

A deep underlying sense of this Spiritual Universe is necessary to the most effective form of mind healing. To the technical work of the mental practitioner there should be added this deep spiritual sense of things. A subtle emanation of Spirit should flow through all the statements which he makes, for every statement must be based on the proposition of One God, One Man, and One Universe—a spiritual system which is complete, Divinely organized, spiritual not only in its origin but also in its manifestation.

The spiritual mind healer must learn to see God in his patient. His conviction of this indwelling Divinity must be more than intellectual. For there is a field of Reality higher than the intellect, and it uses the intellect as its instrument. We should not decry the intellect since it gives shape and form to this inner feeling, but without the feeling nothing comes into being. This has been referred to as the Spirit and the letter of the Law, and we have been told that the letter without the Spirit does not quicken. Applied to mental healing this means that the words we speak must have a deep meaning to us, and we must sense that behind them there is a Power seeking expression.

This Power is infinitely greater than our intellect. The intellect does the best it can, but unless it is directed by the Spirit it finally succeeds in reaching only a gigantic negation, a complete denial of its own existence, a repudiation of the supreme fact of existence which is the act of directly experiencing Spirit.

You could not convince one who has had such an experience that it was an illusion or a hallucination, for this inner testimony of the soul is valid to the one who has it. It is just as much a part of him as is his thought, and the proof of its reality is evidenced by the results which it has produced in the lives of those who have been most deeply sensitive to love, truth, and beauty. To come into closer daily contact with this Supreme Source of wisdom and illumination should be the earnest desire of every worker in this field.

Appreciation of human experience will be quickened rather than retarded through unity with this indwelling Spirit. When a person learns to see God in everyone he will become more spontaneous. He will feel a deep and abiding inner joy.

Our spiritual experiences reach higher levels at some times than at others, and we should seek to bring the inspiration of these moments of illumination into our everyday living. If the philosophy of Christianity were lived, wars would cease, unhappiness would cease, economic problems would be solved, poverty would be wiped from the face of the earth, and man's inhumanity to man would be transmuted into a spirit of mutual helpfulness.

This would not mean the reducing of all persons to one common level. We are individuals in a cosmic Wholeness. Each is a unique representation of the one and only Mind and Spirit, and since this Mind and Spirit is Infinite, Its capacity to individualize must likewise be without limit. Each may remain himself while seeing God in the other.

The spiritual mind practitioner should always have a sense of this fundamental Unity and should realize that it is continuously differentiating Itself through each one of us. Every man becomes a unique manifestation of the Whole, a microcosm within the Macrocosm; rooted in the Infinite, he personifies It. Some part of It, inseparable from It, remaining in It, he is still an individual. The paradox of the many and the One is explained not on the basis of a God apart from man, but on the basis of a God incarnated in man.

The religion of the spiritual mind healer must be one of Unity and Law. He must feel that he is one with the Spirit. Being one with this Self-Existent Spirit, he must sense that he uses the Law. There is nothing arrogant about this, for he knows that should such use be exercised in behalf of duality, he himself must experience the effect of that very dualism which he attempts to project. The Universe is foolproof, and the profane do not enter the Holy of Holies.

Humility, reverence, and adoration are not to be confused with self-obliteration. We are not called upon to consider ourselves unholy; we are neither conceived in sin nor shapen in iniquity. Man's place in the creative order is as a dispenser of the Divine gifts, a husbandman of the indwelling Lord.

The morbidity which has come with the sense of isolation and separation from God must be healed if joy and laughter are to take the place of sorrow and tears. How can we believe in a weeping Universe or a sad God or a melancholy First Cause? Such concepts would contradict the fundamental necessity of Reality, that God is a synonym for Wholeness.

Negation does not belong to the Infinite, and being undivided It is never separated from Its own Good. We must arrive at an abiding sense of our Unity with Good. Much that we have believed must be discarded, for we can never avoid the conclusion that with what judgment we have judged, by that same judgment we must ourselves be judged.

The approach to Reality should be simple, direct, and spontaneous. The Secret Place of the Most High is neither in the holy mountain of Samaria nor at Jerusalem; *for, behold, the Kingdom of God is within you.* This Kingdom is finished, complete, and perfect for eternity, but the manifestation of this Kingdom is the eternal activity of right ideas, law, order, truth, and beauty. Man is given dominion in this Kingdom by a fundamental necessity of his nature. It is impossible that this dominion should be withheld from him.

There is no deific power which either withdraws from man or advances toward man. No more of God is in one place than in another, and in the place where man is, God is, and where man recognizes the Divine Presence, there the Divine Presence responds—not some of It, but all of It.

The communion of the soul with this Over-Presence is a natural act. To feel that a Presence greater than we are is guiding us is normal. To trust this Presence is sanity. To desire that the Divine Eternal shall project Itself through our thought is to be receptive to that greater side of our nature which lies open to the upper reaches of thought. This is religion.

What Is Spirituality?

WE HEAR a great deal about certain people being spiritual, and there is nothing wrong with this provided it does not become a maudlin attitude.

Spirituality is rather an elusive thing. I cannot think of a better illustration to use than to compare it with the idea of beauty which a great artist must entertain if he is to create a worthwhile object of art. We do not say that such a one has great beauty, but that he has great appreciation for beauty. We know that the artist feels beauty, senses its presence, and to a degree communes with it, indrawing it into his own soul that he may outbreathe it through his performance.

Pefect technique alone does not result in great art. We speak of the soul of an artist, that subtle and indefinable something which is the essence of all art. This is a definite feeling, a communion with Invisible Harmony, the Supreme Being, the Mind and Heart of God, or the Creative Essence.

It is the same with what we call spirituality, which is a word too often misused. From our viewpoint spirituality is one's recognition of the Universe as a Living Presence of Good, Truth, Beauty, Peace, Power, and Love. And to this should be added Happiness, Joy, Enthusiasm, and Universal Harmony, which, like the great rhythm of Life, flows through everything.

There is a vast difference between this type of spiritual consciousness and theological dogma, or even logical arguments. It is an Essence diffused, a consciousness transcendent, and a faith that has passed beyond the point of argument into conviction and union and complete acceptance.

Such spirituality we cannot divorce from the highest use of the Science of Mind. It is like the heat in fire, the colors in a prism, the invisible power flowing through a dynamo. It is like something that is caught from the Invisible for the purpose of taking temporary form. It is the background of all spiritual mind treatment, and we should not separate it from our conscious use of the Law of Mind.

Spirituality is a constant, consistent attempt to feel the Presence of God in everything and in everyone. Such an attitude need not be put into words, because words cannot express such a feeling. But out of the feeling words will flow, and when they do they will always be correct.

Spirituality cannot be taught, but it can be felt, it can be practiced, it can be embodied. Each in his own consciousness must experience it in his own way, and his way will always be best for him. Indeed it will be the only way he could do it, because, in the secret precinct of the mind which is alone with God, nothing else can enter.

Listening daily to that which can only be felt, daily sensing and communing with that which is too intangible to put into words, one finds an Essence flowing through one's thought which can be neither analyzed nor described.

Do not wonder whether or not you are spiritual; rather accept the fact that you must be. In a sense, you had nothing to do with it. This is your nature. You are rooted in the Supreme Mind, in the Everlasting Spirit, in the Perfect Presence.

Spirituality is the consciousness that comes through communing with God, for treatment is a definite act and, however spiritual, must still take a definite form. One should not study to be spiritual as much as one should contemplate in order to imbibe the Essence of Spirit, to speak from Its center.

In this, as in everything else, practice will perfect your method, and consciousness will make your method effective.

Desire, Opinion, and Revelation

IT WAS John who said, and rightly, *Believe not every spirit, but try the spirits whether they are of God.* Paul said, *God is not the author of confusion, but of peace.* Possibly he knew that our conscious opinions and our subjective desires so frequently confuse the revelations that when an alleged revelation appears, it is so distorted with conflicting opinions that much of its truth is lost.

If we were to put all of the alleged revelations of the ages together we would be amazed to find how contradictory they are. In fact the contradictions would be so complete that practically the whole revelation would be wiped out, and this in face of the fact that each prophet claims to have received his inspiration directly from the Mind of God. The confusion of such alleged revelations is so great that intelligence compels us to put up the sign: *Stop, Look, and Listen.*

We are amazed to discover that some of these revelations which seem to come from God stimulate man to commit the most atrocious crimes, for many crimes that have been committed in the name of Liberty have also been committed in the name of Truth.

It stands to reason that the Author of Peace cannot inspire confusion. And God is the Author of Peace, since a house divided against itself cannot stand. If God stands for that which is rational, the essence of Peace and Poise; if the Divine means Love, Beauty, Harmony, and Reason; it follows that from this Divine Fountain only pure waters can flow. God could not be the author of confusion inspiring men to acts of destruction. God could not be the author of confusion leading men to irrational mental or spiritual conclusions. Therefore a person who would differentiate between subjective hallucination and opinion, between desire and reality, does well to analyze his own feelings, emotions, and mental reactions. And he does well to

35

analyze the reactions of other people, regardless of whether they are numbered among the so-called great, the little known, or even the unknown.

In the pursuit of Truth one seeks to wed oneself to reason, for she is the only mistress who can lead the soul to the altar of Reality. We do not dispute the idea of revelation, since all truth is some revelation of Reality to the mind of man. We do not deny that there is a Spirit which inspires and a Guidance which directs. What we say is that when it seems as though this Guidance directs us chaotically or counsels men to destructive acts, it is not Divine Guidance at all. It is some form of opinion or desire masquerading as reason, seeking to justify itself by claiming to be the Voice of God.

When someone tells you that he has received a revelation direct from the Almighty you will be wise if you analyze his revelation and see whether it really is inspired by the Divine or whether it is merely a rationalization of his own desire. History records many so-called revelations by which men have claimed to be directed by God to commit such atrocious crimes that sensitiveness shrinks from the fact and intelligence refuses to accept the verdict.

Life cannot will death. Death is the direct opposite of life. Therefore Jesus said, *God is not the God of the dead, but of the living.* Jesus with his clear comprehension of Reality knew that Life cannot will death, but many lesser prophets have proclaimed that the Divine Being inspired them to kill. Most nations at war, worshiping tribal gods, react from their collective unconscious with this same motivation. But whether it be an individual or a collective unconscious, the principle operating is the same.

We may be certain that when Cyrus mounted his chariot and rode in front of his legions crying, "Kill! Kill! Kill! and to God be the glory!" after having attended the divinations of the oracle, what he was really proclaiming, but of course unconsciously, was: "Kill! Kill! Kill! and to Cyrus be the glory!" Even this barbarian shrank in horror before the terrific carnage about to take place. His desire had first to be rationalized in order that his opinion might be justified; therefore he had to receive, through his imagination, evidence for the belief that his killing of men was done for the glory of God and not for the glory of Cyrus.

We take this instance, so far removed from us personally and from our present history, that we may be impersonal about it. But every day this same performance takes place in our own consciousness. We certainly should realize that all is not revelation which masquerades under its name. In the present day, when we are privileged to understand more about psychic reactions, history is better explained on the basis of human will to power.

Today more than ever psychic revelations are imposed upon our consciousness through the sincerity of those receiving such messages in automatic writings, in seances, and by various other media through which such revelations come, and again we must put up the sign: *Stop, Look, and Listen.* To one who has, over a period of many years, carefully studied such apparent revelations, it is evident that too frequently these revelations are largely governed by the mental background of the one through whom they come. Generally we find in them elements of philosophies, the religions, the social, political, and economic systems which the author has believed in or theorized over, toward which he has aspired, or in which he was born. This in no way contradicts the sincerity of those through whom these messages come. Therefore it is not a question of condemning or criticizing the individual; it is merely a question of right judgment and a sane perspective.

We certainly should believe in no revelation which contradicts the final Unity, Goodness, and Perfection of the Supreme Being. In analyzing such revelations we should carry them right back to the point of reason and unity, and whenever they contradict reason we may know that they are not revelations but hallucinations or the rationalizations of desire. They may emanate directly from the consciousness of an individual or from the conscious reactions of an entire race.

We are told that Martin Luther saw the devil. One day he

37

presented himself in Luther's study. Now what was it that this reverend gentleman saw? Not an actual devil, since intelligence compels us to admit that the devil is a mythological figure with no reality outside man's consciousness.

What Luther saw was a personification of the then universal belief about the devil. If we could ask the average man of that period what the devil looked like, his description would be similar to what Luther saw. Strange as it may seem, what he saw was an idea, but this idea had its roots deeper than his own personal consciousness. It arose from the sum total of the opinion of his day. Everybody believed the devil looked like that; therefore the devil did look like that in belief, and what Luther saw was the belief personified; a picture in imagination, but a picture of an imagination more real than his personal one, more dynamic than his individual thought. This picture was impressed upon his psyche, and in some moment when he was subjective to it, it appeared.

With all sincerity Luther may have believed that he saw an actual devil, but with equal sincerity the man who is suffering from a hallucination believes that he sees some grotesque form. It is real enough as far as the experience is concerned, but it is nevertheless an illusion as far as reality is concerned. Luther and all his contemporaries believed in an actual devil, and what they believed in he saw. Hence, seeing, he doubly believed.

This is one of the reasons why many people believe that God ordains suffering, impoverishment, and unhappiness, and that He even demands murder. When we subject such a concept to the rule of reason and common sense we soon discover that the All-Creative Principle could not will martyrdom, suffering, or impoverishment, for this would not be to the glory, but to the degradation, of the Creative Principle. God would not be honored, but dishonored; not made whole, but limited.

Yet what countless thousands of sincere and well-meaning persons suffer the illusion of such a belief and actually condemn the desire for happiness in this world! The very thought of the crucifixion of Jesus has, in innumerable instances, stimulated such morbid introspection that the resurrected form of Christ is but dimly seen through the clouds of darkness and despair. Too often the cross and the tomb overshadow the resurrection.

We must not forget that when we are dealing with this psychic life of ours we are dealing with a very tricky thing. It will just as quickly provide us with an illusion as with a reality. But deeper than this psychic life there is a Spiritual Intelligence which transcends even our objective processes of reasoning, and it can distinguish between illusion and reality.

Our subconscious reactions will coerce us unless we control them, will cause us to believe all kinds of fantastic things unless reason sits in judgment. Therefore we should be careful at all times to study any alleged revelation in the light of this truth, knowing as we do that one's personal opinion may masquerade as any revelation which one's unconscious desire may order, for the entire race thought is more or less active in all of us.

One of the most prolific fields for race hallucination, strange as it may seem, is in the field of so-called revealed religion. Accumulated acceptances of pronounced beliefs have finally created such a subjective reaction to them that people believe all sorts of things, reasonable and unreasonable. Usually it takes a strong new belief to shatter the old. Fortunately, back of most revelations, especially the great spiritual ones, there has always been enough reality—that is, enough of the nature of Truth has been revealed—not only to give vitality to the belief, but to equip it with power and give it a performance which has been good.

Thus in analyzing the great revelations we do not need to recheck them in their entirety, but merely to recheck those parts which arise from human opinion, human desire, or psychological rationalization.

We shall find that reality is at least partly revealed through most of these great systems of thought, but we shall also find a great deal of illusion. Nowhere was this more apparent than in the ancient caste system, which did not rise out of reality since there can be no God who holds one person superior to another. It was an economic thing, and what is more natural than that the dominant-minded should have rationalized their desire and even had it seemingly revealed to them that some were of lower origin than others, and therefore were outcasts. In Psalm 82:6 we read: *I have said, Ye are gods; and all of you children of the most High.* In the days of slavery in America many of our Southern brethren rationalized their belief in slavery as God's will. It could not be the will of God that some men should be free while others were bound, since God is the Author of freedom and not of bondage.

It is interesting to note with what dynamic authority many of our so-called great seers have spoken. With sincere conviction they have proclaimed, "Thus saith the Lord." It was not until the advent of science that reason began to deny these theological assumptions. Science deals with facts and not with opinions, and it must reduce these facts into principles which never vary and which are always impersonal.

With the advent of science we have the beginning of the destruction of superstition. This does not mean that science will destroy religion. Nothing can do that, for true religion is man's immediate experience of Reality. Science will merely destroy distorted beliefs, and in so doing it will render true religion a great service since it will reveal the nature of Reality to be entirely impersonal, responsive alike to each and to all.

As science proclaims the rule of reason and a government of law, new revelations come. These new revelations, even as the old, the student of Truth must carefully scrutinize. He must remain master in his own household. Unless he does so, he will be a mental puppet dancing to other people's thoughts, coerced by the ideas which have already hypnotized them, and if the blind lead the blind, shall they not both fall into the ditch?

Belief, Faith, and Prayer

And the prayer of faith shall save the sick, and the Lord shall raise him up (James 5:15). What, then, is the prayer of faith?

Jesus clearly taught that Spiritual Power works through man at the level of his belief, implying that it would work as he believed and while he believed. He ascribed a mighty power to belief and to faith, and we find that throughout the ages faith has been honored. Most certainly some people's prayers have been answered, but not all persons' prayers have been answered in the way in which they wished them to be answered.

How are we going to account for the fact that one person's prayers are answered and another's are not? Must we admit that there are degrees in which prayers are answered? And if so, why? Is one man's faith better than another's? Is God more pleased with one man's petition than another's?

It seems a pretty tough problem, until we understand what Jesus meant when he said, *Go thy way, and as thou hast believed, so be it done unto thee.*

What did he imply? He implied that it is done unto us by some impersonal Principle, a Principle which knows neither Jew nor Gentile, but knows only Its own ability to do. It will do as quickly for one as for another. The Law is no respecter of persons but works alike for each and all.

Jesus not only said, *So be it done unto thee.* He said, *As thou hast believed.* The impersonal Law, which is the actor, does it unto us, but only as we believe. Immediately we recognize our old friend the Law of Cause and Effect. It is done unto us as we believe, and if we can believe only a little, then only what we call a little is done. But if we believe in what the consensus of human opinion has called a lot, then a lot is done. Not that there is a big or little in the Truth, but that we measure it. Well did the Great Teacher say, *With what measure ye mete, it shall be measured to you again.* It is done unto us, but only as we believe.

41

What is belief? Most surely belief is a certain way of thinking; it is an activity of consciousness. Belief is a thing of thought, and being a thing of thought we can change belief. And if what a man believes decides what is going to happen to him, the most important thing for him to do is regulate his belief so that what happens will be good for him, and he will be glad to have it happen, and joyously welcome it.

What is most likely to change our belief from a negative to a positive viewpoint? What thought, what hope, what expression, what stimulus is most likely to change our belief? This Jesus established in the Sermon on the Mount when he said that the meek shall inherit the earth; that the peacemakers shall be called the children of God. In other statements he showed us how to reform our belief so that it could partake of the nature of Reality and would contain within itself everything necessary for our well-being. This is also what the Apostle meant when he said that we should think on whatsoever things are good, true, and beautiful.

Faith is an affirmative mode of thought. Faith says, "I can," rather than "I cannot" or "I shall not." We can learn to have faith in abundance rather than in poverty. We can change our thought in regard to lack. This is what treatment is for. Instead of saying, "There is not enough good to go around," we say, "All the power there is, is devoted to my good. I am not afraid of poverty because all the power there is, is devoted to giving me abundance. God provides me with every good thing today, every day, always." Such statements as these will change our belief from denial to one of positive faith. Whatever we can have faith in, and having faith in, can understand, we may experience according to the Law of Cause and Effect. This Law is immutable, invariable, unassailable, and absolute.

"But," someone might ask, "is faith in lack equal to faith in abundance?" The answer to this question is that there is neither lack nor abundance, as such; there is merely what is and the way it works. We are so constituted that faith in love overcomes the belief in hate. Our nature is such that faith in life destroys our fear of death. Our nature is such that faith routs all fear all along the line. The great affirmations of life must, of neces-

42

sity, destroy their apparent opposites. Nevertheless we cannot overlook the fact that all statements are positive, all statements are affirmations, since each is a statement of one's belief in something.

Right here is where prayer comes in, and of course we are thinking of prayer in its broadest connotation and its most realistic meaning. We are thinking of prayer as the communion of the soul with the Oversoul, with the Divine Creative Presence which is not only in the soul but which *is* the soul. It is more than an individualization; it is also a Universality.

Prayer in its truest sense is not a petition, not a supplication, not a wail of despair; it is rather an alignment, a unifying process which takes place in the mind as it reaches to its Divine Self and to that Power which is greater than human understanding. In the act of such prayerful and reverent communion with God one senses the Unity of Good, the completeness of Life, and at times the veil of doubt is lifted and the face of Reality appears. This consciousness, which has been referred to as the Secret Place of the Most High, is an experience rising out of the conviction that God is all there is, beside Whom there is none else.

Prayer, then, is communion, and this communion pronounces life to be Good. Prayerful communion ascends to that place where unity has not yet become variety, where the unformed One is ready to take any specific shape. In this act of communion the individual becomes copartner with the Eternal and gives birth to time, space, and conditions.

But what could Jesus have meant when he referred to fasting in connection with prayer? It seems evident that he was not necessarily referring to a physical fact, for one of the accusations laid against him was that he drank wine with sinners. He was also accused of breaking the Sabbath by permitting his disciples to pluck corn on the Sabbath day. In fact he seemed to disregard many of the outward forms which were common in his day. He referred to some deeper Principle which physical fasting was intended to symbolize.

This is what he meant when he said that it was not sufficient to make the outside of the platter clean, and again when he said, *Not every one that saith unto me, Lord, Lord, shall enter into the kingdom of heaven.* Perhaps by fasting and prayer Jesus meant such a complete consecration to the ideal that the Creative Genius of the Universe passed immediately into Self-expression through man's imagination.

Such a high altitude of thought could not be described other than by using the symbol of fasting and prayer, and possibly that is why Jesus used it. Suppose we call fasting a determination to refuse further contemplation of the negative. This would be passing from death into life, from negation into affirmation, from denial into acceptance. In this transformation of thought through faith and belief the communion of the soul with its Source would become a pronouncement rather than a petition. This is the position which the enlightened of all ages have taken.

If a person feels that the act of physical fasting is necessary to the consummation of such a devout communion, let him fast, and no person should be so rash as to deny him this privilege. If, on the other hand, he feels that he is not fighting his way but singing a song, let no one deny him the joyous pathway to freedom. For sooner or later all must discover that it is neither fasting nor feasting, but belief, faith, and acceptance which cause one to transcend the lesser good and ascend into that holy mount within where the eye views the world *as one vast plain and one boundless reach of sky.*

We must never forget to make a practical application of this science. In our philosophy it is not enough merely to state a principle. We must apply such a principle to our everyday living, and wherever a need appears we must meet it, not by accepting the inevitability of such a need but by affirming its exact opposite. The need is met when we no longer recognize it as a need but seeing through it envision that Principle which could just as easily remold the need into an acceptance of good. Therefore we are told to think on whatsoever things are true, lovely, and of good report; we should dwell on these things rather than on their apparent opposites.

To put this into practice should be the desire of every sincere seeker after spiritual truth. He must come to believe that there is such a Divine Power awaiting his use. He must fully un-

44

derstand that he is the one who knows how to use It and then he must proceed defnitely to make use of this Power which is within all men. In actual practice one's life should become a continuous communion with Good.

One's mind should be continuously acknowledging the presence of Good and the Power of Good in one's experience. A practitioner should acknowledge the Power and Presence of this Good in the experience of the one he seeks to help. For the acknowledgment of Good is a creative act making possible its manifestation in human experience. We should *fast* from the idea of lack and *feast* with the idea of plenty. We should *fast* from the idea of poverty and *feast* upon the belief in wealth, and most surely we should abstain from contemplating uncertainties and enter into a long and eternal period of feasting upon certainty. And when the world cries, "Whither goest thou?" something within us should answer, "We know in whom we have believed."

At first this fasting and feasting, this prayer and communion, may seem a little difficult. We all are more or less surrounded by negation and this is where the office of prayer enters. It establishes a serenity within the soul enabling it to have confidence in that spirit of acceptance without which the Divine gift is never complete. For how can the Divine gift become complete until one accepts it? There is no song without a singer. And so we must learn joyfully to enter into our Divine inheritance.

What does all this mean other than that we should learn to have confidence in Life, to believe in the Eternal Goodness, and to accept the Divine Bounty? This transformation of thought from negation to affirmation is seldom instantaneous, so one must maintain a flexibility of thought, being willing to bend somewhat before the storms of life but refusing to break. One's thought should have an elasticity which permits it to spring back into place, but it cannot do so unless it is first fully convinced that it does know in Whom it has believed, unless it is completely convinced that the Universe is a spiritual system governed by a Beneficent Consciousness.

This greater vision seldom transpires in one flash of consciousness, although it may do so. More often than not the ascent from our valley of negation to the mountaintop of realization is slow. But each step on the road entices us with the enchantment of a new vista, and, judging from past experiences and former transformations, the pathway upon which we travel leads to the summit and we press on with joy.

By some Divine interior awareness, call it what we will, there is an intuition within man which pushes him forward. There is some spark which has never been entirely extinguished. The prayer of faith and belief, communion of the soul with its Source, fans this spark into a Divine blaze in whose light dark shadows no longer lurk. This is inspiration. This is illumination. This is the perception of wholeness.

Suppose a man were to prepare himself a mental diet garnished with spiritual realization, his meat the living word, his bread manna from heaven, his fruit the inspiration of hope, and his wine the essence of joy. And suppose in addition to this he should see this table spread before him in the wilderness and waited upon by the Law, the servant of God and man, would he not then realize that he is today in the Kingdom of Heaven, that today God is his Host, and would he not exclaim, ''Oh, Wilderness were Paradise enow!''

The Story of Growth

THE BIBLE symbolizes the spiritual evolution of man, beginning in the Old Testament and culminating in the life and teaching of Jesus, the Christ. As we examine the spiritual symbology of the Bible we should realize that as it tells the story of a race of people it also presents the story of every man's life—yours and mine.

The Bible starts with the fundamental premise that God, the Universal Creative Spirit, is present everywhere and is within man himself. To this concept is added the great Law of Cause and Effect. Then the Bible presents the idea that man is created free, with the possibility of limitless expansion, and let alone to discover himself.

During this process of self-discovery man brings upon himself, through the operation of the Law of Mind, the experiences he images in his thought. We have on one hand the evolution of the individual life under the guidance of Divine Providence, which leads to harmony. In contrast there is the freedom to live under the false guidance of a sense of being separated from Good, which leads to disaster and chaos.

But always the Bible holds before us the great promise of the final redemption of man through understanding the Law of his being and his relationship to the Divine Spirit. It shows us that there is always Something at the innermost depths of our being which never completely loses a sense of Its Spiritual Nature.

Even in the midst of the confusion that followed the misuse of the Law by the Children of Israel, they produced the greatest line of spiritual prophets the world has ever known. These prophets were the ones who always remembered who they really were.

The era of the prophets cannot be divorced from the Kingdom of Israel, its development and rise to power, and its division and dispersal. Nor can the Kingdom of Israel be separated from the Kingdom which each one of us represents. We can relate the development of the Kingdom of Israel to the integration of a personality or the coming into wholeness of any one being.

47

When the Children of Israel came out of the land of Egypt they were an unorganized people. They lived in scattered tribes, warring with other desert tribes. Necessity for self-preservation caused them to band together into greater colonies and this brought forth the need for organized leadership. Here we are introduced to one of the factors that made Israel a great nation.

The first leaders of the Children of Israel were spiritual rather than political or social leaders. The spiritual impulse was fundamental to the nature of their being. Judges were selected to rule over the people—not judges in the sense that we think of for our courts of law, but spiritual judges who represented the Divine Law, the Will of God, or Jehovah. The spiritual Law was, in fact, the civil law of the Hebrew people.

As the nation began to take form it passed from religious into civil leadership and the Kingdom of Israel was established. But we remember that it was a spiritual leader, the prophet Samuel, who raised Saul, the first king, to his throne. And Saul, under Divine guidance, developed the Kingdom of Israel to a power undreamed of. He organized his people so that they worked together effectively in commerce, agriculture, industry, and international relations.

When David ascended to the throne, he was anointed by Samuel the prophet, and undertook to continue the development of the kingdom under Divine guidance. David brought a quality of love to his reign to complement the organizational ability and the intellect of Saul. And the Kingdom of Israel rose to even greater heights.

David's son succeeded him on the throne, and Solomon inherited by far the richest and most powerful kingdom of the world at that time. In the early part of his reign Solomon became noted for his great wisdom and understanding. But later, to satisfy his increasing love of luxury and power, it was necessary for him to increase taxation and conscript more and more slave labor. His people began to grow restless under this oppression, and eventually a segment of them rebelled and seceded from the kingdom. The great nation was divided.

Here is the story of a man who, when his thought was centered on God, erected the great Temple which so perfectly symbolized the meaning of life and the relationship between the individual and the Universal. And then, when he lost the spiritual meaning of the Temple he had built and became engrossed in material force, both his wisdom and his power deserted him. Solomon began to worship two Gods—the god of temporal power and the God of his ancestors, *the one and only true God.* This marked the beginning of the disintegration of a mighty kingdom.

For hundreds of years following the fall of the Kingdom of Israel the Hebrew people were subjected to every indignity known to the human family. But as great as their plight was, never were they without a prophet of the Lord to keep hope alive, to keep before them the promise of a Messiah who would lead them out of their captivity.

There was always an Isaiah to say:

They shall beat their swords into plowshares, and their spears into pruning hooks; nation shall not lift up sword against nation, neither shall they learn war any more (Isaiah 2:4).

And in his prophecy concerning the coming of Christ:

And the spirit of the Lord shall rest upon him, the spirit of wisdom and understanding, the spirit of counsel and might, the spirit of knowledge and of the love of the Lord (Isaiah 11:2).

There was always a Hosea to say:

Come, and let us return unto the Lord: for he hath torn, and he will heal us; he hath smitten, and he will bind us up (Hosea 6:1).

And there was always a Micah to say:

But thou, Bethlehem, though thou be little among the thousands of Judah, yet out of thee shall he come forth unto me that is to be ruler in Israel; whose goings forth have been from of old, from everlasting. . . . And this man shall be the peace, when the Assyrian shall come into our land; and when he shall tread in our palaces (Micah 5:2,5).

All of the prophets who arose during this period of captivity prophesied the final emancipation of the Children of Israel from their bondage through a return to the true knowledge of the Kingdom of God and the final triumph of spiritual Power. They all pointed to the fact that somewhere in human experience some man would arise who would completely reveal the Divine Nature and the Divine Sonship.

Every man is a nation unto himself, a nation inhabited by many thoughts, feelings, appetites, and talents. Every man is a nation of consciousness. All too often, like the Children of Israel, we find it easy to build golden calves and reach with lustful hands to grasp the illusion of temporal power. It is easy for us to forget that there is a Supreme Ruler at the center of the nation of ourselves, whose Sovereignty is fixed in Love and enthroned in the Sonship of God.

It is only as we turn our thoughts away from this Spiritual Sovereignty that our faculties and energies become dispersed. This makes us a weakened nation, subject to the invasion of every fear, doubt, disease, and temptation that presents itself at the borders of our experience.

But, as with the Children of Israel, there is always a prophet in our own minds that gives us hope, consolation, and promise in the knowledge that Life can never destroy Itself and that *truth crushed to earth shall rise again.* This prophet is our own soul, which eternally proclaims the Messiah, even though we may be lost in a wilderness of our own false concepts. We should not forget that the very Power which created this wilderness is the Power that builds the highway for the remnant to return to the Holy Land.

It is the personal application of these great historic symbols presented in the Old Testament in which we are particularly interested. For the ancient race of the Children of Israel has long since departed, but the lesson is as new as the latest invention.

Let us each be sure, then, that the voice of the prophet within does not go unheard or unheeded. Let us right now be still and listen as the Son of God within us proclaims the glory of his Kingdom. Let this Kingdom be real to us in a very practical way. Let us know right now that we are established in the kingdom of health, happiness, and wholeness, because we are established in the Kingdom of God.

Two Great Leaders

JESUS AND Moses are the two outstanding personages of the Bible. It is inescapable, then, that we should find the lives of these two leaders touching the very essence and meaning of the great Spiritual Principles which the Bible represents.

We find the teaching of Moses and the Mosaic decalogue based on the concept of a Divine Presence and an immutable Law of Cause and Effect. But there is a certain warmth, color, and personal relationship to the Infinite which is not as apparent in the teaching of Moses as in the teaching of Jesus. It was the mission of Jesus to reveal this close relationship that every individual has to the Divine Presence and the Universal Law.

It might be said that Moses was the Great Universalist and Jesus the Great Individualist. Moses was the inspired leader who recognized the Universal *I AM*, and Jesus was the one who recognized the individual *I* in this Universal *I AM*. He understood that the abstract Universal Principles must remain concrete and real in our own individual experience, for he said, *. . . as the Father hath life in himself, so hath he given to the Son to have life in himself.*

The people with whom Moses was associated were like children. Moses was like a father to them. Consequently we find in the teaching of Moses a whole category of laws, of ''Thou shalt's'' and ''Thou shalt not's'' born out of his paternal interest in his people. If we carefully look into the deep meaning of these laws we find they were all designed to reveal the One Divine Presence to the undisciplined mind. Our study and reading are a process of disciplining our own thoughts to grow into greater spiritual understanding.

Continually we find Jesus referring to ''the law and the prophets.'' But with his advent, for the first time in human history we find one who balanced the universal Law of Cause and Effect by introducing the personal factor. We find one who boldly proclaimed that the Life of God is in man and the Law of God is operating through man. It was this that distinguished his teaching from that of everyone who preceded him.

Jesus was the greatest individualist who ever lived. He based his whole teaching on the value of the individual life, the significance and meaning of the thought that, as great and wonderful as is the concept of a Divine Presence and a Universal Law, there is at the center of every man's being a revelation of this Presence and an exemplification of this Law. But as great an individualist as Jesus was, he made the claim that behind the individuality is the Spiritual Oneness which holds us all together in Unity and Love.

The whole story of Moses and Jesus finally simmers down to this simple fact: God, the original Creative Spirit, the Universal *I AM*, and the Power of the Law of God are at the center of every person's being. Moses taught the Law but it remained for Jesus to show us how to use It. And this is why we find so many references in the teaching of Jesus to the thought that *I am in the Father, and the Father in me . . . he that hath seen me hath seen the Father . . . the Father that dwelleth in me, he doeth the works.*

Like all great spiritual leaders, when Moses had received the revelation of the Divine Presence he desired to impart it to others. He recognized that Truth Itself is universal and belongs to all people. While Moses was the great law-giver, he undoubtedly realized that there was something beyond even the Law, which is Love. He prophesied the fulfillment of his teaching in the life of Jesus when he said, *The Lord thy God will raise up unto thee a prophet from the midst of thee, of thy brethren, like unto me; unto him shall ye hearken.* And Jesus said, *Think not that I am come to destroy the law or the prophets: I am come not to destroy, but to fulfill.*

When we study the teaching of Jesus, we discover that while Moses had taught the universal Law of Cause and Effect—an eye for an eye and a tooth for a tooth, and that we must all suffer from the mistakes we have made—Jesus added to this the concept of a universal Fatherhood and a universal brotherhood, and the Law of Love.

These two propositions, rightly understood, become the greatest spiritual system of thought ever given to the world. If their universal scope is not understood, they are restricted to a definite time in history and to a few people. The time and the people were merely examples of what should finally happen to the whole world. The teaching of both Moses and Jesus was timeless.

When we find the key to the meaning of their teaching we shall have found the key to our own freedom. Our trouble has been that we have not discovered that this key which unlocks the doorway to the larger life is, as Moses said, in our own mouth. We have not realized that the thing which seems so insignificant in the scheme of things—the personal self—is, as Jesus taught, the keystone of the arch.

Remembering, then, that the Bible is a book of the emancipation of man—which means the freedom of each of us—we must never lose sight of the necessity of combining the teaching of Moses with that of Jesus, and come to realize that the reason why Jesus fulfilled the Law was that he understood the full meaning of the building of the temple, which temple the Apostle said we are.

There is no question that Jesus introduced a whole new outlook on life, a whole new philosophy of living, for he alone had the faith and the courage to announce, without qualification and without limitation, that the same Power that created everything and holds everything in place is also at the very center of our own being.

It is little wonder that, having discovered the inward authority of the Divine Presence, Jesus, like Moses, called others to follow him, proclaiming a way of life and truth. For the secret was not to be to him alone, but a light unto the feet of every man. It was not to be a Power that he alone knew how to use, for he said, *He that believeth in me, the works that I do shall he do also, and greater works than these shall he do.*

54

Jesus laid down the Divine gauntlet. To refuse to pick it up would be to stand in darkness when there is light at hand. And he revealed the fount of living waters from which, he said, if a man drink he will never thirst again. To refuse to drink from this fountain, even though its waters are at hand, is to choke ourselves with the dryness of our own throats.

But how can we drink from this fountain unless we recognize its presence? This is why Jesus told us that we must believe.

What the Mystics
Have Taught

To BEGIN with, the mystics have taught a perennial philosophy, which means that the deep spiritual thinkers of every age have arrived at certain conclusions independently of each other, and we may be certain that in the main their conclusions were correct.

The great spiritual seers of the ages have taught that man is on the pathway of an eternal evolution, the purpose of which is to produce in the individual everything that is inherent in the Nature of the Divine. To feel back to this fundamental Unity, to commune with It, to experience the beneficence of Its Presence, recognized and understood, is what is meant by mysticism.

It would be impossible in the space at our disposal to use exhaustive quotations from the mystics. But you will find a thread of continuity running through them all. You will discover that they all arrived at approximately the same conclusions. It is worthy of note that, throughout all their teachings, evil as a thing in itself disappears and becomes lack of the knowledge of Truth. The theological concept of hell, the morbid teachings of the afterlife are missing from the teachings of the inspired, because they knew that we all are in the process of evolution, and that finally everyone will arrive at the same place, for God is incarnated in all.

It is necessary for a student of the Science of Mind to understand this, for while we are often surrounded by negative conditions which most certainly seem evil, evil is never a thing in itself. Therefore the mystics have taught that Good finally must triumph over evil, even though it appears as though there were a struggle between the powers of Light and darkness.

In the bibles of the world and many other sources, one persistent purpose, teaching, and conclusion runs through them all:

The Universe is a spiritual system and we are some part of it; God is right where we are and is discovered at the center of our own being. Turning from everything that denies this and quietly contemplating the Perfection of the Inner Man, who is an incarnation of God, we meet the Great Reality in the only place we shall ever discover It, within our own hearts and souls and minds.

A Brief History
of New Thought

THE TERM *New Thought* refers to the modern
metaphysical movement whose philosophy teaches that we are
living in a Spiritual Universe here and now. There are quite a
number of such movements. They all base their belief on the
theory that the Universe is a system of Intelligence, the movement of which is Law, the Intelligence being personal and the
Law impersonal.

In reality, New Thought is rather a poor term, since most of
the ideas held in it are hoary with age. Much has been borrowed
from all ancient cultures, from the teaching of the mystics of the
Middle Ages, and from Emerson. The different groups, however,
all unite on one common basis when it comes to using the Principle of Intelligence that they believe in for definite purposes, or
for what we call treatment, meditation, or affirmative prayer.

The original sources of spiritual inspiration are almost identical, even though they spring from different cultures and from
different ages, over a long period of time. We are not particularly
interested in where the forerunners of this movement came
from or what their personal backgrounds may have been.
Neither are we interested in their personalities. What we seek
to discover is something beyond this: what they believed in and
why they have left such a mark on the history of the evolution
of spiritual thought, particularly in America.

For it is really in this country that the New Thought movement originated. No doubt it began with the life and teaching
of Phineas P. Quimby (1802–1866), probably one of the few
original thinkers of the ages. Through a process of thought and
experiment, he came to believe that *mind is matter in solution
and matter is mind in form.* We are not so much interested in
how he arrived at these conclusions as we are in the conclusions
themselves, because the entire New Thought movement is very
largely founded on his philosophy.

It was Quimby who first spoke of the Christ Principle or the

Science of Christ. It was he who first called Jesus a scientific as well as an inspired soul. He said that mind as form and mind as solution are one and the same thing, perhaps in the same sense that Einstein says that energy and mass are equal, identical, and interchangeable.

But Quimby did not stop here. He said that mind as matter, or form, and mind as solution, or an invisible essence, are controlled by what he called a Superior Wisdom, which Jesus understood. He called this the Science of Christ. He taught that Mind or Intelligence, in Its dual form of the visible and the invisible, constitutes the sole and only substance in the Universe. This concept was no different from that of Spinoza, who said, *I do not say that Mind is one thing and matter is another thing. I say they are the same thing.*

Quimby believed that there is Perfection at the center of everything, just as all the spiritual geniuses have believed. He believed that there is a Perfect Man standing back of all our trouble, sickness, and confusion. He said that he could sometimes see this man, but that this man is surrounded by the opinions of the world, and these beliefs take form in the physical body as disease.

That which was so revolutionary in the philosophy of Quimby was his belief that all disease is a result of the misuse of the Mind Principle; that disease is not separate from mind, but is mind in form, and since it is mind in form, mind can change it through thought or, as we would say, through the Law of Mind in Action. He drew no line between disease as a condition and the thought which produced the condition, because the thought and the thing are one and the same. This is what it is important to remember, because it is basic to all the New Thought teachings.

Quimby reasoned that, since disease is a belief or an opinion, it can be changed through changing the belief or the opinion. He was not afraid of either, because he knew that they were mind. He did not say that they did not exist, for he never denied the reality of disease. He said, ''I appear as an attorney for my patient who is the plaintiff, and I explain that he is suffering from a false belief. He is a Spiritual Being and all these opinions that are held against him have no right to be." Then he said, "You ask me what is my cure, and I answer that my explanation is the cure. For if I have completely explained the disease away, then the patient will not have it."

He taught that a series of affirmations and denials leading to an inward spiritual realization can heal physical disease, because disease is thought, while back of it there is a Spiritual Perfection which is not changed, because God's work is already done and He leaves it to man to work out his own salvation. He also taught that statements of Truth work like exact laws of mathematics, while statements of error or untruth work like laws of chance.

This was Quimby's teaching, his method, and his treatment. We are interested in what he believed, what he taught, and how he used it, because without knowing it he was the originator of the New Thought movement in America. Many people believe that Emerson was the father of New Thought. He did teach that God is the Father of all men, and he did reiterate the spiritual philosophy of the ages, but there is no evidence that he had the slightest concept of reducing this theory to a definite concept which could be practiced.

Quimby passed on in 1866 after having healed thousands of people who came to him from all over the country. A record of his conversations, discussions, and letters was kept and published under the title *The Quimby Manuscripts.* *

After his passing, what is now known as the New Thought movement actually got under way. We need mention only a few of the various units of this movement. Let us start with the Unity School of Christianity, one of the greatest spiritual institutions in the world, and one which has helped millions of people.

This movement, originated by Charles Fillmore and his wife, Myrtle, in Kansas City, is built largely on Fillmore's book *Christian Healing* and on *Lessons in Truth*, by Emilie Cady. We are

*See *Phineas Parkhurst Quimby: The Complete Writings*, 3 vols. (Marina del Rey, Calif.: DeVorss & Company, 1988).—*Ed.*

not interested in their theology or their particular religious outlook, but in what they taught and demonstrated. We come back to the same proposition: There is a Spiritual Center in everything, the Principle of Mind or Spirit governs everything, and a series of affirmations and denials will build up a healing consciousness which they called the Christ Consciousness. However, it could just as well have been called the Buddhic Consciousness or the Tao, which means *the way.* Belonging to the Christian faith, the Unity School calls it the Christ Consciousness, and affirms that a series of arguments leading to the conclusion that man is Perfect and governed by Divine Harmony will produce a definite result.

Now let us turn to the Divine Science Church, which has had a profound influence in the last two generations. It was founded by Fannie B. James in Denver. As we study the textbook upon which this teaching is based, and other contemporary writings, we find the same things that Quimby taught. There is a slight difference in theology and spiritual outlook, but when it comes to the use of the Principle, they are identical.

The Church of Truth, one of the lesser of the new spiritual movements, has been both helpful and effective in its work. One of these movements is just as effective as another when it comes to practice, since they all teach the same thing, whether they know it or not. We find them all going back to the same system of affirmations and denials, which, when effective, culminate in the same realization.

Among the earlier teachers was Emma Curtis Hopkins, who taught what she called *High Mysticism.* She had perhaps more individual students than any one teacher, at least several thousand, one of whom was this writer. She had a high degree of Cosmic Consciousness which one could feel. Many of the outstanding leaders in the New Thought movement came under her tutelage. Her method was distinctly one of mysticism, but when it is boiled down to practice and all extraneous material is taken out, we find the same systems of affirmations and denials.

Other great leaders were Christian D. Larson, Orison Swett Marden, and Ralph Waldo Trine. No other three persons have had more influence in the New Thought field, because of the extensive distribution of their books (actually millions of copies) putting them in the same category with the Unity movement. We find that these three men, when it came to actual practice, taught exactly the same thing: argument, or affirmations and denials, building up to a realization.

This movement of New Thought spread to England, and many learned teachers appeared there, probably the two most influential being F. L. Rawson and Thomas Troward. I consider Troward's writings to be the most profound spiritual abstractions of modern times. He taught very little about the application of his belief to practical matters, but he did present the Principle. One can only deduce that it would have to be used, just as in all the other teachings.

Rawson developed a most elaborate system of practice which he and his followers apparently thought to be quite different from the others, since they called it Absolute Science. This really means nothing, because all science is absolute—the thought that two and two are four is absolute. Rawson's book *Life Understood* has been read by many thousands of persons. It is a compilation of varied forms of the New Thought movement. He wrote an elaborate book on *Treatment*, covering practically everything anyone can think of, but when we come to the method, it is identical with other New Thought teachings. It is what it would have to be.

Meanwhile, here in America, a man by the name of Edwin Burrell developed what he called *The Axioms of Truth and Reason*. The presentation of his philosophy was quite involved, fairly interesting, but confusing to most people. Students came to him from across the country, and no doubt they received great benefit, because he was a great man. But when it comes to the actual practice, we return to the same fundamental proposition of affirmations, denials, and realization.

This is a brief and very inadequate outline of the New Thought movement in America. However, it does touch the high spots of a certain wave of spiritual progress over a period of nearly one hundred years, culminating in the beginning of what is probably the greatest spiritual inquiry the world has ever made.

One thing we should remember is that during this process other similar movements arose in America: Spiritualism, Theosophy, occult and esoteric teachings, Yogic and Hindu philosophy, all of which have had some influence on the whole metaphysical field. But these movements have little relationship to practical application, even though some of them are very profound and all of them are interesting.

If it had not been for Spiritualism, we probably would not have Dr. Rhine's experiments in extrasensory perception at Duke University; if it had not been for the New Thought movement, we surely would not have had the modern message that is coming into many of the more liberal churches. The whole mass of thinking has been profoundly influenced by these movements, and today you seldom pick up a newspaper or magazine without finding some reference to them.

It was because of many years spent by this writer in studying these movements, trying to be partial to none and impersonal to all, that Religious Science and the Science of Mind came into being: not as something better than any one of them, but rather as a synthesis of all of them, starting with the proposition that Spiritual Truth cannot belong to any one individual, but, being Universal in Its essence, must belong to anyone who uses It.

The New Thought Movement

THE NEW Thought Movement is essentially spiritual. Dealing with the laws of Mind, it is also scientific. It assumes that God is not only the final Reality, he is the only present Reality. Everything that is real is of Him. Our own being is God manifest as personality.

The New Thought Movement has been likened to applied Christianity. It is both unique and practical, since it seeks to make definite use of spiritual power in everyday living. This attempt to re-evaluate the philosophy of Christianity in terms of practical application definitely originated in the New Thought Movement, and became its chief impulsion, its outstanding characteristic. *It is this practical application of spiritual causation to human needs which has drawn the attention of millions of people in America and other millions throughout the world to a new outlook on life, and to new hope.*

Whatever the New thought Movement may owe to other systems, and it owes much, it is unique in this: It has placed a new and dynamic meaning on the relationship between God and man, between the invisible and the visible. With Jesus, it has insisted that faith shall be made manifest in works; that the Creative Power of God is individualized in every soul. Spiritual faith, belief and conviction, are not merely terms used to designate the devotional life, they are dynamic and creative instruments to be used in everyday living.

While there is a wide range of opinion among the New Thought leaders, teachers, practitioners and laymen, this one underlying purpose runs through the entire Movement: the immediate availability of Good; conscious and practical application of spiritual thought force to the solution of human problems; the inevitable necessity that good shall come to every soul; the belief in immortality and the continuity of the individual stream of consciousness, and eternal expansion of the individual life; the awakening, not to an absorption of man's identity in Deity, but to his complete unity with the Whole. Thus every ~~man~~ becomes an individualized center of God Consciousness, eternally expanding.

The New Thought Movement is metaphysical, but not in a strict philosophical sense. Metaphysics in terms of New Thought means a practical idealism, which emphasizes spiritual causation and the accessibility of spiritual mind power, acting in accord with law and available to all people. From this standpoint, "Christian Metaphysics" means the philosophy of the New Testament, practiced as a science.

It is the purpose of the New Thought Movement to prove the teachings of Jesus relative to the spiritual universe and man's relationship to it. The New Thought Movement in many ways is unlike most of the Oriental teachings, for in following the philosophy of Jesus more closely than that of other teachers of antiquity, it emphasizes the importance of individualism. In this it is quite American, which is natural, since the Movement started here. Yet it would be a mistake to deny the heritage which this Movement has received from many sources. It is an outgrowth of all that has gone before. It has borrowed much from the idealistic philosophies of the ages, particularly Plato, Socrates and the Neoplatonists. It has been profoundly influenced by the teachings of the Old Testament, the precepts of Buddha and the Sacred Writings of the East. It owes an enormous debt of gratitude to many of the spiritual philosophies of the Middle Ages and in our own country is particularly indebted to Emerson and many others with whose writings we are all familiar.

But as much as it owes to other systems of thought, it is still a unique American institution, in that it started in this country, and, although it has spread over the world, it has flourished and grown here more than elsewhere. It probably would be safe to estimate that from fifteen to twenty million people in America today are influenced by its teachings.

The Movement itself is the outcome of a number of contemporaneous systems of thought which have emphasized the inner life. As Dresser stated in his *History of the New Thought Movement*, "The last century witnessed the rediscovery of the inner life. . . . The new age bids us go to the sources for ourselves."

Probably more than on the work of any other one person, the New Thought Movement of America has been built upon the teachings of Phineas Quimby, who was born in New Hampshire in 1802 and who passed from this plane in the state of Maine in 1866. This man was one of the few original thinkers of the ages. He had a deep intuition as well as an unusually pronounced psychic development. He believed that we are living in a spiritual universe now, but that the freedom of our choice, backed by the law of Mind, makes possible the experience of discord and limitation. He said: "Can a theory be found capable of practice which can separate Truth from error? I undertake to say there is a method of reasoning which, being understood, can separate one from the other. . . . Man is made up of truth and belief; and, if he is deceived into a belief that he has, or is liable to have, a disease, the belief is catching, and the effect follows it."

Quimby laid his chief emphasis on spiritual mind healing, rather than on the control of conditions through the creative power of thought. He claimed that disease is but a dream from which one may be awakened. His method, according to his son, George Quimby, was to "change the mind of a patient, and disabuse it of its error and establish the truth in its place, which, if done, was the cure."

He was completely convinced that the Creative Spirit within us is God, and that we have an immediate relationship to the Divine. This relationship is creative. Quimby never sought to control others; he made no suggestions to them. That is, he did not practice suggestive therapeutics. His whole method of procedure was spiritual explanation. His idea was that symptoms would disappear with the changed viewpoint. In this he anticipated the discoveries of modern psychology, except that his was a more spiritual method.

He spoke of mind as *spiritual substance*, and often referred to what he called the real or the spiritual man who needed to be summoned to the aid of the man who is mentally and physically sick.

Quimby believed in a spiritual body. He taught that there is no disease independent of mind. Thus he said, "Disease being in its root a wrong belief, change the belief and it will cure the disease. By faith we are thus made whole."

The New Thought Movement in America today owes much to this man's life, teaching and practice. Most of its early teachers were instructed by him. Thus we find most of them emphasizing the Divine Spark in man, which, despite all appearances to the contrary, is always there.

Shortly after Quimby passed in 1866, several of his devout students, most of whom he had healed, began to teach and write. Each branched out freely and naturally, each added his own ideas to what he had received from Quimby. Among those early teachers were people who had already been theologically trained, several of them in the Swedenborgian Church, and it was not difficult for them to follow Quimby since they had already been taught to believe in a law of spiritual correspondences. Whatever the difference of opinion among these earlier teachers may have been, they all seem unanimous in emphasizing mental and spiritual causation and the thought that the material universe possesses no independent life and intelligence. Of course, this was before the day of the new physics. They all taught that spiritual mind healing of the physical body is a result of touching the DREAMS. springs of life in the soul of the patient. Naturally the different teachers chose different names, such as Divine Science, Metaphysical Clubs, Applied Christianity, Practical Christianity and innumerable other names, and in England the term Higher Thought was used, all of which have a common meaning. The New Thought Movement has always been very individualistic and in many respects has stood for a protest against ecclesiastical or spiritual authority. Finally, an attempt was made to weld the whole movement into a national alliance for the purpose of clarity of thought and the dissemination of its teaching.

The following declaration of purpose is taken from one of its earliest records: "Organized to promote an active interest in a more spiritual philosophy and its practical application to human life. Its spirit is broad, tolerant and constructive, and its object an impartial search for truth. All who sympathize with these purposes, without regard to past or present affiliations of sect, party or system, are cordially invited to cooperate."

In another statement drawn at an early date we read: ". . . It seeks the spark of infinitude in the seemingly finite, and seeks to fan it into a blaze that shall be the light of the world. It is therefore striving to bring into hearty cooperation all the individual potencies that have tended toward the high end which it has in view, believing that thus a resistless impulse might be given to the development of life on the highest attainable plane."

It was the purpose of the New Thought Movement not only to stand for a method of spiritual healing, but for a positive and affirmative philosophic idealism of religion, of applied Christianity, and to emphasize the rediscovery of the Gospel teachings relative to healing and everyday life.

Religous Science

I WAS fortunate in being reared in a home where no religious fears were taught, and where every attempt was made to keep away from superstition and ignorance. It was, however, a religious home, where family prayers were said, the Bible was read daily, and grace was said at mealtime. But it was never suggested that we fear God or the future.

I was a natural candidate for the New Thought philosophies that have sprung up in this country. Having read Emerson, it was easy to realize that Unity is at the base of everything.

Over a period of several years it was my privilege to study the ancient systems of thought, the mystical writings of the Middle Ages, and the modern movements such as Theosophy, Spiritualism, and the various branches of New Thought. I found great interest in trying to synthesize these various systems, with the purpose in mind of finding the thread of unity running through them. It became my persistent desire to put them all together in one system, realizing that we inherit the great thought of the ages and may enjoy the privilege of entering into its meaning.

Probably no one could have had less desire than I to organize or launch a new religion. I am a great believer in all religions, and am firmly convinced that every man's faith is good for him and that the form it takes is best for him at the particular time he follows such form.

I am certain that the great spiritual leaders of the ages, having given their lives to meditation, prayer, and communion with the Spirit, have left a great spiritual legacy to the world. Taken as a whole, they have come nearer to discovering God than any other group of people. Claiming very little originality of thought and not particularly desiring any, I have always been in a position to learn from all sources. Truth cannot belong to any individual, and there can be no religion higher than the Truth.

Out of the years of study and thought emerged the system we call Religious Science because religion is our idea of God, while science is a knowledge of facts, causes, and principles which exist independently of our thinking, just as gravitational force does. Religious Science is a compilation of the great thoughts of the ages, the deep mystical yearnings of minds in search for God, and the modern approach to a faith which can be demonstrated.

This is a brief history of the Religious Science movement which is gradually spreading as though it had a Cosmic Purpose behind it. But there is nothing dogmatic about it. You can add the Science of Mind to your own religion, whatever form it may take, and find it to be effective. For Principles are no respecters of persons, and heaven has no favorites.

A world without religion would be chaos. A world built on dogma alone would be arbitrary. Surely any religion which holds that the Final Truth has been delivered, once and for all, to its own group must contain a large amount of superstition, and thereby prohibits the further evolution of the human mind.

Religious Science is the outcome of what has gone before and, we believe, a forerunner of what is to come. Religious Science is not a personal opinion nor is it a special revelation. It is a result of the best thought of the ages. It borrows much of its light from others, but in so doing robs no one, for Truth is universal.

Taking the best from all sources, Religious Science has access to the highest enlightenment of the ages. Shorn of dogmatism, freed from superstition, and always ready for greater illumination, Religious Science offers the student of life the best that the world has discovered.

The varying faiths of mankind are unnumbered, but the primal Truth of the race is, today as of old, the One Faith: an instinctive reliance upon the Unseen, which we call God. Religion is One. Faith is One. Truth is One. There is One Reality at the heart of all religions, whether their name be Hindu, Mohammedan, Christian, or Jewish.

While the Universal Mind contains all knowledge and is the potential of all things, only as much Truth comes to us as we are able to receive. Should all the wisdom of the Universe be poured over us, we should yet receive only that which we are ready to understand. Each draws from the Source of all knowledge only that to which he inwardly listens. The scientist discovers the principle of his science, the artist taps the essence of beauty, the saint draws Christ into his being, because to each is given according to his ability to receive.

Believing that the Universal Spirit comes to fullest consciousness in man's innermost Self, we strive to cultivate the inner life, knowing that spiritual certainty is the result of an impact of God upon the soul. Like the Methodism of old, we seek the witness of the Inner Spirit.

In its practice and teachings, Religious Science endeavors to include the whole life. It is not a dreamy, mystical cult, but the exponent of a vigorous philosophy applicable to the everyday needs of life, and this accounts for its rapid growth. Men and women find in it a message that fits in with their daily needs.

The conventional idea of the future life, with its teachings of reward and punishment, is not stressed; the gospel is the good news for the *here and now.* Religion, if it means anything, means right living, and right living and right thinking wait upon no future but bestow their rewards in this life—in better health, happier homes, and all that makes for a well-balanced, normal life.

The thought of the ages has looked to the day when science and religion shall walk hand in hand through the visible to the invisible. A movement which endeavors to unify the great conclusions of human experience must be kept free from petty ideas, from personal ambitions, and from any attempt to promote one man's opinion. Science knows nothing of opinion, but recognizes a government of law whose principles are universal. These laws, when complied with, respond alike to all. Religion becomes dogmatic and often superstitious when based on the lengthened shadow of any one personality. Philosophy intrigues us only to the extent that it sounds a universal note.

The ethics of Buddha, the morals of Confucius, the beatitudes of Jesus, together with the spiritual experiences of other great minds, constitute viewpoints of life which must not be overlooked. The mystical concepts of the ancient sage of China

71

keep faith with the sayings of Emerson, and wherever deep cries unto deep, deep answers deep.

Old forms, old creeds are passing, but the Eternal Realities abide. Religion has not been destroyed. It is being discovered. God is the great innovator in His world, and progress is by Divine authority. Through all the ages one increasing purpose runs, and that purpose can be no less than the evolution of the highest spiritual attributes of mankind. It is the unessential only that is vanishing, that the abiding may be made more clearly manifest.

What wonder that religious faith in our day is breaking from the narrow bounds of past teaching and expanding in both breadth and depth. It is not because men believe less in God and the true essentials of spiritual life, but because they must believe more; they are literally forced by the inevitable logic of facts to build for themselves concepts of the Infinite commensurate with the greatness and glory of the world in which they live.

The future religion will be free from fear, superstition, and doubt, and will ask no man where God may be found. For the Secret Place of the Most High will be revealed in the inner sanctuary of man's own heart, and the eternal God will sit enthroned in man's own mind. We can know no God external to that power of perception by which alone we are conscious of anything. God must be interpreted to man through man's own nature.

Who would know God must be *as* God, for He who inhabits eternity finds a dwelling place in His own creation. Standing before the altar of life in the temple of faith, an individual learns that he is an integral part of the Universe, and that it would not be complete without him. That native faith within, which we call intuition, is the direct impartation of Divine Wisdom through us. Who can doubt its gentle urge or misunderstand its meaning?

There is a Presence pervading all, an Intelligence running through all, a Power sustaining all, binding all into One Perfect Whole. The realization of this Presence, Intelligence, Power, and Unity constitutes the nature of the mystic Christ, the indwelling Spirit, the image of God, the Sonship to the Father.

Christ means the universal idea of Sonship; the entire creation both visible and invisible. There is One Father of all. This

One Father, conceiving within Himself, gives birth to all the Divine Ideas. The sum total of all these Ideas constitutes the mystic Christ.

Jesus was a man, a human being, who understood his own nature. He knew that, as the human embodies the Divine, it manifests the Christ nature.

Every man is a potential Christ. From the least to the greatest, the same Life runs through all, threading Itself into the patterns of our individuality. He is *over all, in all, and through all.* As Jesus the man gave way to the Divine Idea, the human took on the Christ Spirit and became the voice of God to humanity.

Conscious of his Divinity, yet humble as he contemplated the infinite life around him, Jesus spoke from the height of spiritual perception, proclaiming the deathless Reality of the individual life, the continuity of the individual soul, the Unity of the Universal Spirit with all men.

Religious Science, following the example of Jesus, teaches that all men may aspire to Divinity, since all men are incarnations of God. It also teaches a direct relationship between God and man. God is incarnated in all men and individualized through all creation without loss to Himself. Within the One Supreme Mind exists the possibility of projecting limitless expressions of Itself, but each expression is unique and different from any other. Thus the Infinite is not divided but multiplied.

While all people have the same origin, no two are alike except in ultimate Essence—*One God and Father of us all,* but numberless sonships, each sonship a unique institution in the Universe of Wholeness. Man is an individualized center of God-Consciousness and Spiritual Power, as complete as he knows himself to be, and he knows himself only as he comprehends his relationship to the Whole.

This overbrooding Presence, this inner sense of a greater Reality, bears witness to Itself through our highest acts and in our deepest emotions. Who is there who has not at times felt this inner Presence? It is impossible to escape our true nature. We stand in the shadow of a mighty Presence, while Love forever points the way to heaven. Behind all is a Unity, through all is a diversity, saturating all is a Divinity.

The Universe is a spiritual system governed by Laws of Mind. There are not two minds; there is but One Mind which is God. The out-push of the Mind of God through the mind of man is the Self-Realization of Spirit seeking a new outlet for Its own expression.

Religious Science teaches that God is personal, and personal in a unique sense, to everyone. It teaches that conscious communion with the indwelling Spirit opens avenues of intuition and provides a new starting point for the Creative Power of the Almighty. Every man comes from the bosom of the unseen Father. As Divinity is awakened, the Divine Spark shot from the central fires of the Universal Flame warms other souls in the flow of Its own Self-Realization.

Religious Science not only emphasizes the Unity of God and man; it teaches us that in such degree as our thought becomes spiritualized it actually manifests the Power of God. Throughout the ages wonderful results have been obtained through the prayer of faith, practiced by every religion. There is a Law governing this possibility, or it never could have been. It is the business of Religious Science to view these facts, estimate their cause, and in so doing provide a definite knowledge of the Law governing the facts.

Religious Science is a religion of joy, free from fear. It is a religion of faith justified by results. Religious Science offers the world what the ages have been waiting for. It is the culmination of the hope, the aspiration, and the faith of the enlightened of all time.

The New Age demands that the fear and superstition surrounding religious conviction be removed, and that the Truth, plain, simple, and direct, be presented that men may learn to live *now*, in the present, with the assurance that the eternal God is their refuge.

A Science of Religion
and a Religion of Science

THERE ARE three general classifications of knowledge, namely, science, philosophy, and religion. By science we mean the organized knowledge of natural law and its application to life. By philosophy we mean the opinions one holds about the world, life, and reality. Although we generally speak of philosophy in relation to those statements which have been put down in writing by men whose opinions we respect, as a matter of fact philosophy is anybody's opinion about anything. By religion we mean any man's belief about his relationship to the invisible universe. Or, we might say, religion is a man's idea of God, or gods—of the ultimate reality.

It follows, then, that there are many philosophies and many religions, since in both instances they constitute opinions. But not so with science, for science is a knowledge of the laws of nature. We also speak of pure science and applied science. Pure science is a knowledge of principles, while applied science is the technique for using universal principles.

A scientist, in whatever field of investigation he may be engaged, is one who uses universal principles. Once a principle is discovered and the laws governing it are ascertained, he maintains absolute faith in that principle.

Science is not an investigation into the why, but into the how. The why of anything, that is, the reason for its being, science makes no attempt to answer. If it should shift its field from the knowledge of principles and facts into the field of inquiry as to why these principles exist, then science becomes a philosophy.

Today, many men of science are beginning to speculate on scientific principles. And as they do this their speculations fall into two generalized classifications, philosophically speaking. These speculations usually lead them either to a philosophic basis of materialism or to a philosophic basis of idealism.

Both the idealist and the materialist believe that the universe is a thing of intelligence. The only difference is that the materialist refuses to admit that the intelligence operating through the laws of nature is backed by or permeated with any form of consciousness; that is, the intelligence is merely a blind but intelligent force, a conglomeration of immutable laws of cause and effect with no element of consciousness, no sentiment, no feeling. He sees only blind force, but he sees blind force intelligently organized.

The idealist feels that back of and operating in and through the laws of nature there is volition and consciousness. He maintains that the manifestation of physical life upon this planet always is in accord with organized intelligence. He feels that organized intelligence can be accounted for only on the basis that there is an engineer as well as an engine.

There are, then, these two branches of philosophy—the idealistic and the materialistic. The idealist believes in consciousness, hence a Spiritual Universe, while the materialist does not. Naturally, the scientist who is philosophically a materialist believes in no God, no Spiritual Universe, and no consciousness in the universe which responds to man. He does not believe in the immortality of the individual soul, nor can he give any real meaning to life. He may be a humanitarian and a very good man, but his ultimate philosophy is: ''Six feet under and all is over.''

The scientist who feels that there is consciousness in the universe finds no difficulty in believing in God or in the universe as a spiritual system, permeated with a consciousness which responds to man. Therefore he believes in prayer, immortality, the value of faith, and feels there is a definite meaning to life. An increasing number of scientific men are taking this position. The scientist who is a materialist has no religion unless it be one of humanitarianism, while the idealist can scarcely get along without some form of religious conviction.

But if the idealist is a scientifc man, believing as he must that everything is governed by law, his religion cannot be superstitious. He cannot believe in a God who specializes on one person more than on another, or who esteems one person above another; nor can he believe that the laws of nature can be broken or modified through anyone's prayer or faith. Therefore the scientific mind which is at the same time idealistic believes that the universe is not only intelligent, but that it is also consciousness, and will be satisfied with no religious concepts which contradict reason, common sense, and a cosmos of law and order.[1]

When the early discoveries of science refuted ancient superstitions and proved that this world was not the center of the universe, that it was round and not flat, the faith which many people had began to wane. The ancient shibboleths, dogmas, and superstitions could no longer be held valid for intelligent men, and formalized religion began to lose its hold on the inquiring scientific mind. Materialism was in the ascendency.

However, today we find increasing numbers of scientific men emerging from that age of materialism. This is due to the fact that modern science has not theoretically been able to resolve the material universe into purely mechanical energy, but has discovered that the smallest particles which it supposes to exist exercise a sort of volition, which of course leaves room for freedom.[2] Once you establish freedom and volition as an operating factor in connection with the energy which becomes form,[3] then you have established a universe of consciousness. And once you establish a universe of consciousness you establish the possibility of communion, and arrive at a logical basis for faith, prayer, the religious and the mystical life.

There has been a tremendous growth of knowledge which has taken place in the world in the last few hundred years. However, the vast majority of people have given but little thought to the implications involved. To most people religion has been either superstitiously entertained—and no doubt with great benefit to those who believed in it—or else it was rejected.

Today, however, there is a certain and rather swift return to

---

[1] "Religion and natural science are fighting a joint battle in an incessant, never relaxing crusade against skepticism and against dogmatism, against disbelief and against superstition, and the rallying cry in this crusade has always been, and always will be: 'On to God!' "—Max Planck
[2] Heisenberg's Theory of Indeterminacy.
[3] Einstein's theory of the equivalence of energy and mass.

spiritual convictions. These new, vital and dynamic spiritual concepts have placed firm foundations beneath man's innate religious tendency, firm foundations which scientific men need not reject and which the unscientific man may accept without superstition.[4]

This is what is meant when we speak of a scientific religion. We do not mean that religion is reduced to coldness, without sentiment or feeling, but rather that law and order are added to the sentiment and the feeling. We have a perfect right to speak of a scientific religion or a religion of science. But upon what could such a scientific religion be based? It could only be based upon the principle of Mind, of Intelligence and Consciousness, which many outstanding scientists today assert is the ultimate and fundamental reality.

Science, in affirming consciousness in the universe, that is, a spiritual Presence and an Intelligence, also affirms that the individual's consciousness is of similar nature.[5] Therefore a scientific religion does not exclude what we call prayer or communion even though it lays greater stress on communion than on petition. For instance, a scientific religion could not believe that man's petitions to God can change the natural order of the universe or reverse the laws of nature.

However, prayer now becomes the communion of the lesser with the greater, which makes it possible for man not to reverse natural law, but to reverse his position in it in such a way that bondage becomes freedom.[6]

We might speak of a pure religious science as we would speak of a pure natural science, which means the study of natural causes. We might speak of pure religous science as that

[4] "The idea that God . . . is not a being of caprice and whim, as had been the case in all the main body of thinking of the ancient world, but is instead a God who rules through law. . . . That idea has made modern science and it is unquestionably the foundation of modern civilization."—Robert A. Millikan

[5] ". . . that consciousness is a singular of which the plural is unknown; that there is only one thing and that, which seems to be a plurality, is merely a series of different aspects of this one thing."—Erwin Schrodinger

[6] "Prayer and propitiation may still influence the course of physical phenomena when directed to these centers."—Sir Arthur Eddington

branch of science which studies the natural principles; the nature of mind and Consciousness. Then we could think of applied religious science as the application of this principle to human needs for practical purposes, and this is where one encounters the study of the nature of prayer, of faith, and of mental actions and reactions.

In the use of faith, prayer, communion, or spiritual treatment, one would be applying the principles of Mind, Spirit, Intelligence, Consciousness, and Law and Order to the persistent problems of everyday life. He would, then, be more than a theoretical religionist; he would have an applied and a practical religion.

This is exactly what we mean when we speak of a science of religion and a religion of science, for we are using this term in its broadest sense. We are using the term religion from the standpoint of universal religion, including all religious beliefs—Christian, Buddhist, Mohammedan, or any other faith—and we are thinking of prayer, communion, and the laws of consciousness as applied to any and all people. In short, we are universalizing the Principle which by nature is universal. Thus each religion approaches the same God, and must basically believe in the same God. But a scientific religion cannot believe in any concept of God which denies a universe of law and order, or which attempts to exclude anyone from its benefits.

It would be unscientific as well as irrational to believe that God, or the Supreme Intelligence, holds one man in higher esteem than another. For as the Bible so truthfully and boldly declares: "And let him that is athirst come. And whosoever will, let him take the water of life freely."

One comes to agree with Robert Browning that "all's love, yet all's law," and that there is an impersonal Law as well as a personal relationship to the Spirit. This Law exists for all, like the laws of mathematics or any other natural law, but the personal relationship is personified through each at the level of his consciousness, at the level of his comprehension of what God means to him.

Intelligence and reason must be the rules of thought, and

God must be accessible to all on equal terms. The scientific religionist could not believe in miracles, but he would not deny the power of spiritual thought. Rather he would think that the so-called miracles performed as a result of spiritual faith have been in accord with natural law and cosmic order, and that they could be reproduced at will. That which the illumined have experienced and that which men of great spiritual power have proved, the scientific religionist feels should be deliberately used in everyday life.

To the individual believing there is a Principle, Intelligence, or Consciousness governing all things, there comes a feeling that he understands the laws, or at least some of the laws, of this Principle; hence he feels that it is intensely sane, as well as humanly practical, to apply faith, consciousness, and spiritual conviction to the solution of human problems. This is what is meant by spiritual mind treatment.

Spiritual mind treatment is based on the belief or the theory, which we now feel has a sound basis, that there is a Principle of Intelligence in the universe which is not only creative, giving rise to objective form, but It is immediately responsive to our consciousness; and being universal, It is omnipresent; and being omnipresent, It is not only where we are but It is what we are.[7] Hence the scientific religionist feels that he understands what Jesus meant when he said: "The words that I speak unto you I speak not of myself, but the Father, that dwelleth in me, he doeth the works."

Just as all pure science, before it can be of any use to humanity, must pass into applied science, so pure religious concepts, before they can have a practical application, must pass into applied religion. And it is the application of religion to the solution of our problems which we may speak of as demonstrating the Principle.

What, then, are the pure and applied aspects of this Princi-

[7] "We discover that the universe shows evidence of a designing or controlling power that has something in common with our own individual minds."—Sir James Jeans

ple? The basis or pure concept is that there is an Absolute Intelligence in the universe—one, undivided, birthless, deathless, changeless Reality. Since no one made God and since God did not make Himself, that which was, is, and is to be, will remain.

According to our first axiom that God is all there is, there is the implication that there is nothing else beside Him. Hence the entire manifestation of Life is an evolution or an unfoldment of form from that which is formless and eternal. This intelligent Cause, this undifferentiated and undistributed God-Principle, one and complete within Itself, is the source from which all action proceeds and in which all creation takes place.

At this point one may logically hold the belief, the opinion, or the certainty that God as man, in man, is man; that when man makes a proclamation it is still God proclaiming, but at the level of man's consciousness. Therefore the cosmos is reflected in, or manifested by or through, the individual. One cannot say, "Why is man?" any more than one can say, "Why is God?" Intelligence exists and man interprets It. Therefore man is Its mouthpiece; man is a personification of the Infinite, governed by the same laws. But man is more than law; he is consciousness.

The application of the principles of such a science of religion to our everyday problems is just as necessary as that there must be a practical application of the theories of any science for them to be of value. It is not enough merely to abstract our thought and announce an Infinite, for the Infinite can never at any time mean more to us than the use we make of It. Just as electricity can never mean more to us than the use we make of It. This is true of any and all principles of nature.

If there is an infinite Creative Intelligence which makes things out of Itself by Itself becoming the thing that It makes, and if man exists and is conscious, then the Creative Genius of this Universal Mind is also the creative genius of Its individualization, which we call man.

From the above-stated propositions intelligence cannot escape, correct induction and deduction cannot escape. Thus, most of the great intellectual geniuses who have ever lived have proclaimed these truths, each in his own tongue, in his own way, in his own day, for his own age. Many believe that Jesus proclaimed them for all ages since he was so universal in his concepts.

Such a way of thinking does not belong to any sect, to any group, to any class, and most certainly not to any person. There is no claim to special revelation; rather, for this particular system of thought there have been gathered together facts from all ages and all people, from all philosophies and religions. And using practical methods, which any other scientific research would use, it is able to, and does, present a Science of Mind with a message of freedom.

What We Believe

Declaration of Principles

We believe in God, the Living Spirit Almighty: One, Indestructible, Absolute and Self-Existent Cause. This One manifests Itself in and through all creation but is not absorbed by Its creation. The manifest universe is the body of God; it is the logical and necessary outcome of the infinite self-knowingness of God.

We believe in the incarnation of the Spirit in man and that all men are incarnations of the One Spirit.

We believe in the eternality, the immortality, and the continuity of the individual soul, forever and ever expanding.

We believe that the Kingdom of Heaven is within man and that we experience this Kingdom to the degree that we become conscious of it.

We believe the ultimate goal of life to be a complete emancipation from all discord of every nature, and that this goal is sure to be attained by all.

We believe in the Unity of all life, and that the highest God and the innermost God is One God.

We believe that God is personal to all who feel this Indwelling presence.

We believe in the direct revelation of Truth through the intuitive and spiritual nature of man, and that any man may become a revealer of Truth who lives in close contact with the Indwelling God.

We believe that the Universal Spirit, which is God, operates through a Universal Mind, which is the Law of God; and that we are surrounded by this Creative Mind which receives the direct impress of our thought and acts upon it.

We believe in the healing of the sick through the Power of this Mind.

We believe in the control of conditions through the Power of this Mind.

We believe in the Eternal Goodness, the Eternal Loving-Kindness, and the Eternal Givingness of Life to all.

We believe in our own soul, our own spirit, and our own destiny; for we understand that the life of man is God.

The following explanation of what we believe, as set forth in the foregoing *Declaration of Principles*, illustrates how Religious Science keeps faith with the spiritual thought of the ages.

We believe in God, the Living Spirit Almighty: One, Indestructible, Absolute, and Self-Existent Cause.

God is defined as: the Deity; the Supreme Being; the Divine Presence in the Universe permeating everything; the Animating Principle in everything, as Love, and the Source of all inspiration and Power, the Source of guidance and of Divine protection.

God has been called by a thousand different names throughout the ages. The time has now come to cast aside any points of disagreement and to realize that we are all worshiping one and the same God.

The Sacred Books of all peoples declare that God is One; a Unity from which nothing can be excluded and to which nothing can be added. God is Omnipotent, Omnipresent and Omniscient. God is our Heavenly Father and our Spiritual Mother; the Breath of our life. God is the Changeless Reality in which we live, move, and have our being.

The Bible says: "I am the Lord, I change not." "Forever, O Lord, thy word is settled in heaven." "One God and Father of all, who is above all, and through all, and in you all." "Know

84

that the Lord he is God; there is none else beside him." "I am Alpha and Omega, the beginning and the ending . . . which is, and which was, and which is to come, the Almighty." "In whom are hid all the treasures of wisdom and knowledge." "God is Spirit: and they that worship him must worship him in spirit and in truth." "All things were made by him; and without him was not anything made that was made." ". . . there is but one God, the Father, of whom are all things, and we in him." ". . . the Lord he is God in heaven above, and upon the earth beneath: there is none else." "For with thee is the fountain of life; in thy light shall we see light." "God is light, and in him is no darkness at all." "Thy righteousness is an everlasting righteousness, and thy law is the truth."

From the Text of Taoism: "The Tao, considered as unchanging, has no name." "There is no end or beginning to the Tao." "The great Tao has no name, but it effects the growth and maintenance of all things." "The Tao does not exhaust itself in what is greatest, nor is it ever absent from what is least; and therefore it is to be found complete and diffused in all things." "Thus it is that the Tao produces [all things], nourishes them . . . nurses them, completes them, matures them, maintains them, and overspreads them."

The Hermetic Teaching defines God as a ". . . Power that naught can e'er surpass, a Power with which no one can make comparison of any human thing at all." This teaching defines God as a Oneness which is the ". . . Source and Root of all, is in all things . . . He ever makes all things, in heaven, in air, in earth, in deep, in all of cosmos [that is, the entire universe]. . . . For there is naught in all the world that is not He." "God is united to all men as light to the sun."

From the Sacred Books of the East: "There is but one Brahma which is Truth's self. It is from our ignorance of that One that god-heads have been conceived to be diverse." "As the sun, manifesting all parts of space, above, between, and below, shines resplendent, so over-rules the all-glorious adorable God . . ." "The One God, who is concealed in all beings, who pervades all, who is the inner soul of all beings, the ruler of all

85

actions, who dwells in all beings . . ." "God is permanent, eternal and therefore existence itself." "All is the effect of all, One Universal Essence." "The Supreme Soul hath another name, that is, Pure Knowledge."

The Zend-Avesta defines God as "Perfect Holiness, Understanding, Knowledge, The most Beneficent, The uncomparable One, The All-seeing One, The healing One, The Creator."

The Koran says that "He is the Living One. No God is there but He."

In Buddhism we find these thoughts: ". . . the Supreme Being, the Unsurpassed, the Perceiver of All Things, the Controller, the Lord of All, the Maker, the Fashioner . . . the Father of All Beings."

In the Apocrypha we read that God is ". . . the Most High who knows . . . who nourishes all. The Creator who has planted his sweet Spirit in all . . . There is One God . . . Worship him . . . who alone exists from age to age."

From the Talmud: "Our God is a living God." "His power fills the universe . . . He formed thee; with His Spirit thou breathest."

In Religious Science *self-existent* is defined as *living by virtue of its own being.* An Absolute and Self-Existent Cause, then, means that Principle, that Power and that Presence which makes everything out of Itself, which contains and sustains everything within Itself. God is Absolute and Self-Existent Cause. Therefore, the Divine Spirit contains within Itself infinite imagination, complete volition and absolute Power.

We are to think of God not as *some power*, but as *All Power;* not as *some presence*, but as *the Only* Presence; not merely as *a god*, but as *The God.* Spirit is the supreme and the only Causation.

This One manifests Itself in and through all creation but is not absorbed by Its creation.

The *Science of Mind* textbook defines *creation* as *the giving of form to the substance of Mind. . . . The Whole action of*

86

Spirit must be within Itself upon Itself. Creation is the play of Life upon Itself; the action of a limitless Imagination upon an infinite Law.

What God thinks, He energizes. The Universe is God's thought made manifest. The Ideas of God take innumerable forms. The manifest universe springs from the Mind of God.

The Bible says that "the Lord by wisdom hath founded the earth: by understanding hath he established the heavens." "In the beginning God created the heaven and the earth." "By his spirit he hath garnished the heavens." "For he spake, and it was done; he commanded, and it stood fast." ". . . the worlds were framed by the word of God." "The heavens declare the glory of God; and the firmament sheweth his handiwork."

The Hermetic Philosophy states that "with Reason, not with hands, did the World-maker make the universal World."

From a Hindu Scripture: "From the unmanifest springs the manifest." "Mind, being impelled by a desire to create, performs the work of creation by giving form to Itself."

Everything that exists is a manifestation of the Divine Mind; but the Divine Mind, being inexhaustible and limitless, is never caught in any form; It is merely expressed by that form. The manifest universe, then, is the Body of God. As our *Declaration of Principles* reads: *"It is the logical and necessary outcome of the infinite self-knowingness of God."* God's self-knowingness energizes that which is known, and that which God knows takes form. The form itself has a Divine Pattern within it.

In the Hermetic Teaching we find this remarkable statement: "All things, accordingly, that are on earth . . . are not the Truth; they're copies [only] of the True. Whenever the appearance doth receive the influx from above, it turns into a copy of the Truth; without its energizing from above, it is left false. Just as the portrait also indicates the body in the picture, but in itself is not the body, in spite of the appearance of the thing that's seen. 'Tis seen as having eyes; but it sees naught, hears naught at all."

One of the problems of Religious Science is to distinguish between that which is temporal and that which is Eternal. God or Spirit is the only Reality, the One Substance or Essence. The material universe is real as a manifestation of Life, but it is an effect. This is why Jesus told us to judge not according to appearances.

The Talmud says that "unhappy is he who mistakes the branch for the tree, the shadow for the substance."

In Hebrews we find: "For Christ is not entered into the holy places made with hands, which are the figures of the true; but into heaven itself, now to appear in the presence of God for us."

And from Colossians: "Let no man therefore judge you in meat, or in drink, or in respect of an holyday, or of the new moon, or of the sabbath days: Which are a shadow of things to come, but the body is of Christ."

Back of all form there is a Divine Substance. Hid within every appearance there is an adequate cause. If we judge by the appearance alone, as though it were self-created, we are mistaking the shadow for the Substance.

In Fragments of a Faith Forgotten it says: "Gain for yourselves, ye sons of Adam, by means of these transitory things . . . that which is your own, and passeth not away."

We are to translate all creation into spiritual Causation. Then we shall be viewing it rightly. The created form has no being of itself, it is an effect. In Ramacharaka we read: "That which is unreal hath no shadow of Real Being, notwithstanding the illusion of appearance and false knowledge. And that which hath Real Being hath never ceased to be—CAN NEVER CEASE TO BE, in spite of all appearances to the contrary."

There is a Divine Pattern, a Spiritual Prototype, in the Mind of God which gives rise to all form. Jesus saw through the form to the Pattern, for he was quickened by the Spirit. "It is the spirit that quickeneth: the flesh profiteth nothing." "For [now] we know in part, and we prophesy in part. But when that which is perfect is come, then that which is in part shall be done away." "Now we see through a glass darkly." That is, our spiritual vision is not quickened to a complete perception of the Divine Reality, the Spiritual Prototype back of the image.

We believe in the incarnation of the Spirit in man and that all men are incarnations of the One Spirit.

All scriptures declare that man is the spiritual image and likeness of God. This is emphatically revealed in the inspiration of our own scripture which says: "God created man in his own image." "The spirit of God hath made me, and the breath of the Almighty hath given me life." "Hereby know we that we dwell in him, and he in us, because he hath given us of his Spirit." "Thou hast made him a little lower than the angels, and hast crowned him with glory and honour. Thou madest him to have dominion over the works of thy hands; thou hast put all things under his feet." "Be ye therefore perfect, even as your Father which is in heaven is perfect."

"Now there are diversities of gifts, but the same Spirit." "There is one body, and one Spirit . . . one Lord, one faith, one baptism, one God and Father of all, who is above all, and through all, and in you all." *One faith* and *one baptism* mean that through faith and intuition we realize that we are living in one Spirit, or, as Emerson said, "There is one Mind common to all individual men."

"Have we not all one Father? Hath not one God created us?" "To us there is but one God, the Father, of whom are all things." "Beloved, now are we the sons of God." "Ye are the sons of the living God." "And because ye are sons, God hath sent forth the Spirit of his Son into your hearts." In other words, there is but one son of God, which includes the whole human family, and the Spirit of this son, which is the Spirit of Christ, is incarnated in everyone. Therefore the Bible says that "he [man] is the image and glory of God."

The Bible continues: "Know ye not that your body is the temple of the Holy Ghost which is in you . . . therefore glorify God in your body, and in your spirit, which are God's." "That which is born of the Spirit is spirit." We could have no more definite statement of the Divine Incarnation than this. Every man is an incarnation of God. Since God is the Universal Spirit, the One and Only Mind, Substance, Power and Presence that

89

exists, and since all men are individuals, it follows that each man is an individualized center of the Consciousness of the One God.

The Koran says: "We created man: and we know what his soul whispereth to him, and we are closer to him than his neck-vein."

In the Talmud we read: "First, no atom of matter in the whole vastness of the universe is lost; how then can man's soul, which is the whole world in one idea, be lost?"

The following quotations are drawn from various Hindu scriptures: "The ego is beyond all disease . . . free from all imagination, and all-pervading." "As from a . . . fire, in a thousand ways, similar sparks proceed, so, beloved, are produced living cells of various kinds from the Indestructible." "If ye knew God as he ought to be known, ye would walk under seas, and the mountains would move at your call." (This is similar to the teaching of Jesus when he said that if we had faith the size of a grain of mustard seed, we could say unto the mountain, "Remove hence to yonder place.") "There is that within every soul which conquers hunger, thirst, grief, delusion, old age, and death."

Perhaps one of the most remarkable sayings in the scriptures of India, relative to the self, is the following: "Let him raise the self by the Self and not let the self become depressed; for verily is the Self the friend of the self, and also the Self the self's enemy; the Self is the friend of the self of him in whom the self by the Self is vanquished; but to the unsubdued self the Self verily becometh hostile as an enemy." (This, of course, refers to the deathless Self, the incarnation of God in us.) "He who knows himself has come to know his Lord." (This refers to the complete Unity of the Spirit, or, as Jesus said, "I and the Father are one.") "And he who thus hath learned to know himself, hath reached that Good which doth transcend abundance."

From the Text of Taoism are gathered the following inspirational thoughts: "Man has a real existence, but it has nothing to do with place; he has continuance, but it has nothing to do with beginning or end." "He whose whole mind is thus fixed emits a Heavenly light. In him who emits this Heavenly light men see the [True] man." Referring to the one whose mind is fixed on Reality, "His sleep is untroubled by dreams; his waking is followed by no sorrows. His spirit is guileless and pure; his soul is not subject to weariness."

In spiritual revelation a calm contemplation of spiritual Truth is held important. The mind must be like a mirror if it is to reflect or image forth the Divine Prototype, the incarnation of God in man. "Men do not look into running water as a mirror, but into still water—it is only the still water that can arrest them all, and keep them in the contemplation of their real selves."

The Hermetic Philosophy tells us that if we would know God we must be like Him, for "like is knowable to like alone." "Make thyself to grow to the same stature as the Greatness which transcends all measure." "Conceiving nothing is impossible unto thyself, think thyself deathless and able to know all—all arts, all sciences, the way of every life." (It tells us to awake from our deep sleep, as though our spiritual eyes were dulled by too much looking on effect and too little contemplation of cause.)

We believe in the eternality, the immortality, and the continuity of the individual soul, forever and ever expanding.

If man is an incarnation of God, then his spirit is God individualized, and as such it must be eternal. Since it is impossible to exhaust the limitless nature of the Divine, our expansion must be an eternal process of unfolding from a limitless Center.

The Gita tells us, "He is not born, nor doth he die; nor having been, ceaseth he any more to be; unborn, perpetual, eternal and ancient, he is not slain when the body is slaughtered."

From the Bible: "He asked life of thee, and thou gavest it him, even length of days for ever and ever." "And this is the promise that he hath promised us, even eternal life." "To an inheritance incorruptible, and undefiled, and that fadeth not away, reserved in heaven for you."

We believe that the Kingdom of Heaven is within man and that we experience this Kingdom to the degree that we become conscious of it.

The *Kingdom of Heaven* means the kingdom of Harmony, of Peace, of Joy and of Wholeness. It is an inward kingdom. Heaven is not a place but an inward state of consciousness. It is an inward awareness of Divine Harmony and Truth.

When Jesus said that we are to be perfect even as God within us is perfect, he implied that there is such a Divine Kingdom already established within man. When the without shall become as the within, then the Kingdom of God shall be established here and now. "The kingdom of God cometh not with observation: Neither shall they say, Lo here! or, Lo, there! for, behold, the kingdom of God is within you." This certainly refers to a state of inner awareness.

The Kingdom to which Jesus referred is not external but within. It is not to be placed outside the self, but it is to be perceived as an everlasting dominion within. The Kingdom of Heaven is something we possess but have not been conscious of. It is neither in the mountain nor at Jerusalem, but within the mind.

No matter how small our concept of heaven may be to begin with, it has the possibility of eternal unfoldment. The power to live is within the self, implanted by the Divine. Ultimately every man will realize his inner Kingdom, which will become to him as the Tree of Life providing food and shelter, perfection and joy.

Again Jesus said, "The kingdom of heaven is like unto leaven, which a woman took, and hid in three measures of meal, till the whole was leavened." Consciousness of the Kingdom of God within acts like yeast, permeating mortal thought and lifting the weight of life's burdens. Jesus referred to the Kingdom of God as the Bread of Life; the Eternal Substance upon which the soul feeds; the everlasting Presence upon which the inner eye feasts.

Let us see what other bibles of the world have taught about this inner kingdom.

In the Text of Taoism we find this: "Without going outside his door . . . without looking out from his window, one sees the Tao of Heaven. The farther one goes from himself the less he knows." "What is heavenly is internal; what is human is external. If you know the operation of what is heavenly . . . you will have your root in what is heavenly." "Take the days away and there will be no year; without what is internal there will be nothing external." "He who knows . . . completion . . . turns in on himself and finds there an inexhaustible store."

The Gita tells us: "He who is happy within him, rejoiceth within him, is illumined within, becomes eternal." And in Fragments of a Faith Forgotten it says: ". . . the Kingdom of Heaven is within you; and whosoever shall know himself shall find it." "Seek for the great and the little shall be added unto you. Seek for the heavenly and the earthly shall be added unto you."

In the Upanishad we read: "As far as mind extends, so far extends heaven." "In heaven there is no fear . . . it is without hunger or thirst and beyond all grief."

The Pistis Sophia says: "Be ye diligent that ye may receive the mysteries of Light and enter into the height of the Kingdom of Light."

We believe the ultimate goal of life to be a complete emancipation from all discord of every nature, and that this goal is sure to be attained by all.

The ultimate goal of life does not mean that we shall arrive at a spiritual destination where everything remains static and inactive. That which to our present understanding seems an ultimate goal will, when attained, be but the starting point for a new and further evolution. We believe in an eternal upward spiral of existence. This is what Jesus meant when he said "In my Father's house are many mansions."

The Koran tells us that God has made many heavens, one on top of another, which means that evolution is eternal. The Hermetic philosophy taught an infinite variation of the manifestation of life on an ever-ascending scale. All evolution proves the transition of the lesser into the greater.

We believe in the Unity of all life, and that the highest God and the innermost God is One God.

The enlightened in every age have taught that back of all things there is One Unseen Cause. This teaching of Unity . . . "The Lord our God is one God . . ." is the chief cornerstone of the sacred scriptures of the East, as well as our own sacred writings.

There is One Life of which we are a part; One Intelligence, which we use; One Substance, which takes manifold forms. "That they all may be one; as thou, Father, art in me, and I in thee, that they also may be one in us."

In the Bible we find these passages: "Now there are diversities of gifts, but the same Spirit." "Whither shall I go from thy spirit? or whither shall I flee from thy presence? If I ascend up into heaven, thou art there: if I make my bed in hell, behold, thou art there . . . If I say, Surely the darkness shall cover me; even the night shall be light around me." "We all, with open face beholding as in a glass the glory of the Lord, are changed into the same image . . . by the Spirit of the Lord." "I shall be satisfied when I awake with thy likeness."

"Know ye not that your body is the temple of the Holy Ghost which is in you?" "That which is born of the Spirit is spirit." "The Lord our God is one God . . . He is God in Heaven above and upon the earth beneath. There is none else." ". . . His word is in mine heart as a burning fire shut up in my bones." "And the Word was made flesh, and dwelt among us . . ." ". . . I will put my words in his mouth . . . the word is very nigh unto thee, in thy mouth, and in thy heart, that thou mayest do it.''

All sacred scriptures have proclaimed the Unity of Life; that every man is a center of God Consciousness. This is the meaning of the mystical marriage, or the union of the soul with its Source. Jesus boldly proclaimed that he was One with the Father. This is the basis for all New Thought teaching, the Spiritual Union of all Life.

The Qabbalah states that ''every existence tends toward the higher, the first unity . . . the whole universe is one, complex. The lower emanates from the Higher and is Its image. The Divine is active in each.''

Unity is a symbol of the soul's Oneness with the Higher Nature, implying complete freedom from bondage to anything less than itself. All positive religions have taught that the supreme end of humanity is a union of the soul with God.

''The Atman, which is the substratum of the ego in man, is One.'' The Hermetic Teaching tells us that ''this Oneness, being source and root of all, is in all.'' And the Gita explains that ''when he [man] perceiveth the diversified existence of beings as rooted in One, and spreading forth from It, then he reacheth the eternal.''

Again the Bible tells us: ''Thus saith the Lord . . . I am the first and I am the last . . .'' ''I am Alpha and Omega, the beginning and the ending . . . which was and which is to come.''

From The Awakening of Faith: ''In the essence [of Reality] there is neither anything which has to be included, nor anything which has to be added.''

In one of the Upanishads we find this quotation: ''The One God who is concealed in all beings, who is the inner soul of all beings, the ruler of all actions . . .'' ''All is the effect of all, One Universal Essence.'' And again in Ephesians, ''One God and Father of all, who is above all, and through all, and in you all.''

In Echoes from Gnosis we find: ''O Primal Origin of my origination; Thou Primal Substance of my substance; Breath of my breath, the breath that is in me.''

From the Bible: ''To us there is but one God, the Father, of whom are all things, and we in him.'' And from another bible,

"All this universe had the Deity for its life. That Deity is Truth, who is the Universal Soul."

From the Apocrypha: "He is Lord of Heaven, sovereign of earth, the One existence." And the Upanishads tell us, "He who is the Ear of the ear, the Mind of the mind, the Speech of the speech, is verily the Life of life, the Eye of the eye."

Religious Science teaches an absolute union of man with his Source. So complete is this union that the slightest act of human consciousness manifests some degree of man's Divinity. Man is not God, but he has no life separate from the Divine; he has no existence apart from his Source. He thinks God's thoughts after Him. He is Divine neither by will nor through choice, but by necessity. The whole process of evolution is a continual process of awakening. It is an understanding of this indwelling union which constitutes the Spirit of Christ.

We believe that God is personal to all who feel this Indwelling Presence. . . . We believe in the direct revelation of Truth through the intuitive and spiritual nature of man, and that any man may become a revealer of Truth who lives in close contact with the Indwelling God.

"Know ye not that ye are the temple of God, and that the Spirit of God dwelleth in you?" "God is in his holy temple." Augustine said that the pure mind is a holy temple for God, and Emerson said that God builds His temple in the heart. Seneca said that "temples are not to be built for God with stones . . . He is to be consecrated in the breast of each."

Every man is an incarnation of God, and since each person is an individual, everyone is a unique incarnation. We believe in the Divine Presence as Infinite Person, and personal to each. God is not *a* person, but *the* Person. This Person is an Infinite Presence filled with warmth, color, and responsiveness, immediately and intimately personal to each individual.

The Spirit is both an over-dwelling and an indwelling Presence. We are immersed in It, and It flows through us as our very life. Through intuition man perceives and directly reveals God. We do not have to borrow our light from another. Nothing could be more intimate than the personal relationship between the individual and that Divine Presence which is both the Center and the Source of man's being.

Whatever God is in the Universal, man is in the individual. This is why all spiritual leaders have told us that if we would uncover the hidden possibility within, we should not only discover the true Self, the Christ, we should also uncover the true God, the One and Only Cause, the Supreme Being, the Infinite Person.

Jesus taught a complete union of man with God. He proclaimed that all men are Divine; that all are One with the Father; that the Kingdom of Heaven is within; that the Father has delivered all Power unto the son; and that the son thinks the thoughts of God after Him, and imbibes Spiritual Power through realization of his Union with his Source.

We believe that the Universal Spirit, which is God, operates through a Universal Mind, which is the Law of God; and that we are surrounded by this Creative Mind which receives the direct impress of our thought and acts upon it.

This deals with the practical use of spiritual Power. In Religious Science we differentiate between Spirit, Mind, and Body, just as all the great major religions have done. Spirit is the conscious and active aspect of God, as distinguished from Law, the passive, receptive, and form-taking aspect. Spirit imparts motion through Law and manifests Itself in form. Thus, the ancients said that Spirit uses matter as a sheath.

Philo, often called Philo Judaeus, born about 10 B.C., one of the greatest of the Jewish philosophers of the Alexandrian school, said that the Active Principle, which is Spirit, is absolutely free, and that the Passive Principle is set in motion by the Spirit, giving birth to form. Plotinus, considered the greatest of the Neo-Platonists, taught that Spirit, as Active Intelligence, operates upon an unformed substance, which is passive to It, and that through the Power of the Word of Spirit this substance takes form and becomes the physical world.

Let us see what different scriptures have had to say on this subject, starting with our own Bible. "In the beginning was the Word, and the Word was with God, and the Word was God." "Forever, O Lord, thy word is seated in heaven." "And, Thou, Lord . . . hast laid the foundation of the earth; and the heavens are the works of thine hands." "Our God is a living God. His power fills the universe . . . with his spirit thou breathest."

In referring to the Law of Mind the Bible says: "Every idle word that men shall speak, they shall give account thereof . . . for by thy words thou shalt be justified, and by thy words thou shalt be condemned." "Be ye doers of the word and not hearers only." "For there are three that bear witness in heaven, the Father, the Word, and the Holy Ghost: and these three are one."

The Koran says that "whatsoever good betideth thee is from God and whatsoever betideth thee of evil is from thyself." And our Bible says of the Spirit, "Thou art of purer eyes than to behold evil, and canst not look on iniquity."

From the Teachings of Buddha we learn: "For the cause of the karma [cause and effect] which conducts to unhappy states of existence, is ignorance." "Therefore it is clear that ignorance can only be removed by wisdom." The Zend-Avesta says, "The word of falsehood smites, but the word of truth shall smite it." And from The Book of the Dead: "It shall come to pass that the evil one shall fall when he raiseth a snare to destroy thee."

From the Text of Taoism we learn: "Whatever is contrary to the Tao soon ends." "He who injures others is sure to be injured by them in return."

We believe in the healing of the sick through the Power of this Mind.

Spiritual mind healing has long since passed the experimental stage, and we now know why it is that faith has performed miracles. We live in a universe of pure, unadulterated Spirit, of

Perfect Being. We are, as Emerson said, in the lap of an infinite Intelligence. There is a Spiritual Prototype of Perfection at the center of everything. There is a Divine Pattern at the center of every organ of the physical body. Our body is some part of the Body of God; it is a manifestation of the Supreme Spirit.

In the practice of spiritual mind healing we start with this simple proposition: God is Perfect. God is all there is. God includes man. Spiritual Man is a Divine Being, as Complete and Perfect in Essence as is God. When in thought, in contemplation, in imagination, in inward feeling, we consciously return to the Source of our being, the Divine Pattern which already exists springs forth into newness of manifestation. When we clear the consciousness—that is, the whole mental life, both conscious and subjective—of discord, we are automatically healed.

The Science of Mind, which is the tool of the Religious Scientist, gives us a definite technique for doing this. It teaches us exactly how to proceed on a simple, understandable basis. It is a science because it is built upon exact Laws of Mind, for the Laws of Mind are as exact as any other laws in nature. They are natural laws. From a practical viewpoint, this is done by making certain definite statements with the realization that they have Power to remove any obstacle, to dissolve any false condition, and to reveal man's Spiritual Nature.

True mind healing cannot be divorced from spiritual realization; therefore the practitioner of this science must have a deep and abiding sense of Calm, of Peace, and of his Union with the Spirit. He must have an unshakable conviction that Spiritual Man is Perfect, that he is One with God, and he must know that in such degree as he realizes, senses, feels, this Inner Perfection, It will appear. The physical healing itself is a result, an effect, of this inward consciousness.

Faith is a certain definite mental attitude. When Jesus said, "It is done unto you as you believe," he implied that there is a Law, a Force, or an Intelligent Energy in the Universe which acts upon the images of our belief. Faith is an affirmative way of using this Law, this Energy, this Force. Therefore, all scriptures have announced the necessity of having faith.

"Be ye transformed by the renewing of your mind." "Be

renewed in the spirit of your mind." "Let this mind be in you which was also in Christ." "I will put my laws into your mind." "Hear, O earth, behold I will bring evil upon these people, even the fruits of their thoughts." "And he sent his word and healed them." "He forgetteth all thine iniquities; he healeth all thy diseases." "O Lord, my God, I cried unto thee, and thou hast healed me." "Then shall thy light break forth as morning, and thine health shall speed forth speedily." "And it shall come to pass, that before they call, I will answer; and while they are yet speaking, I will hear." "I will take sickness away from the midst of thee." "The tongue of the wise is health." "Behold I will bring health . . . I will cure them."

"Jesus turned him about, and when he saw her, he said, Daughter, be of good comfort; thy faith hath made thee whole. And the woman was made whole from that hour." "Then touched he their eyes, saying, According to your faith be it unto you. And their eyes were opened." "Heal the sick, cleanse the lepers, raise the dead, cast out devils: freely ye have received, freely give." "And great multitudes followed him, and he healed them all." "And the blind and the lame came to him in the temple, and he healed them."

In spiritual mind healing thought becomes a transmitter for Divine Power; therefore, the thought must always be kept free from confusion.

It is interesting to note that, while all the great scriptures of the ages concur about the nature of God and of man, and the relationship between the spiritual and the physical, outside the Christian scriptures very little is mentioned about healing or the control of conditions through the use of Divine Power, although they all agree that when the mind reflects the Divine Perfection, healing and prosperity follow.

In the Text of Taoism we find: "The still mind . . . is the mirror or heaven and earth . . ." "Maintain a perfect unity in every movement of your will. You will not wait for the hearing of your ears, but for the hearing of your mind. You will not wait even for the hearing of your mind, but for the hearing of the Spirit." "Purity and stillness give the correct law to all under

100

heaven." And from the Koran: "The Lord of the worlds He hath created me and guideth me; He giveth me food and drink and when I am sick He healeth me." "And never Lord have I prayed to thee with ill success."

There is a Science of Mind and Spirit because there is a Principle of Mind and Spirit. There is a possibility of using this science because we now understand how the Laws of Mind and Spirit work in human affairs. The Principle of Mind operates through our thought, through our faith and conviction, and most effectively through an attitude of Love, of compassion, and of sympathy constructively used. It is impossible to make the highest use of these Laws of Mind without basing such use of these Laws upon inward spiritual perception, upon a conscious realization of the Union of man with God.

We believe in the control of conditions through the Power of this Mind.

While all sacred writings affirm that when we are in harmony with the Infinite we are automatically prospered, the Christian scriptures lay greater stress on prosperity through spiritualizing the mind than any other of the bibles of the world. Our Bible, truly understood, is a book for the emancipation of man from the thralldom of every evil, every lack and limitation.

From the teaching of Moses, running through the thought of the major prophets, and culminating in the brilliant manifestation of the Mind of Christ through the thought of Jesus, over and over this idea is reiterated—that if we live in harmony with the Spirit everything we do shall prosper.

Religious Science teaches that through right knowledge of the Science of Mind we can definitely and consciously demonstrate, prove, or show forth practical results of spiritual thought. Countless thousands have proved this Principle and there is no longer any question about its effectiveness. The greatest guide we have for this is found in the inspired writings of the Christian scriptures.

"Prove me now herewith, saith the Lord of hosts, if I will not open to you the windows of heaven, and pour out a blessing, that there shall not be room enough to receive it." "And he shall pray unto God and he will be favorable unto him." "For every one that asketh receiveth; and he that seeketh findeth; and to him that knocketh it shall be opened." "Ask, and it shall be given you." "And all things, whatsoever ye shall ask in prayer, believing, ye shall receive."

The Apostle Paul said, "I will pray with the spirit and I will pray with the understanding also." This is an instruction for us to combine spiritual intuition with definite mental acceptance. He is telling us that the gift of God is to be consciously used.

We are also told to pray without ceasing, to maintain a steadfast conviction, disregarding every apparent contradiction, obstruction, or appearance that would deny the Good we affirm. "But let him ask in faith, nothing wavering. For he that wavereth is like a wave of the sea driven with the wind and tossed." "To the righteous good shall be repaid." "The minds of the righteous shall stand." "Behold the righteous shall be recompensed in the earth." "The righteous is delivered of all trouble." A righteous man means one who is right with the Universe; one who lives in accord with the Divine Will and the Divine Nature; one who lives in Harmony with Good.

We have the right, then, to expect, and we should expect, insofar as our inner thought is in tune with the Infinite, that everything we do shall prosper.

We believe in the Eternal Goodness, the Eternal Loving-Kindness, and the Eternal Givingness of Life to all.

The Spirit gives Itself to everyone; the Power of God is delivered to all. "Whosoever will, may come." No matter what the mistakes of our yesterdays may have been, we may transcend both the mistake and its consequence through imbibing the Spirit of Truth, which is the Power of God.

This does not mean that we may continue living in the mistake without suffering from it. We must transcend it. That is, we must transmute hate into Love, fear into faith, and a sense of separation into conscious Union with Good. When we have done this, the entire record of the past is blotted out and we are again free—free with that freedom which the Almighty has ordained, and which man may claim as his own.

But liberty is not license, and the Law of Life cannot be fooled. It is exact and exacting. "Therefore," Jesus said, "all things whatsoever ye would that men should do unto you, do ye even so to them." "Give, and it shall be given."

This is a statement of the Law of Cause and Effect which is invariable and immutable, but which is also the plaything of both God and man, for while the Law Itself cannot be broken, any particular sequence of Cause and Effect in It can be transcended. The same Law which, wrongly used, brought poverty, sickness, and death, rightly used will bring Peace, Wholeness, Prosperity, and Life.

This is the great challenge of spiritual faith. Christian philosophy bids us not to look with doleful introspection on previous errors; but, coming daily to the Fountain of Life to be renewed in mind, thought, and spirit, we shall find that we also are renewed in bodily conditions and in physical affairs.

The Scripture boldly declares the triumph of the Spirit of Christ over all evil; "Be ye transformed by the renewing of your mind" by putting off the old man and putting on the new man, which is Christ. "Lo, I am with you always, even unto the end of the world."

We believe in our own soul, our own spirit, and our own destiny; for we understand that the life of man is God.

Man is not only a center of God Consciousness; he is an immortal being, forever expanding, forever spiraling upward, forever growing in spiritual stature. Not *some* men, but *all* men are immortal, for everyone will finally overcome or transcend any misuse of the Law which he has made in his ignorance. Complete redemption at last must come, alike, to all.

What transformations must ensue, what change of consciousness must take place before this is finally brought about, the finite has not yet grasped, but through the whisperings of Divine Intuition we know that, even though we now see as through a glass darkly, we shall some day behold Reality face-to-face. We shall be satisfied when we consciously awake in the likeness of that Divinity which shapes our ends.

"Beloved, now are we the sons of God, and it doth not yet appear what we shall be: but we know that, when he shall appear, we shall be like him; for we shall see him as he is." We are all in the process of spiritual evolution, but there is certainty behind us, certainty before us, and certainty with us at every moment. The Eternal Light will break through wherever we permit It to.

Potentially, everything that is to be exists now, but our spiritual vision has not yet become completely in tune with the Infinite. This is the high task set before us as Religious Scientists; this is the deathless hope implanted in our mind by the Divine.

The trials and troubles of human experience; the blind groping of the finite toward the Infinite; the sickness, poverty, death, uncertainty, fear, and doubt that accompany us—constitute the cross upon which we must offer, as a sacrifice to our ignorance, that which does not belong to the Kingdom of Good. But from this cross something triumphant will emerge, for, as Emerson said, "The finite alone has wrought and suffered; the infinite lies stretched in smiling repose."

Shall we not, then, with joy, go forth to meet the new day, endeavoring so to embody the Spirit of Christ that the Divine in us shall rise triumphant, resurrected, to live forever in the City of God? More could not be asked than that which the Divine has already delivered; less should not be expected.

REFERENCES

Professor Max Müller, one of the greatest European orientalists and editor of *The Sacred Books of the East*, has well said that "the true religion of the future will be the fulfillment of all the religions of the past. All religions, so far as I know them, had the same purpose; all were links in a chain which connects heaven and earth; and which is held, and always was held, by one and the same hand. All here on earth tends toward right and truth, and perfection; nothing here on earth can ever be quite right, quite true, quite perfect, not even Christianity—or what is called Christianity—so long as it excludes all other religions, instead of loving and embracing what is good in each."

As in many other religions of antiquity, the origin of Taoism is more or less obscure. According to some authorities it is said to have begun around 600 B.C., which antedates Confucius, who was born in 551 B.C. The world generally associates Taoism with Lao-Tze, a Chinese metaphysical philosopher who was fifty-three years older than Confucius. It was this philosopher who must have gathered together these teachings. Archdeacon Hardwick tells us that the Chinese word *Tao* ". . . was adopted to denominate an abstract cause, or the initial principle of life and order, to which worshippers were able to assign the attribute of immateriality, eternity, immensity, invisibility."

The Upanishads, the Vedas, the Mahabharata, the Raja Yoga philosophy, as well as the Bhagavad-Gita, are all drawn from the ancient wisdom of India.

The philosophy of Buddha, who was born in the sixth century B.C., is too well known to need any comment.

The Sacred Book of the Parsis is called the Zend-Avesta, which is a collection of fragments of ideas that prevailed in ancient Persia five hundred years before the Christian era and for several centuries afterwards.

The Book of the Dead is a series of translations of the ancient Egyptian hymns and religious texts. They were found on the walls of tombs, in coffins, and in papyri. As in many other sacred traditions, there probably were no written copies in the earlier days; they were committed to memory and handed down from generation to generation.

Some students believe that the books of Hermes Trismegistus, which means *the thrice greatest*, originally derived from ancient Egyptian doctrine. Hermes was a Greek god, son of Zeus and Maia, daughter of Atlas. To Hermes was attributed the authorship of all the strictly sacred books generally called by Greek authors Hermetic (Encyclopaedia Britannica). According to some scholars, the Egyptian Hermes "was a symbol of the Divine Mind; he was the incarnated Thought, the living Word—the primitive type of the Logos of Plato and the Word of the Christians."

Fragments of a Faith Forgotten are taken from the Gnostics, those "who used the Gnosis as the means to set their feet upon the Way of God." Gnosticism was pre-Christian and originated in the ancient religion and philosophy of Greece, Egypt, and Jewry.

According to H. Polano, the Talmud contains ". . . the thoughts . . . of a thousand years of the national life of the Jewish people."

The Koran is the sacred book of the Mohammedans, consisting of revelations orally delivered at intervals by Mohammed and collected in writing after his death (Oxford Dictionary). The Koran is considered one of the most important of the world's sacred books.

The Apocrypha refers to a collection of ancient writings. The Greek word *Apocryphos* was originally used of books the contents of which were kept hidden, or secret, because they embodied the special teaching of religious or philosophical sects; it was only the members of these sects who were initiated into the secrets of this teaching (Encyclopaedia Britannica).

Why Talk So Much about God?

You may ask why we use the words *God* and *Spirit* so frequently and why it is when we explain the Science of Mind that we so often speak about the nature of God or Spirit.

When we use the word *God* or *Spirit* we mean the Intelligent Life Principle which the philosopher calls Reality, and what all religions mean when they refer to that Something in the Universe which responds to our consciousness. It is self-evident that such a First Cause, such an Intelligent Cause, exists.

Haldane says: *Materialism, once a scientific theory, is now the fatalistic creed of thousands. But materialism is nothing better than a superstition on the same level as a belief in witches and devils.* This eminent scientist is telling us that it stretches our imagination more to disbelieve in God, or a Universal Consciousness, than it does to believe that there is such a Universal Consciousness. Or as the sage of antiquity said, *He that planted the ear, shall he not hear? He that formed the eye, shall he not see? He that teaches man knowledge, shall he not know?*

People are more interested in God than they are in religion, because religion has been more or less mixed up with superstition, theology, and ecclesiasticism. But people never have ceased being interested in the nature of God, and there is nothing that gives greater satisfaction than to believe in a Supreme Intelligence with which we may commune, and an Infinite Power with which we may consciously deal.

When we use the word *God* or *Spirit* we do not mean a tribal God, but the Supreme Mind and Power back of all created form, the Intelligence which responds to us, the Intelligence which rises through the mineral, vegetable, and animal kingdoms, and blossoms in the human mind as It approaches the conscious recognition that It is one with this Oversoul. It would be impossible to discuss philosophy, science, or religion without continually referring to the nature of man's being, and the nature of man's being is God.

We wish more than a blind acceptance of God. We need to know with scientific certainty that there is a Consciousness and a Power in the Universe that responds to us definitely, directly, and dynamically. Each individual must arrive at a place in his own consciousness where this contact is so immediate and so dynamic that if every other living soul denied it, he would still know. Without this inner conviction neither faith nor understanding is possible. We would be depending on a forlorn hope which might vanish in the hour of need.

It is enough for the intelligent person to know that the entire planetary system manifests intelligence and organization; that is, it manifests intelligence plus direction, and intelligence plus direction means consciousness. It implies both will and representation; both an Infinite Will and an Infinite Manifestation.

There is within each of us a deep awareness, a subjective and a spiritual consciousness which by pure intuition knows that the Universal Intelligence which we call God exists. We do not need to turn to the Bible for such declarations, for the real Bible is inscribed on the walls of our own consciousness and is *the true light which lighteth every man that cometh into the world.* The inner consciousness of our union with Good is Supreme. Not only is it the highest hope and inspiration of the human mind, but it has ever been its greatest realization.

It is self-evident that we exist because we experience existence. It is self-evident that an Infinite Mind exists, since we can think. It is self-evident that this Mind is a Unity, since as individuals we recognize each other. It is self-evident that we can commune with this Infinite Mind, since we can commune with each other. We cannot disbelieve these self-evident propositions, for we must accept that which it is impossible to deny.

Now everything starts from this certainty of our own being. It is the only fact in the entire Universe of which we are absolutely certain. Man's whole being consists in thinking, and if his thinking is based on knowing, this knowing must be built upon a consciousness of his own existence and of his relationship to the Infinite. It is this spiritual discernment of which Jesus spoke

Individuati̅ Transformation (handwritten, top margin)

when he said, *Ye must be born again*. With scientific certainty the intellect is being led back to the necessity for a new birth.

We must believe in Spirit if we are to use spiritual Power effectively. The consciousness of Spirit, the inner realization of the presence of Perfection, the willingness to meditate upon this Perfection, to understand Its operation and to sense Its presence, is the Power back of all effective mental treatment.

Whether it be the healing of physical disease or the control of conditions, consciousness must be back of the Word. This consciousness does not contradict common sense or the best use of the intellect. It is never necessary to contradict common sense in arriving at the Truth, for fact and faith need never conflict.

We talk about God because everyone instinctively feels that God is, and because human experience proves the necessity of such a supposition in order to explain the facts we do know. We start with the simple induction that since man is and has consciousness, he must live in consciousness. Consciousness or pure Spirit must be the Cause of everything that is, including the physical universe. *(handwritten right margin: ! * Premise I)*

Since the Universe exists as a harmonious Whole, the consciousness back of It must be a perfect, indivisible Unit. *(handwritten right margin: PREMISE II)*

After having established these two simple premises we go on to the necessitative conclusion that since man is, and since there is an Infinite Consciousness, this Infinite Consciousness in man *is* man. Man's thought becomes creative not by well-wishing, prayer, supplication, or desire, but through necessity. *(handwritten: =)*

Consciousness in Its Infinite sense is what we mean when we use the word *God*. Consciousness in the individual sense is what we mean when we use the word *man*. This in no way shuts out any department of knowledge, but includes them all within the realm of consciousness since knowledge could not exist unless someone were conscious of it. Our entire inquiry, then, is an inquiry into the relationship between God and man, and so far as we establish a right relationship we shall have a corresponding power.

When people ask: ''Why do you talk so much about God?''

or when they say something to the effect that they are not interested in religion, be sure to explain to them that you are not offering them a new religion; you are merely seeking to give them an interpretation of life. You are not even trying to convince them that your philosophy is correct; you are trying to give them a reasonable basis for what they already believe.

Always be careful to explain that what you are giving them is just as much theirs as yours; it does not belong to any person, but like the principle of mathematics this knowledge of God can be used by all. Every normal person wishes to believe in God, and you are giving the student a reasonable explanation for that which he already believes, and trying to help him understand what he already feels must be so.

You may be certain that if you approach your teaching from this viewpoint everyone will agree with you. Always make people feel that you are adding to that which they already have, never taking anything away. The very fact that God is already in them as the Principle of their own life needs to be explained.

When you explain to them that the God-Power within them is independent of any other person's consciousness, that they stand alone in the Divine Reality with the Power to demonstrate as much of It as they can conceive at any moment, you will have established them in their relationship to the Universe. Reality Itself must always exceed any individual's understanding, because with an expanded consciousness a larger Good is understood.

Do not be afraid to use the word *God* or the word *Spirit*. All we need to avoid is any superstitious use of the terms, and we most certainly should avoid all dogmatic uses of them. In this work we are making the greatest experiment which the human mind can undertake. We are determining whether or not there is a Universal Intelligence which responds to us in a creative manner. We are engaged in an endeavor to see how much joy we can take out of this Oversoul for ourselves and for others.

The Discovery of God
Is Personal

No ONE can find God for us; each individual must do this for himself. We cannot find God outside the self because we cannot go outside the self. There is no place where we begin and God leaves off. We can find God only within ourselves.

At first this seems almost blasphemous, as though one were setting oneself up as God, but such is not the case. One is merely setting oneself up as a center in the consciousness of God, forever One with God, an Incarnation of the Universal. The gift is not of man's endeavor, but of Life Itself. This is the gift made from the foundation of the world, and is self-evidently true.

It does not look as though we could discover God within the self, because we look at ourselves and say, "Well, look at me! I am poor, weak, miserable, unhappy, disconsolate, and forlorn, and you tell me that I shall find God in the midst of this chaotic mass which I call myself!" It does look discouraging, and like a forlorn hope.

But still we must consider this the starting point, for there can be no other place to begin on the road to self-discovery, the discovery that leads back to the Original Force. Gradually, as we shear the belief in separation from our consciousness, the chaos produced by it, the inhibitions and inner turmoil, we emerge on the other side of this chaotic mass and find that Heaven was waiting there all the time. Nothing had happened to It; as in the experience of the Prodigal of old, the Father's house was still where it always had been.

But just wishing, hoping, or longing will not bring about this self-discovery. There must be a persistent and painstaking attempt to separate everything from us that does not belong to the Spiritual Man.

It might be well to use an illustration here. Suppose we have no peace of mind, no contentment, and no security, are confused and are consequently beset with anxiety and uncertainty and the feeling that the times are out of joint, how shall we proceed?

First of all, we should have at least a sound mental equivalent and psychological basis for a new conviction. How did we get here anyway? We know very well we did not put ourselves here. Nothing is more certain than that man never created himself. He merely awakes to self-discovery.

Therefore, we detach all confusion from the mind by identifying ourselves with the Spirit. God is not poor, not weak, not unhappy; God is not frustrated; God is not in lack; and what is true about God is true about us; therefore, there is no unhappiness to the Real Self. There is no insecurity in the Spiritual Ego. There is no frustration in the Mind of God within us.

Logic and reason conspire to show us that this must be true; no matter what the appearance may be to the contrary, there is still a Spiritual Center. *Standeth God within the shadows, keeping watch upon His own.* We, too, must keep watch, uprooting a false thought here and another one there, until finally, in both intellect and feeling, we reach back to the Center, the Divine Presence within us.

Others may show us how they did this, may even suggest how we can proceed, but there is a path that every man must walk alone. Yet not alone, because forevermore there is a Spirit that beckons, a Presence that feels out toward us as we feel toward It. Some day we shall all rest in Its warm embrace.

Yes, the discovery of the Self is to the self and by the self. There is no use delaying, no use waiting for something to come along or someone who can do this for us, for no such person exists. This is why Jesus told his followers that it was expedient that he go away in order that the Spirit of Truth might reveal to them the meaning of everything he had taught them.

We should not wish it otherwise, for if someone else held the key to our Palace, how should we enter? If someone else had to live for us, we could never live for ourselves. The great and long and meaningful secret of Life is bound up in this self-discovery, and the most fortunate moment in our lives will be that moment when we come to realize that we must take ourselves for better or for worse. Starting right where we are and disregarding time or effort, counting as gain only that which conspires to awaken us to the ultimate Reality, we shall travel back to the Center and the Source.

But there should be no morbid outlook on this, for why need we encounter more unhappiness? Why not think of the opportunity as one filled with peace and fraught with opportunities? Once we are sure there is a goal to reach and the Spirit is directing us, we can be certain that we shall one day arrive, perhaps today, perhaps tomorrow. But is not each step on the road one step closer to reaching our Source?

Let us all, then, accept the simple fact that the road to God is through the self, and that the pathway to an ever-increasing experience can be filled with joy. We can sing as we go along. And why need we deny ourselves the privilege of immediate union, for all the long tomorrows will be but continuations of the short todays. Why not find Life here and now?

YES!

The Silent One within Us

WE FIND this saying in the Upanishad: *The Silent One, the Knower, ever resting in us, may walk, stand, sit, lie down and not do anything at his sweet will.* And in our Bible it says: *I will work, and who shall let* [hinder] *it?* What are these but statements of the Absoluteness of the Supreme as the All-Conquering Power of the Spirit? And this All-Conquering Power of the Spirit finds Self-Expression through man.

This Supreme Being is at the center of each one of us. To It we may come for guidance, and from It we may draw both inspiration and the Power to live, stand, walk, or sit. Every act is an outcome of consciousness, every movement is within the Divine Being, and since the Divine Being is everywhere It must also be at the center of our own life.

It is not only at the center of our own life; It *is* that center. Hence to think of It as the very essence of our own being is clear thinking. To know that Its being is our being is right knowing. And to declare that Its Life is our life is to permit Its Power to flow through us.

The Presence Is Peace, Joy, and Beauty

ALL PEOPLE desire a personal God, and in our system of thought we may be certain that Spirit is personal to everyone who personifies It. If the Spirit is Omnipresent and undivided, It is at the very center of our being, and each one of us is a unique representative of this Omnipresent One.

Kipling said, *Each in his separate star shall draw the thing as he sees it, for the God of things as they are.* Most certainly God is personal to everyone, and the wonderful thing is that each represents God in a unique way. Each individualizes God, and no two individualizations are identical. Thus the Personality of God is not only real to us, but It is uniquely real.

To sense the Divine Person back of each act and the Divine direction back of each thought is both scientific and sensible. Moreover, without such a sense there would be no warmth or color in our work. Every treatment should be filled with the atmosphere of helpfulness, proceeding from our realization that we are recognizing God in our patient, the God who is personified through him, personal to him, individualized in him.

Instead of denying that God is personal to each one of us, we emphasize such personalness. Indeed it is one of the chief cornerstones of this whole spiritual structure, this whole philosophic system of thought.

Not only is there a Presence within us which directly responds to us; there is also a Law operating through us which obeys the will of this Presence. Since this Presence is Peace, Joy, and Beauty, and since It must be Harmony and Wholeness, we may be sure that these qualities seek expression through our activities, seek manifestation in everything that we do, say, and think, or as Jesus said to the woman at the well, . . . *for the Father seeketh such.*

115

God Your Personal Self

THE LIFE THAT IS WITHIN YOU

THE LIFE within you is God; whatever is true of God is true of your Life, since your Life and the Life of God are not two but One. The enlightened have ever proclaimed this Unity of Good, this Oneness of man with God. For this reason many have spoken of this Life within you as both personal and impersonal: impersonal from the standpoint that It is Universal—personal from the standpoint that this Universal Life Principle is personified *in* you.

This Life within you, being God, did not begin and It cannot end; hence you are immortal and eternal. You can never be *less* but must forever be *more* yourself as this Life within you unfolds through your experiences, through your gathering of knowledge and wisdom. Evolution is the *drawing out* of the God-Principle already latent within you. It is this God-Principle within you which Jesus referred to when he said, *Before Abraham was, I am*, and when he said to the one who passed from this life with him, *Today shalt thou be with me in paradise.*

The God that is within you is Truth, Beauty, Harmony, and Wholeness. Every apparent imperfection from which you suffer is a result of ignorance. Because ignorance of the Law excuses no one from Its effects, it follows that the very Power which has bound you, *rightly understood and properly used*, will produce freedom.

The God within you is a Unity and not a duality. This Unity is changeless, forever revealing Itself to each. This is why the God who is already within, even though He is Harmonious and Perfect, has ever appeared as the God we believe in. We might say that the God within, being Infinite, appears to each one of us as the God who is believed in. And we worship the God whom we believe in rather than the God who *is*.

But there is nothing wrong about this, since the God who is *believed in* is at times some part of the God who *is*. Therefore,

116

whatever God you believe in, provided you believe this God is already in you, must respond to you at the level of your belief. This is why it is done unto each one of us as we believe. The Principle is infallible; the practice is what we make it.

There is a great difference in believing God to be *within you* or *outside you*. For if God is outside you, how are you going to reach this God who, not being some part of you, must be separated from you? How can you hope to unite things which are different from each other? But the God who *is already within you*, being forever Perfect and Complete, needs no reunion with anyone; and you need no reunion with this God, because this God already is in your every act, every thought, every movement—in your every plan, purpose and performance.

The God within you creates every circumstance and situation you have ever experienced. You have called these circumstances and situations things in themselves, but they have never been. They have always been the fruition of your thought, and your thought has been dominated by your belief in God ever since you have had self-conscious life.

Ever since you have had self-conscious thought, you have, by your use of the Law of Liberty, created bondage. Not that bondage really existed, but the possibility of using freedom in a limited way existed. You really never *bound* freedom; you merely used it in a *restricted* way. The restriction was not in the Principle but in your use of It.

There is a difference whether you believe in actual limitation or merely in a restricted use of freedom. If limitation were a *thing in itself* you could not change it; but since it is only an outline of experience, why not use your imagination to enlarge that experience? When you do this you will find that the Life Principle within you responds just as quickly to a broader outline. The old outline was *imaginary* only, *never real*. It was like the horizon where the earth and sky appear to meet; as we travel toward this apparent dead end, we find that it disappears.

Whatever you mentally see and spiritually comprehend you may objectively experience, for the God within you is not limited to any one experience. It is the Creator of all experience.

THE MIND THAT IS WITHIN YOU

THE MIND which you use is the Mind which I use; It is the Mind which everyone uses. It is the Mind of God and, because the Mind of God is a complete Unity, It is Omnipresent. Therefore the Mind which you use and which is your mind now is the God-Mind in you. This Mind is in all people, envelops all, and is at the center of every thing. This is why it is that when you know the Truth at the center of your own being you know it within the only Mind there is.

This is why we are told to let that mind be in us which was also in Christ Jesus. The Mind which you possess at this moment is the Mind which Jesus used to demonstrate the Christ Principle. He must have realized God at the center of his being. It is a realization of this Mind of God at the center of your being which gives Power to your word.

Since the Mind within you is the Mind of God, and since the Mind of God has been in all people, it follows that the intelligence within you understands what the great of the earth have been talking about. You already have within you an understanding, a comprehending mind. The Mind of God has no problems, no difficulties, and is never confused. When you know that the Mind within you is God and cannot be confused, then your intellect becomes clarified.

This Mind which is God permeates every atom of your being. It is the governing Principle in every organ of your body. It is the Principle of Perfection within you. Your thought is the activity of this Principle. The Principle is Perfect, Complete, and Limitless, but your thought circumscribes Its action and causes the very Mind of Freedom to create conditions which you call bondage.

As you teach your intellect to believe in the free circulation of Spirit through you, your thought becomes a Law of Elimination to congestion; it purifies stagnation. Your consciousness of the Divine Presence within you, like light, dissipates the darkness. This is the Eternal and True Self at the center of your being. It is the Mind of God manifesting Itself in you, as you. This *you* which It manifests is not separate from Itself but *is* Itself.

118

This Invisible Presence is the Cause of your personality, the light shining through it.

The Divine and Infinite Mind always desiring Self-Expression through you is an insistent urge compelling you to move forward. The Mind in you is also in all people. When you recognize other people it is this Mind knowing Itself in them. This Mind within you is timeless, yet It creates all periods of time. It is the Intelligence back of every action, whether you call such action good, bad, or indifferent. It is always creating form, but It is never limited to any particular form. It is in your every act, but It is always more than any or all of your actions. Even though you appear to be bound, the Mind within you is perfectly free.

Your intellect in no way limits this Mind merely because it conceives of what you call a small form or a little space. It could just as easily conceive of what you call a larger form or a bigger space. Your intellect is doing the best it can with the Mind within you. It reflects this Mind, but not completely. As the Apostle said, *Now we see through a glass darkly.*

The full glory of your Christ-Consciousness does not yet appear at the surface; only a dim shadow or faint echo of It appears. Therefore, you are the Eternal Mind, not caught in time but manifesting Itself through time. You are not merely a shadow of this Mind; you are the substance of It. You are this Mind in action and the enforcement of Its Law. This Law is the Law of your Divinity, and since you are an individual you manifest this Law in a unique way. You project this Mind through experience in a personal manner, different from all others. This constitutes your True and Immortal Self.

Since the Mind within you is the Mind of God, and since the Mind of God not only created everything that has ever existed but will create everything that is ever going to be, you already have within you the ability to project new ideas, new thoughts, new inventions. Therefore, whatsoever ideas you desire, when you pray—when you listen to this inner Mind—know that you are going to receive these ideas, for you are dealing with that Mind which is the Conceiver of all ideas.

When you call upon this Mind for an answer to your problem It at once knows the answer because there is no problem to

It. In this way the answer to every problem already is in the Mind which you possess. *Beloved, now are we the sons of God.*

THE LAW THAT IS WITHIN YOU

THE LAW that is within you is an activity of the Mind Principle in you. This Mind within you is the Mind of God.

All inquiry into any truth, whether we consider such truth physical or metaphysical, leads to the inevitable conclusion that the final creativeness of the Universe is a movement of Intelligence within and upon Itself. This Intelligence already exists at the center of your own being. It really is your own being, and the very power of imagination which you exercise is this Intelligence functioning at the level of your comprehension of It. To think is to create.

The Law that is within you is both Universal and Individual. Since your mind is some part of the Mind of God, there is a place within where you are Universal, where you use Universal Power. That Power is Law.

This Law which is at the center of your own being you no doubt have used largely in an unconscious way; you have used It in ignorance of Its true nature. Consequently, the very Good which you so greatly desire, but which you have been afraid you would not gain, has been kept away from you because you have denied Its presence in your experience. To affirm the presence of this Good is to use the Law within you for the creation of the Good which you affirm.

One of the most fascinating things which you will ever learn is that this Law which exists at the center of your being is creative. You use the same creativeness which brought the planets into being, the same creativeness which produced everything that is. The Law of your life is a Law of Freedom, but you have used It as a law of bondage. You must now use It as a Law of Freedom.

All individual minds, your own included, are different activities of the Infinite Mind. This Mind of God is the Law of your life. When you speak, It speaks within you. Thus your thought becomes the Law of your life because the Law of the One Mind already resides at the center of your being.

To think is to create. You have already been thinking and creating. Now you wish to create Good instead of evil, Abundance rather than limitation. You have this possibility within you, for the Law within you is set in motion by the Mind within you. The Mind within you is God having complete authority over the Law, but you must reverse your use of this Law. You must accept your freedom, announce your liberty, and proclaim your Divine birthright.

Whatever you believe to be true about God, declare to be the Truth about yourself. Know that the Power within you, which is God, is the Law of Good establishing right action in your life. In this manner you will gain dominion and exercise authority.

To think is to create. A thinker is a creator. He lives in the world of his own creation. You are a thinker; therefore you are a creator. Consequently you live in a world of your own creation. At first this does not seem to be true and you may deny it, but finally you will come to see that if this were not true you could not be a free individual. If it is true, then your very bondage is a result of an ignorant use of your freedom.

To think is to create. This is the key which opens the doorway to Wisdom and Power. That doorway is already within you. Somewhere within you the Mind of God reveals the Truth that you were born free, that the will of God for you is one of Goodness, Truth, and Beauty; that all the Power there is, is for you, and all the will there is wills Life. You are the image and likeness of this Life; you are a personification of It; you are the personality of God. The Kingdom of Heaven is already within you, and the Law of that Kingdom is Harmony, Peace, and Joy.

But if this Law of God within you is one with the All-Law, then there is no opposite to It; nothing can contradict Its final, absolute, supreme authority. You must know this. And in knowing it you will exercise that authority which the Eternal Principle has incarnated in you. If to think is to create, thoughts are things and the law of things is a Law of Thought. Change your thinking, then.

This will not be easy at first, because old thought habits are prone to reassert themselves, to claim they have a right to remain in your consciousness, to harass and torment you. But now you are wise and you know they have no such authority. You see them to be exactly what they are—false impressions claiming to be the Truth. They are traitors to your True Self, false representations of the Divinity within you. They are a misuse of your Law of Freedom, but you will cast them out. You will say to them, "I no longer accept you. Begone!" And because they are only thoughts they will evaporate.

What a wonderful thing to realize that this Mind within you is also the Law within you, and that the Spirit within you, which is God, acts through this Mind upon this Law at your direction. You should rejoice that at last you are awakening to the realization that there is no law for you but your own soul shall set it, in the one great Law of all Life, Truth, and Wisdom.

THE POWER THAT IS WITHIN YOU

THE POWER that is within you is the Power of your word operated upon by Law. This Power is not so much a *will* as it is a *willingness*. You will never have to *will* things to happen; you will merely have to *know* that they are happening.

This Law is neutral and impersonal. You are not to think of It as though It were the same thing as Spirit, but merely as a mechanical force which you may use for definite purposes. It is within you and, as the Law of Cause and Effect, reacts to your word. This Law is the way or Creative Medium by which your word is manifested. But this Law, as an aspect of God, is an All-Powerful Medium.

You have been exercising authority through this Law by your word, but you were not entirely conscious of this word because it was just as much subjective as it was objective; it was more or less unconscious, rising out of race suggestion. You are not to think of the Power within you as a person. It is a Principle of nature, a Law of Cause and Effect, a medium.

You have the Power to use this medium in any way you see fit. You have thought that the Law of your being was one of

122

bondage. Now you are going to discover that the very Law which has produced discord in your life can as easily produce harmony.

You have not been using two powers but one Power in two different ways, and experience has already taught you the better way to use this Power. You wish to use It to produce happiness and success, joy, love, and friendship, rather than their opposites. Are you going to realize Good instead of evil? Are you going to use your authority in the Law to create beauty, peace, and joy? They will respond just as quickly as the more ugly manifestations have responded, and you are going to have the greatest possible satisfaction—the satisfaction of knowing that you are a free mental agent in a Spiritual Universe which holds nothing against you but always desires your Good.

No greater good can come to you than to know that the Power already within you is the Power to live, the Power to create. Not only to create for yourself but for others—the Power to do good, the Power to heal, the Power to prosper. You are to realize that the Power within you is a Divine Authority. It is a dispenser of the Divine Gifts. It is a giver of Life, of Joy. It proclaims the Kingdom of Heaven, the Harmony of the soul, and the Unity of all being.

This Power within you responds definitely to direct, conscious thought. It responds as a mathematical and mechanical Law of Cause and Effect. No one can hinder your use of this Power since It is an immediate presence at the center of your own being. No one can reverse your use of It, since nothing can contradict Its authority. Therefore you not only have *some power* at the center of your being; you have access to *all the Power there is*, to *all the Presence there is*, and to *the only God there is*.

You must begin to contemplate this Power within you as answering your every need, supplying your every want, fulfilling your every wish; and you must believe that It does this immediately, right now—not tomorrow but today, because the Law of this Power within you knows no time. When your word directs the Law within you, it must always direct It for today.

You must give conscious direction to this Law and you must definitely expect It to respond. When you say to the Law within you, "Do this!" you must know It is going to do it; you must believe; there must be no doubt in your consciousness. For the Power, Presence, and Law are one and the same thing, and the creative imagination of your own thought is the director of your destiny.

THE FRIEND THAT IS WITHIN YOU

You have a Friend within you who is closer than your shadow. This Friend anticipates your every desire, knows your every need, and governs your every act. This Friend is the God within your own soul, the animating Presence projecting your personality, which is a unique individualization of the Living Spirit.

This Friend within you is Infinite since He is a personification of God. He is not limited by previous experiences which you may have had, by present conditions, or passing situations.

He has no inherited tendencies of evil, lack, or limitation. He has never been caught in the mesh of circumstance. He is at all times radiant, free, and happy.

To your intellect this invisible Friend may seem to be someone else, not your Real Self, but such is not the case. Some have believed that this Friend within you is a mediator between you and Creative Spirit. Others have believed Him to be the reincarnation or the rebirth of your previous self, while still others have sincerely believed Him to be some discarnate soul. But you are not to accept such beliefs, for the Real Person within you is a direct personification of the Universal Spirit. He is your Inner, Absolute, and Perfect Self.

The Friend within you is different from all other persons, yet He is united with all. There is some part of you which reaches into the nature of others, irresistibly drawing them to you and drawing you to them, binding all together in one complete Unity. Right now you are one with all persons, all places, all events.

The Friend within you lives in a state of poise. He is above fear, He is beyond hurt, He is sufficient unto Himself.

The Friend within you is continuously looking after your well-being. He always wishes you to be happy, to be well, to be radiant. Being the very fountain of your life, this Friend is a luminous Presence evermore emerging from pure Spirit, evermore expanding your consciousness. He is the High Counselor, the Eternal Guide. He is your intellect, the essence of its understanding, the nicety of its calculation, the appreciation of its temperament.

There can be no greater unity than exists between you and this inner Friend. He spreads a table before you in the wilderness of human thought. His cup of joy runneth over. He laughs at disaster, triumphs over human failure, and mocks the grave. When this present experience shall be rolled up like a scroll, He will pass on to new and greater experiences. But today He is here. Trust Him today, and you may trust Him for all the tomorrows yet to come. Thus your tomorrow and tomorrow and tomorrow will be but an expansion of your endless today.

Your personality is an outpicturing of the impressions which you have received from this inner Friend, this Deep Personality, this Radiant and Divine Presence whose Life is Light, whose Consciousness is Peace, and whose Presence is Power. You are an incarnation of this Person, this Presence, and this Power.

It may be difficult for you to believe that there is such a Friend, but He is there at the very center of your being directing your thought and causing you to triumph over every defeat, for He is an unconquerable hero. He who keeps silent watch within you lifts your consciousness to the realization that you are forever protected, forever safe, forever perfect.

THE HEALING PRESENCE THAT IS WITHIN YOU

There is a Healing Presence within you. This Healing Presence you must recognize before It can operate for you, because like every other thing in nature It works according to exact and mechanical law.

The God who is within you has already created this marvelous mechanism which you call your human body. The Intelligence which designed and projected this body must have a

125

perfect knowledge of all its parts, It must have a perfect under-standing of all its needs, and It must be able to rebuild those parts and supply their needs.

The Creative Agency within you knows how to re-create. But this Healing Presence, being the very essence of your own nature, must flow out into action through your consciousness of who and what you are. Hence you must recognize the Great Healer, the Divine Emancipator from physical bondage and pain, as your True Spirit.

Since the only final Creative Agency in the Universe must be Mind, and since you are Mind, it follows that this Healing Presence performs Its beneficent act through your conscious-ness. This is why you have always been told to *believe*. If you wish this Healing Presence to manifest Itself you must believe that It *will* do so, and having believed that it *will* do so, you must know that It *is* doing so, for it naturally follows that It can do for you only what It does through you.

You must believe in the Healing Presence within you and within all people, and then you must speak your word in such a way that this Healing Presence may, as It flows through that word, perform the miracle of life which is the giving form to the Invisible. Your word must be definite, conscious, and concrete. You must know that the God within you as a Healing Presence is now the Law of Perfect Life in your physical body. This Heal-ing Presence is reforming your physical body. Continuously It is re-creating all of its parts.

The only way this Healing Presence can create for you is through the images of your thought, through the beliefs which you entertain, whether these beliefs be hope, fear, doubt, faith, or failure. Therefore you must correct all beliefs which deny this Healing Presence. In fact, you must go so far as to deny that there are any negative agencies, and affirm that the Life Princi-ple within you not only destroys all fear in your mind, but dis-solves every object of fear in your physical body.

If you succeed in healing your thought, then this Healing Presence will heal your body as It flows through the new thought pattern. For every denial of physical wholeness you must supply an affirmation of your faith and confidence that the Spirit within

126

you, being Perfect, acts as a Law of Wholeness to your body.

Your body is a body of right ideas. The Healing Presence within you, flowing through all these ideas, lubricates them with the oil of gladness and makes Perfect every organ, every function, every action and reaction. The Healing Presence within you already is Perfect, and it is your recognition of this Perfect Indwelling God which makes possible the execution of the Law of Wholeness.

The Healing Power within you, being the same Healing Presence within all people, may not only become the Law unto your own individual physical experience, but you may use this God-Power within you to help and heal others. And since everyone exists in the same medium of Mind, when you desire to speak your word of healing for someone else you should first recognize the Healing God within you, after which you should recognize the same Healing Presence within the one whom you wish to help.

Then you should make your direct statements for him as though he were yourself. Your statements about him will become the Law unto him just as they have become the Law unto yourself, establishing Harmony in his physical being. State that your word is the Law unto him; that It removes doubt and fear from his consciousness, and with the disappearance of doubt and fear there will be a coresponding disappearance of their manifestation.

The more you use the Law of this Healing Presence within you the more completely aware you will become of Its effectiveness, and the more certain you will be that *it is not I, but the Father that dwelleth in me, he doeth the works.*

THE PEACE THAT IS WITHIN YOU

GOD IS Peace. This Peace which God is belongs to man and is some part of his Spiritual Nature. Whatever God is in the Universal, man is in the particular. The nature of God is incarnated in every living soul.

The Peace that is within you is not something separate from

127

God. It is not something that bombards you from without. This Peace is something that expands from within. Always this Peace has been in you. Always this Peace has nestled at the center of your being, ready to reveal Its Perfection and Harmony.

Peace stands at the door of your consciousness and awaits your acceptance of It. It does not stand outside waiting for entrance; It stands inside waiting to be expressed in everything you do. If the possibility of your peace were dependent upon some external event, some outside circumstance, some objective fact, then you would not have a Principle of Peace within you. You would merely be hoping that one might either develop or be imposed externally.

The Kingdom of Heaven is within you. Within you is the Kingdom of God, and within the Kingdom of God is Peace. A conscious knowledge of this Peace, coupled with a definite use of the Law of Mind, gives to each the possibility of freedom from the bondage of doubt, fear, and uncertainty.

Peace is within you now. The Peace that passeth all human comprehension is there. The Peace that is at the very heart of the Universe is there. The Peace that said to the waves, ''Be still!'' is there. The Peace that healed the lunatic of his obsessing thought is in you. Peace is within you now—the Peace that stilled the tempest and walked the turbulent waters of human discord.

Because God is Peace and because God is in you, the Peace of God must also be in you. You should no longer go in search of Peace, for this is confusion. Search Him not out, but seek Him at the center. He has always been there. The Spirit of Truth, speaking through the understanding of one who realized the Divine Presence, said, *Before Abraham was, I am.* And, *Destroy this temple, and in three days I will raise it up.*

Because Peace is within you, It is available. If It were somewhere else you would never find It. Act as though Peace already possessed your soul and It will possess it. Act as though Peace already emanated from your spirit and It will emanate from it. Speak Peace into confusion, and your peace will heal that confusion.

This Healing Power is to be used and not merely believed in. There is a vast difference between believing in this Principle and using It. To believe in and understand this Principle is essential to the use of It.

Peace is at the center of your own soul; It is the very Being of your being. This Peace which is at the center of your being has never been disturbed. It has never been afraid. It never desired to harm anyone; therefore it has never been hurt. How, then, shall you use this great gift which nestles at the very center of your being?

You are to use it consciously. You are to speak the Word of Peace wherever discord appears. And when you speak the Word of Peace let no doubt arise in your thought. You must know that Peace stills the tempest. You must know that your Peace has all Power because It is the Peace of God within you.

The Peace which is at the center of your being was not born from human struggle, evolution, or accomplishment. It is something that always existed. It was not given by the world. The world cannot take It away. It remains Perfect, exactly what It always has been. It awaits your recognition that you may enter into conscious partnership with It. And when you have joined the forces of your intellect with Its infinite calm your heart will no longer be disturbed, nor will it be afraid.

Above the wind and higher than the whirlwind, enshrined in the Heart of God, there is a Voice within you which says: "Peace! Be not afraid. It is I." This I is YOU. This YOU is God within you. This God within you is Peace.

God Your Impersonal Self

I AM THAT WHICH I AM

I Am that which I Am. I Am the Eternal Presence of your own Self. Thus there is no mediator between you and Myself but your own thought.

This *I Am* has been revealed to you in innumerable ways through the inspired writings of the ages. Each inspiration has been a proclamation that *I Am* is in the midst of you. I Am the writer, the inspirer, and the thing written about. I Am the Creator of history, the One who experiences it. I Am its record and its interpretation. Everything which has ever transpired has but symbolized My Divine Presence at the center of all.

I Am within you is the only Presence there is. I create innumerable centers of My Consciousness personified as people, yet *I Am* is the thread of a Unity running through all, binding all back to Myself. Because I Am a Perfect Oneness, all of Me exists everywhere. Wherever you recognize Me, there I Am. And whether or not you recognize Me, I Am still there. This Divine Visitor, which is your True Self and which is That Which I Am, is both the one who stands at the door and knocks and the one who opens the door.

It is the glory of this recognition which has given to the enlightened true mastership. Do not look for masters outside of Me, or mediators between yourself and Myself. There is but One Self who needs no mediator. This Self is immediate, present, and available.

Any thought or belief which would seek to separate That Which I Am from that which you are would be an illusion, no matter how lofty its concept or how sacred its purpose. For it would seek to deny the ever-present *I Am*, the completeness of My Perfection, the God within you, the inspired thought back of your act.

Your True Self constitutes the only mediator between the visible and the Invisible. I Am that Self. Be still and know that you are one with Me, and My Being in you is your life. It is also your body, mind, and spirit; every cell of your body, every thought of your mind, the glory of your spirit. That which you have so ardently sought has never been separated from you for one moment. My desire within you to be expressed has been the motivating Power impelling and compelling you evermore to reach out, on, and up.

I Am the Christ dwelling at the center of every soul: human, yet Divine; Infinite, yet flowing through that which is apparently finite; unmanifest, yet forever manifesting; birthless and deathless, yet forever being born; timeless, I Am forever creating time. And you, the expression of Myself, appear to be separated from Me merely because you are a unique manifestation of Myself. For I Am that which you are and which all people are. I Am in all and I Am all.

When the recognition comes within you of this *I Am That Which I Am*, you will have discovered your true Savior, your true Sonship, and you will know that this Sonship is a projection of Myself, forever different from any other projection, immortal, yet forever expanding.

Here you find the True Ideal, the Cosmic Pattern, the Eternal Friendship of the soul to itself, the God who is personified, the Person who is God-in-man. And how great is this Divine riddle! How inscrutable is the Sphinx! Men have sought through countless ages to solve this mystery—how can Unity and multiplicity exist together without division?

But now you have solved this mystery. You have compelled the Sphinx to answer her own question; she no longer devours you but, like circumstance, must bow to that Divinity within you; like all created things, must acknowledge the supremacy of *That Which I Am* within you.

This mystery of Unity and multiplicity without division I have proclaimed through the ages, but only the enlightened have understood My meaning; the unenlightened have not realized that those who did understand Me were even as they. They believed them to be great prophets, great mediators governed by invisible masters, controlled by those whom they called saints.

But since I create both saint and sinner, know neither big nor little, good nor bad, and, being ageless, since I create all ages,

I Am that which reveals and that which is revealed. And the stone which the builders rejected has become the chief stone of the corner. The vulgar did not know, and even the high priests failed to recognize, that the Ark of My Covenant was in the sanctuary of their own souls; that the Scroll of Life concealed in this Ark had inscribed on it merely the words *I AM.*

I AM THE ABUNDANCE WITHIN YOU

I Am come that you might have a more abundant Life. To those who know not their True Nature, believing themselves separated from Good, I Am come. To those weary with disappointment and struggle who have sought life outside themselves, I point the way to certain salvation.

I Am in the midst of you is mighty to heal, to comfort, and to prosper. I have come to arouse you from your long dream of separation; from your night of despair. The dawn has come. The sun of Truth rises over the horizon of ignorance. The light dissipates the darkness. The morning dew is upon the petals; they glisten in the sun.

I Am that sun of Truth dwelling within the sanctuary of your heart. I Am the morning star guiding you to the manger of your salvation, wherein lies the child born from your own consciousness. This inner life is your only savior, the creator of your destiny, the arbiter of your fate.

Awake! Become aware of My Presence, for I Am Life. I Am not something apart from your being. I Am your being. Closer than breathing, nearer than hands and feet I Am. You have thought you denied My existence by affirming lack, fear, and failure, but in reality you have merely affirmed My Power to be to you that which you believed. I Am the Reality of your being, but I have always appeared to you in the form of your belief. I Am more than your conscious mind. I Am that which projects the mind which you call *you.* I Am that which creates your being and projects it from the center of My own Divine Originality.

I Am the Power which has bound you to your false belief. I Am the Presence which alone can give you freedom. Bondage

132

and freedom are one and the same. *I Am*, who is in the midst of your being, can project one as easily as another. Bondage does not bind Me; it merely expresses Me. That which you call bondage is My freedom misused.

I have come to awaken you from the sense of limitation; to proclaim to you the eternal days of My Abundance. I have come to acquaint your mind with Truth, to convert your soul by reason, inspiration, and illumination to the realization that *I Am* is all there is, beside which there is none other.

Within you is the Secret Place of the Most High, the Tabernacle of the Almighty, the Indwelling God, the Ever-Present Father, and the Eternal Child. This Ever-Present Father and the Eternal Child are one and the same Being. I Am that Being. I Am the All-Being. I Am your being. You are My Being.

I am that which thou art, thou art that which I am. Therefore you may know that the Universal *I Am* is also the individual *I*. Hence the individual *I* merges into the Universal *I Am*; is Omnipotent wherever Good impels the activities of Its thought. For human thought is as Divine as is its consciousness of Me, and My Omnipotent Law forever obeys its will.

If you can put aside your fear, which is but an expression of your sense of isolation; if you can put aside all negation and turn to Me alone; then you shall be made free. Be still and know that I Am your True Self. Be still and know that I Am the Life Principle. Be still and know that I Am the Truth, dispelling all error. I Am Power, neutralizing all weakness. I Am Abundance, swallowing up all lack. I Am your Real Self.

Nothing that you have ever said or done, no law that you have ever set in motion, is as great as I Am, for I transcend all uses of Law. I, the Creator, re-create. I, the Molder, remold. I, the Maker, remake.

You may trust what I shall do, for I Am God, the Living Spirit in the midst of you—not some-mighty but All-Mighty. There is no law opposed to My Will. There is no opposite to My Nature. There is no darkness which My Light does not dissipate. There is no knowledge which I do not possess, for I Am Wisdom, the Source of all knowledge. I Am Light, the Source of all illumination. I Am Power, the Source of all strength.

I AM THE CREATIVENESS WITHIN YOU

Because I Am the Creativeness of the Universe, and because My imagination is My creativeness, then you may know that to think is to create. Hence were the worlds formed by the Power of My Word. Hence is your world formed by the Power of My Word in you, for your word is My Word in you. Your thought is My Thought in you. Your Power is My Power in you.

I the Universal, and you the individual, are one and the same Being. I the Universal think in you the individual. Thus I the Universal endow you the individual with life, with creativeness —I Am that Life and that Creativeness within you.

Your thought is creative. Your imagination projects form upon the screen of your experience. This is because I the Creative Principle dwell within you, projecting the law of My Creativeness through your imagination.

To know how to think is to know how to create, and this power to create through thought is the execution of My Will in you, the manifestation of My Being through you. This is My Image and Likeness manifest at the level of your consciousness. If you can consciously realize this, you may know that I Am still creating through your thinking.

I the Universal am now individual. I the Impersonal am now personal. And yet in My personality and individuality I still remain Universal. But I the Universal Creative Mind now become at the same time the individual and personal creative mind through your will, through your desire.

Because you are some part of Me you have the Power to think and to create. This Power is My Power; it is also your Power. And because this is so, that which you have believed has come upon you; that which you have thought has transpired. Until now you have not known that the very Power which binds you can give you freedom, that the very Power which has created physical infirmities may heal. I the Eternal within do all these things.

Because you believe that which you experience to be necessary, you perpetuate such experience. This also is My Mind working at the center of your being. *I Am* in the midst of you is

134

the sole and only Creative Agency in the Universe, whether that Creative Agency calls itself your imagination or My Will. It is one and the same. *I Am* in the midst of you can easily dissolve one creation and project another. When your present Universe shall be numbered with the things once experienced, *I Am* in the midst of you will project another Universe and yet another and beyond that more.

Be still and know that I Am within you. Be still and know that every atom of your body is in tune with the Perfect Life. Be still and know that every activity of your physical being moves in accord with My Divine Perfection. I Am not caught in your body but I Am your body. Never limited by its action, I produce its action.

By some Divine Intuition, by some Inner Whispering of your soul, by some Light upon your path, you have progressed. I Am that Light, that Urge, that Whisper, that Voice.

I Am your Real Self. Being the All-Being, I Am the Being of all, from the smallest particle to the greatest, from the lowest form to the highest intelligence.

You must understand that this *I Am* at the center of your being is the *I Am* at the center of all being. When you understand this, all nature will have a new meaning. You will know that the fragrance of the rose is Mine; you will know why the intelligence in the animal responds to you; you will understand the mystery of mysteries. You will possess the key which unlocks the storehouse of nature. You will be bound with an inseparable Unity to all that exists.

I AM THE SUSTAINER WITHIN YOU

In the heart of each I live; at the center of all creation I dwell. I fill all space. I Am All-in-all, over all, and through all. From the mightiest form to the smallest atom, My Presence covers all, pervades all, and animates all.

Beside Me there is no other Presence, no other animating Principle. Wherever you look you will see Me. Wherever you go you will find Me.

God's Will

*Finally, brethren, whatsoever things are true, whatso-
ever things are honest, whatsoever things are just, whatsoever things are pure, whatsoever things are lovely,
whatsoever things are of good report; if there be any virtue, and if there be any praise, think on these things.*
                                        Philippians 4:8

IN THE Science of Mind we are frequently asked these
questions: "What is God's Will? Is it God's Will that I should
be happy, prosperous, free, and self-expressed? Or is God trying
me? Is God molding my character through trial and tribulation?"
Generally speaking, these questions are sincerely asked, and frequently they are made by one whose consciousness has already
suffered deeply from the limitation and unhappiness of human
experience.

What is God's Will? This question is as old as time, and the
answer has been as varied as have been the mentalities of those
who gave it. To the scientific mind the Will of God is manifest
in the Immutable Laws of the Universe. To the overzealous religionist the Will of God appears to come through some special
revelation giving birth to a certain spiritual system of thought
which forever after is to be taken dogmatically and accepted
without question, a truth and a faith once and for all delivered.

If we take a rational viewpoint of this question, shall we not
be compelled to accept, as the only logical conclusion, that the
Will of God must ever be consistent with the Nature of the Divine Being? God's Will and God's Nature must be identical. If
the Nature of God is limitation and bondage, the Will of God
must also be limitation and bondage.

When we use the word *God* we mean the Great Reality, the
Infinite Unity, the Final Truth back of all manifest life, the Absolute or Causeless Cause, the One Unconditioned, Complete
and Perfect Being—Indivisible, Changeless, and Whole. All of
these descriptive terms are synonymous with the word *God*.

If the Nature of God or Reality were unhappiness, then the

136

Will of God would be toward unhappiness. But to suppose that the Nature of God could be toward any form of limitation is to suppose not only an inconsistency but an impossibility. The Truth is Limitless. The Nature of God, then, is not one of limitation or bondage, but one of Freedom; therefore the Scriptures tell us that we have inherited not bondage but Liberty.

Our Divine Inheritance is Self-Sufficiency, Perfection, Peace, Wholeness, and this must include Abundance, Self-Expression, Accomplishment, and Happiness. The Nature of God is Wholeness; the Nature of Wholeness is Happiness; the Nature of Happiness is Peace; the Nature of Peace is Harmony; and the Nature of Harmony is Joy. So whichever way we turn the proposition, we are compelled to understand that the Nature of Reality, the Nature of God, is Perfect; therefore the Will of God, which can never be divorced from God's Nature, must always be a Will toward our Wholeness, Peace, Poise, Power, and Self-Expression.

If the Will of God is the Will of Abundance, it follows that God cannot will lack, want, or limitation. It follows that all bondage is of the human. All bondage is a result of a circumscribed viewpoint of Reality. All affliction is a result of ignorance.

Because of our psychological nature and because that which we think about tends to take place in our experience, it follows that if we believe God's Will is toward unhappiness and limitation we shall experience limitation resulting from such belief. That is why it is so important that our consciousness be clear; that we should know what we really believe about God. Indeed we might say that in the final analysis, what a man believes about God inevitably influences his entire experience in life. It certainly follows that if we believe the Supreme Will of the Universe is toward suffering, we cannot possibly escape the suffering imposed by such belief operating through the Law of Cause and Effect.

But the Will of God is never toward suffering. In the midst of all perplexities the cry for deliverance has ever risen. The intuition senses that deliverance is at hand, but the intellect does not comprehend the manner in which it may become manifest. Hence the intuition proclaims that which the intellect does not understand, and man must constantly reaffirm his belief in the

137

Infinite Goodness if he expects to exclude the idea of evil from his thought.

God's Will for every person is Happiness, Peace, and Joy. God's Will for all creation is Self-Expression, since creation is an expression of this invisible Cause which we call God, nor can it be considered to be anything else. Every constructive desire toward Self-Expression finds its prototype in the Universal need for Self-Expression. The ceaseless struggle for liberty manifest throughout the ages, the constant reaching out toward Reality which has inspired all people to more noble efforts, are expressions of that which is largely an unconscious sense, that hope which *springs eternal in the human breast.*

God's Will is always toward Life and more Life. When Jesus said, *God is not the God of the dead, but of the living,* he was explaining that the Will of God and the Nature of God are Life and not death; for how can the Principle of Life produce death? We might add: How can the Principle of Harmony produce discord? We must believe that the Will of God is Happiness. Then we shall have a strong spiritual and psychological background for our conviction that we too should be happy. In the quest of the soul for its greatest Good, which is an inner contentment, we must know that the Will of God is Serenity, Security, Certainty.

But some may say, "That all sounds very grand, but is it not a subtle argument of the devil, trying to lead us astray? Is it not really our own lustful and willful wishing, seeking to escape the dire penalties of our rash acts?"

We must patiently, persistently, and insistently show people that the Will of God cannot be toward anything other than that which is Good; that the Will of God and the Nature of God are identical and must forever remain so; that there is nothing in the Universe which opposes their Good except their misuse of the Law which of Itself is Good. This Law must present Itself to each individual according to his belief.

God's Will most certainly is toward Abundance. If we enjoy life, God is that much more completely expressed; the world is to that extent a happier place in which to live. There is no God who tries men's souls or beats them over the head with a cosmic

138

club, seeing how much they can stand. There is no sin but a mistake, and no punishment but a consequence. By the same token, virtue is its own reward. If some sincere person says to you, "Then if all this is true, I can do exactly as I please since God has no Will for me," explain to him again that God's Will and God's Nature are One, and one part of God's Nature is the immutable Law of Cause and Effect. Every man must reap as he sows.

There can be no new harvest without a new seedtime. If we have been suffering from unhappiness, thinking it to be the Will of God, we must realize that our thoughts are so formulated that our unhappiness is an inevitable result. Our emotions are so directed that they must create unhappiness. In other words, we suffer from ignorance.

Now if the Will of God is toward Peace and Joy, and if the Nature of God is identical with this Will, then the Law of God, which is also the Nature of God executing the Will of God, is toward Joy and Happiness. Consequently, when we begin to think Joy and Happiness they will rush to us, claiming us as their own.

Thus it is that the Father advances to meet the Son and enfolds him in His embrace. They were never really separated; the Son had merely misdirected his energy. The most beautiful thought of all is that when he redirected this energy into a constructive channel, his evil experience was terminated, and a new use of the Law was put into effect. In this simple but most profound lesson did the great Wayshower teach the simple Truth of our relationship to the Parent Mind.

Every moment that a man is unhappy and unexpressed he is tearing down his personality. The moment he becomes inwardly contented he begins to build it up again. The Will of God is toward the more abundant life because that life expresses God. The life that is cramped, warped, timid, and fearful does not express the Divine Being so completely as the free-swinging self-expression of the soul pronouncing God's Work to be Good, announcing through every experience the ecstasy of self-expression.

We do not honor God by being poor, weak, and unhappy, nor do we limit God by such experiences. What we do in our negative experiences is misdirect the positive energy which is already in us, for there is only One Final Energy, just as there is only One Final Mind. This Final Mind and this Final Energy are always manifesting through us at the level of our consciousness of Life and our comprehension of Its meaning; hence the importance of re-educating the mind to a more direct perception of its relationship to God.

All men seek Self-Expression, as all men seek life, because the God in us is Freedom and must be expressed. If our outlet for this Self-Expression, for this Divine Urge, is a constructive one, no evil results can ever follow, and through our Self-Expression the world will be benefited. Every form of morbid argument arises to slay this great hope within us. God is trying us, the devil is tempting us, experience is too much for us, and on and on through the limitless category of human morbidity this argument of the serpent seeks to win us from our Garden of Eden.

Through every subtlety, by every illusion, by the logic of human experience, we are led from Reality into our dream of separation. It takes resolute thought, a poised mind, and a confident spirit to overcome this. It takes calm faith and quiet confidence in the Supremacy of Good and in the Omnipotence of the Law of Good. Freedom from bondage is a thing which we must inwardly perceive. This perception is the greatest of all perceptions.

The Nature of God, the Will of God, and the Power of God are one and the same thing. It matters not that countless millions of people through endless generations have misinterpreted this Will of God, and thought that It meant limitation and suffering. The Nature of God is demonstrated when It is understood. It is proved when It is *known*.

If the Truth about God is Happiness, Joy, Self-Expression, and Abundance, then this is the Truth we should seek to demonstrate in our own lives. This is done by *knowing* that every thought within us abounds with Peace, partakes of the Divine Bounty, includes the idea of Wholeness, and is shot through with Eternal Light.

God the Self-Evident Truth within You

IT IS self-evident that we live. Descartes said, *I think, therefore I am.* This might be called an axiom of reason whereby one perceives that he exists. An axiom of reason is a Truth so self-evident, so universally experienced, so immediately known to the mind that reason cannot deny Its existence. That there are such final Truths is self-evident.

We wish to establish our identity in the Universe, the limitless possibility of self-expression, and the certainty of eternal unfoldment. We wish to establish identity, individuality, unity, completion.

Our first self-evident proposition is that *the Truth is that which is.* We are using Truth in the sense of Its absolute meaning—not *some* truth or *a* truth, but the Truth, the ultimate Reality. The Truth being that which is, there can be nothing unlike It, different from It, or opposed to It.

While it is true that our present finite comprehension does not grasp such an Infinity, and appearances seem to contradict this fundamental premise, we may be certain that even the judgment of the senses is no final criterion. The earth and the sky do not finally meet anywhere. We all have such apparent horizons attached to our experience. But we must postulate an absolute, unconditioned Truth somewhere. This is the Truth Jesus referred to when he said, *Ye shall know the truth, and the truth shall make you free.* What this Truth is and how It operates through us is the nature of our inquiry.

That which reason cannot doubt, that to which the essence of reason can find no opposite, but in which clear thinking must have complete confidence—by the very fact of its inability to conceive an opposite—that is Truth. The Bible tells us, *For by thy words thou shalt be justified, and by thy words thou shalt be condemned.* The concept of Truth formulated in our thought becomes our word, becomes the affirmation of our relationship

141

to the Universe. For instance, we believe that God is all there is, or we do not believe that God is all there is.

If clear reasoning does deliver the perception of the Allness of Truth, and if Truth is a synonym for God, then we may say: God is all there is. And we may add that it is impossible to conceive any opposite, otherness, difference, unlikeness, in what we call the past (which is memory), in what we call the present (which is experience), or in the future (which is anticipation). For past, present, and future are but a continuity upon which is threaded the sequence of experience.

If God is all there is, then past, present, and future—time, experience, and form—if they exist at all, must exist as some part of Truth. If this Truth is all there is, we also must be included in It, and we should identify ourselves with It. Thus the Allness of Truth automatically includes the Reality of our own being.

We arrive at the proposition that *Truth, being all there is, must be Universal.* Spirit plus nothing equals Spirit. Since there is no such thing as that which is not, a lie merely becomes a denial of Truth. A lie has no vitality, no power, remaining merely a suppositional opposite to that which of itself is positive, absolute, and eternal. Truth is Universal. Cancelling what is not and leaving what is, we arrive at the conclusion that nothing has happened to the Truth. It was not born, It will not die. It did not come, It will not go. It has no degrees of being. It is universally present.

Next we prove the theorem that *Truth is Indivisible.* Having nothing unlike It with which to divide It, being All, it remains a complete Unity. Therefore, every announcement of being is an announcement of Truth. The Indivisible Wholeness of Truth includes All that is, and since I can say I am, Truth includes myself.

Emerson tells us that no power of genius has ever yet had the smallest success in explaining existence. The perfect enigma remains. Truth is not explained nor is It explainable. Our Unity with It is not something which we acquire. It is a Reality which we discover. This is a conclusion at which we arrive, not by intellectual processes alone, because the genius of the intellect has never explained its own existence; it has merely experienced it.

If the Truth is all there is, if It is Universal and a Unit, then nothing came before It and nothing came after It, but Itself was, is, and remains All. The Indivisibility of Truth guarantees Its Unity, and Its Unity guarantees not only our Oneness with It and Its Oneness with us, but the inseparable Allness of this Oneness. Transcendent even while it is immanent, the Truth unifies transcendence and immanence. The perceiver and the thing perceived are united in One Common Mind and Existence.

Individual - Process.

Something cannot be divided by nothing. If the Truth is all there is and if there is nothing unlike It, then there is no dividing line between God and man. Hence the self-evident perception of Jesus when he said, *I and my Father are one.* Such Allness announces independence. That which we call the attributes of Truth are not attributes of something which projects such alleged attributes, but are activities of that which constitutes such attributes. Essence and performance are identical. Truth and attribute are one.

Interdependi

This must have been what Jesus had in mind when he said, *The words that I speak unto you, they are spirit and they are life.* He was not thinking of his word as reflecting or transmitting some over-dwelling power, but that Power Itself was undivorced from the word. His word was that Power, not merely an expression or an extension of It. The attribute was the essence. Hence Power is never separated from Itself, and the Mind which conceived the Cosmos, giving birth to Its infinite forms, is identified with the plot in the latest play—the same Mind, because all Mind is One.

Ego's will?

Within all people and within everything that lives there is an impulsion toward self-expression. This impulse is dynamic and irresistible. The very fact that there is an insistent urge for self-expression in all individuals proves that this urge is Cosmic. The apparent parts substantiate the characteristics of the Universal Wholeness if our axiom of Unity is correct. Therefore

yes Adler.

the desire for self-expression is not only legitimate; it is irresistible. To seek escape from this desire would be an unconscious attempt toward self-annihilation.

Each individual must interpret the Universe for himself since he has to interpret It to himself. The Universe can interpret Itself for him only by interpreting Itself through him. God can give us only what we take, and the taking is the Self-Expression of God in us—not something other or different from God, not something which has succeeded in passing a dividing line, but Itself is God.

The urge which causes us to say *I am* is more than an urge causing us to express a Power which extends Itself through us or an Intelligence which uses us as an instrument for Its activity. This urge in us which causes us to say *I am* is God. Hence our self-awareness is Its Self-Awareness. This perception of Unity has been basic to the spiritual genius of the ages, and is but another way of saying that God is all there is. The enigma of Unity is solved in such degree as one perceives Unity in multiplicity and multiplicity in Unity.

We are using this illustration of axioms not to confuse nor to mystify, but to show that, through all of the attempts which ever have been made to teach the Truth, this one central theme has run—the Indivisible Unity of God and man. Every sacred literature of the ages contains it.

To realize that this Indivisible Wholeness is at the center of our own being is to understand that the Power of our individual word is an activity of the Infinite and Eternal *I Am*, the Everlasting and Perfect Spirit. That Spirit in us is us. No greater Unity could be delivered than that which by the very nature of being cannot be withheld. This deliverance is not partial but complete.

Next we arrive at another proposition, which is that *the Truth is unchangeable*. This is self-evident, since there is nothing for the Truth to change into. It cannot change into nothing because there is no such thing as nothing. It cannot change into Itself because It already is Itself. It remains, persistent, permanent.

If the Truth cannot change, if It is permanent, if It is ever-present, then It is always reliable. There is nothing but stability and nothing but security. The Truth is faithful. Truth has no birth, evolution, or decay. Because the Truth is eternal and changeless, and because I exist, and because that which I am is It in me, it is self-evident that I am eternal. Such is the perception of immortality, deathlessness, and everlasting being. This is but another way of saying that God cannot die, that God is all there is, that God is the essence of my life and is my life; that I am an immortal and an eternal being now.

We next arrive at a conclusion which tends to liberate the mind from the thralldom of circumstances: *The Truth, being all there is, is both Cause and Effect.* It is self-evident that Truth has no cause and that there is no effect external to It. Therefore Cause and Effect are one and the same thing. There is neither cause nor effect external to Truth. Hence any belief in the cause and effect of bondage has no substantiality, for, if it had, bondage would be permanent, changeless, and inescapable. If Truth were bondage, freedom would be unthinkable.

The Truth which sets us free is not the introduction of some higher power on a lower plane. It is the knowledge that there are no higher and no lower planes in Truth, no higher and no lower laws in Truth. There is merely *what is*, and the self-action of *what is* proclaiming Itself to be that which It is. If Truth were bondage instead of freedom, the very knowledge of Truth would create more bondage. But since Truth is freedom, then a knowledge of Truth is freedom. To know the Truth is to be free. Truth and freedom are identical.

Cause and Effect, therefore, become a plaything, a something to be used. Karma and Kismet become bubbles to be blown about. Such is the perception of Power. Such is the realization that the knowledge of Truth is Power. Power is that which compels, necessitates, authorizes, commands. *He [Jesus] taught them as one having authority and not as the scribes.* This was because he understood the nature of the spontaneous Spirit within him and realized that the Law of Cause and Effect is the mechanical method through which the Word of Power proves Its authority.

We arrive next at the perception of *person, individuality, personality,* and *humanity,* for again we may say, "I think, therefore I am." Also, our fellow man may say, "I think, therefore I am." The *Allness* of Truth delivers the message that, in a certain sense, each is *All* because of the indivisibility of Truth, and *All* is in each. Such is the mystery of individuality which the mask of personality but dimly reveals. The Truth, being *All,* means that each individual is forced to be Truth and nothing but Truth. Truth does not deny individuality, personality, or humanity. It affirms that each exists in his apparently separate star, maintaining an eternal, changeless, and perfect identity in the *Allness* of Good. Each is an individualized expression of the One.

There is nothing which separates one individual from another, even while there is nothing which can annihilate, subtract from, or add to the individuality of each. Such totality in individuality and such individuality in totality is perceived, not so much by an intellectual process as by the very axiom itself which delivers the necessity of accepting the Principle of Omnipresence.

The Principle of Omnipresence also declares the Principle of Omniscience. Truth is not only All-Presence; It is All-Knowledge. Because this is so, an inventor can say, "I know the answer to my problem"; the author can say, "My plot is worked out"; the organizer can say, "My organization is complete." By consciously practicing Omnipotence, Omniscience, and Omnipresence, we prove in some measure that these self-evident abstractions are real necessities, reliable, substantial, and available. We need labor under no illusion that it is necessary to deny individuality, personality, or humanity in order to affirm the Allness of God.

But if Truth is all there is, then Truth is Intelligence, Truth is what we call Mind, Truth is Idea. Idea becomes absolute. Idea reflects experience. The Allness of Idea destroys the belief in any physical, mental, or material universe external to concept. Creation becomes the contemplation of Truth. Such is the perception of creativeness. Forms are real, but not self-sustained; they are nothing in themselves. There is nothing in such a reflected idea to have control even over itself.

Having established Unity, Indivisibility, Permanence, Power, Omniscience, Omnipresence, and Omnipotence, we arrive at the conclusion of *Eternal Dominion.* It is self-evident that, if the objective world were a thing in itself and we were in no way connected with it other than by experiencing it as an external fact, we could not possibly exercise dominion. The Truth would be in fragments which we should never be able to put together; hence we never could attain Wholeness. The greatest teachings of the ages contradict the fragmentary theory and insist on resolving all apparent multiplicity into a final Unity. This Unity is not some far-off event, but a present fact. Modern science tends in the same direction.

The Allness of Truth, stated in the simplest manner, affirms that God is all there is. God never changes. God is in me. God is that which I am. God is in the Universe. God is the Universe.

At first, man is ignorant of his True Nature. The Word has become flesh, but self-conscious life has not yet emerged. The fusion of will, desire, and volition, without which there can be no personality, has not taken place. Finally the Word not only becomes flesh; it also becomes person. Man awakes to Life, turns toward the Light, and triumphs over limitation.

Therefore our final self-evident proposition delivers the perception of *Bliss, Wholeness, and Perfection.* The Universal *I Am* and the individual *I* are One in Peace, Joy, Love, Wisdom, Beauty, and Power.

In the beginning was the Word, and the Word was Life, and the Word was Light. And the Light through Law produced form, and the created form turned to the Light, and the Light of consciousness dawned. And man beheld the Light and walked in It, and the Light was All.

The Lord Is My Shepherd

An Interpretation of the Twenty-third Psalm

Centuries ago the Psalmist caught a Divine Inspiration and began to think about God as the Good Shepherd. And as he did so, a great wave of peace flowed through his whole being, a feeling of trust and confidence, and his soul began to sing within him.

Of all the inspired writings of the ages none is more beautiful than the Twenty-third Psalm, none more filled with quiet contentment and complete assurance, none more replete with the comfort and consolation of the thought that we are not left alone to buffet our way through life, here or hereafter.

THE LORD IS MY SHEPHERD; I SHALL NOT WANT . . .

A shepherd cares for his sheep lovingly and kindly; feeds and shelters them and tends them if they are ill. Throughout the Bible we find references to the shepherd as a loving Presence, guiding, guarding, and keeping. The sheep do not worry; they are not afraid, for they have a sense of being cared for, a feeling of security. When we let the Lord of all creation take care of us we are following the Good Shepherd, who knows his sheep and loves them.

HE MAKETH ME TO LIE DOWN IN GREEN PASTURES . . .

To lie down in a pasture suggests relaxation in the midst of abundance, an abundance which is already provided, a good which is Divinely given. The words *green pastures* refer to a place of rest. Green is the most restful and comforting color in nature. It brings to our minds the picture of a shady nook where we can rest in the middle of the day.

148

HE LEADETH ME BESIDE THE STILL WATERS . . .

To complete the picture the Psalmist tells us that this pasture is beside still waters, referring to the River of Life in which there is no conflict, no turmoil.

HE RESTORETH MY SOUL . . .

Just let all the cares of yesterday flow out and all the burdens go with them, for the soul cannot be restored by the River of Life unless it lets go of the past and discovers that a new future is forever flowing around it—something fresh and clean and new and wonderful.

HE LEADETH ME IN THE PATHS OF RIGHTEOUSNESS FOR HIS NAME'S SAKE . . .

When we follow the pathway of righteousness, which means right-use-ness, and when we take the name of God with us, then we are in line with the great Harmony of the Universe and we are restored in body, mind, and soul, because the Spirit makes everything new.

YEA, THOUGH I WALK THROUGH THE VALLEY OF THE SHADOW OF DEATH, I WILL FEAR NO EVIL: FOR THOU ART WITH ME . . .

Death is but a shadow cast by life. The Divine Spirit brought us into this world; It has never deserted us, and It will remain with us forever. We cannot wander away from God. It is destined by the Divine Will that good shall come at last alike to all.

THY ROD AND THY STAFF THEY COMFORT ME . . .

A rod or staff was used by the shepherd to protect himself and his sheep. Like many other symbols in the Bible it refers to the staff of Truth or our complete reliance on the Law of Good.

THOU PREPAREST A TABLE BEFORE ME IN THE PRESENCE OF MINE ENEMIES . . .

The table of the Lord is forever spread and on it are the gifts of Life, including health, happiness, joy, and success in living. Good can be found anywhere, if we look for it. Abundance can spring from want, peace from confusion, and joy from unhappiness, right where we are. The table of God is eternally spread, but, if we are too busy to come and eat, then we cannot expect to partake of the Divine Bounty.

THOU ANOINTEST MY HEAD WITH OIL . . .

The Eastern custom of the host anointing the heads of his guests with oil was a symbol of complete hospitality, of perfect welcome.

MY CUP RUNNETH OVER . . .

God's abundance is an extravagant abundance; It is limitless. Our cup could be filled and running over if we would only hold it right side up. Too often we reverse this process because we do not realize that the Divine Spirit wishes us to have everything that is good and withholds nothing from us.

SURELY GOODNESS AND MERCY SHALL FOLLOW ME ALL THE DAYS OF MY LIFE; AND I WILL DWELL IN THE HOUSE OF THE LORD FOREVER.

Goodness will always be available to us, and there will always be mercy for our mistakes. This goodness and this mercy will never forsake us, because there is a Presence and a Power that goes with us and is within us—the loving Presence of the Divine Spirit and the all-conquering Power of the Law of Good.

The Individual
and the Universal

WE INDIVIDUALIZE the Universal and Universalize the individual.

This sounds like rather an abstract statement until we understand its simplicity. The ancients said that every man is a microcosm within a Macrocosm, a little world within a Big World, or an individual within the Universal. Jesus said: *Believest thou not that I am in the Father, and the Father in me? The words that I speak unto you I speak not of myself; but the Father that dwelleth in me, he doeth the works.*

What does this mean? The answer is simple, and yet it is that type of simplicity from which the most profound conclusions are reached.

There is no such thing as an individual anything in the Universe. For instance, we as individuals do not have an individual gravitational force that holds us in place. We do not possess an individual law of mathematics or principle of harmony. Rather we are immersed in all of these things, and they individualize through us in accord with the use that we make of them.

When Emerson said that there is One Mind common to all individual men he reached one of the highest perceptions of the ages. Nor was he denying the Reality of our own being. He was saying in substance: "You are because God is. You live because God lives in you." Each one of us individualizes the Universal Mind by our use of It. The sum total of our mental and emotional reactions surrounds us with a field of thought which is operated upon by a larger field of Mind, Law, and Action.

This is why you do not send out thoughts or hold them, or will or wish or concentrate when you give a treatment. You make a definite statement in this Universal field of Mind, which individualizes for the person, place, or thing you identify your statement with. Your treatment is an individualization of the

Universal Mind, but the moment it is given it becomes a Universalization of the individual mind.

This sounds abstract, so we shall make it more understandable by way of an illustration. When a farmer sows grain he is individualizing the creative soil of a Universal Medium. The creativity was there before he used it. It would be there if he did not use it. It is, was, and will remain just what it was, nothing more and nothing less.

Without being consciously aware of the fact, the farmer has learned that he as an individual can sow the seed of his choice. The Universal is now individualizing for him at the point of decision in his personal life.

But the moment he sows the seed, a Universal process is set in operation, and that which was individual passes from a point of his conscious volition, selectivity, and will into a Universal field of creative reaction. He actually is individualizing the Universal, but the moment he does so his individualization is acted upon by the Universal, and thus it becomes a Universal operation.

This is true in everything we do. We are individual points in the Consciousness of God or the original Creative Spirit of the Universe. We are points where It thinks through us as us, or, as we say, God as man in man is man.

But the God that is in man is the same God that is Universal. There is no wall of separation, no barrier, no place where one begins and the other leaves off. All is One and One is All. The creativity of thought is not dependent upon the thinker. Only the choice of thinking is dependent upon the thinker. The creative activity of thought belongs to the Universe.

This is one of the fine points in our philosophy, and one of the main points in the Science of Mind. Every advance in science is built on the simple proposition that nature obeys us when we obey it.

It is said by those who understand ancient symbology that this is why Jesus washed the disciples' feet. It was as though he were saying to them, "If I, your master, wash your feet, ought you not to wash one another's feet?" Everything that Jesus did was to demonstrate the Divine Reality and the Laws which govern Its operation. The Lord or the Law serves us, but first we must obey It. Therefore when one of the disciples protested and told Jesus he could not permit him to wash his feet, Jesus answered: *For I have given you an example, that ye should do as I have done to you.*

I hope you will think long and deeply upon this idea of the individualization of the Universal and the Universalization of the individual, always remembering that in no way does this contradict either the supremacy of God or the Reality of man. Man as an individual does not disappear because God is incarnated in him or because his life is God, nor does the Universal Law dominate him in his personal choice. It is complete cooperation based on Unity.

If we had to make things happen, or push our thought out, or influence or dominate and beat down the opposition, we should be faced with an impossible task. We never try to coerce anything in dealing with the laws of nature.

One of the things we must come to understand in dealing with the Laws of Spirit is that we are still operating in a realm of Law and Order. We are operated upon by gravitational force. While it is true that we can change our individual position in it, it is also true that whatever position we take we are still operated upon by it.

So it is with our word, our treatment, our prayer, our affirmation. It operates in a larger field and is operated upon by a Supreme Law. This is why we can have faith in it and patiently, cheerfully, and expectantly await the outcome, knowing that as a man sows, so shall he also reap.

The Ego

OUR IDEA of the ego is different from the average concept held by psychologists, particularly the materialistic one which holds that the ego is the reservoir of instinctive impulses dominated by the pleasure principle, as it comes in contact with the external world through the senses and becomes imbued with consciousness.

They believe that the ego is not a spiritual reality, but is something acquired. They are partly right, in that the ego which shows is a result of our experience. This is why the ego ideal is a standard of perfection formed in childhood through self-identification with persons who are admired.

They have another theory of an alter ego, which is developed out of a need for self-expression derived from the whole human race.

Without denying or seeking to minimize the psychological concept of the ego, we have something to add to it. We believe that there is a real Spiritual Ego back of the psychological one. The psychological ego acquired in living is a projection of the Real Ego and what we experience in life.

There is an Ego, or an *I Myself*, which was not created by experience but only expressed through it. There is a real and dynamic Spiritual Ego. If there were not, the psychological ego could never have functioned.

This Real Ego the Bible calls *the Christ in us*, the Hope of Glory. At the center of every man's life the impersonal becomes personal; the generic becomes individualized. The Universe or God is incarnated in each individual in an entirely different and unique manner. This is the hidden Source of Life, the place where Christ in us blends on one side with the Divine, and on the other side with the individual. This is why the Bible tells us there is but one mediator between God and man, which is Christ.

The reference to Christ is not a reference to the man Jesus but to the Divine Incarnation in all people. It is through this Divine Ego that we reach back to the Universal Wholeness of which this Ego is a part. It was not created as our psychological ego or our alter ego or our ego ideal is created. It was not created by experience. It is that which produces experience.

We go along with the psychological concept and accept all the discoveries that have been made, but we cannot accept the Ego as something we ourselves created. This would be contrary to our concept of life.

If you read the Book of Job in the Old Testament, you will discover that is exactly what he did. He thought he had an ego separate from the Thing Itself, and the narrative states that he got into all kinds of trouble because of this. He was on his own and finally ended up in sackcloth and ashes, and his wife told him that he might as well curse God and die.

But at that point Mr. Job remembered something that Mrs. Job apparently had forgotten: that there is an integrity to the soul, a reality to the Spirit. With this deeper self-awareness, this spiritual identification, he reached back through himself to the cause of everything that is, and discovered God.

Egocentricity is the result of a sense of separation between the ego that is objective and subjective, and the Ego that is super-conscious; the Ego that is hid with Christ in God. If, like Job, we refuse the false ego and acquire the true, we shall find that the external ego will no longer be false, but will become an instrument for the Real that is back of it.

Anything that separates us from an understanding that we are One with the Whole bars It from coming to Self-Expression through us, and all we have left is the acquired ego, which is not enough to meet the issues of life. It soon flounders and becomes submerged.

We must clear the track back to Life Itself, the Power and the Presence and the warm, colorful Reality of the Universal Spirit incarnated in us. *What is man, that thou art mindful of him? and the son of man, that thou visitest him? For thou hast made him a little lower than the angels, and thou hast crowned him with glory and honour* (Psalm 8:4,5).

What Do We See
in the Mirror?

I ONCE read an article called *The Scent of Fear*, in which it was claimed that fear exudes a scent that an animal can smell. The author claimed that this scent of fear arouses an antagonism within the animal, and he often attacks in self-defense

A geologist friend told me he was sitting on a rock one day out in the desert, drawing a map. He happened to glance down and noticed a rattlesnake coiled under the edge of the rock on which he was sitting. I asked him what he did when he saw the rattlesnake and if he was afraid of it. He said, "Not at all. I had no desire to hurt the snake, and it had no desire to harm me." So he sat there and leisurely completed his plans.

This reminded me of a passage in the Bible which says: *Behold, I give unto you power to tread on serpents and scorpions, and over all the power of the enemy; and nothing shall by any means hurt you.* And in another place: *They shall take up serpents; and if they drink any deadly thing, it shall not hurt them; they shall lay hands on the sick, and they shall recover.*

Dogs feel our personal atmosphere, and if it is one of trust and confidence, if it is one of understanding and love, they respond to it. And I wonder if it is not true that when we feel antagonism for others, they in turn feel it and their response to us becomes antagonistic. Perhaps this is why the Bible says that a soft answer turneth away wrath.

There is a subtle atmosphere around us which, unperceived by us, is silently attracting people to us or repelling them from us. I have no doubt that some form of fear is the cause of most of our troubles. What the animal smells, because of its acute instinct, we humans feel when we contact each other.

An atmosphere of failure attracts failure. The person who always has the feeling that no one likes him surrounds himself with an atmosphere that pushes people away from him. It seems as though our mental attitudes are contagious, as though we go around more or less enveloped in them. The silent influence we exercise on others is something that takes place automatically. Friendship attracts friends, while antagonism not only repels people, it actually awakens a feeling of distrust and dislike within them.

Here is one of the keys to successful living and right relationships among people. It is only when we are whole within ourselves that we can help others. It is only when we have faith that we can instill faith. It is only when we have hope and enthusiasm that others respond to us with an equal hope and enthusiasm.

You have often noticed that when you spend considerable time with people who are depressed and afraid, you feel as though the weight of the universe were on your shoulders, as though everything were hopeless. On the other hand, in company with those who are buoyant and confident, you feel a lightness, a sense of joy, a feeling of enthusiasm.

It is almost as definite as going from fog to sunshine, and from sunshine back into fog again. It is as definite as the wind in your face. Sometimes, as you talk with people who are depressed, and try to bring them comfort and courage, you feel their atmosphere lift, as though a fog were clearing away. You feel the sun coming out again. Almost invariably these people will tell you how much better they feel for having talked with you.

If we could come back to see that life is like a mirror, tending to reflect back to us the images of our own thinking, then we should realize that by changing our thinking we can change the reflections in the mirror.

Next we should ask: What do we want to see in this mirror? And have we the courage to admit that what we are looking at in the mirror is a reflected image of our own outlook on life? Are we looking at antagonism, resentment, confusion? Are we looking at fear, failure, unhappiness? And are we actually willing to look into this mirror of life and say, "That is I"? And then, if we do not like what we see, have we enough confidence to believe that we can change it? If so, we have made the right start.

Our starting point is to recognize God at the center of our

own being, to have faith in this Divine Presence within us, and to have an equal faith in the Divine in everyone else. We must come to see that God is the one eternal Presence in everyone and in everything, and we must learn to think from this basis.

How wonderful it would be if we were never afraid of anything! We fear people because we think that in some way they can harm us. So the very antagonism we have for others arouses a like antagonism in them for us. But turn the proposition around, change fear into faith and antagonism into love, and we shall have reversed the whole process.

You see, the mirror is merely something that reflects. You cannot scratch the reflection out of the mirror, but you can change the image in front of it. And you are the image-maker. So let us create new images which will reflect new patterns. And we must be definite in our conviction, and deliberate in our aim if we expect happy results, for theories are no good unless they are applied.

Let us take the case of an individual who feels that everyone is against him. He always seems to be at cross-purposes with people and with events. This has gone on until people avoid him, because they feel the resentment in his mind, and it arouses an equal antagonism in their thoughts about him.

Let us make believe that we are teaching this person what is actually taking place, and that he is accepting our explanation. We understand what is wrong with him. We know that his suffering is self-imposed and we wish to help him. So our explanation will have to be very kind and considerate. It will have to be like leading a child or helping an invalid, for he really is a sick person. We are acting as a doctor to his mind, and doctors should not harshly judge their patients. They should try to help and encourage them to the place where the great restoring power of nature can resume its natural function.

We are acting as physician to this person's mind. We, too, will have to be kind and considerate and willing to let him explode a little, because we understand what is eating at the vitals of his being. Deep inside him he is afraid, scared to death, and unconsciously he is reacting in self-defense. This we must explain to him.

He is longing for love and friendship. He would rather have it than anything else in the world. He wants people to like him, but he is afraid of them. So we tell him how the mind works and how it is that he must come to have faith in something bigger than he is. This he will like, because he is looking for strength; he longs for happiness even as blind men long for light.

We must be very gentle about this, with the simple, sincere desire to be helpful and with no criticism whatsoever. We might even be able to say to him that there was a time when we felt exactly as he does; a time when we thought everything was against us. But one day the light broke, and gradually a transformation took place in our lives. This will cause him to feel that we are sharing our innermost secrets with him, and when we take him by the hand he will respond with confidence.

The change may not take place in a day, a week, or a month, but it will take place if we persist. Let us give him certain affirmations to make for himself each day, similar to the ones we use at the close of this article. Let us help him to make them; let us make them with him. He will begin to feel that he has a partner, and this is a feeling we all need; someone understands him. It will not be long before he will be working with us with an enthusiasm equal to our own, and by and by the signs will begin to follow. His mirror will begin to change its reflection.

This will create hope, and it is only a short step from hope to faith. Through this experience we shall learn the great lesson of life, that the good we have must be shared with others if it is to be increased. For when we have made a friend of a person who is friendless, and have made it possible for him to acquire friends, we have multiplied our own friendship by that number of persons. When we have brought good to some person, and have shown him how to extend that good in his own experience, we have brought that much more good into our own life.

MEDITATION

As I look out into my world I see that there is nothing to fear. And as I look back into my own mind I know there

159

is nothing in me that is afraid. My thought is filled with confidence, with hope, with trust, and with the acceptance of Good.

I expect the mirror of my experience to be filled with joy, and as I turn the magic lantern of my mind into the great Mind and Spirit of the Universe in which all things exist, I know that I am One with all Peace, all Power, and all Good.

I affirm the presence of Good in everything I do, the guidance of Love everywhere I go. I affirm that strength, enthusiasm, and vitality forever flow through me from the all-sustaining Life of the Universe.

I affirm my union with God, and I know that there is nothing in the entire Universe to be afraid of, nothing to avoid, nothing to run away from. I am at home in the Universe—one with God, one with people, one with that perfect and abiding faith that knows no fear.

Thought, Feeling, and Emotion

MAY I start the discussion of this subject by interjecting a personal opinion and one which I quite frankly admit may be wrong? It is for you to judge. I believe that the heart of the Universe, the essence of Reality or God, the Living Spirit, is of the essence of pure feeling. I believe that feeling is back of every creative impulse, whether in God or man.

This feeling in human beings and to some degree in animals breaks down into what we call the emotions. I think that feeling is a fundamental essence in the Universe; it is a part of the nature of Reality. Our emotions are this Original Feeling flowing through us as the Universe individualizes Itself in us. There cannot be anything true about the individual unless it is first true about the Universe. By the same token, anything that is true about the Universe must be true about the individual, for the individual is a microcosm within a Macrocosm, or a little world within a big world, or as we state the proposition, an individualized center in the Creative Consciousness of God.

In psychiatry and psychosomatic medicine it is believed that there is a definite, fundamental, irrepressible emotion or feeling back of everything, an urge to flow through everything creatively. This has been called the libido or the emotional craving back of all things toward self-expression, the repression of which leads to psychoneurosis. Psychoneurosis means a congestion of this emotion. That there is such a feeling back of everything I do not doubt, and whether we call it the libido or the urge makes no difference. There is an emotional craving for self-expression back of everything, and when it is repressed it does lead to trouble, and pretty serious trouble—perhaps to a large percentage of all our troubles.

But even emotion and feelings are things of thought because they cannot function without consciousness, and the movement of consciousness is thought.

161

I realize that this proposition can be contested, and elaborate explanations can be written to prove it is not true and that thought itself is only the result of some kind of stimulus. This, however, has never been scientifically proved, and the whole tendency today is away from it rather than with it.

As far as we are concerned, then, we shall assume that there is a thinker, an ego, an entity, a person, and that behind him is an irresistible impulsion to express Life. In a certain sense he must live or die; he must create or perish; he must express Life or the Life seeking expression through him will flow back inside him. There will then be a pressure from within out, and a pressure from without in. It is in this inner or between point that unconscious conflicts occur.

If we can accept the proposition that feeling and emotion are certain ways of thinking, and actually reduce them to thought or to Mind in Action, then we can see how it is that thought can change them. As a matter of fact this is what psychiatry and spiritual and mental counseling do. This may be done through having the patient talk his troubles out of himself with the kindly guidance of a wise counselor, or it may be done as in our method by the practitioner's thinking back to the Spiritual Reality of his patient and identifying the patient with It.

The results will be the same except that in ordinary counseling the logical implications of the Spiritual Nature of the patient are not emphasized. But if we are rooted in this deep Reality, which we know that we must be, it follows that our thought should reach back even through the feeling and the emotion to Reality Itself.

We recognize that we cannot do this by the intellect alone. Our work has a feeling about it, a feeling of the Divine Presence and the emotion of Infinite Love. As metaphysicians, or those who believe in spiritual mind healing, we do not deny physical facts or psychic facts, nor do we hesitate to affirm that there are spiritual facts. We should put them all together. The emotions affect the physical body, and the mind can be destructive or constructive according to the way it is used. For this is the Law of Mind in Action. But back of it all is the Actor.

Wise counseling leads from the act to the actor, and brings the patient to what is called self-awareness, to a place where he sees why he acted as he did and why he can just as well act differently. It takes him back through all his emotions to the place where he was when he was an infant before all of his troubles started.

But just taking him back there is not enough, even though it does have a salutary effect. He must consciously recognize his Union with the Infinite, his Oneness with Life, his Partnership with God.

Here is an interesting thought to speculate on. If feeling and emotion acting through the avenue of consciousness can produce such havoc, what would happen if the same feeling and emotion were constructively employed? What would happen if we could convert the energy of fear to faith, the energy of doubt and uncertainty into a feeling of belonging to the Universe and being safe in It? Would not the Original Artist Himself go forth into new creation through us?

God Talks to the Heart

WHILE WE admire the intellect, we must realize that the intellect is not the creative factor in the Universe. Rather, it is feeling that is creative.

Coué said that when the imagination and the will are in conflict the imagination invariably wins. And that suggestion must become auto-suggestion or self-realization before it can become effectual. This is why he coined the phrase *Day by day in every way I am getting better and better*, which was to be repeated so rapidly as to break down the self-conscious or intellectual barriers, and in a sense hammer itself through to self-realization.

The real creative power of the mind is deeper than the intellect. It passes into the realm of feeling and acceptance, yet it is the intellect or the self-conscious faculties that must speak the word in order that every obstruction may be cleared away. We could coin no better expression than to say that God speaks to the heart through a language of feeling, a feeling which is affirmative.

You will frequently find people who have splendid intellects, whose logic is almost perfect, but who seem never to penetrate the deeper mind where the creativity resides. To all treatments, no matter how intellectually or analytically correct they may be, there must be added this deep feeling and conviction that enable one to commune with the Invisible.

As I have so frequently said, the best comparison I can think of is the feeling that an artist has toward beauty, for beauty is an invisible essence, an all-pervading, all-penetrating something that cannot be adequately expressed in words but only in thoughts. It is an inward emotion of the mind which reaches out until it strikes some corresponding chord emanating from the Universe Itself.

This is what an artist feels. In a sense he weds himself to the essence of beauty and draws it into his own being until beauty becomes diffused through his technique and makes an imprint that the intellect cannot analyze. Then intellect stands in awe before the supreme Reality, yet still knowing that It is the essence of its true being waiting to become articulate.

Perhaps this is the real and true meaning of communion; something beyond prayer as ordinarily thought of; something which cannot be described but can be felt. God does speak to the heart more than to the intellect, and this is why it is that often you will find a person who apparently can give no reason for what he believes. He says, "I know that God is all there is and there is nothing else." By some inward, childlike faith, his intellect has surrendered to that which is greater than he is, and the miracle takes place.

One frequently meets such persons. It seems to the over-intellectual that they are entirely inadequate, and such simplicity might even be rejected as being incapable of fathoming the depths of Reality. But their word is powerful because they listen with the heart. Through some unknown avenue the heart reaches a depth that the intellect can penetrate only mathematically.

Of course, it is well to combine the intellect and feeling and to use both the head and the heart, for the intellect gives a definite form to the feeling. But unless the feeling is there, the intellect will merely have provided the empty mold.

It is interesting to know that the best psychological balance is the balance between the intellect and the emotions, the conscious mind and the feelings. We want not only to feel but to think. We wish not only to think but also to feel. Be certain, then, that in all your work you combine this subtle essence with the conscious word you speak until the two become one.

As a practitioner you will put these qualities together until they fuse into one, and then the head will speak through the heart and the heart will feel through the intellect. This we believe is psychological wholeness.

The River of Life

SOMEONE HAS said, *There is a river of life, clear as crystal, flowing through the body of humanity, uniting every part into one great being in Christ.* Jesus spoke of the well of water, from which if a man drank he should never thirst again. Throughout the Bible we have this simile of water, typifying the flowing Power of pure Spirit. It is impossible to think of Spirit as being anything solid. It is always fluid.

In line with this thought it is interesting to note that modern physics has theoretically resolved all physical form into lines of energy, and these lines of energy must be directed by some intelligence or they would never take definite form. Therefore we say that the River of Life forever flowing through us is ever ready and willing to take the form which we give it.

It appears that we have the ability, at least temporarily, to pollute this Stream of Life with the consciousness of hate, despair, or any negative thought which denies its purity. But of course we do not really have the power to destroy, only to mold and remold.

It is fortunate indeed that this is true. For in spite of all our misdirection we are still being carried forward on the bosom of this Infinite Stream to a harbor of perfect safety. We may rest in absolute assurance that Good will be the final goal of all things.

We can hasten the advent of this Good by definitely clarifying our thought and by daily meditating upon the invisible Source, the wellspring of Life within each one of us.

Our Spiritual Identity Forever Expands

IN SPIRITUAL mind practice evil is never treated as an entity, but as an operation of thought. The practitioner never deals with evil as though it were big or little, and he must be careful not to locate it anywhere, in any person, or any group of persons. It is easy enough to see that the mentality of a practitioner must be kept free from the belief in evil, which unfortunately obsesses most persons' thoughts much of the time.

Limitation is not a thing of itself; it is a way of belief. Unhappiness is a condition, but it is not something of itself. Every man has an Identity in Spirit, and this Idea will eternally unfold; It will never grow less but will always be more of Itself. What man knows about God, the Universal Truth, constitutes his real Spiritual Being, constitutes his personification of the Infinite; therefore the more completely conscious he is of God, Spirit, Truth, Beauty, the more perfectly will he evolve.

Since the Truth is Infinite, there is room for eternal expansion, so that man passes from glory to glory, from one plane to another, or as Jesus put it, *In my Father's house are many mansions.*

The Spiritual Identity Itself remains individual and unique though forever expanding. We cannot now visualize what the future development may be, but it is inevitable that we shall pass from this state of being into ever-ascending states forever.

It does not seem at all necessary or advisable that we spend much time wondering what is going to happen hereafter, since our evolution will take care of all those things as we come to them. What seems most important is that we be happy, well, and prosperous here and now, and that we maintain our Spiritual Identity wherever we go and whatever we do.

Your Own Understanding

Your consciousness of Good is the Law of Elimination to every discord. Your treatment enforces the Law and is the activity of Its power. Be sure you do not deny your own understanding.

The inertia of human thought, rising as it does from the morbidity of race consciousness and the mesmeric grip of race suggestion, seeks to claim that you do not have the power to heal, the consciousness to heal, or the spiritual capacity to heal. Recognize this false argument for what it is. It is nothing claiming to be something. It is a lie, claiming to be the truth. It is a habit of thought, unwilling to surrender itself.

You must know that the thought of Truth dispels this mental inertia, and frees the consciousness. Heal the thought and the Law of Perfection will establish harmony.

Know that It does this immediately. Every treatment must incorporate within it the consciousness of Completion, of Perfection, in the here and now.

Use positive statements to declare that the Divine Power which you use frees you from the hypnotic belief that would deny you the privilege of helping all who come to you. A practitioner must continuously be conscious that all the Good there is, is his; not *some* part of It but *all* of It. It is not only available; It is workable. It is not only ever-present; It always responds to him.

You Have Dominion

WITH AN understanding of this science fear should disappear. And with direct application of this Principle to your problems you will discover that they will begin to seem less insistent.

Begin to act as though you already had Dominion over evil, as though all fear were a phantom, and as though everything you have been afraid of were unreal. Declare the Truth by saying there is nothing to be afraid of; that you no longer entertain any images of fear; that Good is the only Power there is; that this Good which is the only Power there is, is now operating in your affairs.

Know that Good is Omnipotent. Know that the Truth instantly, effectively, and permanently destroys every fear and every effect of fear. Know that you are governed by Infinite Intelligence. Know that you are directed by Divine Guidance, and that you are compelled to think and act constructively. Therefore you may know that everything you do, say, or think carries with it a Divine authority.

Freedom already exists, but your freedom is in your own thought. Hence it is not enough to say, "God is free," which, of course, is a true statement; but this statement must be made personal: "The Freedom of God is *my* freedom, the Power of God is *my* power, the Presence of God is *in me*. The Mind of God is *my* mind, the Strength of God is *my* strength, and the Joy of God is *my* joy."

Be Yourself

PEOPLE ARE the most interesting things in the world. While it is true that we do not always get along with them as well as we might, it is also certain that we could not get along without them. We need each other more than we realize. The world is made up of people, and human relationships are merely reactions of people to each other. Many business firms maintain human-relations departments for the purpose of helping their employees to appreciate each other and get along together in their work.

We are told that the two things people are most interested in are love and personality. This is not strange, because everyone wants to love and be loved; everyone wants to feel needed. Every individual wishes to feel that he plays an important role in life. All are attracted to the person who has a winning personality.

One thing is certain—whatever our personality may be, or whatever it is to become, is wrapped up in the one idea that there is a Spirit in man, and God Himself is incarnated in every living soul. This Spirit within us is the gift of heaven, and without it we would not be alive. It is a recognition of this Spirit within us that is the true starting point for the development of personality.

We often think we have to pattern our lives after the lives of others. But our personality, no matter how winsome it may be, or how convincing, or how dominant, is more than a mask we wear; it is a manifestation of an inner, hidden Principle, a Divine spark within us which uses both the mind and the body for Its own Self-Expression.

We could think up all the beautiful things to say and the most wonderful and best method of approaching people, and study all the arts of personality development that have ever been taught, and still fall flat on our faces as far as the real personality is concerned. For personality is not the clothes we wear, nor is it our physical appearance alone. It is not just a dominant or domineering something so powerful that it brushes everything else aside.

Personality is the flowering of the Spirit within us, the coming forth of a secret relationship that we all hold to God. The people who have most completely influenced the human race throughout the ages are those who have known this, and who have made but little effort to influence others. They are the ones who have had the deepest feeling of the Divine Presence within them.

No one will ever be satisfied or happy or secure in developing a dominant personality. Those who win their way through life by force eventually become weary with the struggle, the purpose of which never reaches its final goal. Personality is not an external thing, for everything we do and say and think, and everything that we appear to be outwardly, is always the result of some hidden fire burning at the center of our being, some Divine Reality which we did not create but which we may discover.

I think we can say without hesitation that the person who finds himself in God will discover at the center of his own being something which dominates without effort, something which does not have to assume a false front, something which, by the very nature of its being, is both human and Divine.

But someone may say, "Now you are introducing religious ideas that we don't want to be bothered with. What we want is something that can take us into the activities of life in a triumphant manner."

Now this is both right and wrong; right, in that we wish to be successful in living; wrong, if we think that of ourselves we can add to or take from what God already has given. For while we can, and should, develop an outer personality, back of this there is something you and I never thought up—we did not plan it, we did not create it. Finding this something is like exploring a new land. This country already existed before we discovered it. There are heights and depths to our own being which we have not plumbed.

There is a Divine Person back of our personality—a unique manifestation of the Living Spirit. It is never alike in any two people. This is proved by the fact that no two persons' thumb prints are alike, no two blades of grass are alike, no two anythings are identical. And yet everything is rooted in One Life,

171

One Presence, and One Power. Why, then, should we expect that any two individuals should be alike? God Himself has placed a unique stamp on everyone. We should not study to be alike, but rather to develop what we really are.

Unity does not mean uniformity. Our unity with other people does not mean that we must think and act as they do. All it means is that we should get along with them. We should unify with everything, while at the same time keeping intact and whole that God-given something at the center of our being which is the Spiritual Ego.

To find this true center is the end and aim of our search. This Divine Person within us has, in a sense, one hand placed in the hand of God and the other outstretched to humanity, for the person who finds himself in God will discover God in others. He will see things in a different light than will the one who thinks he is alone. He will draw strength and inspiration from Life Itself, for no man can live without God and be whole.

Since everything is included in God—for God is the only Presence and Power that there is—the person who wants to be the most himself will have to be the one who has discovered more of himself in that which is greater than he is. Our capacity to think, to live, and to move is nonphysical. There is an invisible Presence hidden within us which has Its source in a higher Power, and which acts through our actions, wills through our minds, and reveals Itself in what we are doing.

At the center of our being there is a Divine Person, a unique incarnation of God. This is the Source of all real inspiration; here, and here alone, at the center of our being, is the real Creative Power. The question is whether we are living from this center, or whether we are thinking of ourselves as detached, separated, divided, alone, and inadequate. We all have direct access to the Infinite Presence, the Universal Person. There could be no more beautiful thought than that the Divine Spirit Itself, infinite as It is, is also within us.

And with this acceptance of God there must come an acceptance of the real self, that self which blossoms in our relations with others and finds fruit in its own action.

How Old Are You?

How OLD do you think you are? How old is old? And when does a person get too old to enjoy life? Could it be possible that even age is something that happens to our minds rather than to our bodies? And could a person be as young at eighty as he is at eighteen?

We are told that each cell of the physical body is completely replaced every fourteen months. It seems funny, does it not, to think that no one is even a year and a half old, physically.

We are also told that there is no reason to suppose that our minds grow old; that the mind is as young at ninety as it is at nine; that the only thing that is added to it is experience. Most psychologists agree that we learn less rapidly as years advance, but just as certainly and just as accurately. Some of the scientific minds today are telling us that, while time exists, age does not; that in reality time is not a way of measuring years and months and days, but rather a measurement of experience in a limitless life.

If it is true in a broad sense that neither the mind nor the body actually grows old, it is time for us to ask what produces this aging process.

Suppose we think of mind in the same way we think about space. Space is everywhere. Many things exist in space. But space itself is never crowded and it never gets old. No matter how much stuff you put into it there is still just as much space. You cannot wear it out. It never grows tired and it never becomes burdened with care.

And now let us introduce another thought that we have often talked about. God's Mind is the only mind there is and God is Eternal. The whole proposition is this: We live because God lives in us, and we are able to think because the Mind of God is in us.

Our trouble is that we have thought of ourselves as separate from God, and in doing this we have stored up a burden of care and worry in our minds. We also take on a feeling of responsibility which we are not equipped to handle when we come to

173

the place where we think, "I am separate from God. If I am facing life and all its problems with my little mind I feel inadequate to handle the situations that come along, because I am working all on my own, alone and without help from the Power that is greater than I am."

What a load we shall get off our minds when we learn that there is but one Mind that carries every load. Is not this what Jesus meant when he said, *My yoke is easy and my burden is light?*

And now let us consider what wonderful miracles Life is always working in our bodies. When even one minute cell is injured there is an Intelligence that immediately puts all the chemistry of our body to work to replace it with a new cell, one that is whole, complete, and perfect. This is how wounds heal.

It is almost startling how Divine Intelligence works for us to give us health and comfort. Even in such a simple instance as stepping from a warm room into cold winter air, if we had eyes to see it, we would witness a miracle of the One Life at work for our comfort. This Life immediately causes the circulatory system, the respiratory system, and the digestive system to go to work in such a way as to bring about an inner balance of temperature to counteract the cold wind and keep the body free from pain and discomfort.

But nature does not seem to interfere with our thought processes in the same way, and this is because we are individuals and have the right of self-choice. And so we are permitted to store up liabilities in the mind which tend to perpetuate our discomfort.

Life maintains a wonderful factory in the human body. It has a furnace room to generate heat. It has a chemical plant to purify and dispose of poisons. It has a maintenance crew that keeps the machinery in order. It even has a lubricating system which keeps the joints oiled. And there is a transportation system that carries supplies from one part of the factory to another; and an inter-office communication system that would stagger the imagination of the greatest engineer.

This One Mind, which is God, is capable of running the

174

factory of this human body in perfect order. When Jesus said, *Consider the lilies*, he could have been saying to us: See how beautifully the factory is run when there is no interference with the Laws of God. It is self-evident that God's Mind would be capable of running this factory of ours which we call our bodies if we would not throw wrenches of fear and doubt into the machinery, and if we would not overload the communication system and the transportation system with the burdens of grief and worry.

This is so simple that we should ask ourselves: "How is it, and why is it, that we have arrived at a place where we have stopped trusting in the Divine Architect who created the factory and who is capable of operating it so perfectly?" I think if we could answer this question we would know what is wrong with us.

In Job 33:23 we read: *If there be . . . one among a thousand, to shew unto man his uprightness: . . . His flesh shall be fresher than a child's: he shall return to the days of his youth.* Of course we should not interpret this as meaning that we want to go back to childish ways or former years, but that we do wish to keep the child always with us and not be burdened with the years that have passed. This is what repentance means. It means *to think another way*. It means a new birth in the mind of that Life that comes fresh and new every moment of our existence. Every day is a fresh beginning, every day is the world made new.

Nor does this mean that we have to recapture the physical body we possessed years ago, but rather that we recognize the youth of the physical body which we now have because there is not one cell in it that is over a year and a half old. Youth is in every muscle and in every fiber of our being. It is no wonder Jesus likened the Kingdom of Heaven to a child. So let us consider the mental attitudes of a child if we would recapture the dream we seem to have lost.

When we were young we had so much to look forward to. The days were crowded with happiness and fulfillment. We could hardly wait to get up in the morning to begin over again, because we had such enthusiastic expectation. The first third of a person's life is spent in the enjoyment of the day in which he lives, always with something more ahead. He is learning, studying, finding out how to do things, getting ready to live in a larger way. He has the security of home and parents. He is not afraid.

He reaches maturity, and the world is still ahead of him. He falls in love, gets married, has children, and the cycle repeats itself—he lives in his family, and all the things that he has done for himself he now does for them, only in a bigger way. This is about what happens to the average person for the first half of his life. People do not grow old when they are busy with the pleasures of living, the enjoyment, the expectation, the enthusiasm, and the thought of the more that is to come.

But too often, when these first two periods have passed, there is not enough left to look forward to. The kick has gone out of life. For no man is happy who chases mad ambition. We are happy only in creative things, and in those things where we share the joys of living with others. We must keep our interest in life so active that there will be an element of wonder and surprise in simple everyday things.

Life is activity, and when we stop being active we turn away from the newness of life. And the person who grows old in years without an inward expectation and assurance that he is going to live forever, somewhere, will find the last part of his life burdened with the thoughts of yesterday. Let us make up our minds that yesterday is gone. Tomorrow has not yet arrived. But today can be filled with wonder if we know that we stand on the threshold of that which is wonderful and new.

I have never yet met a single individual who maintained this attitude in the last part of his life unless he had faith. And I am talking about the kind of faith we all understand the meaning of—faith in Something bigger than we are, in a Power greater than we are, and a complete assurance that we are going to live forever, somewhere.

It is an interesting fact that whether or not we know it, and whether or not we like it, our lives are so tied in with God, the living Spirit, that we cannot even remain young and enthusiastic unless we know that we are one with that which knows no age and has no burdens.

176

Youth is not a time of life—it is a state of mind. Nobody grows old by merely living a number of years. People grow old only by deserting their ideals. Years wrinkle the skin, but to give up enthusiasm wrinkles the soul. Worry, doubt, self-distrust, fear, and despair—these are the long, long years that bow the head and turn the spirit back to dust.

Whether seventy or sixteen, there should be in every man the love of wonder, the sweet amazement at the stars and the star-like things and thoughts, the undaunted challenge of events, the unfailing childlike appetite for What next?, and joy in the game of life.

You are as young as your faith, as old as your doubt; as young as your confidence, as old as your fear; as young as your hope, as old as your despair.

The Door That You Alone Can Open

It is said that at the entrance to Solomon's Temple stood two pillars called Jachin and Boaz, and that those who wished to enter the Holy of Holies must first pass between the two pillars. These pillars are symbolic of the Law and the Word, or the Universal Principle and the Universal Presence. The Temple represents the self. In order to understand the true self we must first realize that the Universe is built on the two great Principles of Reality, the Personal as Presence and the Impersonal as Law.

It is also said that the High Priest met at the Temple doorway all those who had passed between the pillars and conducted them to the Holy of Holies. The High Priest represents the Divine incarnation in every man. This is the High Priest who must conduct us to the Holy of Holies in which reposes the Ark of the Covenant. *Ark* means a vehicle containing the Life Principle, while *Covenant* means the eternal Laws of God that are forever established. In this Ark is the Scroll of Life upon which is inscribed the name of God, the *I AM*.

Whether we look at this as a fable or a Reality makes no difference. It was most certainly someone's attempt to describe the nature of the Universe and our relationship to It, and how we are to discover the Secret of Secrets, which is a knowledge of the Spiritual Truth about our own being.

First of all we must come to realize that the Universe is a balance between the Impersonal and the Personal; the Principle and the Presence, or the Law and the Word. Or if we wish to put it another way, between the mechanical or mathematical and the personal or spontaneous.

This is the nature of Reality as proclaimed by the great of every age. This is the first and basic Principle of our whole science, philosophy, and religion.

178

We are some part of the Whole, but we must discover our true relationship to It. If we are to be admitted to the Temple, which is the self, and find entrance to the Secret Place of the Most High within us, which is the Holy of Holies, we must meet the High Priest, who is our own Spiritual Being or the incarnation of God within us. The door to the Temple must be opened by the Self. You are the only person who can open this door for yourself, and I am the only one who can open it for myself.

At first this may seem difficult or altogether impossible because we all like to believe that someone else can live for us or be happy for us or find God for us. Such is not the case. Each individual is a unique institution in the Universe.

There never was a *you* before just like the *you* that you are, and there never will be another one. Nature never duplicates her creations, even though she multiplies them. There is a doorway or an entrance through which the mind must pass on its way to spiritual realization, and that door can be opened by none but the one who is to enter. Within each of us is the Secret Place of the Most High, the Holy of Holies, the Ark of the Covenant, the Scroll of Life, the Sacred Name of God.

There is only a certain amount that can be taught; the rest must be learned through the doing. Every man must discover God in his own way, but always within himself.

Now there are many approaches to the door, and no doubt many entrances to the Holy of Holies. Every great spiritual leader has found a door through which he has entered. As we study the spiritual systems of the ages we discover that, though the approach has been varied, the Temple of the Spirit is One. God is all there is, and there is none beside Him. This statement includes everything.

In all the kingdoms that exist, in all the planes that exist, and deep within the self, hidden and yet felt, there is a High Priest ready to conduct us to the sacred and secret chamber of the self, where God and man are One. The search for union passes into the realization, not that we are just *with* or *in*, but that we are *of* God. One *with*, or One *in*, implies separation. The great realization is that we are *of* that which is; we are some part of It.

Many have found entrance to this door through deep spiritual meditation, some through high inspirational enlightenment; others by just sitting still and letting something happen to them, as symbolized by the Descent of the Holy Ghost.

The end, the aim, and the whole purpose of our study is not for the salvation of the individual life, because Life cannot be lost, but for the discovery of the Self which the Scripture tells us is hid with Christ in God. We have studied our techniques and we have come to understand something about how the Science of Mind works and how to use it, what to do, and why. These, however, are but guideposts on the way to the real discovery of the Self, the Self that is hid with Christ in God, or the Son begotten of the only Father.

The opening of the door to the Temple often calls for patience and waiting, painstaking and watchful prayer and meditation, for continual communion with That which is both the Oversoul and the Inner Spirit. The end and aim of our search is to discover that Universe which is individualized in each one of us, and that individuality within each one of us which now has the possibility of expanding to the universalization of the Self.

What Is Your Dream?

Did you ever have a nightmare? I once ran across a cartoon which showed the picture of a man sound asleep, and apparently having a terrible dream in which he saw a gigantic figure at the foot of the bed leaning over him, as though it were about to seize him. The man was nearly prostrated with fear and said to the phantom, "What are you going to do with me?" The phantom replied, "I don't know. What are you going to do with *me*? I am your dream, you know."

How many phantoms we all carry around with us in our imagination! How often we have such morbid and unhapppy thoughts that they actually appear as gigantic and menacing figures about to seize us in a deathlike grip. And how seldom do we face these fears and try to find out exactly what they are and where they come from. What a shock and what a surprise it is to us when we realize that we are the ones having the dream; we are the ones who are creating the phantom, and in a certain sense running away from the shadow of our own fears.

What, then, are our dreams? Are we dreaming of success or failure? Of happiness or misery? Of sickness or health? For our dreams are mental patterns that can lead us into a fuller and richer life, or can create phantom monsters that make our lives a nightmare, whether we are asleep or awake. Every man is the dreamer of his own dreams, and within each is the Spiritual Power to choose the patterns that he wishes to experience in life.

Psychosomatic medicine has been developed to help people get rid of the monster-phantoms that come up out of their own minds. For what is a neurosis other than a group of mental images that arise to disturb the mind? Take the case of a person who feels that no one likes him. Just think of the monsters that he creates in his own mind through his feeling of being rejected. He looks at his fellow men and imagines that they do not like the way he wears his clothes, the way he talks; he feels that they are criticizing him in their own minds.

The fact is that his own morbid dreams are putting negative

181

ideas into the minds of everyone he meets, for there is a mental contact we have with others which registers in them. He begins to shrink from life, and instead of throwing back his shoulders and facing life openly and squarely, he begins to round his shoulders and close in on himself. The passing world looks at him and says, ''Here is a person who is defeated and miserable.''

The dreamer who feels that he is unliked is so blinded by the monsters of his own mind that he does not realize that everyone around him is simply responding to the way he feels. He does not know that the phantom of hostility which he encounters is in his own mind and is actually following the dictates of his own thought. One of the interesting things that we learn in the Science of Mind is that the very thought patterns we create, in a certain sense gradually obsess us. They can reach a point where we become hypnotized by them, and we go around in a dream state, imagining that everything and everyone is against us.

The unfortunate thing about this is that the dream is real enough to the one who has it. The man who was asleep and having the nightmare which nearly paralyzed him with fright, awoke in the morning and was greatly relieved to know that there was no ominous form threatening his safety. He was relieved to find that it was only a dream. And so it is with most of our troubles. They are real enough to us while we are having them.

But there is another part of us that was never caught in this dream. And just as the man who saw the gigantic figure at the foot of his bed finally awoke to the realization of its unreality, so there is some part of us that can awake to the unreality of most of the things that bother us. The very fact that one can rouse a man who is experiencing a nightmare shows that there is something about him that is superior to the experience he is having.

One of our most common dreams is that we are unhappy, that nothing ever works out right for us, that people do not like us, that life is against us, and that nothing good is ever going to happen. And because there is a Law of Mind which operates on our thought, we begin to create situations which look like our dreams. And in reality they are our dreams. Then we bow down before them in fear, and feel that we are the victims of a fate beyond our control.

A parable is told of an angel who came to visit the earth. He found himself in the usual stream of human activities and he listened to the conversations of people. For the first time he heard negative comments. Someone who was supposed to be an authority said that there might be a war and human life would be destroyed. And he read in the newspaper of a great epidemic of illness. And someone who certainly should have known explained in great detail that financial hardships were certain to limit all of us. He heard that there was not enough good to go around, the world was not going to be able to produce enough food for everyone, and people were going to starve to death.

He began to wonder if these things might not be true, and even as he entertained the thoughts of negation to which he was listening, the brightness of his angelic presence faded into dark shadows. His form seemed to shrivel, and looking at himself he saw that he was dressed as a human being, walking the earth in fear, doubt, and uncertainty.

And so the weary years went by, years of unhappiness and impoverishment and dread, years so filled with anxiety that he wished he were dead, that some oblivion might forever swallow him up. And yet, even in the midst of all this, something within him remembered that he was once an angel of God, living in a heaven of Beauty and a place of Peace and Joy, living in a Garden of Eden which God had provided for him. And, remembering, a determination arose within him to somehow or other find his way back to this lost paradise.

This determination grew into a great hope, and as hope was renewed, a Light seemed to shine in the distance; and he seemed to have the courage to travel toward the Light. And gradually a miracle took place. As he traveled toward the Light, he found that shadows were being cast behind him, until finally he so completely entered into the Light that no shadows were cast at all, and he realized that he had been asleep, that he had had a bad dream from which he was awakening.

To what extent are we all dreaming, and in our dreams seeing the monsters with terrible forms that we have unconsciously built up in our own minds? And we too are asking these forms, "What are you going to do with me? What terrible future do you have in store? What awful experiences are to come now?"

Perhaps we are still asleep and have not had quite the courage to ask these phantom forms what they are going to do with us, or to listen to the only reply they can make: "There is nothing we can do to you. What are you going to do to *us*? We are your own creations, you know."

St. Paul said, *It is high time to awake out of sleep.* So let us wake up, and let us be certain that we no longer drug ourselves with the sleeping potion of fear and uncertainty and doubt, but awake into faith and confidence, into peace and joy, into love and happiness. For there is something in us too, like the angel in the fable, that has never forgotten. There is a Silent Witness at the center of every man's being which evermore proclaims with the great and beautiful Jesus: *Come unto me, all ye that labor and are heavy laden, and I will give you rest.*

Getting Along with People

NO ONE can live to himself alone. Other people are so much a part of our lives that we cannot think of living without them. People who feel themselves excluded from society are maladjusted.

On the other hand, much of our trouble comes because of others. In our relationships with others two things must happen if we are to be happy. We must be with others, enjoy them and act with them, without in any way seeking to control their actions.

This is not always the easiest thing to do, particularly with our closest friends. But you may be certain that the one who has the largest number of friends is the one who can work and play with them while at the same time letting them alone.

This is true even in family life. For the family is made up of individual members who must live in close relationship with each other and work and play together, while at the same time remaining individuals. It is a fortunate child who is born into a family that understands this and that gives the child as much freedom as possible while at the same time teaching him to cooperate with others.

The overprotected child loses his self confidence, when he grows up he lacks self assurance. The child who feels neglected, unloved, and unwanted is likely to grow up with the unconscious feeling that everything and everyone is against him. He is apt to develop either an over-aggressive or an under-aggressive attitude toward life. When his attitude lacks the proper amount of aggressiveness he continually lives in dependence on others and gets along well only with those who are protecting and caring for him. When his attitude is over-aggressive he finds it difficult to get along with others for he generally seeks to dominate them.

The well-adjusted person is one who has been permitted to be an individual, but who also has learned to cooperate with others. This attitude probably was formed way back in the early family life. For it is here that we become conditioned for the years ahead.

But we cannot be born again physically, nor can we actually return to the days of our infancy. However, modern psychology does, in a sense, do this for the poorly adjusted person. He is taken back in imagination to infancy, and his mental and emotional reactions which well up from the underpart of his mind and memory are brought to the light of day.

This is a slow and expensive process. Few people could afford either the time or the money to go through with it. Moreover, there are not enough analysts in the world to handle even a small fraction of the ones who need help.

But there is another thing that we can do, something that Jesus knew about—something he referred to when he said, *You must be born again.* And when they asked him how it could be possible for a man to be born again, he said, *You must be born of the Spirit.* This is the new birth that comes through a new outlook on life, a new way of thinking, a new sense of our relationship to our environment, to the people around us, to ourselves, and to God.

It was this relationship to God that Jesus placed first, for he said that if you find this, everything else will be added. Today we know that the psychological, emotional, and mental readjustments which are necessary to our well-being will be made if we experience this new birth that Jesus was talking about.

In order to do this we must have a firm conviction that all people live in God, and we must have a deep realization that we are all One in this Universal Spirit which is God.

There is a place where we begin and leave off physically, but there is no place where we begin and leave off mentally or spiritually. Our minds merge with the minds of others and, as they meet, some silent force within us attracts or repels automatically in accord with our accepted thought patterns.

If we do not merge with others in cooperation, in unity, and in happiness, we may be certain that there is something in us that still feels it has been rebuffed.

Here is where the adjustment has to be made. What we must

do is to see that we ourselves are adjusted to others. We neither wish to dominate them nor wish them to dominate us. We wish to get along with them happily. They have opinions that are different from ours. We must be flexible enough to recognize that their opinions are right for them, even though they do not fit into our scheme. This is what Jesus called *nonresistance*.

When he spoke of nonresistance he did not mean that we must agree with every person's opinion. He meant exactly what he said—do not resist it, let it alone, do not even try to dominate it. If we do not resist it, it will depart from us, it will not disturb us. If we can get over this idea of trying to control other people's thoughts or actions and still live with them in happy relationships, we shall be well on the road to readjustment. And above everything else, if we can trace our own origin back to its original Source, which is God, and do the same for everyone else, we shall find that we are getting along with others.

If you want sunshine, step out into the sunshine. If you have locked yourself away in a dark closet, why not come out into the light? If you have been feeling that everything is against you and no one really cares for you, know that God is in everyone, and meet the God in others and see what happens.

It is remarkable how Jesus approached this subject. It is as though he said, "You think that you were born of flesh and blood. You think that your parents gave you life. You think that everything that has happened to you since you were born is held against you. You think that all the negative thoughts you have ever had are operating against you. You think that all the fears and failures and doubts and uncertainties you have been carrying around for years are something over which you have no control. Why not try something else?

"I have a method which will work for you if you will let it. Just forget all the past. Forgive yourself and everyone else for everything that has ever happened. Try to feel that everyone is doing about the best he can. Come to realize that, while you were born into this world through your parents, you really are a Spirit. You really are born out of Life. The thing that entered into you when you were born was God, the living Spirit. Why not get back to the true center of your being and think and act and live from the point of view that you are One with everything because you are One with God?"

Jesus gave to us the secret of complete adjustment when he said, *Seek ye first the kingdom of God . . . and all these things shall be added unto you.*

Go back in your thought and your imagination to this central idea: I am One with God; all people are One with God. We all live in God. When I meet others it is God in them I meet— God individualized, God personalized, God as my friend.

Jesus added the Spirit to the knowledge of what today we call psychology, or the way the mind works. He did not deny that people are unhappy or badly adjusted to life. He did say: "You do not have to be this way. Seek first things first and everything else will be added." And, by *first things* to which everything is added, he meant—find God in yourself. That is why he said, *Blessed are they that do hunger and thirst after righteousness: for they shall be filled . . . Knock, and it shall be opened unto you . . . Seek, and ye shall find.*

If people look drab or uninteresting to us it is because of the way we look at them. If we have not received joy from others it is because we have stifled joy at the center of our own being. Joy must go forth to meet joy. Love must go forth to meet love. All people are rooted in God, and it is only as we go down to the roots of our being that we unify with others in Spirit and Truth. Everything that follows is the play of Life upon Itself.

MEDITATION

Because I am One with God, I am One with all people. Because I am One with Life, I am One with everything that lives. I feel my union with people and with nature. I feel that I belong to Life.

I love life and I enter into the joy of living. I enter into companionship with others, into cooperation with them. And I know that something within me reaches out and embraces the whole world. Something within me blesses everything it touches, brings life and happiness and joy to everyone. Something in me acts as a healing balm, restoring everything to its natural and native Perfection.

As I silently listen to the Spirit within me and think of Its Perfection, I know that I am being born again—born into joy and hope and gladness, born into love and faith and assurance.

Silently I release every negative thought from my mind. I loose it and let it go. And I, too, pray "that they all may be one; as thou, Father, art in me, and I in thee, that they also may be one in us."

How to Build
Your Tomorrow Today

LIFE IS an adventure in which we never know what is going to happen just beyond the turn of the road. But too often our today is filled with regrets over the past. If we could convince ourselves that the limitations of the past need not be carried into the future, what a happy outlook we should have.

One of the outstanding things that Jesus taught was that the mistakes of yesterday can be canceled, that God's creation is always taking place, and, no matter what the experiences of yesterday may have been, they can be changed.

Jesus did not seem to think that this change required months and years of strenuous effort. Unlike those around him, he knew that God, or the Divine Spirit, wishes only Good for everyone. He knew that we are all rooted in pure Spirit, in Perfect Life, and that at any moment we can so unify ourselves with the Power of Good that evil will disappear from our experience.

Even as what we did yesterday set the Law of Life in motion to create what we are doing today, so what we are doing today sets this same Law in motion to create what will happen to us tomorrow. What we did yesterday is carried over into today only because we give our consent to it. What we are thinking and doing today can create the kind of tomorrow we wish to experience if we will change our outlook on life.

But since today is the only day in which we live, and yesterday has forever passed, the change that we need to make within ourselves must be made today. And so we have to live each day as though it were Complete and Perfect within itself. We have to live each day as though all the Joy there is in the Universe were ours *now*. And we have to live each day as though all the Joy we ever expect to experience were ours *now*.

If we make every day a day of praise and thanksgiving, a day in which we recognize the Divine Bounty and the Eternal Goodness, and if we live today as though God were the only Presence

190

and the only Power there is, we would not have to worry about tomorrow.

We are all human and we have all made mistakes. The starting point for creating a better future for ourselves is to deliberately free our minds from the mistakes of yesterday and feel that they need no longer be held against us; they need no longer be a liability.

Too often our minds are so burdened because of the mistakes we have made that we do not take time to forgive ourselves and others and start over again. And so it is wise to occasionally review the past and try to find out just what we have been thinking and doing to create this burden in our minds.

Suppose we have had a deep sense of animosity toward others and because of this find that we are not meeting people in the right spirit; they, naturally, respond to us the way we meet them, and our whole set of human relations is out of harmony.

We cannot go back over the past and relive it. We cannot make adjustments in the past. We have to make them in the present. It is not going to do us any good to sit around and cry over the past and bemoan our fate, because in the very day in which we are living we are creating our tomorrows, which will become monotonous repetitions of our yesterdays.

So today is the time in which we should cut loose from the threads of previous experiences, wherever they were negative, and deliberately make up our minds that we shall no longer create our future out of the old past. If we have had antagonisms and resentments in the past, today is the only day in which we can change them.

How, then, shall we do this? We must arrive at some practical way, some definite and concrete method, and deliberately use the Law of Good just as we would any other law in nature. In doing this, the one who is suffering from his past mistakes of resentment and animosity merely turns quietly to himself and says:

I have decided to change all this. I want to like people and I want them to like me. I want to get along happily with others. I forgive myself for everything that has happened up until now. I loose it and let it go. I not only forgive myself, I forgive everyone who I feel has held anything against me. I forgive and I am forgiven.

And back of this simple statement we should know that all the Power in the Universe conspires to help us. We should feel that we live in an Eternal Presence of Pure Spirit whose whole purpose is Good, whose whole desire is constructive, and whose whole feeling toward us is one of Love and compassion. Therefore we should say:

Knowing that God is the only Presence and the only Power in the Universe, and knowing that God is Love, I deliberately turn from everything that is unlike this Love. I desire that this Love and compassion and well-wishing for others shall be the whole theme of my life.

It does not seem possible that so simple a method as this can produce such a dynamic result. But experience has definitely proved that it can. Anyone who tries this method will experience definite results. The most wonderful thing about it is that we do not have to change anything but ourselves. For every man is the cause of his own experience, whether he knows it or not. We are all carrying the negative experiences of our past into the future merely because we have not disconnected them from our minds. If we are creating a negative future it is because we have not changed our thought about it.

We have seen the same thing happen to people who have failed in the past, as though nothing could ever work out right for them. We have seen them deliberately change their thought, disconnect their memory from failure, push it aside mentally as though it no longer belonged, as though it were no longer a part of them, and affirm that Good alone accompanies them, that Life is made to live successfully and happily. Accepting this and daily affirming it, we have seen failure and defeat turn into success and triumph.

We have not the slightest doubt that when we do this we are using an all-powerful Law, the Law of Good we talk so much about, the Law which controls everything. We are swinging into line with the great Harmony of the Universe.

But before we can entirely disconnect ourselves from the negations of the past, we have to learn to fill the mind with positive acceptances which are so much greater and deeper than the negations we have been entertaining that they consume them by their very presence, just as light dissipates darkness.

It is not going to do us any good just to make a lot of idle resolutions or to make up our minds that we are going to create such a dynamic personality that nothing can withstand it. This is too much like a person whistling in the dark because he is afraid. What we have to do is get back to some fundamental proposition which ties us directly into the Mind of God and, with the simple acknowledgment that there is a Law of Good in which we have complete confidence, reverse our whole mental outlook on life.

If we disconnect ourselves from the past and find ourselves firmly rooted in God today, in Love, in hope, in joyful expectancy, and in grateful acknowledgment, and if we learn to harmonize with everything that transpires today, tomorrow will blossom like a new flower in our experience.

Or we might think of it another way. When we are weeding our gardens we often find certain plants that are choking out the growth of the things we wish to harvest. So we pull them up, throw them aside, cultivating only those plants that we want to mature. We do this today. Yesterday is past and tomorrow has not yet arrived. So the only time we can weed our garden is today.

And one other thing we have to realize is that we did not make the Laws of Life; we only use them. The Power that makes the garden is a Power greater than we are. All we do is use It. Of necessity the creative soil had to produce the weeds that hamper the growth of the desirable plants, and of necessity the same law has to stop creating them when we uproot them.

Now if we can shift this whole scene into the mind, into our thinking, then we shall have a key to the situation. This has to do with the moment in which we live. Are we permitting Love to blossom in our lives? Of course we want it to, but are we deliberately uprooting everything that denies Love, and trusting to the Lord of creation to produce the desired harvest?

What if we are confused and distraught and upset and all out of sorts? What if the pressure of the past has appeared to cloud the sunlight of the present? The past is gone and the sun is shining on the other side of the clouds. And so let us deliberately resolve to change our thinking today, and make up our minds that we can have confidence in life.

No one can be hurt by doing this. We have everything to gain and nothing to lose. We can uproot all the unhappy thoughts of the past, all the thoughts of failure, all the doubts and fears, all the little petty animosities and disagreements, if we really want to. And we can create our own future today just by carefully guarding our thoughts. But how can we do this unless our faith in Life is greater than our fear, unless hope rises triumphant over despair, or until Love cancels everything unlovable?

This takes us back to what is the great need of the world, the world that somewhere along the line has lost its vision of God. We have gone on our own too long. We have separated ourselves from the Source of our being. We are like persons lost in a fog. The one great resolution we should make today as we turn from the mistakes of the past and look to the future with hope—the one great resolution we need to make, above and beyond all others and more important than all—is that we will find God.

And since we must deal with people and events, and since our lives must be spent with others and in doing things, how can we expect to find God outside His own creation? How can we expect to realize Him in the emptiness of space if we have refused to see Him in those we meet? And how can we find Him in those we meet and in the events that transpire around us unless we have first discovered Him at the center of our own being? We cannot.

The starting point is at the center of our own being. When

we awaken to the Divine within us, It will reach out and embrace everything around us, and It will discover the same Presence in people and in events and in all nature. For God is not separate from what He is doing. The Divine Life is in everyone and in everything.

This is the secret that Jesus discovered. This is why he was able to speak as no other person ever spoke. This is why he was able to perform the miracles of Love and healing, and in so doing prove a fact so simple, so fundamental, but so powerful that people stand in awe before it—the simple fact that God is right where you are.

Cause and Effect

WHILE IT is true that science must deal with cause and effect in practical applications, it is also true that in physics the old idea of cause and effect has been eliminated, which means that things do not always work in the way they are supposed to, basing the performance on precedent.

Here is a very interesting philosophic proposition, because we know that science cannot get along without dealing with cause and effect any more than a farmer can get along without planting crops if he expects to reap a harvest.

But at the same time we have to consider another proposition: the Universe is not merely a gigantic machine. There is injected into Its mechanism a Will, a Choice, a Volition. From a scientific viewpoint it is no longer held that anything is predetermined or foreordained.

We still have the farmer, planting time, and harvest season, but we also have an alternative. He might plant his grain in May with the foreknowledge that, all things being equal, it will mature in September. But on the last day in July, being a free agent, he might decide to plow it up and plant something else. There would be a sequence in the continuum, and there would be cause and effect operating unless it is intercepted, but there would also be choice and volition introducing a personal factor and spelling freedom.

This is the viewpoint the spiritual mind practitioner must take in working for himself or for others, whether for the healing of physical conditions, the betterment of circumstances, or whatever. He is to follow the injunction of Jesus and judge not according to appearances but judge rightly. Whatever effect the appearance has on the mind, he is to say: "What if I do have a piece of ice in my hand? It will melt as it contacts the warmth of my flesh. What if there is an apparent obstruction in the physical body or in the body of my affairs? There is a Truth which can dissolve it."

New causes bring new effects, and every sequence of cause and effect takes place in Something which is greater than cause or effect. Freedom is where it is perceived and in such degree as it is perceived.

Such an attitude is scientific and mathematical. It is also intuitional and revelational, and from the standpoint of practicality gives us a vision that nothing is solid, everything is moving, shifting, changing. Emerson said that even though we view the Universe as a mass of solid facts, God or the Supreme Cause views It as liquid laws, for matter is Spirit reduced to Its greatest thinness.

Direct Contact
with the Infinite

IT IS written, *But the natural man receiveth not the things of the Spirit of God, for they are foolishness unto him; neither can he know them, because they are spiritually discerned.* This means that the objective senses, the intellect with all its arguments, might easily keep us from the Kingdom of Good unless we are careful to remember that spiritual things must be spiritually discerned.

There is an inner meaning to everything, an inside to every fact, a hidden Cause within every visible effect. This Cause is Spirit.

If we spiritually discern this hidden Cause, if we inwardly know that It is operating for us, then we are thinking from the recognition of the Allness of Good. We all have direct access to the Parent Mind, but we do not all use this direct access because we are so used to judging from external facts. It is difficult for us to get away from the apparent long enough to judge the real.

When we know that there is but One Spirit in the entire Universe we shall know that there is but one Source for all forms. We shall know that every form is some manifestation of this Source.

When we have found that this Source is also centered in us we shall know that we can come directly to It and, discerning that Its "Spiritual Nature" is Love and Truth and Beauty, and particularly that It is responsive, we shall make known our requests with thanksgiving, with complete mental abandonment.

The Sequence
of the Creative Order

BY THE Law and the Word we mean the operation of our spontaneous word consciously and volitionally spoken, and the reaction of a mechanical and mathematical but Intelligent and Creative Force which is the Medium through which the Law of Mind in Action operates. The Principle of the Science of Mind is exact and mathematical, while the use of it is personal.

Our Bible starts with this initial statement: *In the beginning God* . . . In the beginning of all creation there is nothing but pure, Absolute Intelligence. The Bible then refers to the Spirit moving upon the face of the deep, which means Absolute Intelligence thinking within Itself. This is but another way of saying that the starting point of every creation is the Word of God or the Word of a Universal Intelligence.

The Word moves upon the face of the deep, or in our language it moves upon the Subjective Law of Mind which receives the impress of our thought, always tending to bring this thought into manifestation. As the starting point of creation this is what is meant by the sequence of the creative order, or an Absolute Intelligence thinking, or the movement of Mind or Spirit within Itself, knowing something, realizing something, affirming something.

Next we have the face of the deep, or the waters of the Spirit, or the Creative Law set in motion by the Word. We have the Law automatically producing the situation, the condition, or the creation implied in the Word. Therefore the sequence of the creative order or the way the Law and the Word work is: first of all, Absolute Intelligence; next, Its Word or thought; following this, the Law is set in motion, for the Word is the Law of Mind in Action; then, at the end of the sequence, is the creation or the formation of the Word in definite and specific circumstances, situations, or creations which are the logical, inevitable, mathematical, and mechanical reactions of the Law to the Creative Word.

Our Bible and the original spiritual systems from which all religions have sprung assume that there is such an Infinite Intelligence; that It does create through Its word or by Its meditation; that there is a Law which reacts to It, producing the object of Its desire. In this way the Original Spirit comes into the fruition or the realization of Itself in and through what It does. Thus it has been said that creation is the meditation of God. *For he spake, and it was done,* or *In the beginning was the Word, and the Word was with God, and the Word was God. . . . All things were made by him; and without him was not anything made that was made. . . . And the Word was made flesh, and dwelt among us.* The Centurion came to Jesus and said, *Speak the word only, and my servant shall be healed.* And in Psalm 107:20: *He sent his word, and healed them.* You will also remember that Moses said, *But the word is very nigh unto thee, in thy mouth, and in thy heart, that thou mayest do it.* Isaiah said, *So shall my word be that goeth forth out of my mouth: it shall not return unto me void, but it shall accomplish that which I please, and it shall prosper in the thing whereto I sent it.*

Throughout our Bible and all sacred books we find this same idea that the Word acting as Law produces a definite result. But right here we must remember that the Word is not something that speaks itself. There is an Intelligence that speaks the Word; therefore the initial movement of the creative sequence is Absolute Intelligence speaking a Word which also becomes Absolute, because it sets an Absolute Law in motion for the purpose of producing a definite result.

Next we must remember that all these sacred writings refer to God as the Macrocosm (the Universe), and man as the microcosm (the individual), and they all teach what Jesus taught when he said, *For as the Father raiseth up the dead, and quickeneth them; even so the Son quickeneth whom he will . . . For as the Father hath life in himself; so hath he given to the Son to have life in himself.* Intelligence compels us to recognize that there must be One Self-Existent, Self-Propelling, Self-Perpetuating, Self-Energizing and Self-Expressing Spirit. This and this alone could be the Origin of Creation.

200

But the Bible states, as other sacred writings do, that man reproduces this Creative Order on a miniature scale. Jesus said, *The Son can do nothing of himself, but what he seeth the Father do: for what things soever he doeth, these also doeth the Son likewise.* What could this mean other than that we as individuals are not separate from the Original Creative Cause? It is upon this premise (which seems rather abstract, but is simple enough if we do not become confused over the thought that it must be too profound) that the Science of Mind is based.

Let us then state it in more simple terms, after this manner: We are centers or points in a Cosmic Universal Consciousness which is the Origin of all things. On the scale of our individual lives we reproduce the Divine Order in Its entirety. This does not mean that we are God, but we find in Psalm 82:6: *I have said, Ye are gods; and all of you are children of the most High.* The whole Divine nature is reproduced in us, but we are ignorant of the fact. Our thought is creative, but in our ignorance we use it destructively.

Theology has called this the problem of evil. We call it a misuse of that which is Good. We as individuals are centers of consciousness in a Power infinitely greater than we are, but which is placed at our command by the very nature of things. From the consequence of our use of this Power we cannot hope to escape, because It is the very Law of Life Itself.

Let us restate our proposition: We are thinking centers in a Cosmic Mind. Our lives reproduce the Original Life. Everything that happens to us must start with the movement of Intelligence within us, which is a movement of our word or contemplation or meditation within ourselves. So let us say of ourselves or to any individual: "You are a center of Intelligence; you did not make it this way, you cannot change it. This is the way it is. You must accept it. You are using a creative Law from which you cannot and do not wish to escape, because It contains the possibility of all freedom when you learn how to use It. To learn to think in the right manner is to learn to create that which is Good, and which gives complete expression to the self without ever containing anything destructive or negative."

201

The beginning of our individual word follows the same Law, the same sequence, and the same order as that of the Supreme Mind, because it is in It and of It and like It. No matter what conditions may be around us, even though they appear to be negative and unhappy, they can be changed if we retrace our mental steps and start with the proposition that our word is also the Law of our lives. Everything that follows the word is an effect of the consciousness that speaks it. Therefore we start with the simple fact that we are consciousness speaking its word, thinking a thought, to which word or thought the Law of Mind reacts creatively.

If we can get this simple proposition firmly fixed in mind, simply stated and as simply believed in, we shall see that everything surrounding us is in the nature of an effect, and effects can be changed when we set new causes in motion. Therefore instead of being confused by the situations around us we should be calm, tranquil, and confident that through re-forming our word and changing our whole body of thinking, we can as easily change the existing conditions as perpetuate them.

This calls for a whole change of thinking. What we need is a complete assurance, an inner conviction, a faith, a confidence to know that we can proceed with definite, deliberate determination and that there can be no question about the results; they will be inevitable.

It was this consciousness that enabled Jesus to perform what to those around him seemed miraculous, or the intervention of a Divine Providence on his behalf. He was consciously and definitely using a Power that he knew about, the very Power of God Himself. And now it is up to us to follow in his footsteps, for as the Bible states: *If ye know these things, happy are ye if ye do them.* To know of this Principle and to understand the way It works is not enough. We must use It.

In actual practice we must be quiet and calm within ourselves and begin to think new thoughts even though they contradict everything that appears, for that which created can recreate; that which molded can remold. The Principle we are using is not limited by anything that is happening, because all external things are in the nature of effect while the Principle Itself is Absolute Creation, creating new effects whenever It receives a new impulsion.

This is what we mean by the Law and the Word, or the sequence of the Creative Order. We can initiate a new creative series by the definite and deliberate contemplation of our own minds, and out of the new thoughts will come new things, for the Law is a reflector only. While It is Intelligent and Creative, Its whole business is to receive the impulsion of the Word that dominates It. This is an apparent paradox, but it is true. We shall discover that the very Law that bound us will now free us; the Power that seemed to stifle us will bring emancipation. The very Power which appeared to produce evil will produce the opposite if, as, and when we change our thought patterns.

The changing of these thought patterns is more than a thing of the intellect; it is also a thing of feeling, of a deep, inner conviction. We must feel that we are One with the Eternal Reality, and that our word is spoken in complete reliance on It; therefore It cannot fail.

Gradually, as we re-form our thoughts they will become subjective; they will sink into that place in mind which is the Power within us and which must constitute the meeting place between the Absolute Cause and the relative effect which It projects.

It may take time to do this, but think of the reward, the gift, the outcome. Keeping the goal in mind, refusing to be baffled or defeated, with uplifted thought and calm but definite purpose, we cannot fail.

What Goes Out Must Return

AFTER THE newcomer to this field has learned of the creative power of thought, he is intrigued by the wonder of it. He is fascinated by the fact that thought is creative; that what he thinks takes form in his experience. What could be more natural than that he should begin to use this Law for every purpose possible for the benefit of himself, as well as others? There is nothing wrong with this, for salvation does begin at home, and only the one who has proved this Law for himself is in a position to use It for others with any hope of success.

At first we are prone to treat everything and everyone around us, in an attempt to influence our environment and other people, and to exercise control over things to our own liking. Most of us pass through this phase, but it is only a phase. As we progress in this science we come to realize that the aim of scientific treatment is not control of people and things. We treat ourself, our own mind, our own consciousness, no matter what the desired end may be, and gradually we learn that, as Emerson said, *we must stay at home with the cause.*

Our thought does not go out to influence persons or things. What it does is readjust our own consciousness, our own thinking, to include a larger and a more harmonious field of action. We learn that when we get our own consciousness straightened out, things in our external world adjust themselves to meet our new and better inward awareness.

Now there is a reason for all this and, like everything else, the process is governed by an exact Law. When Einstein announced that everything bends back upon itself, even time, space, and light, he was scientifically and mathematically approving what the Divine Intuition of the ages had always taught, that everything which goes out will come back again. This is why Jesus said, *For all they that take the sword, shall perish with the sword.* And why Emerson said, *If the red slayer think he slays, Or if the slain think he is slain, They know not well the subtle ways I keep, and pass, and turn again.*

That which goes out will again return. Why? Because everything travels in circles. This Einstein has proved; this the great teachers have taught us. Everything moves in circles. Therefore the outflowing or the beginning of any sequence of action and reaction will have to be equal to the inmoving or the backflowing or the return of that sequence.

In a certain sense we can say that, since what we push out must move in a circle, it must move back to its original position, and in completing the circle reunites with itself. What we push out from this one point will return to the same point from which it was pushed.

For an illustration let us take a person who has learned that he can use the Law. If he has been more or less lonely and without friends, it is quite natural for him to start treating people to get them to like him. He might say, "Wherever I go I shall be met by love and friendship, I shall be received with joy, and I shall be appreciated." He feels that his thought is going out to influence those whom he contacts.

Now he is right as far as he has gone, and he will get definite results, but sooner or later he will discover the real secret, which is that if he is friendly he will attract friends; if he is happy he will attract happiness. He will no longer expect to influence people. His consciousness of Love will have so expanded that out of the fullness of his heart he will exclaim, "I love everyone, I am Love; I am a friend to everyone; nothing that is good is excluded from my consciousness." He has set up a center within himself that automatically radiates to every circumference in his experience, and because everything moves in circles it will again return to him.

The burden has been removed from his mind, and he knows that he can stay at home with a cause which operates upon nothing but himself to produce the desired result. This is one of the greatest secrets of this science.

Of course this same Principle can be applied to everything we are doing. "I am success; I am happiness; I am joy. I am one with all the good there is. I understand everyone and everyone understands me."

The real secret is that everything moves in circles. Everything bends back upon itself. What goes out must return. What is embodied within will complete its own circle, and if we wish to enlarge our experience we must increase our capacity to understand, to feel, to embody, and to know.

Again we are brought back to the saying of Jesus: *Ye shall know the truth, and the truth shall make you free.* In other words, if we really know the Truth, the Truth will make us free, because the Truth Itself is Freedom; It is Wholeness. The Truth is God.

The Law:
Schoolmaster or Servant?

Wherefore the law was our schoolmaster to bring us unto Christ, that we might be justified by faith. But after that faith is come, we are no longer under a schoolmaster (Galatians 3:24,25). This means that the Law of Cause and Effect is a taskmaster while we are ignorant of Its operation, and being ignorant we use the Law destructively.

Experience teaches us what is best. We learn that Good alone can be Eternal and that Love overcomes hate by the same Law of Cause and Effect which made hate seem real. Thus we are justified by faith and we are no longer under the schoolmaster of the Law.

This does not mean the Law is destroyed. It means that we have reversed our use of the Law. We have brought chance into compliance with Love, Reason, and Faith. We have caught the lightning and made it turn the wheels of industry. We have engaged the laws of nature and harnessed their energy to our purposes.

The Law which was our schoolmaster is the same Law, but now It is our obedient servant. To know this is what constitutes the difference between spiritual wisdom and spiritual ignorance. The unwise have no alternative, they are subject to the Law of Cause and Effect as a schoolmaster until they learn Its nature and until they discover that they may transcend all previous negation, and through Christ or Truth enter into a new heaven and new earth, a different consciousness. When Consciousness is changed, experience automatically changes.

207

Specializing the Mental Law of Cause and Effect

YOU ARE already familiar with the Mental Law of Cause and Effect, with the idea that Mind in Action is Law, and with the Principle upon which all mental practice is based; that we are surrounded by a Universal Creative Mind which receives the impress of our thought and acts upon it. This Mind is entirely impersonal, neutral, and plastic. It is subjective or subconscious to our thought, which means that It must receive the impress of our thought as we think it, and must, because of Its nature, tend to create after the pattern of that thought.

This Universal Subjectivity, once it is set in motion, continues to work until the tendency set in motion in It is neutralized. But we cannot neutralize the Law Itself. Laws are eternal, changeless, and immutable. We cannot neutralize the Law but we can reverse our position in It. We cannot change Its nature but we can specialize that nature.

Law as specialized by personality is represented by the two pillars that stood in front of the Temple of Solomon—Jachin and Boaz, one meaning the Law, the impersonal creative medium, and the other the Word, or personal element. Here we have personality and law combined, and it is through these two pillars that we must enter the Temple, which symbolizes the nature of Reality and our innermost life.

The Word of personality and the Law of impersonality, symbolized by these two pillars, constitute the great Mental Law of Cause and Effect which Emerson called the High Chancellor of God, and to which the Bible refers when it says, *Whatsoever a man soweth, that shall he also reap.*

We should not forget that this Law is a Doer and not a knower. It has no choice of Its own, nor does It have any desire of Its own. It is a blind, intelligent Force, creative but not directive. The personality dominates the Law. Both Law and personality (Principle and Presence) are necessary to a Universe of Self-Expression. The understanding of how best to balance these two, the personal and impersonal elements, is what constitutes a correct knowledge of our relationship to the Invisible. From our use of this relationship we reap either bondage or freedom.

We should not confuse the Law as an Impersonal Force with God the Universal Spirit. God is Infinite Person individualized in each one of us, making our nature like God's and giving us the same dominion in our field of action that the Universal Spirit has in Its field.

The Law is the servant of the spirit of man even as It is the servant of the Spirit of God, and our word moves upon the face of the deep just as truly as the originating Creative Word moved. *In the beginning* means the eternal process of creation.

We are always specializing this Creative Law, but generally in ignorance. Ignorance of the Law excuses no one from Its effects, for that which we call good or evil, abundance or lack, are but two ways that one fundamental Principle operates. It neither lacks nor is limited, nor can we say that It is less in a small form or greater in a large form, since our idea of size is entirely relative.

For example, if the physical plane upon which we are living were suddenly reduced to a mile in diameter, and everything else were reduced correspondingly, we should never realize that anything had happened. If, on the other hand, it suddenly expanded to an infinite diameter, and everything else expanded correspondingly, we should never know that this had happened.

But we know big and little, or think we do. Hence we set the Law in motion for the creation of what we conceive, and we say that bigness expands our experience and littleness contracts it. Therefore the experience is contracted or expanded according to our concept. This is the personal element working upon the impersonal, and it is just this possibility which guarantees our freedom.

When we know how this Law works and how to use It we can specialize It for a new purpose. We can use the Power which has bound us to create the freedom we desire. We wish joy instead of tears, gladness instead of sorrow, peace instead of disturbance, success instead of failure, life instead of death. We cannot change the nature of the Law, nor can we change the nature of our being, but we can think and act differently, and the Law, being subjective to our thought, must change Its tendency toward us. In no way do we neutralize the Law of Cause and Effect; we merely use It in a different way.

The Law, having no purpose of Its own, having no intention of Its own about us, is compelled to take the color of our dominant thought and create after that pattern. We, being persons, can change our thought and thereby remold our conditions. Indeed this is the great realization of freedom, and to understand this is to understand how we may become released from bondage. Not to understand this compels us to remain in bondage until enlightenment comes.

The Law, undirected, does nothing. It is merely a natural energy in a spiritual world or a spiritual energy in a natural world. Whichever way we think of It, It is the Law of Cause and Effect, and we are using It every moment of our lives. Of course our greatest use of It is through the subjective channels of our thought. Hence these subjective channels must be clarified and reorganized. The unconscious mental reaction must be redirected, for it is this subjective side of the individual which at all times reflects itself into the Universal Creative Law, and the Law in Its turn molds the image into form and passes it back to us as an actual everyday experience.

It seems self-evident that the Law knows us as the sum total of what we believe ourselves to be, and when we add to this the fact that what we know ourselves to be, or think ourselves to be, is largely subjective or subconscious, we realize that the Law knows each individual from the viewpoint of what the race thought proclaims to be true about all individuals: that is, about each individual as one of a class, plus what the individual has learned to believe about himself.

We should think this over carefully and come to a definite understanding of what it means, for it is of the utmost importance that we come to see that, as individuals, we have not really thought ourselves into limitation. What has happened is that the belief in limitation has operated through us, and our *agreement* with this belief has tended to vitalize it.

We must reverse the whole process definitely and deliberately. This is exactly what Jesus meant when he said that it is done unto us *as* we believe. The new patterns of belief must be found in a higher consciousness and a deeper realization of man's position in the creative order as dispenser of the Divine Gifts and as the recipient of the Infinite Will and Willingness.

We need to repudiate the belief that we are bound. We need to know that the Spirit within us is now free, complete, and perfect. There is not a person living who cannot change his thought, at least somewhat. We can all improve and broaden our mental reaction right where we are, and with each new and better mental outlook there will come a corresponding reaction in our objective world.

In actual practice we must be definite. One of the main troubles with us is that we fail to realize that abstractions are not all that is necessary. The study of philosophy, no matter how spiritual it may be, will avail us but little from a practical viewpoint unless we definitely use the knowledge which we have acquired. To understand the working of the Law is knowledge, but to use It constructively is wisdom.

Daily we must consciously reverse our position in the Law, knowing that we are no longer subject to the race suggestion of lack, limitation, want, or fear; knowing that the Spirit is with us and for us and operating through us; knowing that all good is ours, and specifically declaring that the particular good we desire is now made manifest.

A person who has everything which he desires in life except friendship should accept the good he already has and add friendship to this good. The individual who may be enjoying all good friendships, but who lacks supply, should accept these friendships and add to this idea of life a belief in the presence of supply. The one who may have friendship and supply, but lacks physical well-being, should accept friendship and supply, but continue to specialize the Law for physical healing. There is nothing too great and nothing too small; whatever the need is we should seek to meet it through specializing the Law.

In teaching others to do this for themselves, be careful to explain to them that they should not accept this philosophy as merely a scientific belief or a beautiful system of thought, or as a new attitude toward religion. All of these things it is, but the fact that it is all of these things will never cause it to do anything in particular for anyone. It must be used.

When the pioneer settlers discovered the prairies it would not have been enough for them to exclaim, "What fertile soil! What wonderful harvests it will bring forth! How bountiful is nature! How beautiful the scenery! How marvelous is its vastness and how good is God to have led us here!" All such exclamations would have been true, but they would never have produced a harvest.

We have followed the old patterns of thought so long that transformation from the old to the new position is generally rather slow, and the mental ascent into the consciousness of completion seems beset by many obstructions; hence faith and expectancy are necessary, and above all, a great inner flexibility.

If you are teaching these principles you should insist that those to whom they are taught must use them and must never take *No* for an answer. The Law knows only to agree. It reaffirms our negation and presents us with bondage as easily as with freedom. But is not the knowledge that we can change bondage into freedom one of the greatest joys we can contemplate?

Thought into Action.

The Law
of Mental Equivalents

IN OUR field we hear a great deal about what is called
the Law of Mental Equivalents. We sometimes wonder what
this means, and we shall keep on wondering until we have reduced it to its greatest simplicity.

The Law of Mental Equivalents means that everything that
is consciously and subjectively embodied in our thinking tends
to radiate an atmosphere, a vibration, a current of thought, an
inward acceptance which automatically attracts to itself that
which is like itself.

We are getting back again to the idea of everything moving
in circles. The Law of Mental Equivalents means that there shall
be within the body of our thinking not only an acceptance of the
good we desire, but an inward experience of the meaning of that
good, a real sense and a real feeling that we now possess it.

It is easy enough, then, to see that the Law of Mental Equivalents means a subjective embodiment even more than it does
a conscious statement. It means that when we do make a conscious statement there shall no longer be anything in us that
denies or repudiates it.

But this subjective embodiment of ideas is something that
can be consciously generated. Not only can we change our objective thinking, but by a process of careful treatment we can
change the whole subjective field of our thought, because most
of our thinking is unconscious. Therefore the mental embodiment of an idea or the true mental equivalent of something is
not so much the word we speak as it is something we feel in the
heart.

We all have a definite content of unconscious thinking, of
unconscious expectation, of unconscious frustration and desire.
This is just as much a part of the process of our thinking as the
words we use consciously, and it is just as certain to be operated
upon by the Law of Life. This we sometimes overlook. But if

these things are true, then the first thing we must change is ourselves.

This is sometimes a long and arduous process, for a person does not change all of the patterns of his thought in a moment. Rather it takes place little by little, until gradually the old thought patterns become transformed into new ones by some inner alchemy of the mind, the operation of which we do not see but the manifestation of which we do experience.

For instance, an individual who has not met with as much good and happiness in life as he desires should select a definite time each day to treat himself. The treatment should be something like this:

> *I know that all the Good there is belongs to me. God is Good, Good is God. I am surrounded by Good, I am enveloped in It; I feel Its presence.*
>
> *There is nothing in me that can reject that Good. My whole inner feeling entertains It and experiences It. My whole expectation is one of joy and pleasurable anticipation. All the old thoughts of fear and doubt and uncertainty have vanished. Within me is the Secret Place of the Most High; within me is the Presence and the Power and the Will to know and to do and to be.*
>
> *There is nothing in me that can deny this statement or refuse to accept it. There is nothing in me that can limit me. My memory is one of happiness; my anticipation is one of joy; my experience is one of pleasure.*

This would be a broad-gauge treatment and, practiced over a period of many days, would be very effectual.

This would be true of any idea we wish to embody. We should think about it and feel it, envision it, and try to think of the meaning of each word. Accepting it consciously, we should let it sink deeply into the unconscious, until the subjectivity of our thought shall have accepted its meaning; then we shall have arrived at the mental equivalent of the idea.

Principle and Precedent

ALL MANKIND is more or less following the patterns of thought in which it is immersed. Whether we choose to call this the collective unconscious, the carnal mind, or the influence of race suggestion makes no difference. Most of us follow the patterns of thought as they have been laid down through the ages. We say things must happen today and tomorrow because they happened yesterday and the day before. Psychologists contend that a neurotic thought pattern will repeat itself with monotonous regularity until the pattern is changed.

Advances in science and civilization come through breaking down the belief that things have to be the way they are because they have always been that way.

But the laws of nature or the Principles that govern life know nothing about precedents. At one time we used tallow candles; now we have electric lights. There was nothing in nature that prohibited the world from having had electric lights ten thousand years ago, but no one knew anything about them. When the day arrived on which somebody discovered the new possibility, the laws of nature complied and delivered the secret which made the new possible.

The world has always said wars must continue to be because they always have been. People have always believed that the different countries could not settle their difficulties by peaceful methods. This precedent is of such long standing that it is a difficult thing to overcome. Yet sooner or later it will have to be overcome if the world is to survive.

The same thing has happened throughout the history of spiritual evolution, or the unfoldment of man's thought about his relationship with God. People have prayed to a Power higher than themselves and occasionally their prayers have been answered affirmatively. Perhaps they have always been answered in accordance with the way they have prayed. However, it has always been accepted that some prayers are answered while others are not. Because of this belief, a precedent was established which made the answer to prayer an unpredictable thing.

215

This is one of the precedents which need to be broken, for we must allow spiritual activity a larger scope. When we realize that all the spiritual Power there is is at our disposal, and that no matter how limited a viewpoint we may have had yesterday (with the limitations that follow that viewpoint), today we can increase our field of inward awareness, then we make possible a greater influx of the Divine through the human, that is, through our own thinking.

But we can never do this unless we believe that we can, for the belief that we cannot binds us back to the old precedents and compels us to accept only as much good as has been experienced in the past. If we can get it firmly fixed in our mind that Principle is never bound by precedent, that the doing of new things in science through new discoveries always existed as a possibility, and that there was nothing in nature which prohibited the larger experiences, we shall no longer be hypnotized by the past.

It is probable that most of us go through life more or less hypnotized by what everyone has believed. We say that the good we desire cannot come to us because we have never experienced it. Or we say the good we desire is too much to expect, or there is not enough good to go around, or that God does not hear our prayer. Too often we turn over the possibilities of the individual life to the acceptance of the collective group.

We should do the exact opposite. We should break down the hypnotic suggestions that bind us, and create new avenues in the mind for a fresh approach and a new outlook to the Spirit. This is something that every person must do for himself. But there must be a method or a way to begin.

We should start with the firm conviction that we are dealing with a Power which is not bound. It is not limited. It is not only some power; It is All-Power. It is not difficult to convince the mind of this, since plain reasoning compels one to accept such a viewpoint.

Next we must assure ourselves that we have access to this Power. We could never do this if we felt that the Power were external to us, if It were something apart from or different from our own being. We discover that God is immediate and personal,

216

a possibility latent within the self but ready to be called upon and used.

Our next step is to identify the self with this Power. *I am that which thou art, thou art that which I am.* We are One with this Power, in It, with It, and some part of It.

Having identified ourselves with the Power which is the Law, and the Presence which is the Spirit, we must consciously increase our expectation and deepen our realization. This is done by meditation, communing with the Divine, until gradually we so extend our concepts of life and the possibilities of living that we are no longer bound by our old thought patterns.

There are simple techniques which help us to do this. As an example, we might say:

> *I am One with all the Power there is; I am One with all the Presence there is. There is One Life, that Life is God, that Life is my life now. This Power, this Presence, and this Life are Perfect, Complete, Whole, Happy.*

We identify the mind with this Wholeness, with this Happiness, with this Perfection, affirming Its Presence and embodying a certain feeling about It, an inward awareness. This practice must continue until the idea becomes real to us, not as though we were something apart from or approaching the Reality, but as though we were operating from the very center of It, which of course we are.

Then we can continue by saying:

> *There are new thoughts, new ideas coming to me. I open my whole consciousness to the influx of that which is larger and better. I identify my mind with inward Peace and Joy.*

At times we may be confronted with negative arguments of set mental patterns which circumscribe, limit, and depress the mind. Our senses may try to insist that we follow the old established precedents as our true guide, since they have been adhered to by mankind from time immemorial.

Right here a certain amount of adventure, of imagination

must be brought into play to create a feeling of acceptance which will break down these old thought patterns. We must understand that they are not the Truth of God's Being but merely monotonous repetitions of all of the negative thought of the ages. We must know that our new declarations of Truth have the Power within themselves to completely destroy the old thought patterns.

An argument similar to the following is a good one to use in such cases:

> *I am no longer hypnotized by the old thought patterns; I am no longer bound by these precedents; I am no longer limited to what everyone has believed, because I now know it has no Truth, no Reality, and no Law to support it. It is but a phantom.*

Such an argument in mind will tend to destroy old beliefs and give us the leeway that is necessary if we are to initiate new, larger, better, and less limited ideas. Imagination and feeling will play a great part in overcoming the old limitations, and our newly acquired inward awareness will proclaim to us that we are and always have been a part of God's Universe. The words which we speak will connect us with that which is greater than our previous experiences.

We must come to know that no past experiences need bind the possibility of new and better ones, until finally we think more and more completely from the standpoint that God is all there is and that all things are possible to God, and also that, through our new knowledge, the greater possibility is ours today.

Identifying ourselves with this more complete life, we begin to specialize this universal concept by identifying the things we are doing with the greater possibility. In a certain sense this is "letting fire down from heaven," or bringing light into a darkened room.

In actual practice it is a consistent process of identifying the personal self with the impersonal, man with God, life with living, prayer with performance, the Universal Spirit with our own spiritual being, which is part of that Universal Spirit; and then bringing these larger thought patterns to bear upon the things we are doing in everyday life.

Principle is not bound by precedent. There is no law in the Universe that seeks to perpetuate old limitations, but there is a Law which responds to our greater vision at the exact level of that vision. The mind should be kept in a buoyant, expectant, enthusiastic attitude; all weightiness and confusion must be eliminated, and we must think back to that which is boundless and free.

This is a secret we hold with ourselves and with Life, or God. Do not ask that someone else justify you in your belief, for this is confusion. Do not ask by what authority we do these things, for this would be to limit our activities to the way other people have done them. Here is where the mind must work alone, increasing its own sphere, reaffirming its own position, awakening itself to the greater influx.

Just as surely as we do this we shall find that the prison walls of the lesser self begin to crumble, the horizon of experiences begins to push itself farther away, and, because more Spiritual Territory is taken in, greater experiences are bound to follow.

Disease Is Not First Cause

THE BASIS for correct spiritual treatment starts with the idea that Being is already Perfect. The idea of Perfection is the Spiritual Power which heals.

From the standpoint of pure Spirit, an unknown or hidden false cause would be just as unreal as a known or revealed one. Therefore we must know that disease is neither cause, medium, nor effect. From the standpoint of pure Spirit, wrong action had no beginning, it has no duration, and it will have no climax.

The treatment we give is an activity of the Law enforcing this Truth. Your use of the Law, being on a higher plane of consciousness than the state of thought which produced the discord, must therefore erase it, and you must know that it will do so.

You know that Mind, or Spirit, is Pure, Perfect, and Complete, manifesting Itself in physical form in and throughout all nature. The government of Good is enforced through the Law of man's own Divinity.

Power exists, and the action of this Power is upon your word, or your word acts upon the Power, no one knows which. For all practical intents and purposes, the Power acts upon your word.

How Does God Know
What I Am Doing?

FREQUENTLY PEOPLE ask, "Why should God be interested in my little affairs?" I remember once speaking to one of our Trustees, who had been ill for several weeks. I asked him why he had not requested treatment. He said, "I did not wish to bother God with such a small thing."

This is a natural enough reaction, and yet it is built on ignorance of Cosmic Laws. We might ask, "Is there more life in an elephant than in a flea?" Or from the standpoint of the Infinite, "Is a giant sequoia of more importance than a rose blossoming by the wayside?" Of course not. There is no big and no little, either to the Divine Presence or to the Law which governs everything. Is not the rose rooted in the same soil in which the tree is rooted? It is merely a different type of manifestation of life, taking a separate form but rooted in a common Unity.

We should eliminate the ideas of big and little or hard and easy, because they do not exist in the Creative Mind of the Universe. Things exist there as ideas, and it is the nature of the Law of Mind to cause these ideas to take forms native to such ideas. All ideas are brought into form or fruition through the One Medium. A person running a peanut stand on some street corner and affirming the presence of activity in his business is invoking the same Law as the builders of a railroad or an Empire State Building are invoking.

The Law always takes the form that we give It. We may call it big or little, or important or unimportant, but the Law as such knows nothing about comparative degrees. The very nature of this Law is such that It cannot say "I am big" in one place and "I am little" in another. It can say only "I am, and that also I am," including what we call big and little, as it automatically flows through everything, taking the form of all things.

In our treatments we entertain an idea and accept a form, because from the viewpoint of the Law one thing is as important

221

as another. When we ask ourselves how it is that God knows who we are and that our little affairs are important, the answer is that God knows everything, not as big and little, but only as action and reaction, only as contemplation which produces its own reaction.

All great spiritual teachers have told us this, and they were right. All thought of big and little, hard and easy, can and cannot, must be divorced from our treatment. Remember that the same ingenuity, the same Creative Power that flows into the largest form also creates the smallest form.

Comparatives do not belong to the Universe. They are merely differentiations in our own mind. Dropping them completely out of our thought, we contemplate neither the big nor the little, but the Thing Itself taking particular form.

A great load will fall from our mind if we will stop thinking about big and little or hard and easy. If you set a spool of thread in front of a mirror, it will be reflected, or if you stand in front of the mirror yourself, you will be reflected. This larger form will be reflected as readily as the smaller form. The mirror knows nothing about size, but reflects automatically the form held in front of it.

We are told that there are many heavenly bodies millions of times larger than the earth; there are many that are smaller, but the same Cause created them, not as big or little but merely as expressions of Itself.

In a certain sense this makes the creation of a mud cake by a child as important as the building of an empire, not that it is fraught with as much significance to human experience, but that from the standpoint of the Creative Genius of the Universe they are just creations.

Is a sunset of less importance than an epic poem? And in reality would the healing of tuberculosis or cancer be of greater importance than the healing of an ordinary cold, or the removal of a wart?

We are told in psychosomatic medicine that warts are easily removed by suggestion, and yet a wart is a definite form rooted in the physical body. How do we know but that, if our idea of cancer were as lightly held as our idea of a wart, a simple suggestion would dissolve cancer as quickly and as easily? We do not. From the standpoint of the ultimate Spirit of creativity there is no reason whatsoever to deny the liquidation of one as easily as another.

It must be, then, that the obstruction is in our own consciousness, or from our unconscious resistance created by the thoughts of big and little or hard and easy. This is what we must overcome.

Energy and Mass

ONE OF the propositions in physics is that energy and mass are equal, identical, and interchangeable. Now this is a harmless-sounding phrase, but very few people understand the mathematics behind it. However, we can understand its meaning and apply it to our own science.

Saying that energy and mass are equal, identical, and interchangeable is quite different from saying that energy energizes mass or that energy operates upon, in, or through mass to do something to it. When we say that energy and mass are equal, identical, and interchangeable, we are saying that energy, which is invisible, is the actual substance of the mass which is visible, and that the visible and the invisible are the same thing; they are equal, identical, and interchangeable. It is equal to saying that what you see comes out of what you do not see; what you do not see becomes what you do see; and what you do see and what you do not see are the same in essence.

Applying this to the Invisible Principle of creation, we find that it is no different from what we read in Romans 1:20: *For the invisible things of him from the creation of the world are clearly seen, being understood by the things that are made.* . . . This is also equal to saying that what you see comes out of what you do not see.

Let us look at this proposition in a different light. Emerson said that there is one mind common to all individual men, and that we are all inlets to this mind. Spinoza said that mind is not one thing and matter another; they are the same thing. Quimby, upon whose teaching the New Thought Movement in America was pretty much founded, said, *Mind is matter in solution and matter is mind in form.* But he added that there is a Superior Wisdom, which he called the Science of Christ; mind as matter and mind as form are the substance that this Superior Wisdom uses.

It is of great importance that a student of this science understand the meaning of these rather abstract statements; that he reduce them to their utmost extremity and accept them as a part of his basic Principle. He must be careful not to become so absorbed in some mystical or imaginative concept that he will be too confused or too far away from Reality to think straight.

Einstein was a mathematician. Emerson was a logical thinker and a great philosopher. All of the greatest teachings of the Bible are inspirations and intuitions. Quimby gave us the key to spiritual mind treatment.

There could be no such thing as psychosomatic medicine or body-mind relationships if the Ultimate Substance on which Mind works were different from the Mind that works on It. A spiritual mind treatment is not a process whereby thought spiritualizes matter or materializes Spirit. Your thought can have no effect for, in, around, or through anything if it is unlike the thing that it affects.

Fifty years ago, to have said that mind and matter were the same thing would have caused people to think that one might be slightly out of balance mentally. But when a man like Dr. Einstein proclaimed that energy and mass are equal, identical, and interchangeable, we could not laugh it off.

Remember again that Einstein was not saying energy energizes matter or influences it or hypnotizes it or does anything to it. Energy does not do anything to matter, nor does matter do anything to energy. They are the same thing. If either one does something to the other one, it is because the two are one and not two, and the one is all there is.

Let us then apply this simple but abstract, profound but understandable, proposition to our own science. Thought does not energize matter, nor does thought restore matter or a material form to a material harmony. There is no material universe.

This is true whether we are dealing with the Science of Mind or with Einstein's equation. Physical science no longer deals with a material universe. It deals only with a universe of undulating waves or streams of particles in some mysterious way hitched to a continuum or an endless stream of time. The sequence is not bound necessarily by any law of cause and effect such as science used to deal with, because at any moment it can be changed.

This is no attempt at a scientific or technical explanation of the new physics, but it is a new picture drawn for our imagination, and we might as well lay hold of it and apply it to our own science, for our philosophy is no more to be laughed off than is theirs. The time to laugh at one who deals with the Science of Mind passed on when physics discarded the theory of a material or a mechanical universe.

Translating the terms *energy* and *mass* into terms *mind* and *matter* we have the same equation. But continuing with Quimby's theory that mind in solution and mind in form are the same thing, and that they constitute the matter of a Superior Wisdom which he called the Science of Christ, we see that we are using a Force and Energy that are both visible and invisible, and we are using them in such a way as to cause the invisible to become visible and the visible to become invisible.

Einstein's equation does the same thing in effect, because it views energy and mass as equal, identical, and interchangeable. But we must also take into consideration that which views it, the physicist, the person. Here is one of the finest points in spiritual mind healing and in using the Science of Mind. Just as energy does not energize mass but is mass (or energy in form), so in our science there is considered to be no difference between the thought and the thing thought of or about. One becomes the other.

However, we must realize that back of all form or at the center of all creation there must be a Divine Pattern which is the Reality of that thing. What we change is not the Reality but our perception of It, or quoting Ecclesiastes 7:29: *Lo, this only have I found, that God hath made man upright; but they have sought out many inventions.*

Your Invisible Forces

IT IS said that the average man draws on only about 10 percent of his real capacity; the other 90 percent is mostly submerged and unused. Well, you and I would think it wonderful if we could multiply our talents many times. I have no doubt we can do this if we try.

So let us take a simple lesson from nature. Perhaps from where you are sitting you can see a tree in full bloom. If so, remember that the roots through which the tree draws its life are entirely invisible. And unless the tree drew on this invisible source it would never flourish.

Our roots are in the Mind of God. Our individuality, everything that we are and do, is an effect of our Invisible Forces—Forces which continually draw on the Infinite. But in our ignorance we limit the flow of Divine Power into our lives.

Of course this is not intentional, for we all want to make good in life; we want people to like us, and we desire to be worthwhile. But too often when we make an inventory of our assets we depend only upon the circumstances that surround us. We say, "How can I better myself? I haven't the personality," or "I haven't the natural attractiveness which is necessary to making good in life."

Right here is where our faith in the Power greater than we are must be brought into play. For we as individuals are rooted in this Power. It was his great claim on a Power greater than he was that enabled Jesus to become a Divine Man while still living on earth. Did he not say, *Of mine own self I can do nothing . . . the Father that dwelleth in me, he doeth the works.*

Yes, we must come to believe that the Father does dwell within us, and that the same Creative Spirit that is back of all things flows through us. Jesus said, *Consider the lilies of the field, how they grow; they toil not, neither do they spin: And yet I say unto you, that even Solomon in all his glory was not arrayed like one of these.*

God has need of us or He wouldn't have put us here. The

227

Divine wishes to express through you and through me or we would have no existence. We have no existence of ourselves alone. It is only because we live in God that we live at all. If we think of ourselves as rooted in God and expect Divine Power to flow through us, our every thought and act will be animated by the same Life and Power and Beauty that clothe the lily of the field.

We once knew one of the country's leading cartoonists. The nature of his work was such that he had to produce new ideas daily and make pictures of them for a newspaper syndicate for millions of people to read. I asked him how he accomplished so much, and he told me that he had a room with four blank walls, and the only furniture in his room was a table and a chair; that when he needed ideas he would go into this room, sit down, and become quiet.

He said that sometimes he would sit there for two or three hours and nothing would happen. Then all at once something would begin to flow up from within him, a new thought, a new idea, and he would take a pencil and write his impressions. What he wrote and what he drew was like the bloom of a plant as it draws upon the soil.

The creative artist and the inventor do this. And why should we not do the same? We have to start with the proposition that all things are possible to God; that God makes everything out of Himself by the simple process of becoming the thing He makes, just as the tree grows out of the ground and the invisible forces of its life turn into foliage, into blossom, and into fruit, all through a silent process of nature.

Did you ever ask yourself this question: *How is it that I can eat mince pie and ham sandwiches and maybe a salad, and have it turn into flesh and blood and hair and fingernails?* Here is the miracle of Life, the Invisible becoming visible. We are so used to the process that we never question it; we take it for granted. Why should we not take it for granted that God will give us ideas, that the Spirit within us, as Jesus said, knows what we have need of even before we ask?

Let us get back to the tree again. Suppose every time it thought of putting forth a new branch it would say, "How am

228

I going to do it? I have only a certain number of branches. I don't know how to make a new branch, anyway." Now just for the fun of it, let us suppose this tree is a person, and it is bemoaning its fate because it would so greatly like to have a few more branches, but it doesn't know how to make them.

And thinking of the tree as a person, let us assume that every time it says, "I don't know how to make a new branch" it is blocking off the possibility of drawing its life from the soil. If this should happen, the tree would never make any more branches; it would begin to die from that very moment.

But the tree is not a person. All it does is to depend on nature. All it knows is to grow. So it never short-circuits the Divine Energy that gives it life. But we are people and we can short-circuit the Divine Energy that ought to be flowing through us. We short-circuit It when we deny that It is there. And the reason we deny It is because we do not see this Energy, and therefore we do not believe in It.

If we believe that the Father is within us, and if we believe that all things are possible to God, then we should no longer deny that God knows what to do with His own creation, and we should include ourselves in that creation.

All right, then, let us see what would happen to us if we should include ourselves in God's creation. Right at the start we should learn to have a little better opinion of ourselves. I am not talking about a conceited opinion, for we have learned that we can do nothing of ourselves — we live because we are drawing on the invisible Source of all Life. The only way that God can work for us is by working through us, and God cannot give us anything unless we take it. He has made the Gift of Life or we would not be here. Only God can give Life, as only God can make a tree. But we are not living like the tree, because we deny the very Power by which we live.

And now we want to change all this. We wish to draw on these Invisible Forces, to let our roots run deep into that Life which already is Perfect and Complete, and we want to live happily and without fear. For fear short-circuits this Divine Energy, while confusion and uncertainty cause It to produce bondage instead of freedom.

If we want to change this let us start by accepting ourselves for better or for worse. But in this instance let us be sure that we accept ourselves for better, because we are thinking of that deep, hidden Self which the Bible tells us is hid with Christ in God.

Here is where prayer and meditation make possible the miracle of Life. Remember we are talking about affirmative prayer, for there should be nothing negative in our communion with God. It should always be affirmative. We should never say God cannot or will not, but always God can and will and does. And having cleared all doubt from our consciousness we must learn to affirm that all the Power and all the Presence and all the Life that there is, is for us and with us and in us.

And there is one more thing we certainly should not forget to add: The higher Forces of Life always work constructively. When we use them constructively there seems no limit to their possibility. But the moment we begin to use them destructively, they appear to block themselves.

This seems to be the only condition that the Divine has laid down which might be considered limiting, but which is not. We could not expect to use the Power of Good for evil purposes, nor could we expect through hate to generate Love, nor could we hope for God to give us that which we refuse to pass on to others. These are the only conditions Jesus laid down when he told us that we would always receive if we would pray aright.

Let us take a simple illustration to demonstrate this. We can love without limit—we can love everyone and everything and feel kindly disposed toward people and circumstances and situations—and this attitude toward Life will never hurt us, nor will it block the flow of Life through us. Rather it will tend to accelerate it. But the moment we begin to hate we block the passage of Life, and gradually this negative attitude stifles us; it short-circuits the flow of Energy from the roots of our being into the things we are doing.

When we are on the right track there is no limit, but when we get on the wrong track we go on to where the trail runs out and stops. It would seem as though God had imparted His own

Life to us, placing no limitation or condition that would restrict us other than this: Life must be lived constructively, in Unity and Love and Sympathy with everything around us if we expect to live It to the full.

There is no other condition imposed on us from the Divine. Everyone is born to be creative and to live to the fullest and to enjoy Life, to be happy and glad and prosperous and whole. We do not believe that God is a failure. God never makes any mistakes. We are the ones who err.

If we are certain that our lives are constructive, and if our whole desire is to live in such a way as to harm no one but to bless all, then we should place no limit on the possibility of our future. This great Gift of Life is to be accepted, even as the lilies of the field and the birds of the air.

Let us try this simple experiment, daily saying to ouselves:

All that the Father hath is mine. There is nothing in me that can deny His Presence, His Power, His Wisdom, His Guidance, and His protecting Love. Today and every day I shall live Life to the full; I shall sing and dance and be glad. And always within me there is the Power and the Presence and the the Life of God. And unto this Presence be Glory and Honor, Dominion and Power, both now and forever. Amen.

Your Spiritual Bank Account

WE ALL know that we have to have money before we can spend it. And how comfortable it makes us feel to have a good fat checking account, an account big enough to draw on in emergencies without impoverishing us when it comes to paying for our ordinary needs.

Let us talk about another kind of checking account which is equally important. We are calling it *Your Spiritual Bank Account* because we believe there are great spiritual forces that we can draw on and deposit in our own minds, and which can be used in any emergency, in any stress or strain of life.

Life has enough of everything to spare. It contains love and faith and peace of mind and joy. Would it not be wonderful if we could build up a spiritual bank account and hold it in reserve—an account which we knew would be sufficient to meet any emergency in our lives? For we are always being called on to meet emergencies—times when we need more love and tolerance, more kindness and understanding, a deeper faith and a higher hope.

These are the real crises in our lives. And at such times, unless we have a vast amount of good stored up, we not only become impoverished, but we sometimes become destitute of hope. And then despair takes the place of hope, and fear takes the place of faith. This is what we want to avoid.

How would it be if we all opened a spiritual account with the Bank of Life and, realizing that we were drawing on the Infinite, each day deposited enough hope and happiness and faith to more than meet any emergency that might possibly arise? The wonderful part about this is that we know Life contains all these things and It wants to give them to us. It is intended by the Divine scheme of things that we should have them.

How would we go about it to open up such an account and be sure that we had enough of these qualities on deposit so that our checks would be honored whenever any emergency arose? We know that we have to deposit money in the bank in order to draw checks. We know that the money is in a safe place and that the checks will be honored unless we overdraw the account. In our ordinary affairs we have to earn the money, and in a certain sense this will be true of our spiritual bank account. But the earning of the supply or the substance for our spiritual bank account is a little different, for we earn the ability to draw on the Bank of Life only through having practiced Love.

This is where many of us fall down because we do not quite realize that Love is the base of everything. We have had so much experience that seems to contradict this that we become skeptical and cynical and sometimes wonder if Love, after all, is the greatest Reality in Life. And yet we know that we could not live without Love, for life is absolutely meaningless unless its whole motivation is built on Love and Givingness.

Why can we not think of it this way: God has already made the initial deposit—and a big one—for everyone who is ever born into this world, because God has given Himself to us. He has imparted His own Life and, in a mysterious way which is beyond our comprehension, has endowed us with the capacity to Love. If God is Love—and no sane person can doubt this—and if each one of us has, as we must have, immediate access to the Love of God, then we earn the ability to draw on the Bank of Life in such degree as we become loving.

We shall earn the ability to draw on this bank through constant meditation and prayer and communion with the Infinite, using statements in our meditations similar to the following:

> *God is Love and all the Love there is is mine now. I shall endeavor to see something lovable in everyone I meet, in every situation in which I find myself, and as I do this I shall accumulate a great degree of Love to be deposited in my bank. And then when some experience comes along which seems unkind or unlovable, I shall be able to write a check on my Bank of Life which will cover every liability of hate or of unkindness.*

And here is one of the great secrets of nature—the person who has taken the time to harmonize himself with Love will find that, when some incident that seems hateful or discordant arises in his experience, he can draw on a reserve Force which

233

he now has. He can actually apply this to the situation when it arises.

If you have accumulated a certain amount of Love and then meet some situation where discord and strife seem to enter, get quiet inside yourself and say, "I am bringing Love to bear on this situation—a Love which comprehends and includes everything, a Love which has no hurt in It, a Love which is not afraid, a Love which is calm and confident and sure of Itself."

Right here is where the Law of Mind in Action comes into play. When you apply your thought of Love directly to discordant situations, and there is nothing in you which is afraid, your thought of Love applied to that situation will heal it. If you have deposited enough Love in your checking account you will find that you can meet the situation, your check will be honored by the Bank of Life, and the situation that confronts you will be healed.

First of all you must have a firm conviction that God is Love, and an equally firm conviction that when you apply this Principle of Love to any human problem the very words you speak in your meditation or treatment or prayer will operate as Law in the condition that confronts you, and will neutralize or overcome everything that opposes It.

This is not an act of will. It has nothing to do with holding thoughts. It has nothing whatsoever to do with concentrating your mind or influencing people. It has to do with this one thought: God is Love. God has deposited Love at the center of every man's being, whether he knows it or not, and this Love which I now use is not only the greatest sentiment in the world; It is the Supreme Power, It is the Perfect Law, It is Reality.

And because you have deposited a Love which can see around everything that contradicts It, and because you have ample Love left in your own thought, you will find that the Love you use, acting as Law, will definitely overcome the fear and the hate and the sense of insecurity that come where there is a sense of lack of Love.

Perfect Love alone can cast out all fear. Love is always greater then fear. Fear is not really an enemy of Love. All that fear can do is cast a shadow across your pathway. But this shadow is dissipated when you look at it with Love. You are not dealing with two opposing forces but with only One Force, which is Absolute and Positive and Conclusive.

But first you must have made the deposit with the Bank of Life. You must have spent much time with yourself straightening out all the little animosities and resolving them into the one great Love which is God. God never fails and Love never fails and you will never fail if you use the Love that God is.

And now let us think of some other things we want to deposit in the Bank of Life. Perhaps one of the most important, next to Love, is faith—faith in God, faith in ourselves, faith in what we are doing, and faith in those around us. A person without faith is so insecure, so shaken by circumstances, that he becomes unstable in everything.

Let us see, then, if we cannot draw upon the great reservoir of faith which comes only through implicit, complete surrender of all our fears, whether they be big or little. Faith is natural; fear is unnatural. Faith is positive; fear is negative. Faith is affirmative; fear is a denial of life. And we need a great deal of faith if we are going to meet all the fears and uncertainties that we are sure to encounter.

Only a little faith cannot do this. Just as we cannot pay a thousand-dollar debt with five hundred dollars, so it is impossible to meet a trying circumstance unless we have sufficient faith to cover all the fear. As a matter of fact, we have as much faith as we use. We have as much faith as we believe.

When Jesus stood before the tomb of Lazarus he was confronted with the fear of death. He was confronted with the weeping and wailing of the family. In a certain sense he was confronted with the whole human belief in death. And you will remember that they told him he dare not roll away the stone from the tomb of Lazarus.

This stone is a symbol of the obstruction that confronts us sometimes when we attempt to use our faith for definite purposes. How often we look at the stone. How often we think of the tomb, with the dead inside. How seldom do we realize that there are no obstructions to Divine Power.

But Jesus lifted up his voice in communion with God; he

raised his thought above the fear of the moment. He could not have done this unless he had spent much time drawing on the Bank of Life and depositing large amounts of faith to his own account. For on another occasion he said, *This kind goeth not out but by prayer and fasting*—by communion with God. Jesus had spent so much time alone with God that what to us seems unreal was to him the one solid Reality—God is Life, God is Power, and this Life and this Power are available right *now*.

Jesus must have gradually accumulated a storehouse of faith, and when the emergency arose he was able to stand calm and certain, uncaught by the fears of others. He looked up and not down, and offered what seems to us to be the greatest short prayer of the ages: *Father, I thank thee that thou hast heard me. And I knew that thou hearest me always.* What sublime confidence! What infinite trust! What limitless assurance!

God always came first with Jesus—*Father, I thank thee.* How many of us have enough faith deposited in the Bank of Life so that when fear confronts us we can boldly proclaim, "My faith is sufficient. My trust is complete. My assurance is absolute. Father, I thank thee that thou hearest me." There is no doubt here, no uncertainty, no hesitation.

And I knew. . . . What Power and possibility is caught in the two simple words—*I knew.* There is no question, there is no doubt, *I knew that thou hearest me always.* Not once in a while; not by and by; not yesterday; but here, today, as I face this tomb. In the midst of all this doubt and fear and uncertainty, *I knew.*

And now carefully note what happened next. It is written that Jesus cried with a loud voice: *Lazarus, come forth.* He could not have said this with such confidence if he had been depending on his human will power. He was standing still and watching the glory of Life with a calm assurance that his words were honored by a Power greater than he—that Power which we all have access to, Life Itself.

There are many other things that we must accumulate and deposit in the Bank of Life besides Love and faith. Important among them are joy and happiness. For Life intended us to be glad. There is always a song when we know how to sing it, and always a joy if we can find it.

And, of course, we need to deposit a large amount of Peace, a Peace that rises above the storm of confusion and doubt and uncertainty that so often confronts us. If you listen to Peace you will hear it, and it will flood your whole being. Then when you meet confusion, just write out your check on the Bank of Life and do not be afraid to sign it in the name of God. This is God's bank. And just as surely as you do this you will discover that your words of Peace, acting as a Law of Good, will draw upon a Power greater than you are and liquidate the confusion.

This is practicing the Presence of God, coming to know that we are in partnership with the original Banker, the One who made the Bank of Life, but the One who, in a certain sense, must wait for us to join in this Divine Partnership.

There is a Power that honors our faith. There is a Love that meets Love with Love, a Law that meets faith with faith and Good with Good. We did not create this Law, this Power, this Divine Presence. We had no more to do with It than we did with the creation of the North Wind or the North Star. It was there before we recognized It; It would be there if we had no existence. But It does not *seem* to be there until we believe in It and use It.

Let us, then, be certain that we open up our account with this great Bank of Life. For here, and here alone, is the real substance that we can draw upon to purchase every good and beautiful thing that Life has in store for us. Here alone are peace and joy and certainty. Here alone is freedom from fear and doubt.

Deliberately close all your accounts with the lesser banks, throw away the old checkbooks, and forget them, and learn to turn daily to the one and only Supreme Source, which is God.

MEDITATION

Believing that God is all the Presence there is, I am learning to feel this Presence in everything and in everyone.

Dwelling on the thought that God is Love, I permit my mind to become filled with the consciousness of this Love. I permit this Love to envelop everything and everyone, bringing with it a sense of peace and joy and certainty.

Realizing that God is Life, I open my whole thought to such a complete inflowing of this Divine Life that I see It and feel It—the One perfect Life which is God—in people, in nature, animating every act, sustaining all movement. My faith in this Life is complete, positive, and certain.

Knowing that all things are possible to faith, I say to my own mind: Be not afraid. Faith makes your way certain. Faith goes before you and prepares the way.

Believing that God is in everyone, I meet this God in people and I am One with everyone I meet.

Knowing that God is Peace, I open my mind to the quiet influence and the calm certainty of this Peace.

And knowing that God is Joy, I meet every situation in happiness. I commit my life unto that Power which can do all things with complete assurance.

How to Create
a Spiritual Chain Reaction

No ONE lives entirely by himself. We are all individual parts of humanity, and whether or not we realize it, each is influencing those around him, and each in his turn is being influenced by others. No doubt the thoughts and opinions and actions of the whole world finally are based on what everyone thinks and believes.

Since the explosion of the first atom bomb we have read a great deal about the possibility of a physical chain reaction that might destroy civilization as we understand it. Dr. Einstein and a number of leading physicists who understand these things better than we do have told us that there is such a possibility, and that consequently the nations must learn to live together in peace and harmony or face the other possibility, the very thought of which makes us shudder.

But science has also told us that this same power, if properly used, can become an instrument for the most rapid advance in civilization the world has ever known. The limitless energy that they now know how to loose can be used for the purpose of irrigating all the wastelands of the world. It can even be used in the field of medicine for the purpose of healing disease. It certainly can be used in industry everywhere. This energy may some day take the place of coal and oil and all the other natural energies that we use in modern life.

It appears that nature has placed before us the possibility of the greatest blessing the world has ever had or, wrongly used, the greatest destruction. And so modern scientists are telling us that before we go any farther in uncovering and utilizing the energies of nature we had better stop, look, and listen, and be certain that every new advance in science is used for the betterment of humanity and not for its destruction.

We happen to know of another kind of energy which we feel is even more important than the physical energy created through the explosion of the atom. And this is the energy of faith, of affirmative prayer and spiritual meditation. There is no reason to doubt that in the field of spiritual consciousness a chain reaction could be created which would bless the whole world. And since the world finally acts the way it thinks, should a majority of people come to believe in Spiritual Power and the benefits that can be obtained from It, they would all have a great desire to try a new kind of experiment, one that would bless instead of curse humanity.

Did you ever notice the contagion of a happy person; one who has an enthusiastic joy in living? His spirit permeates those around him, and the contagion of his personality influences his environment to such an extent that it finally changes it. Have you ever noticed the effect that a calm and poised person has on others? How they feel safe in his presence?

We are sure you have had the experience of finding yourself more or less frustrated and confused and beginning to wonder what it is all about. Then you have had the privilege of sitting down quietly with someone whose atmosphere is permeated with peace and confidence, and gradually you have felt the rough edges of your agitation disappear until finally your own atmosphere changes, and you are filled with hope and confidence.

One of the most remarkable evidences of how this silent Spiritual Force works was exhibited in the life of the late Mahatma Gandhi as he sat quietly before perhaps a million people. In these great public meetings a combined atmosphere of confidence and faith was created which they called *darshan*, which means the united Spiritual Force of a great multitude of people. Vincent Sheehan, who wrote a book about Gandhi called *Lead Kindly Light*, said that he had felt this spiritual realization so completely that it was as though he had bathed in some refreshing stream of life.

This is an example of how spiritual reaction can work. It reaches out to all around and sets in motion a chain reaction to which there is no limit.

We know that the Power that does this is Good; it is a Power of Life, Love, Truth, Beauty, and Peace. It is not only a power; It is the final Power in the Universe because It is God. And It is

240

God present everywhere and in all people. For just as there is an energy caught from the Universe and locked in the physical atom that can be loosed, so there is a Spiritual Energy caught in every person's mind and locked up in the individual life waiting to be used.

Faith and conviction are the instruments through which this Energy is used. And just as in physical science natural energy is hooked up to run a machine or a streetcar or to create light and heat for definite purposes, so we can use the Spiritual Power that is within us to heal, to bless, and to prosper those whom we think of.

It is wonderful to realize that we can sit in the quiet of our own being and consciously direct a Power greater than we are for the definite purpose of helping ourselves and someone else. This Power should be used for both purposes. For we have to get back to this simple proposition—we must use the Power to help ourselves first, in order that we may establish a realization of our ability to use It for others.

If you would bring happiness to those around you, you must first become happy yourself. But before you can become happy something has to happen to you that causes you to know that God is right where you are, that Good is the final Power in the Universe, and that Love is an all-conquering Force. You have to have confidence and self-assurance. And this kind of confidence and self-assurance comes only through having proved to yourself completely that there is a Power greater than you are, that It is a Power for Good, that It is available, and that you actually know how to use It. And the only proof you will ever have is what It does to you and to others.

Jesus understood this perfectly. He explained it simply. It is what he meant when he said, *As thou hast believed, so be it done unto thee.* In a certain sense he was a very scientific man in that he placed complete reliance on the Law of Good. And he was a practical man in that he said, *These signs shall follow.* . . . For he knew that anyone who uses the creative energy of faith will receive a direct answer or will see a sign following the use of this Power.

Jesus took the ideas of faith and prayer out of the realm of speculation and theory and put them into the realm of fact and experience. He made his religion and his spiritual conviction come alive and move through him into action. Through him It healed the sick, raised the dead, multiplied the loaves and fishes, turned water into wine, stilled the wind and wave, and above everything else It brought a consciousness of peace and security to those whom It touched.

It is this proof that we need and must have, and fortunately for us we do have this proof in an ever-increasing volume. We can pray effectively if we decide to. We can build up a faith within ourselves if we have the will. We can learn to live with a sense of confidence and security if we will just get over our fears. And we can prove that Love is the greatest healing Power in the world.

The laboratory in which we work is our own mind, the instruments are our own thoughts, and the method is affirmative prayer and meditation. Meditation draws us close to the Divine Reality so that we sense Its atmosphere and feel Its presence. When we think about Peace we become peaceful. And it is out of this feeling of Peace that we speak our affirmation of Power. It is from this Peace that we affirm the presence of Love and Truth and Goodness. Because our prayer of affirmation works exactly like any other law in nature, signs will follow our belief.

We need such signs. If a scientific man announced that he had discovered a new principle in nature but was never able to prove it, how would we know whether or not he was right? He might possibly be just dreaming about something that had no existence, and we should lose all confidence in him. But if he proved it to us we should know that he was right.

And so it is with the life of the Spirit. We say that God is all there is, Love is an all-conquering Force, faith will produce results. This is our theory. Certainly it is the most beautiful theory in the world—God, Love, and faith. But now we have to prove our claim. And in so doing we shall double our capacity to use this Power.

We should use this Power in everything we do. The Power that holds a grain of sand in place is the same Power that holds the planets in their places. There is nothing big or little or hard or easy as far as the Power is concerned. It is the same Power working in and upon everything. This is the Power which we use.

Do not hesitate to use affirmative prayer for any good purpose and for all purposes that are constructive. For in so doing you will most certainly be starting a chain reaction in that particular direction. Do not think it unimportant for you to be friendly to everyone you meet, because your friendliness will start a reaction in them which will cause them to be friendly to everyone they meet, and the thing will multiply and expand. It might even reach around the world. Let us, then, do everything we can to increase our own faith and conviction, and be equally certain that we are using this faith and conviction in everything we are doing.

If you want to start a chain reaction that will help those around you—realizing that it must begin at the center of your own being—suppose you take time daily to say these words to yourself, very simply and sincerely, and perhaps repeat the process a number of times each day:

> I know that nothing but Good can go from me and nothing but Good can return. It is my inward desire that everything I touch, every person I think of, shall be blessed and helped. It is my affirmative prayer, which I completely accept, that even as I pass people in the street some silent influence of Good shall reach from me to them.

If we make a practice of this we shall find something new and wonderful beginning to happen, for we shall be silently broadcasting our own conviction and silently starting a chain reaction which must finally accomplish its purpose, because it is dealing with a Law of Good. We must be careful to avoid thinking that we are unimportant in the scheme of things. We are the most important persons living, as far as we are concerned.

This is not egotism, not conceit; it is a simple statement of the conviction that each one of us is rooted in the Living Spirit, that we have access to the Mind of God and the Love and the Power and the Peace of the Spirit. It is a simple conviction that no matter how humble our walk in life may appear to be, it must of necessity influence its own environment. We may not be important to men, but we certainly are necessary to God.

Placing our entire trust, our complete faith, our whole conviction in this simple thought, we should walk in confidence and speak our spiritual convictions with complete assurance, knowing that there is a Presence and Power with us and for us and operating through us—a Presence and Power that knows no defeat.

Healing Is a Revelation

THE PRACTITIONER should know that at the center of every man's being there is an absolutely perfect Life, a complete Wholeness, and a deathless Principle. The work of the practitioner is to mentally uncover this ever present Reality, this Changeless and eternal Perfection.

In the uncovering process the practitioner may use many forms of thought. His thought may take the form of reasoning, logic, argument, affirmation, denial, or realization. The form of mental procedure is not important. The all-important factor is whether or not the form which he uses causes his own mind to believe, to understand, and to accept the Perfect and Spiritual Nature of his patient.

Suppose we were told that a beautiful diamond ring lay at the bottom of a trunk filled with rubbish and that it was to be ours when we should succeed in uncovering it. Should we care very much what method we used to remove the rubbish? The main thing would be to find the diamond. We should feel justified in using any method which would enable us to do this. This is equally true in spiritual mind healing. We must uncover the Perfect Man; we must remove every obstruction of thought which denies His Presence.

Spiritual mind healing is a revelation even though we go through a process to arrive at it. Each one must work out his own method and pursue his own logic. If his method and logic lead him to the right conclusion he will be rewarded by an affirmative answer.

One Healer

THE BELIEF that we do not have the ability to heal arises out of the mistaken idea that *our* power does the healing, or that the intellect does the healing. All that the will and the intellect could do is to behold or watch the process. The mind fixes its gaze steadfastly upon the Principle and then declares that this Principle is operative in human affairs, and particularly in the affairs of the one being treated.

There is but One Healer. This is the Spirit of Truth. There is but One Life Principle. This is God in us. There is but one final Law. This is the Law of Good. There is but one ultimate Impulsion. This Impulsion is Love.

That which really does the healing can never fluctuate, can never change in Its nature. It is not more one day and less the next. It is at this moment absolutely all there is and It is ever available.

We must forever rid ourselves of the idea that it is the personal man who does the healing. We must know that it is not I *but the Father that dwelleth in me, He doeth the works.* Principle operates irrespective of personal opinion, and when through acquiescence we agree that It is operating, then It must operate.

It is not enough for the practitioner to know this or to state it as his belief or to affirm it as a conviction. This is but the foundation upon which he builds his edifice of faith. These are the materials which he molds into the form of definite desire. He must not only know that God is all there is, but he must know that God exists right where the need is—not in the form of the need but in the form of an answer to the need.

The Divine Spirit is the only Actor, the true Savior, the All-in-All, and is now manifesting Itself. Being All-in-All, It has no opposition, competition, or otherness.

The Consciousness
That Heals

IN THE Fifth Chapter of James we read: *And the prayer of faith shall save the sick, and the Lord shall raise him up.* When we analyze what the prayer of faith means we discover that it is a statement of belief in some power which is able, ready, and willing to do the healing. At first this may seem like a rather cold-blooded analysis, for to pick a prayer of faith apart seems to rob it of its sentimentality. Nevertheless if we would arrive at a state of consciousness that heals we must be willing to analyze some of those things which seem so intimate and so holy that we dislike even to mention them.

The prayer of faith may be thought of as a petition, as a beseeching, or as an agonizing cry of the soul for deliverance, but whatever we term it and from whatever viewpoint we look at it, we discover that it still is an attitude of thought, a way of thinking, a movement in consciousness. If the prayer is one of faith, then this mental movement is one of acceptance, for *faith is an acceptance unqualified by denial.*

Complete faith is absolute and positive. Faith is the attitude of one who makes a complete mental surrender. It can arise only through a consciousness of complete abandonment. To the consciousness of faith there are no longer any arguments against its conviction. Faith has no opposites; it is an uncompromising mental attitude, and this is exactly what the prayer of faith is. It is a prayer, a petition, or a beseeching stated in some form of mental acceptance, unqualified belief, unquestioned trust.

While the burden of petition and the necessity of faith rests on the one making the petition or having the faith, the *response* to this petition and this faith is made by some creative agency which has the power and the willingness to perform the act. It is God who raises him up.

What is this but a statement of *spiritual cause and effect*, for it plainly states that we have our part to play in creative faith, and that as a result of our belief some principle in nature

247

responds by accomplishing the desired result. This result is obtained without further effort on our part. Another parallel statement to this is: *And ye shall know the truth, and the truth shall make you free*, which implies that there is a truth which, known, automatically becomes demonstrated.

Surely in these two statements, *The prayer of faith shall save the sick, and the Lord shall raise him up*, and *Ye shall know the truth, and the truth shall make you free*, a definite principle is involved which all can understand and use. It is the understanding of principles with the ability to make conscious use of them that constitutes what is called the scientific method in any and all research into the secrets of nature.

There are several things which happen in the pursuit of this scientific method. First someone evolves the theory that a certain principle exists in the Universe. Perhaps through observation, possibly by intuition, he conceives his theory. Having conceived this theory he begins to experiment with it, and if his theory is correct he discovers that there are certain laws involved. These laws flow out of his principle, so to speak.

Having discovered his principle, he experiments with it until he learns more of the laws which govern it. Next he uses these laws for definite purposes. What has he done? He has uttered what might be called a prayer of faith. He has felt that certain things must be true, and he has had such faith in his belief that he has actually set about to discover the laws governing his theory. If his theory is correct his faith is justified. He uncovers the natural laws of cause and effect relative to that theory. The scientific researcher always finds that there are no variations whatsoever from this result. When he uncovers a principle of nature it is changeless and invariable—he can always depend upon it.

Civilizations may come and go, empires may flourish and decay, time may pass, and change may deface all previous experience, but law is eternal. Thus the scientist learns to depend on law. His prayer of faith to his principle is a willingness to comply with the operation of its law. His cooperation and his understanding teach him how to use this law for specific purposes. We might say his prayer of faith enables him to use the principle intelligently and definitely. Thus his prayer of faith causes a response on the part of the law, and the operation of the law accomplishes the desired result. What is this but another way of saying that the prayer of faith shall save the sick and God shall raise him up?

The two ideas are identical, but because we have been so accustomed to thinking of spiritual things in unnatural ways, and because we have been so used to divorcing natural things from the spiritual, we have believed in a dualistic universe and have failed to realize that Spiritual Causation is in reality the invisible end of every objective fact.

To whom does any principle of nature belong? We have never yet heard of a sane scientific man declaring that the principle of mathematics or chemistry belongs to him because he happens to be of some particular religious conviction.

Science knows no race, no particular generation of men, and no separate dispensation. The only revelation that science knows is that revelation which comes to the listening ear, the expectant thought, the intelligent uncovering of nature's laws. When a scientific principle is uncovered it belongs not to the scientist who uncovered it, but to the God who gave it and to any individual who has sense enough to use it.

Let us take our scientific method and return to the thought that the prayer of faith shall save the sick and the Lord shall raise him up. The prayer of faith is a consciousness of acceptance, a mental conclusion in a person's mind, based on the belief that the Creative Spirit responds directly to him.

In the words of Jesus: *What things soever ye desire when ye pray, believe that ye receive them and ye shall have them.* When we bring the two words *soever* and *them* into bold relief, what do we have? We have what we might call a conscious specializing of the Law for definite purposes. The prayer of faith is a prayer which expresses faith about *some particular* thing. *What things soever* include our specific wants, our definite needs. If a man were praying for a home he would not be asking for an automobile. If he were praying that his neighbor be healed he would not be asking for money with which to take a trip.

When we return to our central thought that the prayer of faith shall save the sick and God shall raise him up, we must remember that the prayer of faith is definite—it is faith *in some-*

249

thing and *about something.* This type of prayer is not generalized, but specific. It is conscious and definite.

This brings it into line with the scientific method, for the scientific use of any law is always conscious and always definite. The principle governing the law is universal, but the use of the law is always individual. It is this element of personality injected into the Universal Law which differentiates it when we use it for specific purposes. The consciousness that heals is definite and deliberate; it is a specializing of the Universal Law. In this Law we may have absolute and implicit confidence, but we must also remember that the Law can do *for* us only what it does *through* us. Its energy and creativeness must be interpreted through our belief and imagination.

We should add another proposition to our general statement, which is: *And as thou hast believed, so be it done unto thee.* We now have these words—*what things soever, them,* and *as.* This is but another way of saying that if we want the principle of electricity to light our living room we must provide a fixture which makes it possible for the electricity to become a light. This is what is meant by the *as.* When we pray in faith we receive *what things soever* we pray for. If we believe that we shall receive them, we shall receive *them.*

There is a specific, definite thing we are to receive, but we are to receive it *as* we believe. Let us say that we are praying for supply. Because we are praying for supply we are to receive supply, according to the principle that what things soever we believe when we pray, we shall receive. If we are praying for supply, we shall receive supply, but the supply will be measured *as* we believe. The quantity of the supply must take the mold of our mental equivalent of supply.

Since we know that this, like all other principles, must be subject to definite law, and since we now understand the Law, let us again inquire into the consciousness that heals. It is recognition of the Principle, faith in the Principle, conviction that It will always respond, plus the knowledge that It can respond only by corresponding to our mental attitudes. This is the secret of the consciousness that heals.

Someone might ask whether we have left God, the warm, pulsating Divine Presence, out of this discussion. The answer

250

is: "Certainly not." It is impossible to leave God out of anything, for do we not realize that God means the very Intelligence by which we understand this Law, the very consciousness by which we use It? Never forget that this Law, being the Law of Cause and Effect, is merely a mechanical force in the Universe, though an intelligent one. When it comes to the Law of Mind we must think of It this way, for this is the way to work. God is not left out. The very inspiration which causes us to inquire into this Law is the ever-present Spirit of God forever seeking Self-Expression through us. Unless our use of this Law is impulsed by Love and Unity, we shall be automatically shut out from the most effective use of It.

Let us once more remind ourselves that the Universe is foolproof and that the Holy of Holies is entered only through the sanctuary of the heart, purified by Love, directed by Reason. The more feeling we put into our conviction, and the more faith we have in Divine Givingness, the more perfectly we shall be complying with the Law; hence we shall have greater power over It.

We should return, then, to our central theme with renewed hope and increased vigor, and most certainly with exuberant enthusiasm; with something of the spirit of an adventurer or explorer who goes out to discover new countries. The untold Good which the Creative Spirit has placed at our disposal awaits the magic touch of our consciousness to spring into expression for us, filling the cup of our desire with Its manifold gifts. Who does not wish to be well, happy, and prosperous? Is there any normal person who desires to be inactive, impoverished, and in pain? Of course not! And is there not a voice within each of us forever proclaiming and insisting upon this Divine potentiality? This urge to express is natural.

Feeling unexpressed is frustration, but energy converted into action is accomplishment, and we can be certain that the Eternal is with us and never against us when we are never against anyone else. Moreover, we can be certain that the prayer of faith will save the sick and God will raise him up. Let each, then, in his own way, lift up the chalice of expectancy for the outpouring of the Spirit, that he may receive from It all that his soul can contain.

251

Let Us Not Fool Ourselves

In the Science of Mind we do not say everything is all right when it is all wrong. We do not say peace when there is no peace, but rather we try to discover what is wrong and why we do not have peace. We do not say that people are not poor, sick, or unhappy. We ask why these things should be if the Original Cause of all things is Harmonious, Perfect, Radiant, and Happy.

In the practice of spiritual mind healing we do not deny that people are ill, nor do we minimize the need of sanitation or of medical or surgical help. We seek to aid these other agencies by uniting with them in their efforts, by being grateful for their help, and by cooperating in every way possible with what they are doing. Some day, when these things are better understood, there will be complete cooperation between all these agencies, for man is spirit, mind, and body.

The body must be properly cared for, and we should come to understand body-mind relationships. In addition to this we must never forget that man is primarily a Spiritual Being with a mind and a body. It is only when these three are brought together that we can hope to have health, happiness, and success.

A person in our field would be deceiving himself if he refused to recognize that something could be wrong with the body and the mind even though nothing could be wrong with the Spirit. This would be saying peace when there is no peace, and we must avoid such an assertion.

The spiritual mind healer recognizes the need of physical care. If he is intelligent he will never deny or seek to minimize the splendid work being done in the fields of medicine, surgery, and psychiatry. But he does have something to add to these: He has the assurance that man is One with the Living Spirit.

If many of our physical troubles come from an inward sense of uncertainty and insecurity, it follows that we must find a security greater than that insecurity which comes from a sense of being isolated from the Universe, separated from the Cause of our being, or apart from God.

252

One of the chief offices of spiritual mind healing is to relieve the mind of fear, to compose the thought and permit it to reflect the deep inner feeling that comes from conscious union with the Spirit. Science and religion should walk hand in hand in the accomplishment of this purpose.

We have no one to denounce and nothing to antagonize. Seeking cooperation with all, we should endeavor to relieve the mind of the burden of fear, doubt, and uncertainty. All of these attitudes could be wrapped in one package and labeled *a lack of faith in ourselves, in each other, and in Life.*

Let us not fool ourselves by thinking that a few idle statements will do this. This calls for a calm, insistent determination to reorganize the whole body of our thinking, until at last the little irritations and vexations of life, the too harsh differences of belief, and the disagreements with everything and everyone are redeemed. This redemption can come only through a conscious sense of our union with Something greater than we are.

In doing this we shall discover that Love is the lodestone of Life. There is nothing cold or unfeeling about the philosophy of Religious Science and the practice of the Science of Mind. To be effective, it must pulsate with deep feeling. As it reaches back to the Original Source, it must bring some knowledge of the Kingdom of Heaven into the consciousness of man. Coldness, criticism, unkindness have no place in this philosophy or in this science.

The spiritual mind healer is always humble before the Great Whole, even though he speaks with the authority of faith in that Wholeness. He must be willing to place himself in the other person's position and, with true compassion, enter into the thoughts and feelings of others, not as one caught in them or distraught by them, but as one who comes as a redeemer, a savior, to bring the Light of Truth to those who have lost the way.

If we think we can approach others in their need and help them without this deep inward feeling and desire, we are fooling ourselves. We shall find ourselves mumbling a lot of empty words which find no corresponding chord in the heart of suffering humanity. Those who engage in this practice must have a deep desire and willingness to sympathize with the person who suffers.

There is no place in this practice for arrogance or the holier-than-thou attitude. The great have always been humble. The great have always been kind. The great have always been lovers of humanity.

A New Look
at Psychosomatics

I ONCE knew a man who developed arthritis in his feet to the extent that he was unable to put on his shoes. After a little questioning I found that one of his duties was collecting rent from people who were unable to pay. He was a very sensitive person, and unconsciously he developed a physical condition which made it impossible for him to walk to the places where he must meet a situation that was so distasteful.

I have in mind a woman who became so anemic that she was at the point of exhaustion. Her real emotional trouble was loneliness. Her family had grown up, married, and established their own homes. She was left alone, in beautiful surroundings but with no inward, enthusiastic interest in life. We might say that Life had gone out of her—as though it had flowed away.

Well, these are mind-body relationships that we are hearing so much about under the general heading of Psychosomatics. *Psychosomatic* is rather an ominous-sounding term until we understand what it means. *Psyche* means the mind, and *soma* means the body. But the Greeks, from whom these terms come, also spoke of the *pneuma*, by which they meant the spirit. This we do not hear very much about in psychosomatics, but the Greeks evidently considered it of importance. They felt that man was, as our New Testament says, <u>spirit, soul, and body</u>, and that these three together constitute the whole man—the man who is a spirit with a mind and a body.

One of the ancient philosophies of China taught that man has a spiritual body, a mental body, and a physical body. And to show how intuition often precedes scientific discovery—and by thousands of years in this case—this Chinese philosopher said that the physical body cannot be in health unless there is physical circulation. Today we know that there must be proper circulation, assimilation, and elimination if the body is to be normal.

Our ancient philosopher said that man also has a mental body, and unless the mental body circulates through the physical there will be improper circulation, physically. This, too,

255

precedes our modern knowledge of body-mind relationships, particularly as they pertain to our emotional reactions to life. For we now know that most mental and emotional congestions, with their inner repressions and unconscious conflicts, are due to a lack of proper assimilation of emotional ideas.

But to get back to the ancient Chinese idea. It concludes that there cannot be proper circulation in the mental body unless the spiritual body, to which the mental is attached, circulates through the mental; that we cannot even be physically whole until there is a circulation of the spirit through the mind, and the mind through the body. This is why the Greeks spoke of the whole man as made up of *pneuma*, which is spirit; *psyche*, which is mind; and *soma*, which is body; and why the Chinese said that the three are one and must have proper interaction.

Let us now take a look at the ideas of one of the chief exponents of the teaching of Platonism, a man by the name of Plotinus who lived somewhere around the third century A.D. and who is considered to have been one of the most illumined souls of all the ages. Plotinus said that our physical organism is attached to a Spiritual Idea, which he called a Prototype or a Divine Pattern, and that when any physical organ becomes detached from its Pattern it begins to have pain and longs to return to that which will make it whole.

And we have this idea expressed in still another way in our own Scriptures, where it says that we should be perfect, outwardly, even as the Divine Spirit already is perfect, inwardly. *Be ye therefore perfect, even as your Father which is in heaven is perfect.*

This is what we call taking a new look at the modern idea of psychosomatics, upon which so many books have been written—books well worth reading that deal with body-mind relationships. And let us see if we do not find something missing even in this new outlook on life. Not that it is not wonderful as far as it goes, and altogether true, but it so happens that man is a spirit, having a mind and a body. So it is not enough to say that there must be proper relationship between the mind and body. There must be proper relationship between the spirit and the mind also. And I think we may coin a new expression (one that is entirely intelligent and without which the idea of psychosomatics can never be quite complete), which is *spiritual psychosomatics*.

We believe that man is rooted in pure Spirit; that he is a Spiritual Entity, right *now*, *here* in this world, and that it is impossible for a person to be completely well physically unless he is happy mentally. Equally we believe that it is difficult for him to be happy mentally unless his mind has the assurance that it is rooted in something stable and permanent, something transcendent and altogether whole within itself.

Man is spirit, soul, and body. To try to live in the physical organism without the mind is impossible. To try to live on intellectual thoughts without feeling is equally impossible. But not to realize that even the mind, wonderful as it is, is dependent upon something greater than itself, is disastrous. For if many of our physical troubles are the result of an inward emotional conflict based on a sense of inadequacy or defeat, and an unconscious feeling of guilt and rejection, then nothing is more certain than that the mind and the feeling must have the assurance of a Power greater than themselves, governing, guiding, and enveloping.

We get right back to the old thought, so simple yet so direct, and one of the most exalted concepts the human mind has ever conceived—*In Him* [*in God*] *we live, and move, and have our being.*

We do not deny the body, nor do we deny the mind. What we do is affirm the Spirit. We believe the body should be properly cared for   that is the office of the physician. We believe the mind should be oriented—that is the office of the wise counselor. But in addition to this we believe in the Spirit which should govern the mind. Consequently we have developed what we call a new order of spiritual meditation, where an individual takes time definitely each day to remind himself that he is a spirit, that he is one with God, and to try to bring about a deep realization that there is a Power greater than himself sustaining him; a Wise Counselor guiding him; a generous Provider who is ready and willing to meet the needs of everyday life.

No, we do not deny either the body or the mind, but we do affirm the Spirit as the Supreme Presence and the Superior Principle of all life. We do come from this thing that we call Life, or

257

God, and we are fundamentally Spiritual Beings even while in the flesh. How, then, can we hope to be whole unless we establish a right relationship within this trinity of our being, which is thought, feeling, and action?

Spiritual psychosomatics is a reality, and all our modern systems, wonderful as they are, must fall short of the ultimate goal unless and until the whole man is recognized. We try to live from the viewpoint of Divine Government in human affairs—Divine Life flowing through the physical body; Divine Intelligence governing the thoughts of the mind. For it is in God, and in God alone, that there is absolute security. Every great and gracious soul who has ever lived has recognized this and taught it.

Let us, then, think of *spiritual* psychosomatics, and consciously and deliberately unite the mind with the Spirit. For if so many of our troubles, physically, are due to inward conflicts that arise as a result of feeling isolated, unwanted, unneeded, and unloved, with the attendant sense of guilt, how can we find wholeness without first discovering some Wellspring of Life within us, some Divine inward assurance that we are all on the pathway of an eternal unfoldment? It is my belief that it would be impossible.

Perhaps Jesus had this in mind when he said we do not live by bread alone. And yet he realized the need of bread, for he fed the multitude. He never denied any of the objective things, nor any of the things which today we call subjective and unconscious, which he understood better than we do. He included the lesser within the greater, and said that if we seek the Kingdom first, all these things will be added.

It is evident that since he went about healing the sick and doing good, Jesus never rejected the idea of our objective lives as though they were illusions. He knew that the body must be fed and clothed and the mind comforted. But he knew where the real Substance came from. And so he taught a most simple method of practice—to go into the inner chamber of our thoughts and feelings, meditate upon the Divine Presence until It becomes a reality, and then conform our whole thinking to this invisible Pattern of ourselves, which the Bible tells us is *hid with Christ in God.*

Psychosomatics
and the Infant

THIS IS obviously not a complete treatise on the subject. Many books are available that fully explore the various theories of psychosomatics.

In reading these books note the few fundamental principles underlying most of them. It is the synthesis of ideas we are looking for rather than the more elaborate explanations of any one author. While they are interesting reading, they necessarily constitute only the opinions of the one writing such books. What we are interested in is putting the meaning of all of them together in one concise form. When we do this we shall discover the thread of consensus which they all hold.

To begin with, all people are born with a predetermined desire to express Life, to come to self-fulfillment through love and accomplishment, and to live creatively. We call this the Cosmic Urge to express something that seems to be inherent and fundamental in man, in animals, and in all nature.

In reading these books you will discover that two of the basic principles back of the emotional drive which everyone has are that the ego must not be rejected, and the libido must find an object.

By *libido* we mean the emotional craving for self-expression. This is based on the idea of love seeking an object upon which it may lavish its affections, and thus finding fulfillment in the object of its desire. This impulsion seems to be born with life itself, and we are told that from birth, and even prenatally, the infant should be surrounded by an atmosphere of love and attention.

Of course the infant does not reason these things out; it merely feels them. This feeling is born with the infant; it is put there by nature. The infant born into a home where it is unwanted feels an unconscious repulsion, and everything in its life becomes conditioned by this feeling. Often such infants shrink from the very touch of the hand. This is why many hospitals

259

now place the babe beside the mother where she may reach and touch it.

The whole atmosphere of the home should be one of wanting and needing and loving the infant. Otherwise the emotional reaction of the infant is that it is not wanted, needed, or loved. Its libido, which means its emotional craving for finding a love object, is pushed back into the infant mind, and unconsciously it feels itself to be an alien in its environment. This early conditioning is a great influence throughout its life, because these are the first impressions the infant receives.

This law of our emotional being, that the ego must not be rejected, is fundamental. If this is true the infant should be welcomed at the time of birth as though it were a gift from heaven, a gift of God, an offering of Love to humanity, the greatest treasure on earth, and the hope of the future.

The infant should be held not only to its mother's breast but in its father's arms. There is no danger of spoiling the child through love. Quite the reverse. The future life of the infant may be wounded without it. What more wonderful concept can we entertain than that of Jesus, who said, *Suffer the little children, and forbid them not, to come unto me: for of such is the kingdom of heaven.*

It is better to have no children than to have those who are unwanted and unloved. Parents assume a tremendous obligation when they permit themselves to have children. From the earliest point of conception there should be preparation in the parents' minds, an atmosphere of thinking, feeling, and longing for the new birth. There should be definite, daily meditations centered around the idea that the child is conceived in love and welcomed with joy. Such daily meditation will relieve tensions and assist nature in making the birth normal, natural, and easy. There must be no confusion or anxiety. Everything should flow along with a calm and delightful expectation of wonderful things that are going to happen.

The mother should feel that she is carrying a Divine treasure, the highest gift of Life. She should daily sense the formation of this embryo into a Perfect Being, and always with a great tenderness in her heart and mind.

The father should have the same mental attitude, for he is a part of the mental and emotional family life and without him the child could not be born. Some part of him enters into this birth since he is an instrument of nature in its accomplishment.

The ego must not be rejected, which means this: In the early formative years particularly, the child must feel itself to be a part of the family life. This does not mean that the child is to have its way willy-nilly, but it does mean that it is not to be harshly rejected as though it were of no importance. The counsel of children should be sought by parents, that they may feel a community of interest and spirit, for they are working out the family life together. They all are now some part of it.

Particularly when another child is born, the older one or ones should feel that they too are playing an important part in the birth. The new babe has not come to take their place in the affections of the parents, but rather that they all may enjoy it together. This is of vital importance. Too often this process is reversed and the older ones feel something is taking their place. With this inward feeling comes the unconscious sense of antagonism toward the newcomer.

All of this, too, must be taken up in quiet meditation, in spiritual unification of the family life. If these two fundamental needs are fulfilled the child will be conditioned early in life to meet anything that may come up in its experience. This is why people who speak with authority on the subject maintain that these early formative years are of vital importance.

To show how true this is, there are cases on record in which an unconscious resentment of the wife to the husband centers in the child, and babes have been known to suffer with continual diarrhea when this unconscious treatment exists. It is known too that in early life children often have attacks of asthma in order to gain the notice, affection, and care of the parents.

These things are worth your special notice as you read the books on psychosomatic medicine. We agree thoroughly with the findings of those who are giving their whole endeavor to the subject. We not only agree with them; we will go a step further and introduce the idea of spiritual values, the deep inward feeling that the family is a household of God, a Kingdom of Heaven on earth in which the parents are seeking to play the role of Heavenly Father. How can this take place unless the parents themselves believe there is such a Divine Presence, unless they believe that all conception is immaculate and that all birth is holy?

Psychosomatic medicine is wonderful. What it teaches is of vital importance to all of us. But we would add this other thought: everyone is in partnership with Life, with Love, with God, with Truth, with Beauty. To rear a family without some spiritual concept that is adequate, whatever religious form it may take, is going contrary to the first Law of our being, which is that we are all rooted in the Divine Spirit, in Perfect Life. We are all children of God.

The Doctor, the Psychologist, and the Metaphysician

WHEN THE physician and the metaphysician come to understand each other better they will cooperate with each other. It is self-evident that each is seeking to alleviate human suffering. No intelligent person would deny the need of physicians, surgeons, and hospitals. On the other hand it is generally agreed that a large percentage of our physical troubles are mental in their origin, and that all have some relationship to mental processes. It is important, then, that we understand and appreciate the work of the sincere metaphysician.

It is not at all probable that the psychologist can take the place of the metaphysician. For just as the healing of the body without an adjustment of mental and emotional states is insufficient, so the adjusting of mental and emotional states without introducing spiritual values will be ineffectual. Hence there is an important place for the metaphysician, and his cooperation should be sought.

In the early days of spiritual therapeutics it was believed that a practitioner could not successfully treat patients if they were being attended by a physician, or if they were using material methods for relief. Now we know that this was based on superstition. We no longer give it any serious thought. The metaphysician feels it a privilege to be called into consultation with a physician or with a psychologist. He has learned to appreciate the fields of medicine and surgery.

The day is certain to come when the field of medicine will recognize, deeply appreciate, and gladly cooperate with the metaphysical field. Such cooperation is far more common even today than the average person realizes. When the metaphysician stops denying that his patient is ill he will find a greater inclination toward cooperation from the medical world.

Today most physicians recognize the power of thought in

relation to the body. All realize the dynamic energy of the emotions. Just as psychology and psychiatry have been introduced into the medical world, soon the metaphysical field will be gradually understood, accepted, and appreciated.

Already there is a tendency among many psychologists to affirm the necessity of a spiritual life. Spiritual values must be introduced into the healing art, and who is going to meet this need unless it be the metaphysician?

In our experience here at the Institute of Religious Science we have been most fortunate in this connection. Our practitioners have had the opportunity of cooperating with many of the leading physicians in our community, and this experience has been happy and beneficial to everyone concerned.

In such friendly cooperation the metaphysician has the opportunity of receiving a correct diagnosis from the physician, which enables him to do better mental work. There is also an added comfort in the mind of the patient when he knows that he is having proper physical care, proper diet, and right medical and surgical attention when necessary. His mind is in a more composed state, and this enables the mental practitioner to do more effective work. It is easier to work for one whose mental attitude is poised than for one whose thought is distraught. If a patient must undergo a serious physical operation, what is more important than that his mind be at peace? This alone would reduce the element of risk.

Progress is inevitable, and cooperation among all right-minded workers in the healing arts is certain. Let us do all that we can to remove superstition, intolerance, and bigotry, which are the result of ignorance.

All should unite not only to alleviate physical suffering, but insofar as possible to remove its cause. If much of this cause lies hidden in the realm of mind, then surely those who are equipped to work in this realm are contributing their share to the meeting of a human need.

Not only should the physician recognize this, but the clergy should as well, and religious institutions should have a department for this purpose. The reason that this has not already taken place is that few such institutions have recognized the possibilities of this work.

When it is more thoroughly understood that trained workers in this field should be recognized as professional men and women entitled to compensation for their services, then something very interesting will happen. This has already been done in some religious institutions, but many have not yet recognized the necessity of making a definite profession of the practitioner's healing work in order that men and women may give their entire time and attention to it, just as physicians and psychologists do.

We look forward to the day when there will be full cooperation between physician, metaphysician, and religious leader. When the misunderstanding and superstition which separate these three fields are removed, inestimable good will be accomplished. The dynamic energy of spiritual conviction can be definitely used for the purpose of healing, but this should be done by trained workers who must be compensated for their work if they are to give their entire time and thought to it.

Someday this more or less embryonic vision will become an actuality, with the physician, the metaphysician, the psychologist, and the clergyman all working together for the common good, each in his own field, each cooperating with the other. Today wherever the inclination toward such cooperation is manifest from any pulpit, that church is packed with eager and expectant people ready to support the institution which is bringing to them this new hope through a restoration of faith.

The Story of the Lost Word

IT IS said that once each year, during the great celebration in the temple at Jerusalem, the high priest would stand on the temple steps and, amidst the shouting of the multitude, proclaim the sacred name of God, which was the word of Power. But he spoke the name only when there was such a din that no one could hear it.

It is also said that this word of Power was deposited in the Ark of the Covenant in the Holy of Holies. Frequently someone would discover it. But two lions guarded the gateway to the temple and when the one who had discovered the word of Power came through the doorway, the lions roared in such a terrific manner that he became so frightened that he forgot it.

And even today it is commonplace for us to think of some people as possessing powers beyond others. Actually there have been those throughout the ages who have exercised a power so far beyond the ordinary that they have stood out almost as gods.

Jesus never claimed to have any secrets that were kept from others. He plainly said: What I do you can do also when you learn how. He undoubtedly possessed the secret word, the lost word, or the key that actually unlocked the door to a secret chamber which revealed the mysteries of the Kingdom of Heaven. But the secret that Jesus possessed and taught was so simple that it has taken nearly two thousand years for its very simplicity to reveal itself to us.

Moses said that the word of Power is not afar off but in our own mouth, that we should know it and do it. But very few ever believed that Jesus meant exactly what he said and said exactly what he meant, or that he knew what he was talking about. The teaching of both Jesus and Moses has eluded us because whoever would believe that the lost word is in his own mouth? Whoever would believe that the Power he is searching for he already possesses, or that the secret is no secret at all?

The Bible, from beginning to end, is an elaborate method of disclosing exactly what the lost word is and what the Power is that we all are searching for.

266

Our first conclusion, then, should be that there is such a word of Power. There is a Truth which can deliver us from evil. There is a way to know this Truth and use this word in such a manner that Good, and only Good, can follow.

Now the approach to this lost word is, first of all, one that brings us back to a God of Love and Intelligence. There is but one final Power and Presence in the Universe, which is <u>God</u>; there is but one final Law in the Universe, which is <u>Good</u>; and there is but one final Impulsion in the Universe, which is <u>Love</u>. It is only through Love that we find the Presence in Its greatness and can use the Power in Its fullness.

The next thing we discover is that, having come to realize that Love alone opens the doorway to the secret chamber, we should realize that this Power must be used affirmatively. We cannot use It while we deny It. We cannot use It while our minds are filled with doubts and uncertainties about It. Love is a feeling. Faith is the key to use this feeling. Love has nothing in It that could hurt anything; faith has nothing in it that can deny any good. This is the starting point; a Love that cannot hurt and a faith that will not be denied.

When, through Love, we use faith affirmatively, a Law of Good operates on our word and brings into our experience, or into the experience of those we are thinking of, the Good we have accepted. Jesus, who revealed the Divine Presence in everything, discovered the lost word and found the Kingdom of God, which is the <u>Kingdom of Love</u>.

Jesus located this <u>Kingdom of Heaven</u> in the only place anyone can find it—<u>in our own heart and mind</u>, in our own <u>soul</u> and <u>spirit</u>. Just as Einstein discovered the secret energy caught in the atom, so Jesus discovered the dynamic, the Creative Power of the Kingdom of God in the human atom, in your life and in mine.

It is the use of this Power that we are interested in because there is a possibility here beyond our fondest dreams and our highest hopes—the possibility of knowing the Truth that can set us free from fear and want and limitation. And, the Bible tells us, finally from death itself.

But having discovered the Power and learned how to use it,

we must next apply it to every problem in life. We must not be merely idle dreamers, lost in a maze of theories that, however beautiful, can have no practical results in our everyday living.

First of all, we must realize that the Power exists and that it operates from the center of our own being, in our own minds; next, we must approach it in Love; and then, we must use it affirmatively. In actual practice the method would follow somewhat along the following lines:

We should take certain definite times every day to recognize the Divine Presence within us and around us. But even this must be more than a vague thought. It ought to resolve itself into definite statements such as:

God is the only Power and the only Presence there is, and God is right where I am. I live and move and have my being in God. God's being moves through me and manifests itself in what I am doing.

There should be no *ifs*, *ands*, or *buts* about this, no confusion. It should be simple and direct.

These are the conditions Jesus laid down. But to be effective they must now be followed by another instruction, which is: when you pray, when you state your desire, do so affirmatively. Instead of saying, "It may be that good will come to me," or "It is possible that it might," or "Perhaps it will; I hope so," we should say:

The good I desire I already possess. That which I ask for I now receive. That which I want and need I now have.

The thing that happens when we pray aright is simple. We create an attitude of complete acceptance in our own minds. When we do this, the Law of Good, which is All-Powerful, begins to operate on this acceptance and begins to rearrange all the facts and activities of our lives in such a way that what we have accepted will actually transpire in our experience.

It is important for us to remember this part of Jesus' instructions, for really it is no different from saying: If you want a garden, plant one; bury the seed in the ground and nature will take over and produce the plant. It is as though God said to the hen: Sit on the egg and I will give you a chicken.

How wonderful to realize that the lost word has been found, and found in the only place that you and I could use it—in our own mouths. How wonderful to realize that at last we have located the Divine Presence at the only place we could recognize it—within ourselves, and within everything. And how wonderful it is to know that at last we have reached our goal.

But this does not mean that we have reached the end of all things. Really, this Truth we have found marks but the beginning of a new day, a new experience, a new life—a life no longer disturbed by fear or haunted by doubts or filled with regrets of the past or misgivings over the future—a life that can be lived in its fullness today, and a life that will extend through all our tomorrows in an ever-broadening arena of experience, an ever-deepening realization of a Presence and a Power and a Peace that gives us complete security and an ever-greater vision of the more that is yet to come.

You Are a Spiritual
Broadcasting Station

DID YOU ever stop to think that you are a spiritual and mental broadcasting station, and that messages are going out from you in all directions, perhaps even while you are asleep—messages which have an influence on your environment and the people around you? And since everything moves in circles, the messages you broadcast will come back to you.

We are told that the mental atmosphere of a home can influence a dog, a cat, or a canary to the extent that they become neurotic when surrounded by unhappiness or criticism. There is a place where our physical bodies begin and leave off, but the mind has no such limitations, and our thoughts penetrate everything around us.

We are all broadcasting stations, whether or not we know it. Our thoughts, feelings, and emotions, our faiths and fears, tend to make an imprint on our environment. We are also receiving sets, but it does not follow that we must tune in to every program being broadcast. When we want to listen to a certain program we tune our radios to its wavelength. The program already is within the ether in the room, but it does not affect our instrument until we tune in to it.

It is fascinating to think that we are both mental broadcasting stations and receiving sets. And it will be even more wonderful when we learn to broadcast only the kind of messages that we wish to have return.

If a person's mind is filled with animosity and resentment people will feel it, whether or not he says a word. This animosity arouses within others who have resentment and animosity a feeling like his own. His thoughts tune in to theirs, and theirs immediately respond by flowing back into him. One accentuates the other.

On the other hand, if you are surrounded by people who have resentment and animosity, but you have none, you will not tune in. Their vibration bypasses you, and their antagonism does not arouse an equal antagonism in you because you are not broadcasting on the same mental wavelength.

It is the same with everything in life. A person whose thought is filled with the fear of failure tunes in to and picks up vibrations of failure wherever he contacts them; to his own negative thought there is added a great mass of negative thoughts, until finally it seems that the only thing he can think about is failure. In a way both his will and his imagination become hypnotized, because he is tuning in to so much negation. When a person's mind is upset, disturbed, and unhappy, all he mentally hears is discord because his inner ear is listening to a continuous turmoil.

Conversely, a person whose thought is filled with the idea of success, who has faith and confidence in himself and what he is doing, will tune in to the successful thoughts around him, the thoughts of faith and optimism and happy expectancy.

A person who confidently expects good things to happen, who expects everyone to like him, and who expects to find happiness in life wherever he goes, will not only be broadcasting these thoughts which will make other people happy; he will be receiving them in return. Because he feels friendly, people will respond with friendliness.

We all wish to be like this. We not only want to be whole ourselves, because no one can be happy unless he is whole, but we want to help others. We not only wish to broadcast good news; good news is what we want to receive.

We should decide to think on the affirmative side of life, or accentuate the positive and eliminate the negative. In doing this we must make up our minds that we are not going to receive the criticism or the negative state or the animosity of anyone. And let us not forget the importance of keeping our minds in a state of good-natured flexibility. If a tree did not bend with the breeze it would break under a strong wind.

We have to be flexible and tolerant as well as positive and affirmative. And even if someone throws a brick at us we need not catch it. It is far better just to step aside. When we catch the

271

bricks that are thrown at us it is generally for one purpose only—to throw them right back. And the first thing we know, the air is full of bricks, and what a mess that makes. It will help if we decide to play the game of life in a happy way.

Another thing we can learn is not to dwell on the obituary notices. Remember that for everyone who passes out of this world someone else comes in. Life is a river always flowing, and Life Itself never gets tired, worn out, or exhausted; It never depletes Itself. Yes, there are a lot of things in the papers besides the obituary notices. We do not have to morbidly scan all the accidents any more than we have to listen to negative conversation. More and more we are coming to see what it means to accentuate the positive and eliminate the negative.

It is true enough that birds of a feather flock together, and birds do come home to roost. But if we use the mind that God has given us, we can build our own roosts. We can even change the color of our feathers, if we want to. For the Divine Mind has created a plumage for each one of us, and has built a nest in the Secret Place of the Most High for every living soul.

All of us are rooted in the Mind of God. We did not plan it this way; this is the way it is. God is still the Supreme Power, and the Divine Spirit is still present with us no matter where we are. We must learn to tune in to the Mind of God, for when we do we are tuning in to the most dynamic Reality in the Universe.

Do not be afraid to talk to God, always remembering that God speaks a certain kind of language and there is nothing negative in it. We believe in prayerful, affirmative meditation above everything else. We believe in actually talking to God and then letting God answer. But perhaps in our confusion we talked *at* God rather than *to* Him. We have told Him how terrible everything is, how unhappy we are.

Try this: Sit or lie in complete repose, and then tell God how wonderful He is and how glad you are, how grateful. It is at times like these that we are really tuning in to the Divine, and the Divine will always respond to us. We shall always receive the comfort and consolation we need, the inward sense of security and well-being that everyone must have to be happy and whole.

Let us find a new wavelength for our mental instruments,

and as surely as we do this we shall begin to broadcast on this wavelength. We shall discover that we are not only helping ourselves but are helping everyone around us. Let us tune our mental instruments to success and happiness, to the idea of physical wholeness, and above everything else to the comforting thought *yes!* that there is a Love in the Universe which by Its very presence dissolves all hate; there is a faith that neutralizes all fear; there is a confidence that brushes aside every doubt.

God never deserts us, and we shall never have to convince God to be Good. All we have to do is reverse our whole mental and spiritual outlook on life and then the miracle will take place, because what goes out must return.

The skeptic may call this a Pollyanna-ish attitude and say that we are living in a world of unreality. Well, I have dealt with skeptics all my life and I have no awe of them—none at all. They are forlorn and unhappy people who have no guideposts to go by, no chart, no compass, and no pilot. Learn to say with Samuel Walter Foss:

> Let the howlers howl,
> And the growlers growl,
> And the scowlers scowl,
> And let the rough gang go it.
>
> For behind the night
> There is plenty of light,
> And the world's all right,
> And I know it.

No, this is not an empty or an idle dream. This is an intense Reality. Somewhere along the line we must find a faith greater than all our doubts and fears and uncertainties. Somewhere along the line we must find a Love greater than all animosity. And we must find a Peace beyond our confusion. This is the pathway that we are all seeking, whether or not we know it, and we are being guided by a loving Intelligence which evermore seeks to bring us peace and comfort, cheer and good-will, happiness and success, health and abundance.

First of all we must be sure that we are right inside, and then learn to trust ourselves because we have faith in God. We must learn to get our own broadcasting station in order. We must re-tune our own receiving set. It may take time and effort, but the goal we seek is worth the journey, and the prize that is offered is worthy of our effort. Heaven is lost only because we lack the idea of harmony; it was destined from the foundation of the world that Right should finally win, and that Love should conquer all.

We all are spiritual and mental broadcasting stations. There is a Silent Force flowing from us in every direction at all times. How necessary it is that we assume the role of the announcer and the broadcaster. How necessary that we write our own program and deliver it ourselves.

When a person speaks into a microphone in a broadcasting station his words are carried to the far corners of the earth, where they are reproduced. But the force that carries them is mechanical. It is a law, a vibration. And it is a law which actually reproduces the words he speaks, the intonations, the inflections.

And now along with this word which is broadcast goes a picture, an image of his personality. This is what we see in television, as though he were suddenly present everywhere, and the picture looks like him because it was his image, his likeness, that created it.

And so it is with the reaction of the Law of Good from a Power greater than we are. It always tends to bring back to us exactly what goes out. But we are always the broadcasters, and we can always change the pictures if we will.

MEDITATION

"Out of the abundance of the heart the mouth speaketh." Today I am keeping careful watch that I think and speak only those things that I wish broadcast from my mind and returned to me.

I desire that everything I think shall be from the heart as well as from the head. I wish to broadcast kindness and love, sympathy and understanding, peace and joy. No condemnation, judgment, or fear shall go from me to anyone or anything.

Tuning my mind in to the Divine, I draw into my own soul the essence of everything that is Good, True, and Beautiful. I draw into my own mind the realization of the Divine Presence and the Power of Good until my whole being responds.

And this is all I wish to broadcast to the world—something that will help and heal and bless, something that will cause everyone I meet to feel a new strength, a new hope. Desiring to receive the Divine Blessing in my own life, I wish to broadcast it to the whole world. And so I say to the whole world:

The Lord bless and keep thee: The Lord make his face to shine upon thee, and be gracious unto thee: The Lord lift up his countenance upon thee, and give thee peace, both now and forevermore. Amen.

Your Word Operates Instantly

SOMEONE HAS said, *Rest in faith that your thought reaches the person or condition to which it is sent.* Now we know that the objective person, place, and condition are all effects following Invisible Causation, which is Mind. And we know that thought is the instrument of Mind. We know that Mind is ever-present and is never divided; It is a complete and perfect unit. Therefore when we give a treatment we say, "This word is for this person," or "It is for this condition."

From this viewpoint the word does not have to reach any objective place; it merely describes the place. Identifying itself in Mind with the place, it is instantly at that place.

Some of the ancients have said that the Truth is that whose center is everywhere and whose circumference is nowhere. This is a good idea for us to keep in mind. It will help us to have a complete conviction that our word will always reach the desired condition; it will never fail to objectify where it should, when it should, and in the right way.

Nothing but absolute faith in the Law of Cause and Effect can give us this confidence. If we do not have this confidence we must start at the beginning again and ask ourselves the simple question: "Where did anything come from?"

It is self-evident that all things come from the Invisible, are projected by It, and remain within It. Our thought is an activity of this Invisible Causation, and when we say, "This word shall manifest in this place," we may be and we must be certain that it will do so.

The Principle of Mind
at Work

UNLESS THE one studying spiritual mind healing practices this Principle he will neither understand its nature nor appreciate its value. Therefore its practical application becomes of prime importance, and each of us should become a practitioner even if he himself is his only patient.

Like any other principle in nature, we must use this consciously and deliberately. The practitioner resolves things into thoughts, for it stands to reason that only thought can reach that which is the result of thought. We do not expect thought to reach some physical condition independent of mind. If there is such a thing as mental healing it must be based on the supposition that all form is a manifestation of mind and that mind controls its manifestation.

From the standpoint of the mental practitioner disease must be seen as primarily a thing of thought, and the diseased condition as a mental declaration of discord, an argument of confusion, or a mental experience of negation. It is the wrong kind of manifestation, and whether or not we believe that it originates in mind, the mental practitioner must confine his work to the operation of thought, for this is his field.

The mental practitioner resolves things into thoughts and proceeds to untangle the wrong thought through the recognition of the Omnipresence of God or Truth. Mind can never operate outside of consciousness, and if the practitioner believes that disease or conditions are external to consciousness, and treats them as if they were, he will soon discover that he is trying to bombard them from without. He is trying to make mind reach something which is not mental, or trying to make thought reach something which is outside of mind. He is doomed to failure.

When he realizes that everything is either Mind in an absolute state, or mind in a concrete form, he has no difficulty in rearranging thought positively instead of negatively. This is exactly what a spiritual mind practitioner does. He does this deliberately and consciously. The name of a disease signifies to him merely the thought about the disease, whether a person believes it to be curable or incurable, whether he believes it will take a long time or a short time to heal, and it signifies the mental reaction of the race consciousness. This is the only significance the name can have to the practitioner, for in this field he cannot treat one disease as organic and another disease as functional, since from the standpoint of our practice all disease is a negative statement in mind.

Now I am fully aware that the thought that all disease is a negative statement in mind is a rather difficult one to understand and is likely to produce considerable confusion in the minds of those who hear it for the first time. But let us remember that this field is entirely different from other fields. Here we have a practitioner who treats through the instrument of thought alone. He is not antagonizing any other form or method of practice; he is not refusing his patient the right to have any other form of practice while he is being treated mentally.

He is a spiritual mind practitioner, and from his viewpoint, no matter what the condition is and no matter what it has been pronounced to be, it must remain a thing of thought, for as already stated, if it is not thought, how is thought going to reach it? And the practitioner is thoroughly convinced that thought does reach it, that pure Mind exists everywhere, and that pure Mind is at the very center of the diseased condition.

The practitioner must conceive of pure Mind as being in a state of harmony. Instead of feeling that he is treating some terrible disease, he feels that he is explaining why this negative condition need not be. His explanation is to himself about his patient; it is never to his patient. What, then, is he doing? He is clearing up his own consciousness, and in order to do this he must resolve the disease into a thing of thought.

The practitioner uses any statement about a particular case which will untie the mental knots in his own consciousness about his patient. Generally, he is confronted with the idea of fear, and he should begin his treatment by removing all sense of fear. He must know that there is nothing of which to be afraid and he must make a definite statement not only that there is nothing of which to be afraid, but that there is no one to be

278

afraid. He must say this for his patient, not *to* his patient but *about* him. When giving a treatment he never addresses the patient by name or speaks to him personally in mind; he merely identifies his treatment with his patient by saying, "This treatment is for so-and-so," and then he forgets all about his patient objectively and gives the treatment within his own consciousness.

If God is All in All there is nothing of which to be afraid, for perfect love casts out fear; where love is, fear cannot enter. The practitioner knows that fear cannot operate through his patient or through anyone around him. Man is a spiritual entity; therefore he has no disease, nothing which is opposed to life assails him, nothing is operating through him which can produce death, since there is no death.

If he is using the argumentative method of treating he brings an array of arguments to support his position that God is All in All, and to reject the belief that it is necessary for his patient to suffer from this particular disease, or any other. The form of the argument and the power of the argument is merely to produce realization. Argument itself is not realization any more than musical technique is harmony. The argument merely gives form, definite intention, specific direction to the treatment. Argument leads toward a realization of the Allness of Good. Probably more people are helped through argument than by any other method, although in every instance one should seek a growing conviction and an increasing realization of the meaning of one's argument.

The Life Principle Itself is the healer, or if one chooses to put it this way, God is the healer. The patient is a spiritual entity and there is nothing about a spiritual entity that needs to be healed. Disease of itself is not person, place, or thing, and has no location. It did not begin in time, it has no duration in time, it does not end anywhere in time. It is no longer being experienced in the consciousness of the one who has been affected by it. These are merely suggested arguments for the purpose of clearing up the mind of the practitioner, for his thought is the only thought that he can heal in this practice.

The practitioner assumes that the Body of God is perfect, including every manifestation of Itself. Man is the Body of God. For instance, the idea of vision, of speech, or of any other faculty or organ of the body is an Eternal Idea, an Infinite Idea, and an Omnipresent Idea.

The practitioner treats to know that there is only one Perfect Pattern of lung or heart; there is only one Idea of lung or heart, because there is only one Spirit, one Absolute *I AM*, one Eternal God, or one everlasting Reality. The heart God made is a perfect heart, the lung God made is a perfect lung. It may help to realize this better when one knows that the physical vibration of heart or lung is the same wherever the manifestation of heart or lung takes place, whether it is in an animal, a bird, or a man. It shows the universality of the idea of heart or lung and helps him to realize that when he declares for the oneness of any Divine Idea, he is declaring the Truth about that Idea.

The practitioner, then, treats of the oneness of manifestation, and it is about this oneness that he makes his declaration, always declaring that this oneness is true about his patient. It would not be enough to say the Heart of God is perfect and there is only One Heart, but he must complete this statement by saying, "This Heart of God is the heart of this patient. Nothing ever happened to it, it didn't enlarge; there was never any tension around it, there was never any pain in it; it never caused pain and there never was any emotional state that caused it to pain. It was never repressed, depressed, or suppressed. It was never tired or worn out, it never broke down, and the whole circulatory system, being a part of the Divine Life Impulse, never was impaired."

Heart is a Divine Idea, and the Heart of Reality is the heart of this particular person whom you are treating. The Divine Reality must be considered as perfect, complete, ever-present, always active, ever-available, and the negation of this must be reversed in the mind of the practitioner; that is, the denial of it must be understood to have no power.

Thus the spiritual practitioner converts things into thoughts. He can think not only of *our Father which art in heaven*, but also of our perfect body and perfect organism which are in the Kingdom of Reality now, and to the practitioner this must be an intense reality. He must believe what he says. He must understand that the Kingdom of Heaven is at hand. He cannot do this unless he contradicts much that is experienced. Mentally he never deals with a material condition or a diseased condition, but he knows that since Spirit is the only Power there is, there is no mind which has been hypnotized into believing that there is or can be any opposite to Spirit.

The practitioner must know that Creative Mind hears and answers his thought because Creative Mind is ever-present. He knows that right idea is the operation of true Principle, whether it be in the science of mathematics or the Science of Mind. The Principle cannot help hearing. The mind which makes the request is the Mind which fulfills the desire, since there is but One Mind. If the practitioner can bear in mind that what he is destroying is belief, he will do well.

Now right here the uninstructed will say, "Do you mean to tell me that I do not experience discord or disease?" We do not deny that man experiences discord or disease. What we affirm is that the experience is the belief in form and that the disintegration of the belief will produce a corresponding disintegration of the form. That is why we so continuously say: *Turn things into thoughts and heal the thought.* In mental practice the practitioner must deal with belief or with thought, and he must deal with form as though it were belief and thought, else, as we have already stated, how can he conceive that thought can reach that which is not of the nature of mind, thought, or thinking?

For instance, if someone should draw a picture of a horse on a blackboard, and others seeing it should believe it to be a horse, it still would be nothing other than a picture. Now you come along and take an eraser and rub out the picture. Where is the horse? It was never a thing in itself, it only appeared to be an entity. Your knowledge that it could be rubbed out and your act of rubbing it out were but two ends of the same thing. So the mental practitioner must realize that his argument or his realization rubs out the argument of negation which projects discord. He cannot do this unless he understands that the projection of the discord is just as much a thing of thought as what he calls the thought behind such projection.

It is perhaps a little difficult to make this clear, but it means that the practitioner works in a field of mind and thought alone, and all he has to neutralize is thought, never things. It is one of the most subtle parts of this entire system of practice, one to

281

which we should pay the most careful attention. For the root of all evil is in mental conviction, not in evil itself. The axe of Truth has to be laid at the root of evil and the false condition chopped away, so to speak. Therefore spiritual enlightenment in the mind heals the body because the body is mind in form and because spiritual enlightenment changes the form of thought in mind.

If this is true there is no adversary, no opponent, no opposition. When in the mental argument a practitioner reaches the place where he perceives or understands the Truth of his argument, his argument ceases as argument and begins as realization. It has passed from analysis into conclusion. It is this realization which is the creative power in treatment. And what is it that is to be realized? The perfection of the patient, the perfection of all people, the harmony of the condition. Furthermore, whether one is treating to heal physical disorders or treating to heal financial disorders, or any other disorders, the operation of the Principle is identical.

Substance is supply. There is but one Substance, this Substance is Omnipresent, It is right where the need appears to be, and It meets the need according to the acceptance of the one who experiences the need. It could do neither more nor less than this. One must accept supply if Substance is to interpret Itself as supply in one's experience. The practitioner realizes the Omnipresence of Substance, hence the ever-availability of supply.

This in no way turns Spirit into matter, nor does it materialize Spirit. It merely gives form to Substance. As the physical universe has been likened to the Meditation of God, so our individual experiences may be likened to our meditations of life. And our meditations of life are our awareness, our realization— an inner feeling and conviction which transcends the experience taking place in an objective world. From the standpoint of practice, there is but one Substance, but this Substance is forever active as supply. Just as there is but one Heart, which is forever active as perfect circulation and perfect impulsion, so there is one Substance forever operating as supply.

The practitioner does not necessarily need to treat his patient for specific things. He realizes the activity of Substance in the experience of his patient, and that whatever mental equivalent his patient has will automatically be filled. It is well that we understand this, because it is self-evident that the patient brings his bowl of acceptance with him. In other words, he has thoughts and desires which he wishes to have fulfilled, which are personal to him and individual with him. The practitioner pours his realization of abundance over the entire situation, and wherever there is a mold it is automatically filled, for since Substance is Omnipresent It can fill all molds without depleting Itself.

So the practitioner declares that there is but one Substance and his patient's need is supplied out of this Substance today—whatever his patient needs, everything he needs, and all that he needs is amply supplied. The limitless activity of the Infinite now manifests in form in this man's experience. His activity always produces good results; it always produces abundance because Infinite Substance is limitless supply.

Now this Substance cannot be depleted. It remains exactly what It is and Its nature is to flow forever. Therefore, wherever there is an acceptance there is a manifestation. Wherever there is a belief which inhibits manifestation, the manifestation is limited to the acceptance. That is, through unbelief we still believe in a limited form of that which we deny. The practitioner treats the form of lack as a belief in lack. He heals the belief. He works to know that Substance is Omnipresent, is forever flowing into the experience of his patient as supply, as right action.

The patient himself brings the mold of money or house, of automobile or a suit of clothes, of position or environment. The practitioner does not have to supply the mold for his patient. To assume that he has to do so would be to assume that he must take control of his patient's thought, which would be an attempt to hypnotize his patient. Naturally, he would be unsuccessful.

The practitioner does not supply the mold of thought for his patient in any instance. He merely realizes that the mold which his patient supplies is filled by the Substance which forever flows into form. Therefore the practitioner has no personal responsibility. It is his business to realize the flow of Substance; it is the privilege of the patient to receive that Substance in the form of his own desire.

How to Give
a Spiritual Treatment

FOR *PHYSICAL HEALING*

TAKE A definite time at least twice each day to be alone, sit down, compose your mind, and think about God. ~~Try to~~ arrive at a deep sense of peace and calm. Then assume an attitude of faith in a Power greater than you are.

Say: *The words I speak are the Law of Good and they will produce the desired result because they are operated on by a Power greater than I am. Good alone goes from me and good alone returns to me.*

You are now ready to give a specific treatment for yourself. Begin by saying: *This word is for myself. Everything I say is for me and about me. It is the truth about my real self.* (You are thinking about your spiritual nature, the Divine Reality of yourself, the God in you.) Say: *There is One Life, that Life is God, that Life is perfect, that Life is my life now.* Say this slowly and with deep meaning.

Next say: *My body is a manifestation of the Living Spirit. It is created and sustained by the One Presence and the One Power. That Power is flowing in and through me now, animating every organ, every action and every function of my physical being. There is perfect circulation, perfect assimilation, and perfect elimination. There is no congestion, no confusion, and no inaction. I am one with the Infinite Rhythm of life, which flows through me in love, in harmony, and in peace. There is no fear, no doubt, and no uncertainty in my mind. I am letting that Life which is perfect flow through me and become my life. It is my life now. There is One Life, that Life is God, that Life is perfect, that Life is my life now.*

Next, deny everything that contradicts this. Follow each denial with a direct affirmation of its opposite. In a certain sense you are presenting a logical argument to your own mind, based on the belief that there is but One Life, which is perfect and which is your life now. The evidence that you bring out in your argument should reach a conclusion which causes your own mind to accept the verdict of perfection. Remember you are not talking about your physical body as though it were separate from the spirit, but about God in you; therefore you will have no difficulty in convincing yourself that this God in you is perfect.

You have now reached a place of realization in which you enter into a feeling of assurance that comes from a consciousness of the Divine Presence in, around, and through you. This period of realization should last for several moments, during which you sit quietly accepting the meaning of what you have said. Then say: *It is now done. It is now complete. It is now perfect. There is One Life, that Life is God, that Life is perfect, that Life is my life now.*

Between these periods of meditation try to keep your mind poised in such a way that you do not contradict what you have said in your treatment. Keep your mind open at all times to a Divine influx of new inspiration, new power, and new life. Accept what you have said with joy and gratitude.

FOR *BETTERMENT OF CONDITIONS*

In TREATING for the betterment of conditions you are using the same Principle but for a different purpose, therefore you would say something like this:*

Everything that I do, say, or think is governed by Divine Intelligence and inspired by Divine Wisdom. I am guided into right action. I am surrounded with friendship, love, and beauty. Enthusiastic joy, vitality, and inspiration are in everything I do. I am aware of my partnership with the Infinite.

Every thought of not being wanted, of being afraid, of uncertainty and doubt is cast out of my mind. My memory goes back

---

*NOTE: When treating another, say: "This word is for him (or her)," then continue exactly as though you were treating yourself.

to God alone, in whom I live, move, and have my being. A complete sense of happiness, peace, and certainty floods me with light. I have confidence in myself because I have confidence in God. I am sure of myself because I am sure of God.

The Spirit within me knows the answer to any problem which confronts me. I know that the answer is here and now. It is within my own mind because God is right where I am. I now turn from the problem to the Spirit, accepting the answer. In calm confidence, in perfect trust, in abiding faith, and with complete peace I let go of the problem and receive the answer.

I know exactly what to do in every situation. Every idea necessary to successful living is brought to my attention. The doorway to ever-increasing opportunities for self-expression is open before me. I am continuously meeting new and larger experiences. Every day brings some greater good. Every day brings more blessing and greater self-expression. I am prospered in everything I do. There is no deferment, no delay, no obstruction or obstacle, nothing to impede the progress of right action.

I identify myself with abundance. I surrender all fear and doubt. I let go of all uncertainty. I know there is no confusion, no lack of confidence. I know that what is mine will claim me, know me, rush to me. The Presence of God is with me. The Mind of God is my mind. The Freedom of God is my freedom.

Today I bestow the essence of love upon everything. Everyone I meet shall be lovely to me. My soul meets the Soul of the Universe in everyone. This love is a healing power touching everything into wholeness. I am one with the rhythm of Life. There is nothing to be afraid of. There is nothing to be uncertain about. God is over all, in all, and through all. God is right where I am. I am at peace with the world in which I live. I am at home with the Divine Spirit in which I am immersed.

Treatment Deals
with Thought

TREATMENT DEALS with thoughts rather than with people. We must be careful never to associate a negative condition with the person who suffers from it. It does not belong to your patient nor to anyone else.

Perfection is already accomplished; It was and is and will remain. There is a Perfect Idea behind every organ and there is a Perfect Actor behind all life. The more completely you realize this the more effective will be your mental treatment, because this treatment is a conscious pronouncement about the Spiritual Self and Its relationship to the Universe or God.

The treatment should be simple, unlabored, calm, but designed to convince the thought of the one who gives it. The person who gives the treatment must *believe* that there is one Perfect Body of God and that this Body is made manifest through his patient.

The practitioner does not feel that he must create this Perfect Body; his business is to *reveal* It, to announce It, to pronounce It. He knows that his treatment will reach the person for whom he is working without any effort on his part other than the statement that it is for that certain person.

One Mind in Three

MAN HAS one mind, but for convenience we separate it into three classifications: the conscious, the subjective (or subconscious), and the Christ Consciousness. We must be careful, however, that we do not divide man into three parts, for his conscious mind is the use he is making of his 'Spiritual' faculties, while his subconscious mind is the unconscious use he is making of the Universal Law of Cause and Effect.

It is an interesting fact that we can reach the subconscious and give it direction by use of our conscious faculties. The conscious faculty is what impresses the subconscious reaction.

The subconscious of itself, being merely a part of the Law of Cause and Effect, may be reorganized by the conscious direction given it. This is why mental treatment is a definite act of thought and not a haphazard or chaotic arriving at confused conclusions.

The entire theory of the control of conditions through the conscious use of thought rests on the proposition that conscious thought activity may reorganize subjective reactions, and that subjective reactions will return as objective situations as directed.

Hence we see that spiritual mind treatment is definite. It always has a conscious purpose in mind. To believe this, to understand it, and to know how to use it enables us to rise above old situations and to create new ones.

Mental Technique
for Spiritual Treatment

UNLESS THERE were a definite method of procedure in spiritual mind healing, it could not be considered scientific. Unless a definite technique could be delivered, there would be no intelligent approach to the subject. Unless one could learn this technique and consciously apply it, it would not be universally applicable. But the Science of Mind is just as definitely scientific and just as positively based on an actual principle as any other science.

The fact that we are dealing with invisible forces makes them no more intangible than any other force of nature with which we deal. All life is invisible, all energy is invisible, all causation is invisible. The Principle of Mind is invisible and Its practice is invisible, but Its results are the Word made flesh.

Since the modern approach to mental science has developed simultaneously along both the psychological and metaphysical fronts it is well to analyze our position and determine where we agree with the psychological method and where we depart somewhat from it. For whether or not we are conscious of the fact, we more or less combine both methods.

Unfortunately, many people in the metaphysical field do not understand this, and in their ignorance of the subject deny psychology a place in their system, and just as unfortunately many psychologists do not understand the metaphysical viewpoint, and in their ignorance deny its place in their field. With the broader understanding of both fields there will be a more conscious cooperation, for each in its own way is seeking to help and to be helped.

The approach of psychology to mental healing has already passed through several distinct stages. Starting with mesmerism it developed into hypnotism; next into mental suggestion; and finally into mental explanation, which is the method employed by most psychologists; that is, if we reduce their methods to the simplest interpretations.

Neither psychiatry nor analytical psychology is hypnotic, nor do they practice mental suggestion. Their entire field is one of explanation. In analytical psychology the explanation is drawn from the patient's consciousness in such a way that he self-sees his trouble, and by this self-seeing the difficulty is supposed to be dissipated.

In the earliest stages of analytical psychology it was thought necessary that the analyst should draw out of the consciousness of his patient every trivial incident which might have led to his mental and physical undoing. This has made of analysis one of the most subtle of arts, as well as one of the most difficult practices. If one expects to draw out of the consciousness of one's patient the most trivial incidents of his life, the method becomes painstaking, laborious, and more or less cumbersome; generally the treatment must cover a long period of time.

There is a tendency today among many practicing analysts and psychiatrists to short-cut this method somewhat, and to drain more quickly the psychic confusion from the unconscious memory of the patient, thus producing a quicker response.

In spiritual mind healing we do not have to uncover every unconscious cause of mental confusion with its attendant physical distress. We know that broad, generalized statements often effect a healing of disease without either the practitioner or the patient having any specific knowledge of its cause. We know that the clearer one's consciousness is and the more definitely certain one is that Spirit is the Absolute Cause of all, and that Good alone governs, the more quickly will healing take place. We know that silent recognition and realization elevate the consciousness to a place of greater power and make possible a more immediate manifestation. Jesus did not analyze; he announced.

In actual practice we combine analysis with realization. Sometimes we use one and sometimes the other, but more often we combine the two. It is probably safe to say that, in most practice, the combination of these two methods has been more effective than the use of one to the exclusion of the other. No one appears to be in a continual state of conscious Spiritual Power, but we all have the capacity to give scientific mental treatments. We must resort to our definite technique for practice, and through mental statements arrive at a spiritual conclusion, a consciousness of the Allness of God and the ever-present availablity of Good.

We claim to have a science which can be delivered to all intelligent persons, and we claim that the average person can effectively use this science provided he complies with its Principle and Law.

It is therefore necessary to deliver a definite technique and a conscious method for procedure. That is why we start with the proposition of Perfect God, Perfect Man, and Perfect Being. This is the spiritual Principle which the mind, through right ideas, seeks to demonstrate, and in so doing it will probably combine argument with realization. Just what do we mean by argument in mental treatment? We mean the phases of thought through which the mind goes to arrive at a conclusion. The following example may help to clarify this point:

A person suddenly finds himself feeling greatly discouraged and mentally depressed. He knows that God is neither discouraged nor depressed. He knows that nothing has happened to the Divine Reality. He might, by sitting in quiet contemplation for a few moments, so fill himself with this Spirit of Reality that his negation would disappear as mist before the sun. This of course would be the ideal way. But suppose in contemplating this he fails. His next step is to resort to his mental technique. He begins to make definite statements, similar to the following:

God is neither sad nor depressed. There is no life apart from God; therefore my life is God. Consequently I am neither sad nor depressed. God is not afraid of anything. My mind and the Mind of God are One Mind; therefore my mind cannot entertain fear.

At this place in his treatment, the image of fear or some memory of fear may arise. Immediately he would say:

This fear is not person, place, or thing. It has no law to support it, no power to uphold it, no consciousness to conceive it, no law to enforce it, no person to express it.

He would be repudiating the negation, and would follow such repudiation by the affirmation:

My Mind is the Mind of God—calm and peaceful, unafraid and certain. All Presence, all Power, all Peace, and Joy are mine today. I am not afraid of anything because I now see that there is nothing to be afraid of. The images of fear cannot operate through me. I am completely separated from any belief in fear. I do not remember anything in the past of which I was afraid. I do not anticipate anything in the future of which I shall be afraid, and I am not conscious of anything going on today of which I am afraid.

There is no discouragement. I am protected by the only Power there is. I live in the only Presence there is. This word completely neutralizes, obliterates, casts out, expels every thought of fear and every belief that there is anything to be afraid of.

A person making statements similar to these would probably find himself gradually lifted up mentally to the place in thought where he would begin to feel at ease. The images of doubt would no longer assail him. Calm and peace would accumulate in his thought. In such degree as he embodied the meaning of the words which he had just spoken, a sense of realization would fill his consciousness with peace. This sense of realization he should mentally hold in his consciousness for a period of time, and finally it would become permanent.

One thing, however, we must be careful to avoid, and that is fooling ourselves. Our work rests upon demonstration, and whatever method we use, how much argument we employ, or whatever state of realization we may reach, we must prove our position. We must actually demonstrate that thought manifests in form, in actual conditions, in objective life. If thought is not manifesting in this way in our experience, we must work with ourselves until it does. We must never take *No* for an answer. To do so would be repudiate the Principle in which we believe, and wreck our faith in It.

Therefore we must persist in our effort until the purpose we have in mind is accomplished in actual fact and not merely in fancy. We must always remember that proper use of the Science of Mind is not a practice through which we fall into a mental reverie as an escape from objective life. Our work is not done properly unless something happens as a result of it.

This something that happens we can always weigh and measure objectively. For instance, if we are treating someone who has high blood pressure our work is not accomplished until the patient can go to a physician for proper and thorough physical examination and receive the verdict that the blood pressure is normal.

Treatment is not for the purpose of helping us either to avoid reality or to endure unhappy situations. It is for the express purpose of changing situations, and unless situations or conditions are changed as a result of the treatment, we have missed the mark. Always we must insist that we demonstrate our proposition, for our motto is: *To do is to know, and to know is to do.*

Right Thought Will Always Externalize Itself

EVERY TREATMENT should be a Law unto itself. When you give a treatment you must know that your word is the Law unto the thing which is spoken. Since we are dealing with a mental or a spiritual Principle it follows that the one using this Principle must do so mentally; his operation is a thing of thought; therefore his thought can have only as much Power as he knows it to have.

Words of doubt have no affirmative Power. We must know that our treatment is a good treatment, a successful treatment certain to accomplish. Every word you speak is the Presence, the Power, and the Activity of the Law within you. It is the Law unto the thing whereof you speak. It cannot and will not return unto you void, but will accomplish the purpose you have in mind. It can and will heal and demonstrate; It can and will produce the desired result.

You are not willing this to be so; you merely have a willingness that it should be so, a willingness to believe. There must be a persistent belief in the Power of your own word. You must know that the Law of Good is All-Powerful, and that no evil is ordained or intended. You must realize that your knowledge of the Law of Good dissipates all evil and all manifestation of evil.

You must know that right thought will always find an objective form and will always externalize itself. You must believe the Will of God is always toward Goodness, Truth, and Beauty. Goodness, Truth, and Beauty cannot be reversed because they have no opposites, but your knowledge of the Truth can reverse every so-called law of evil.

Direction and Intention

NOTHING IS more definite than mental work. Mental work is not daydreaming or fantastic wishing. It is a deliberate act of the mind, a conscious, moving action of thought in a certain definite direction, and we should think of it from this viewpoint. The conscious mind chooses what it wishes the subjective Law to act upon. It gives direction to a Power which is Infinite compared to its own conscious capacity.

But is this not true of all laws of nature? We are always using laws which of themselves do nothing for us until we consciously use them. If we would think of the laws of thought in the same practical manner as we think of other principles in nature, and if we could free ourselves from all superstition in using Spiritual Laws, realizing that they also are natural, we should have the Power at our command which we so greatly feel the need of and which we so deeply desire to know how to use.

This is what differentiates a practical, experienced, and scientific worker in this field from one who merely hopes, wishes, or wills things to happen. A scientific worker always knows what he is doing. He always has a method of procedure. He has a definite technique and he follows this technique specifically. He uses thought, not as will power, not as concentration, not as coercion, but always with definite direction and conscious intention.

The Use and Meaning of Words in Mental Treatment

THE ENTIRE basis for spiritual mind healing lies in the assumption that we are now living in a Spiritual and Mental Universe; that Law is Mind in Action; that thinking and action are the same. And if thinking and action equal the same thing, certain kinds of thinking must constitute certain kinds of action. It logically follows that if one kind of thought produces a certain effect, then an opposite thought must produce an opposite effect.

Mental treatment is Mind in Action. A person should use those words which convey a meaning to his own thought. For instance, if he says, "This word is the law of elimination," he must feel that any condition which does not belong is actually being eliminated.

Since it would be impossible for him to believe that Mind could operate upon some matter or substance which is unlike Mind, he must first have resolved things into thoughts. For the practitioner does not treat a body separate from consciousness; he treats consciousness alone. Hence the state of inaction which he seeks to remove, so far as mental treatment is concerned, is neither a state of material nor physical inaction; for he has reduced the whole process to a state of mental inaction. It is evident that unless he could do this he could not give an effective mental treatment.

Thought alone can reverse thought, thought alone can handle thought, and only thought can demonstrate over that which is a result of thought. Therefore the mental practitioner theoretically resolves everything into Mind and proceeds upon the basis that Mind is form, or takes form, and that the form which it takes is still Mind. Our work is done in the realm of Mind alone. The words that we use should be simple, direct, and to the point, and should signify a meaning to our own consciousness.

The process of reasoning in treatment must be one which

establishes man upon a spiritual basis, enthrones him in a Kingdom of Good, and gives him dominion over all apparent evil.

If you say four and four make eight, and eight has a meaning because you have already experienced handling eight marbles or eight oranges or eight chairs, then when you say four and four make eight you understand what those words mean. But do you understand what saying four million and four million means, even while your intellect announces eight million to be the answer?

Words must have value to the inner comprehension. I am sure Jesus understood this when he spoke of his word as being Spirit and Life. He spoke of his words as though they were entities. The thought and the thing cannot be separated. *The words that I speak unto you, they are spirit, and they are life,* implies that the words possess not only power but almost a degree of personalness.

In mathematics a person can correctly use his principle only as far as his understanding goes. This is also true in mental treatment. What is this understanding which he must have and which he must pour into the words which he speaks? He must understand his relationship to Being Itself, to God, to the Universe, and to Reality. There must be an interior awareness, a realization that Good is all the Power there is.

A practitioner uses words which imply to his own imagination the idea of movement, of explanation, of action or reaction, or whatever the desire is. That is, when he uses the word *elimination* he must know that something is being eliminated. He must have unqualified faith that there is a movement toward the desired elimination simultaneous with the word he uses. The practitioner must come to realize that thoughts and things are not separated; they are identical.

If he says, "Substance is supply and supply is money," and if he desires to demonstrate money, when he uses the word *substance* he should feel the presence of substance. Otherwise he is merely using a lot of words which have no meaning.

Surely we cannot separate thoughts from things in our treatment and hope to demonstrate things through thinking. For unless thoughts were things, then thoughts could not change what we call *things*. Indeed they would have no power over them whatsoever. It is upon this proposition that our whole science is based. Since thoughts are things, different kinds of thoughts are different kinds of things. When the practitioner uses the idea of substance and supply in his imagination, the idea should not be divorced from the actual presence of whatever he thinks supply is, or whatever supply means to him.

Suppose he were conceiving the idea of *home*. It would not be enough for him to say, "I'm but a stranger here, heaven is my home." In this world *home* means house, tent, a place of residence, a place to live. Therefore if he wishes to demonstrate a home, when he uses the idea *home* there should be some corresponding reaction to the word which means the actual presence of a right place in which to live.

What words we can really use with spiritual meaning, significance, and reality constitute the stage of consciousness we are entertaining at any particular time. As a matter of fact our state of consciousness is what we are, and if we happen to be in business and wish to treat for right action we must realize that right action means being busy in the thing that we are doing. Business is the activity of consciousness, and the business of Mind is never inactive. Nor is the business of Mind limited to two, four, six, eight, ten, twelve, etc. It is as limitless as is our concept of it. Spirit is Good, therefore business is good, and we should know that our business represents our oneness with supply, with the Creative Cause, with the Creative Givingness, with the limitless activity of the Creator.

Our business enterprise is the demand which we make upon supply, and since the demand is answered, and can be answered, only in terms of the demand made, and since there is no gap between, because both supply and demand are mental or spiritual, then it follows that supply follows demand, while demand does not limit supply but measures it out at the level of the demand made.

One man working for success might have the idea of enough money with which to pay the rent; another might have the idea that after the rent was paid he would have a few dollars left over; while still another might have the idea that paying the rent was merely attending to a detail and that out of the limitless abundance he should have money left which he could share with others.

There must be some reason why some succeed and others fail if the Universe in which we live is Intelligent. It is impossible to conceive of Mind as ever being unexpressed, and wealth and poverty are expressions of Mind, fulfilling an idea. The thought of success will create success. Mind thinks and it is done. Man's business is God's business and God's business is man's business, and there is only one business, which is the business of Life. Life is never inactive, never inadequate; it is always perfect, and your consciousness of right action is perfect. Your word is perfect and the thing to which the word gives form is perfect, and abundance is the only law there is—but your words must have meaning, and their meaning is their power.

If you are treating to heal a physical disease, you should realize that material appearance is a mental formation rather than a law unto itself. Your realization that this formation is not necessary, and the significance of the statements which you make in declaring that your word is the law of elimination of the condition, should have the same reaction in your own thought as that which would be produced if, while you were looking at something, it should disappear. You would immediately recognize the omnipresence and the omnipotence of God, and to such degree as your recognition of the omnipresence of Good signifies to your own thought the annihilation of the negative physical condition, the condition will cease to be.

When the practitioner says, "This word is for so and so" or "for such and such a purpose," his definite intention specifies the place or the purpose, and this is all he needs to do. From then on his work is within himself, and his work is a combination of thinking, which through argument or realization brings about a complete acceptance of the desired fact. It would be impossible to do this unless facts could be reduced to states of consciousness.

That which needs to be externally changed is not a thing in itself but a physical state of consciousness. This is the crux of the whole matter; it is the finest of all points in metaphysical practice; it is the essence of the subject, but unfortunately it is too often overlooked. The external condition is not a thing but thought externalized, and thought externalized is still thought. A mental conclusion objectified is still a mental conclusion.

This is the meaning of argument in giving mental treatments. The argument is for the purpose of convincing the mind of the practitioner that the condition which needs to be changed is not a thing in itself; that back of it is a perfect Universe, God, the All-Being. But unless the words used by the practitioner in such argument have a definite meaning to him, implying life and action, they will have no power.

If we can understand that objective nature is a thing of thought, a Divine language, still plastic in the imagination of its conceiver, we shall know how to liken the laws of nature to the laws of thought, for this a metaphysician must do.

His work is specific in that it meets and repudiates a claim where the claim is—it denies it where it is and affirms the opposite—for he must meet the false argument either with an argument that is directly opposite to it, or by a realization which denies the argument without controversy. This is called *spiritual realization*. Therefore the condition must be met as though it were the surface form of a mental argument or state of consciousness, a suggestion rather than a thing itself.

Affirmations and Denials in Treatment

THERE ARE two methods of giving a mental treatment, two ways in which one may approach spiritual mind healing in its practical application. These two methods are called *argumentative* and *realization.*

The argumentative method is one wherein a series of mental arguments is used to erase a negative mental conviction. In the method of realization no argument is used, but a state of consciousness is induced, the result of which is such a harmonious reaction that the physical discord disappears. Let us consider, then, the use of affirmations and denials in spiritual mind healing.

As we have frequently stated, Science of Mind practice is built on the supposition that Spiritual Man is Perfect, Nature is Perfect, God is Perfect, Being is Perfect. Spiritual Man is a part of Spiritual Being. Spiritual Man is the manifestation of Spiritual Being. Spiritual Man is the Consciousness of God as man.

In spiritual mind healing it is necessary to establish a consciousness of this foundation of Truth. The treatment seeks to bring man back to the Principle of his being; to the Perfection of his being. In doing this the practitioner meets what we call the argument of negation.

It may seem strange to speak about the argument of negation, but this idea is rapidly being accepted by many psychologists. Out of years of practical experience they have learned that the inertia of thought patterns is so great and so difficult to remove from the consciousness of the patient that they sometimes speak of these thought patterns as actually arguing back, refusing to be dislodged.

When we speak of the argument of negation we are speaking of a very real mental activity, and the practitioner must meet this argument of negation by an opposite argument. If a child says two times two equals six, the teacher explains to him

301

that two times two equals four, never more and never less. There is no emotional strain in delivering this message to the child, but there is the necessity of convincing the child's mind that two times two really does equal four, always and under every circumstance.

So the practitioner starting with this Principle of Perfection argues that disease is neither person, place, nor thing. It has no law to support it. The condition from which his patient suffers has no location; it has no duration; it has no beginning and no development and no end. His argument is as definite in his own thought as though he were explaining that two and two always make four. There never began to be a time when two and two made five. Two and two put together never evolved to a place where they made six, and no matter how many people believe to the contrary or experience the negative result of such a belief, two and two never made seven.

In the wrong working out of an example it is the teacher's duty to point out where the mistake arose. This is what the argumentative treatment is. It is the activity of thought establishing not only a correct premise, but an equally correct conclusion.

Diagnosis in mental treatment is for the purpose of discovering why the person thinks as he does, upon what false premise his thought is based, what belief in the opposite of Good he is entertaining. Of course the negative beliefs which he entertains are mostly subjective. As they are subjective he is not conscious of them; they are operating through him. To the all-embracing Intelligence, the Infinite Mind, man is held as being Perfect and Complete, and two and two never equals anything but four in this Intelligence. There is no negation of mind in this Intelligence, and as the practitioner reverses the negation, the wrong argument disappears from the patient's thought.

By the wrong argument we mean that which attends the wrong argument, which is the negative condition. The practitioner does not feel that he is fighting an adversary or contending with a real opponent. He rearranges the facts which his patient has misarranged. He reverses the mental process by knowing that two and two make four; he knows the Truth about them.

Each individual who presents himself to a practitioner represents an individual problem to be solved, or an individual opportunity to be met. The practitioner denies that Perfection can produce imperfection. He declares that his patient is a Spiritual Idea forever Perfect. He knows that health is indestructible, while disease is a negation. He knows the belief that two and two equals five never was the Truth; therefore it does not have to disappear nor can it reappear—it has no appearance. He knows that from the standpoint of the Spiritual Man, disease never started; lack, want, and limitation never had any beginning, operation, or ending in the Spirit of Truth.

The practitioner handles the experience of negation as though it were only a belief in negation. And this is an important point in mental healing, for unless the practitioner of this science could resolve things into thoughts he would have no mental method of procedure which would sound reasonable, sane, or scientific. Unless disease originates in consciousness, consciousness cannot change it. Whether we are aware of the fact or not makes no difference—it has nothing to do with the Truth of the matter.

In dealing with negation the practitioner does not feel that he is separating the negative from the Real as though they were two different things, for that would be to fall under the hypnotic suggestion that No is equal to Yes, that evil is lord over the Kingdom of Good, and that the Infinite has a rival equal in Power to Itself.

The practitioner deals with That Which Is, and not with that which is not. Therefore when That Which Is appears in the form of negation, even this negation is part of the activity of That Which Is, but is a wrong use of It. This wrong use of That Which Is implies no negation of That Which Is, no separation from That Which Is, and no disunity with That Which Is. It implies merely a negative use of It. Hence the practitioner never deals with the negative as though it were a thing of itself—it is but a state of consciousness.

In analyzing a case for argument (that is, for the affirmation and denial method of procedure in spiritual mind healing), the practitioner starts with this premise: A patient has presented himself for help. It follows that something is wrong. The argument is that there is a place where this negation is experienced. There was a time when he began to experience this negation. There is a real substance which takes the form of this negation. This substance is separate from Mind, Spirit, or Perfection. Consequently he is actually experiencing a negation, and the negation which he experiences has a form. This form is seen by others. It is a fact even though it is not a Truth or an eternal verity. This negation may have taken the form of disease, unhappiness, poverty, domestic infelicity, loneliness, fear, or any other of the myriad forms which deny Good. This is what the patient presents to the practitioner.

Having accepted the premise, how does the practitioner proceed? He begins to deny that anything is wrong. He knows that negation is not person, place, or thing. He knows that negation never began, just as two and two never began to be five. He knows it in the same way, dispassionately but with absolute certainty. He knows that there is no place where negation can be true, nor is there any place where it can be thought to be true. It has no one to support it, no one to believe in it, and no one through whom it can operate. It is exactly nothing and is cancelled by knowing that it is nothing.

There is no time but the Present, and the Present is Perfect. The practitioner knows that the Allness of Truth precludes the possibility of any opposite. Then he pays particular attention, in his thought, to affirming the Presence of the desired Good. From this viewpoint the specific negation is met by the opposite and specific affirmation. The denial is used to clear the consciousness; to sweep it out, as it were, and to make room in thought for the opposite affirmation, which recognizes God as the Only Presence, Power, and Person.

The practitioner deals with the argument of negation which appears as wrong things, or wrong conditions, by using the opposite argument of Truth based upon the Reality that God is All there is. The mental argument continues until the mind of the practitioner is satisfied with the evidence he has produced. In this practice it is evident that the practitioner deals with the negation more as though it were a hypnotic suggestion than as though it were a Reality. He is conscious that his patient is suffering from this condition, but he is equally conscious that he need not suffer from it.

Suppose a patient came to a practitioner and said, "I am an elephant." The practitioner would not believe that he was an elephant; he would not believe that he ever began to be an elephant or ever developed into an elephant. He would not believe that there was any law compelling him to be an elephant.

But suppose the patient should tell the practitioner that there was such a law and that that law was inherited; that he had inherited a tendency toward becoming an elephant. What would the practitioner handle—the elephant or the wrong belief in the patient's mind? It is obvious that he would handle the wrong concept. The practitioner knows that his patient is not an elephant. He knows that he does not inherit any tendency toward being an elephant, but he does know that he suffers from his wrong conception. He heals him, not from being an elephant but from the illusion that he is an elephant.

Now suppose the patient were to tell the practitioner that he is an elephant because he was born on the second day of July and that the stars control the whole thing—it is a matter of fate. Would the practitioner treat fate or the belief in fate? The answer is self-evident. He would deny that the stars had anything to do with this man's being an elephant or not being an elephant. He would know that the only sign is the sign of God or the sign of Perfection. He would deliberately remove the hallucination, he would not try to remove the influence of the planets because they have no influence.

But suppose on reading the history of humanity he should have discovered that many millions of people had believed that at certain times in their lives they must become elephants because of the time of year that they were born into this world. Would the practitioner agree to this hypnotic suggestion? Not at all. He would say to himself, "It does not matter how many people believe that this man is an elephant, or that because he was born under a certain sign he must become an elephant; I know that this is a lie. He is not an elephant, never was, and never will be."

Let us carry the proposition into a more subtle field of argument and suppose that millions of people were to say, "We can prove to you that this thing works mathematically: All people born under certain signs have the inclination to become elephants." What would our practitioner do in a case like this? How would he detect this subtle argument of negation? By following this line of argument: *I realize that whatever the whole race holds to be true about itself appears to be true, because thought works with creative power and with mathematical precision. But even so, I know that the whole thing is an illusion; that even though thought does work with mathematical precision and with creative power, and even though countless millions of people have acted as though they were elephants and believed that they were, they never have been elephants at any time.* This line of argument may be used to heal any belief in horoscopes, inherited tendency, prenatal influence, or race suggestion.

The practitioner must never be tempted to believe that the negative condition is a thing of itself or that it ever had a cause. He denies every aspect of belief about it. In the argumentative method he affirms that Man, Being Perfect, is not born under race belief and does not suffer from signs in the heavens. Two and two are always four no matter what anyone believes. His entire argument is affirmation and denial swinging around the central theme of Spiritual Being and Perfection, and that God is All there is, ever was, or ever will be.

The practitioner recognizes that we all suffer from race consciousness and that what millions of people have believed in operates to some extent through all of us. But this does not make it so. He must learn that much which appears to be true in experience is not true in Principle, and he must reverse the use of thought until the experience is transcended. In doing this he resolves everything into mind—planets, people, peanuts, kings, and cabbages. The entire human experience and the latest event in the experience of his patient are theoretically resolved into mind and into thought.

Next he knows that the only activity of mind is thought. He knows that the activity of his thought destroys the activity of the negative thought, and that what is left is Perfect. Hence the sooner he recognizes that what is left is Perfect, the sooner his denial becomes an affirmation. Affirmation always follows denial in order that realization may be built up. This realization is a realization of the Presence and the Perfection of God.

The practitioner deals with the mentality alone. Having theoretically resolved the physical universe into a thing of thought, he handles thought. Negative thought is not evil of itself and is not a law unto itself. It is merely a mistreatment of Principle and belongs to no one. Therefore it must be dealt with as though it were an impersonal thought force operating through someone's belief. Correct mental practice means dealing with this negative thought force as though it were a belief, and removing it as though it were merely a mistaken conclusion.

The practitioner, then, deals with the negative condition, whether it is impoverishment or physical illness, as though it were an objective argument or combination of wrong thoughts. Seeing it in this light he untangles the wrong thought, leaving the field to that nature which is Perfect. He seeks to arrive at a realization and recognition of the Allness of God, the Omnipresence of Good.

In this entire process the practitioner deals with nothing but his own thought. His affirmations, denials, and realizations take place at the center of his own consciousness, and he never attempts to project or suggest. He makes no attempt whatsoever to concentrate. His treatment is a moving, conscious, animated thing.

This practice would be impossible unless the practitioner could sincerely and truthfully resolve things into thoughts in his own imagination and proceed upon the basis that all manifest life is a thing of thought in form. He must be thoroughly and sincerely convinced that there is a Spiritual Man and that this Spiritual Man is Perfect; that the Kingdom of Heaven is now, and that a statement of Truth has actual Power.

Moreover he must be certain that as far as he is concerned the answer is taken out of It, not put into It. Otherwise he will be trying every form of mental coercion, will power, suggestion, and concentration.

Arguments Logically Presented to Mind

Arguments logically presented to Mind will produce definite results. What does this statement mean? It means that we are surrounded by a Universal Mind which is creative, which receives the impress of our thought and acts upon it. It receives the conclusion of our thought and acts as though it were true. Hence a mental argument logically presented to Mind in such a way that its conclusion is definite must produce a definite result.

The argument should be made with a consciousness of harmony, of wholeness, of peace, of power, and of perfection. When we make the statement that God is all there is, our argument must support this statement by strong mental proof that since God is all there is, there is nothing else. We must know that both Cause and Effect are spiritual, and our every argument should tend to demonstrate this position in our own thought. For whatever we demonstrate in our own thought is logically presented to Mind to be acted upon and projected into form.

Creative Mind of Itself has no specific intention as far as we as individuals are concerned. We give It the only intention It has for us, and the fact that we find ourselves in confused and limited circumstances, instead of disproving this theory, is a positive proof of it.

These uncertain circumstances in which we find ourselves are themselves a direct result of confused thinking. When we reverse the process and start with the proposition of the Allness of Good and logically present to Mind the idea that Good is the only Power, we shall see definite changes take place in outward manifestation.

Simple Acceptance

UNTIL A person has demonstrated the Truth so completely that he can never again be shaken in his conviction about It, he should not talk much to others about his belief. For the conscious and subjective reaction of their doubt might confuse him unless his own mind is already so firmly planted in understanding and faith that it remains calm in the midst of confusion and doubt.

Particularly is this true when one is making a demonstration for one's self. It seems to scatter his force. Some Power seems to go out of him. It seems as though there were cracks in his mind through which conviction oozes. Others will see the evidence of his demonstration when it takes actual form.

Remember: the intellect argues, but the Spirit *knows.* The intellect examines; the Spirit has no opinions. This is why Jesus likened the Kingdom of Heaven to a child, for a child expects his parents to meet his needs. When he asks his mother for a drink of water he expects a drink of water, and he would be the most surprised person in the world if he did not receive it immediately. Equally, the mother expects to give it.

It is the nature of the Creative Mind to respond to us, to give us what we ask when we ask it, and in the way in which we ask it. Thus the childlike mind of absolute acceptance is likened unto the Kingdom of Heaven. In actual practice we must let go of the mental images which we dislike, and cling to only those which are more nearly after our heart's desire.

When you give a mental treatment you should feel that all the Power there is in the Universe is flowing into your word. It is impossible to feel this way if you think that you are dealing with will power, mental coercion, or even mental suggestion. It is equally difficult to do so if you feel that you are dealing with some masterful mental concentration, but it is very easy if you simplify it in your thought and realize that you are dealing with an Eternal Presence which when called upon responds to you.

Because God Knows, I Know

THE MIND which states a problem is the mind which knows the answer. Throw the problem into mind for solution and the answer will rise to consciousness.

In actual practice one does this by stating that he already knows the answer to his problem. The Intelligence within him knows, and this Intelligence within him which knows causes him to *consciously* know. It is not enough merely to state that Intelligence knows. We must combine our statement that there is an Intelligence which knows, with a conscious acceptance that this Intelligence is now functioning in our conscious thought, causing us to know.

It is scientific to say, "I know. I know because I know that God knows; and because God knows, I know." Use any statement which will convince you that you really know. We are directed not by a blind force, but by an Infinite Intelligence which is not only willing, but whose very nature compels It to give us Guidance.

All the prayers which men have uttered, no matter under what religious or spiritual banner they may have marched, have been effective not because of the peculiarity of their theology or religious belief, but because through this individual approach they used a Principle that exists at the center of every man's being.

Naturally, and humanly, they have told us that they received results because of their particular belief. But we know it was because they contacted an impersonal Principle. We know there is such a Principle involved, and we know how to make conscious use of that Principle.

Feeling, Organized and Directed, Is Creation

MIND MUST know all things, being Omniscient; hence whatever is, Mind Knows, and Mind is the Principle back of all treatment. Treatment is enforcement of Principle. The words, thoughts, phrases, and statements are the way in which one makes known his feeling of the Divine Allness at any particular time.

Mind comprehends everything. Mind is at the center of man's body and at the center of his affairs, and comprehends both body and affairs. We are to demonstrate that this comprehension is Perfect, Harmonious, Whole, Prosperous, Happy, Complete, and Eternal.

When we use such words we must feel their meaning. The feeling without the words may have a meaning but no direction, and meaning without direction will produce no creation. Feeling, organized and directed, is intelligent creation.

The practitioner knows that nothing is hid, and that the ideas of Mind are perfect. He knows that Absolute Intelligence has nothing hid from It; there is nothing covered which shall not be revealed. Everything is visible to It.

The practitioner knows that his word, being the Presence, Power, and Activity of Mind, does uncover, reveal, make known, proclaim, and manifest itself. His word is the Law of Mind unto any case. Hence if a practitioner feels that he does not know what words to use he should immediately know that he does know what words to use.

Spiritual diagnosis exposes to thought that which is Eternally True and declares that Allness is *now present* and *now manifest.*

Treatment and Feeling

THAT WHICH is felt cannot be taught, while that which is taught may be felt. This is one of the most vital things in mental and spiritual science. A treatment has no Power unless it has a meaning to the one who gives it, just as we know that a public speaker cannot convey a message which he himself does not understand.

If we wish to convey a message we must feel it, just as the musician feels the atmosphere of harmony back of his technique. Yet technique is equally necessary in order that he may give definite form to his feeling.

The practitioner recognizes the whole condition as a thing of thought and in his own mind straightens out this thought about his patient. In so doing he reveals the Eternal Harmony back of the negative appearance. The straigthening out of thought is *technique*. It may be taught, analyzed, taken apart, and put together again. It consists of words, phrases, thoughts, ideas, all of which are understandable, teachable, and learnable.

The *essence* of the treatment, the feeling which the practitioner has, his interior sense of the Divine Allness, of that Spirit which is closer to him than his own breath—this cannot be put into words, this cannot be taught. It can only be felt.

By using right words, statements, and phrases, and dwelling upon their subtle meaning, one may come to feel the meaning back of the words.

What Must Be Felt

WHAT is it that must be felt in spiritual practice, the feeling which is beyond words, statements, and phrases? It is the *essence* of Life, the *Spirit* of the thing from which the mind automatically draws an intellectual conclusion. This feeling results in words which are an activity of the feeling, the enforcement of the Principle back of it. In this way the word becomes Spirit and life.

The practitioner assumes that the Truth is all there is; hence all appearances of evil are but wrong interpretations of the Truth. They are not the Truth in reverse, neither need we consider them as opposites to the Truth, because the Truth has no opposites. Negation is a false statement of the Truth, a false belief about the Truth.

Treatment corrects the wrong use through its right knowing. Right knowing is an intelligent activity of mind which plunges beneath the surface and reveals Pure Spirit as the Invisible Cause of creation. The words that a practitioner uses should imply a feeling which lifts him above the appearance he wishes to change.

The practitioner makes a series of statements about the Truth. The feeling that he has must be that the Truth is all there is, and he must sense that the words that he speaks are the enforcement of this allness. Hence he must feel something which cannot be merely stated in words; he must feel the allness of his treatment, not as mental suggestion but as spiritual realization.

In such degree as he does sense this allness his word will have Power.

The Practitioner Clarifies His Own Thought

STRANGE AS it may seem, after you have listened to the negative statements of your patient in which he presents the case for materiality and produces evidence to prove that he is convicted, you as a practitioner are the first one who needs to be healed of the belief that he must necessarily remain in his prison.

The entire condition of lack, evil, and limitation which he has described must be repudiated. You must silence his belief in your own consciousness. You must recognize that what has been operating through him is neither person, place, nor thing; it is not cause, it is not medium, it is not effect. And you should know that your word completely expels it from his consciousness.

But your word cannot expel it from his consciousness unless at the same time it expels the same condition from your own thought. Again we must reiterate the all-significant fact that the practitioner treats himself to remove the patient's false belief from his own mind.

It would be impossible for any practitioner to do this effectively unless he were first thoroughly convinced that Mind alone is the final creative factor in the Universe, and that all movement takes place in consciousness.

Therefore clarify your own consciousness about your patient. And when your statement has clarified your own consciousness (healed your own thought about him), he will come to you and tell you that he is receiving benefit.

Watch this simple process as you silently practice it, and you will be amazed at the dynamic results which will follow.

Divine Ideas

WE MUST know that the doorway of opportunity is never closed. Man is always receptive to the Divine Ideas. It is never too late for him to manifest opportunity; it is never withheld from him for a single moment; there is no sense of limited or restricted opportunity.

Treat to know that your patient is at the doorway of limitless opportunity, forever expanding in his experience. Everywhere he goes a new and better opportunity for self-expression opens before him; he is compelled to recognize this opportunity and to act intelligently upon it. His imagination is continuously increasing, new ideas come to him every day, and he knows how to execute these ideas.

And right here be sure to remember that nothing can come out of a treatment that is not first put into it; hence it is not enough to state that God is limitless, for though this abstract statement is undoubtedly true no concrete manifestation of it can take place in the experience of your patient until you specifically designate that it is taking place.

Know that your patient is receptive to the influx of ideas. Feel that he is now the object of every infinite solicitation, that friends are impelled toward him, that he is compelled to recognize them, and that his talents are appreciated and he is adequately compensated.

Free every belief about him which he has brought to you. Ask him why he thinks he is not getting along better and then deny every negation which he affirms, immediately affirming its direct opposite. Handle the case specifically and definitely; formulate your statements in such a way that if the words were actual things and immediately formed before you, the form which they would take would be desirable.

Make Each Treatment Complete

ALWAYS FEEL that the first treatment you give will meet the case, while at the same time never taking *No* for an answer even in a series of treatments.

Each time a treatment is given the practitioner should feel that it is Complete and Perfect; that it is Finished and Done. His treatment is not complete until his own consciousness accepts the verdict as Final and Perfect.

In actual experience the practitioner may have to do this day after day over a period of time, but he must be careful to avoid the feeling that the performance must go on forever.

He must be equally careful that he knows that right thought continually poured into consciousness will heal. So what he does in practice is to make each treatment complete; to draw a final conclusion in each treatment, and then be willing to keep on until the case is met.

Do Not Deny the Physical

In spiritual mind healing we do not deny that the patient has a stomach, lungs, arms, etc. We affirm that they are Ideas of Divine Mind; that they are spiritual substance. The only thing we deny is a material sense of the physical body. The Spiritual Body is in Divine Mind and is pure Spirit.

The practitioner does not deny the body. He affirms that body is a combination of Divine Ideas; that right action takes place in every organ. He supplies the material sense with an opposite spiritual realization. The body is the sum total of Divine Ideas, and all Divine Ideas are Eternal, Universal, and Perfect. Therefore God, or Spirit, is the Life of the Real Body and the Essence of It.

We must be careful to tell our patients not to condemn the human body; certainly never to deny its Reality or the reality of any of its organs or functions. There is nothing wrong with the sum total of Divine Ideas which make up the Real Body, which is Spiritual. Every organ and every function of the human body has a Universal Prototype behind it. It is an Idea in the Mind of God, and a Perfect Idea.

To dwell morbidly on any organ or function of the body is to condemn it, to retard its action, to congest its movement, to impede the circulation through it, and, of course, wherever the circulation is impeded the elimination is also impaired. We must know that there is Divine circulation, perfect assimilation, and right elimination.

The function of the body is not something apart from God but is something *within* God. We must learn to love all of these functions as being attributes of Spirit, and to sense the Divine Universal Harmony underlying all.

Spiritual Mind Treatment Is Not Well-Wishing

WHEN YOU give a spiritual mind treatment you are not wishing that someone will be healed. You are not hoping that someone will be healed. You are not asking that someone shall be healed. You are making definite statements in the Mind Principle about some person or situation, or you are entertaining a state of realization in your own consciousness for someone or something. You are not petitioning God to please do this, or that, or something else.

Not that there is anything wrong with this, because any sincere petition to one's God will have a Power equal to the conviction of the petitioner. The Principle of the Law of Mind in Action must act on the mental attitude entertained and the words used, because this is Its nature. In doing this It must correspond with the acceptance of the one making the petition.

When we say that spiritual mind Treatment is not well-wishing we are in no way criticizing the sincerity or the Spiritual Power of any form of petition. What we are doing is restating our own position by saying that we cannot believe in a Supreme Power which acts more favorably for one than for another. Such a belief would immediately take us out of the realm of Law and Order into the realm of chaos. We should never criticize any person's form of prayer, nor should we try to convince a person that our method of communion with the Invisible is superior to his.

But when it comes to a conscious use of the Principle of Mind we must not forget that we are dealing with such a Principle. Therefore our method of procedure is different. Instead of asking for something, we are accepting something. Instead of hoping that something will happen, we are endeavoring to know that it has happened or is happening. This is a fine point in the Science of Mind and it should not be overlooked.

We believe in Spiritual Communion, which is the drawing of the essence of Reality into our own minds through keeping the thought uplifted and in tune with the Ultimate Harmony. We believe that the Divine Presence is immanent in everything and in every person. This of course is the very basis of our assumption. It is the rock or the foundation upon which our edifice is built. Man not only can talk with God but he can receive a direct answer through intuition. Through such communion he enters into the realm of Reality and imbibes the Spirit of Truth.

In giving a treatment we proceed on the assumption that there is an intelligent Creative Principle in everything and in everyone which responds to our word exactly the way we speak it. There could be no Science of Mind unless this were true. Therefore a spiritual mind treatment in actual operation is a series of statements logically presented to the Principle of Mind, based on the assumption of Perfect God, Perfect Man, and Perfect Being.

Looking away from the appearance, no matter what the appearance may be, and turning to Reality, our statements are made to conform with the Realities felt. God is all there is; therefore this negative condition need not be and should not be and is not.

In the argumentative method of treatment the argument proceeds along this basis until the practitioner comes to the logical conclusion that, since God is all there is, and since harmony constitutes the only Reality, this person or this condition does of necessity conform to Reality; this word is the law of elimination to everything that disputes or denies that which is Perfect.

A combination of feeling the Divine Presence and making statements in the Law of Mind constitutes both inspirational and scientific spiritual mind treatment. Therefore it is plain that such treatment is not well-wishing, hoping, or longing. It is not a petition. It is a bold, flat, definite, predetermined statement, concise, clear, and dynamic.

But we hasten to add that it is not as though a large amount of Good were now to be hurled at an equal amount of evil. It is not storming the gates of Heaven with an affirmative petition. It is more like the calm contemplation of the mind which says there is a light, and because there is, darkness disappears.

We do not question the physical diagnosis of the doctor or the mental diagnosis of the analyst, provided they are true. We do not deny either mind or body. We do affirm the Spirit as transcendent, having the ability to create new thoughts while new thoughts create new situations.

The practitioner should always know that his statements transcend not only the physical or objective conditions, but subjective or unconscious causes as well. They are transcendent of both the cause and the effect of the negative condition, rising to a position in Mind which starts new and clean and fresh.

This is what Jesus meant when he said in effect that there is a Truth which known will prove itself. *And ye shall know the truth, and the truth shall make you free.* He recognized a Truth transcendent of all negation.

Mind, the Only
Creative Energy

No MATTER how seemingly impossible any situation may be or how difficult any problem may appear, the practitioner should never become discouraged. He must continue to do his work, knowing full well that he is dealing with the Invisible Essence, the Invisible Substance, the Great Reality back of everything.

It would be impossible for a person to do this unless he were firmly convinced that Mind is the only Creative Agency in the Universe and that he has direct and conscious access to Its creativity. Moreover, he must be conscious that right thought and true statements are the enforcement of this Law of Mind.

Man's thought is the activity of Mind, for Mind without thought or directed consciousness would have no real existence. There can be no existence apart from consciousness; or, if there be any existence apart from consciousness, then there is no one, no thing, and no intelligence to be aware of such existence. It is evident that without self-awareness there is not only no realization of Life, but no Life to be realized. Hence we affirm that Mind in action is Law.

The practitioner who understands this will not become discouraged. He will know that if he perseveres in declaring the Truth, the pathway to Reality will be cleared, obstructions will be removed, wrong forms will be dissolved.

It follows that he will be both courageous and happy in his work. He will be happy because he is sure; doubts no longer assail him, fear does not possess him, negation no longer obsesses his thought. He continues to make his declarations with calm confidence and with Divine assurance.

Treatment Is Independent
of the One Who Gives It

Spiritual Mind healing is based on a definite Principle and one that works mathematically. In no way should this concept interfere with the beauty of it, or determine whether it is spiritual. The Universe is a system of law and order plus the Infinite Presence or Person and, from the standpoint of the human being, personalities. We are persons living in a Mind Principle that reacts mathematically upon our acceptance. Throughout the ages this has been the secret of faith and the answer to prayer.

Just what is the position of the person in this Principle and how does a spiritual mind treatment operate in such a way as to be independent even of the one who gives it? This consideration is of deepest importance, for we should never feel that when we give a treatment we must compel it to operate, any more than we feel that if we plant an acorn we must compel it to become an oak tree. The personal element is volition, which makes it possible for us to plant an acorn instead of an apple seed and with complete certainty know that the answer will be an oak tree and not an apple tree.

As far as the creation of the tree is concerned we have nothing whatsoever to do with it. We have merely used a law of nature that responds to us, that operates upon the particular concept, or the seed we buried in the ground, that some invisible force might operate upon it to produce the exact correspondence to the idea of our seed, and not something else. We plant and cultivate the ground, but we do not really grow the garden. Nature does this for us.

When we come into the field of spiritual mind treatment, we have not entered a field of chaos where nothing happens in accord with law. If this were true, we could place no reliance upon our treatment, or the Principle operating on it. We should be dealing with some whimsical fancy or with the caprice of some law in nature that might or might not respond to us mathemati-

322

cally and with complete certainty. It is in this sense that the treatment is independent of the one who gives it.

You can plant a garden for someone else in his plot of ground and it will grow if he cultivates it and waters it. You can plant one in your own ground and it will grow. You can scatter seeds by the roadside and they will grow. All about us in nature we see the variations of such plantings. Perhaps the wind has blown the seed, perhaps it has been accidentally dropped, possibly it has been consciously planted, but always the creative Law produces in complete independence of the avenues through which the seed was planted.

A person giving a spiritual mind treatment should know that he is using such a Law. There can be no argument against the existence of this Law because It is invisible, any more than there could be a valid argument against the operation of any law in nature. All laws are invisible. We see only the effect, never the cause. We know that certain effects will follow certain uses of the laws of nature, and we place complete reliance on the operation not of our will or our desire, but of the actual operation of a law.

Now there is such a Law as Mind in Action, and it is this Law that we use when we give a treatment. Our word is operated on by a Power greater than we are, an Intelligence superior to ours, which is entirely independent of us as personalities. Therefore a practitioner, when he has said that his word is for a certain person or a specific situation or condition, gives his treatment feeling that it is entirely independent of precedent or anything that has happened before; that in a certain sense it becomes an actual entity in the field of Universal Mind that operates upon it.

Every sense of personal responsibility or individual obligation, other than the obligation to do one's work to the best of one's ability, must be dropped from the mind. There should be no thought of anxiety, even as there should be no feeling of uncertainty. The Law operates on the word you speak, not because of your wishing or willing, but because that is the way the Law works.

This is the Principle you are dealing with. This is the Power you are using, and this is the certainty upon which you can rely.

There is a vast difference in our mental reaction when we know that we are dealing with a Law that operates upon our word, than there would be if we felt we had to push that word to make it do something or go somewhere or become something. And so again we come right back to the very foundation of the whole theory upon which this practice is built: that we live in a Universe which sustains Itself, by Itself, out of Itself, within Itself.

Every scientist must follow this same rule. He uses a certain law. It is the nature of the law that he uses to respond in the way he uses it. We have the obligation to do the best we can. The responsibility rests in the Law of Good.

Spiritual Mind Healing
and Mental Suggestion

WHILE IT is self-evident that some degree of mental suggestion enters into all human relationships, we must be careful not to confuse spiritual mind healing with the popular concept of mental suggestion. In this practice, suggestion disappears and explanation takes its place.

Someone might contend that explanation itself is a form of suggestion. We admit that there is some basis for this claim if by mental suggestion is meant changing one's thought after receiving instruction from another. From this viewpoint, would we say that a teacher is practicing mental suggestion when pointing out to a student their error in working a mathematical problem, and then explaining how it should be solved? We would not consider this mental suggestion, but explanation.

It is certain that suggestion plays a subtle role in all life. If we go out into the desert we receive a suggestion of its calmness; if we look at a glorious sunset there is a suggestion of infinite peace and beauty. It is impossible to read the daily newspaper or a book without receiving some suggestion. When we read advertisements in the newspapers or in magazines, the principle of suggestion is operating.

It is not so much a question of whether suggestion is playing this subtle role in human life; rather, it is a question of whether the dominant suggestions of human life are constructive. In this analysis it is necessary to understand whether we think of mental explanation as being a suggestion. For instance, if someone says two and two make five and we explain to him that two and two make four, do we consider our explanation a suggestion? If so, then every teaching of Truth becomes a suggestion. Undoubtedly we should all agree that the teaching of Truth is an explanation rather than a suggestion, and in drawing our line we realize that if the teaching of Truth is a mental suggestion, then it is a most desirable one. The only suggestions we need to avoid are the destructive ones, those which coerce the mind.

The question might be asked, "Is faith-healing mental suggestion? Does the atmosphere of a particular shrine suggest some positive conviction that can heal?" Another question almost inevitably follows, "Is this exchanging one belief for another?" Since we are finite I suppose we are generally exchanging one belief for another, but if we make a good bargain by trading lesser beliefs for greater ones, I presume we have done well.

There have been long and varied discussions on this subject, as to whether or not spiritual mind healing is based on a principle of mental suggestion. Those whose entire interest is in the field of psychology claim that this whole field is one of mental suggestion. They call it spiritual suggestion. On the other hand, the average metaphysician will disclaim any element of suggestion in his work and tell you that he heals through the knowledge that God is All.

It is certain that in the practice of mental suggestion the one making the suggestion must be present with his patient, and the patient must be consciously receptive to his suggestion. In our field the practitioner does not have the slightest need of knowing where his patient is when he treats him. In his treatment he does not mentally address his patient. For instance, he does not say, "John Smith, you are thus and so," or "You are going to be thus and so."

We all know that the average suggestive therapeutist must be in the room with his patient, but in our form of healing we do not care where the patient is or what he may be doing when we are giving a treatment for him. Therefore suggestion, as it is commonly practiced, would not be effective in what we call absent treatment, and we know in our field that absent treatment is just as effective as is present treatment.

In ordinary methods of mental suggestion it is considered advisable for the patient to be relaxed, receptive, acquiescent, but the practitioner in our field does not consider these points in his practice. In some cases the patient does not know that he is a patient, the reason being that in this field the practitioner does all his work within himself.

In treating he recognizes the one he is seeking to help, by saying: "This word is for John Smith or Mary Jones or Martin Andrews." He specifies the person the treatment is for; he identifies the treatment with the person. All his work is done within his own mind, in his own thought, with complete disregard of where his patient may be or what he may be doing, or what he may be thinking about at that particular time. The practitioner clears up his own consciousness. That is what spiritual practice is. Jesus did not suggest anything to the paralyzed man when he told him to get up and walk.

Of course we do not deny that much disease is the result of suggestion, whether that suggestion be self-suggestion or whether it arises spontaneously from the consensus of human opinion, which we might call collective suggestion. We do not deny that suggestion plays not only a subtle but a powerful role in human life, individually and collectively, and that in all probability it is impossible to escape some of its effect.

What we affirm is that in this form of practice one does not try to suggest anything to one's patient. He does not say, "You are getting better," even though such a statement might be salutary. The practitioner must know that he is dealing only with the Spiritual Man, and the Spiritual Man does not get better; he is already Perfect.

This form of treatment is a revelation of the Self to the self and is arrived at instantly through realization, or by stages through the reversal of consciousness.

But whether we are able to recognize instantly the Truth for someone, or through the process of affirmation and denial arrive at the same conclusion, makes no difference. In neither instance do we try to suggest anything to the patient, and yet we realize that in some way the recognition which we make must operate through the patient if it is to heal him.

Just how this happens no one knows, but that it does happen without any attempt on the part of the practitioner to do anything other than arrive at a realization for his patient, is certain. Treatment contains no element of mental coercion, practices no form of conscious suggestion or mental concentration.

Treatment is a series of statements about some person, an argument in mind about some person, or a realization of what we call the Truth about some person. But whether it takes the form of a series of statements, an argument in mind, or a realization, it is effective to such degree as the practitioner becomes inwardly conscious of what we call the Truth about his patient; that the patient is now Complete and Perfect.

It is our belief that wherever spiritual mind healing has been successfully practiced or demonstrated, one unifying and identical principle has run through all such practice; an element of both conviction and acceptance.

Now the question might be asked, "Does faith pass into the certainty of understanding?" The answer is both *Yes* and *No*. Faith in electricity passes into the understanding that the energy which we call electricity exists, and we may use it. But even understanding that it exists is faith that it will always respond to us according to what we have discovered to be the law of its being.

All sciences ultimately resolve themselves into a series of faiths in natural laws discovered and demonstrated. Faith may pass into understanding. Applying this principle to spiritual mind healing, we announce that faith in God or Good has throughout the ages definitely demonstrated the Presence of a Universal Principle of God. Thus faith may pass through experiment to scientific certainty which is knowledge.

From this standpoint we would not say that faith, as exhibited throughout the ages, is merely a mental suggestion, for it is definitely more than this. It has been and it is an unconscious mental union with Reality. It would be absurd for a modern metaphysician to deny that this experience has come historically to people of varying spiritual convictions, and it would seem intelligent to recognize that the Universal Principle always works wherever, whenever, and in such degree as anyone consciously or unconsciously, in ignorance or in wisdom, in superstition or in fear, provides an avenue through which It may work.

Thus we arrive at a concept of the Universality and Impersonality, the Changeless Reality of Natural Principles. Faith has been the most dynamic Power throughout the ages, and it should not be denounced as mere suggestion; but understanding that faith has demonstrated a Principle, we should seek to understand that Principle, and we should make every endeavor to reproduce at will the too infrequent experiences which result from an attitude of faith.

We agree that while mental suggestion plays some subtle role in spiritual mind healing, it is not the dominant factor, and as far as the practitioner is concerned, it does not enter into it at all since he makes no attempt to suggest anything to his patient at any time or under any circumstance.

If someone tells us that the practitioner of this science does his work in the field of mental explanation, we may agree with him, but we must hasten to add that this explanation operates through some Universal Field which needs no coercion; which is independent of time, place, and circumstance; which knows neither big nor little, hard nor easy, past nor future, but appears to exist in an Eternal *now* and in an Everlasting *here*. In practice this *now* and *here* are in the mind of the practitioner.

Moreover, when we apply the ordinary concept of mental suggestion to another phase of our work, which is the control of conditions through right thinking, we find it impossible to accept suggestion as an explanation. For while we might suggest to an individual that he is successful, how could this make him successful in actual objective fact unless thought also operated in a field entirely independent of the immediate environment?

For instance, to what or whom would a grocer give suggestions if he were working for prosperity? Suppose he has no customers, then there is no one to receive his suggestions. We must fall back upon the idea that his suggestions are made to sacks of potatoes or bags of beans. These inanimate objects, the commodities which he has to sell, together with the cases in which he displays his goods, are apparently the only things open to suggestion, and who ever heard of a man suggesting to a can of beans that it could sell itself or that it could go out and find a customer?

Of course we are not denying that most advertising is suggestive, or that many methods of suggestion are used in all business. We are not denying that one may, to some slight degree at least, influence others. What we are doing is affirming that this is not the method used in this form of practice. Our grocer who has no customers to receive his suggestion must know something which will bring him customers. This he does through the activity of right ideas, realizing that the activity of right ideas is the real activity and that there is no solid fact, that all facts are fluid. He resolves things into thoughts and handles the thoughts, not the things.

Suppose one wishes to attract new friendships. He starts out by having no friends to whom he can offer suggestions of friendship. There is nothing to coerce because there is no one there to be coerced. He can influence no one because there is no one in his environment to be influenced or to influence. He starts from scratch, and unless there were a Principle which acted independently, he could not attract new friendships into his life. It is self-evident, then, that this part of his practice is not mental suggestion. It is mental realization, which brings us right back to the central theme of our whole philosophy.

We are brought back to the fundamental proposition that Self-Realization is based on Self-Existence, and Self-Existence, from the Universal standpoint, means that the Generative, Productive, and Projective Power of the Universe is at the point of man's self-recognition, and responds to man's self-recognition.

Love Dissolves Fear

TO UNDERSTAND that Love overcomes both hate and fear is one of the chief requisites of a scientific mental practitioner. Love does not overcome hate and fear by argument or force, but by some subtle Power of transformation, transmutation, sublimation, invisible in Its essence but apparent through Its act.

As light overcomes the darkness, as the presence of heat causes the atmosphere of the room to change until it is warm and comfortable, so the radiant presence of Love and Peace dissipates fear, hate, and confusion.

In every series of treatments the practitioner should bring out these points of Being relative to his patient. His patient is dominated by Love and appreciated in Love by everyone who contacts him. Fear and hate cannot motivate him, cannot operate through him, cannot do anything to him, do not belong to him, and are not part of him. Nothing enters his consciousness but a sense of peace.

The practitioner does not fight evil. He knows there is no evil. He knows there is no reversal of his thought; that the statements which he has made about his patient are the Truth about him. He knows that the Truth does absolutely, positively, immediately, and permanently uproot, cast out, and forever obliterate every negation about his patient. He knows that his patient is not controlled by material laws or governed by others' thoughts. He covers him with Love.

Love is the victor in every case. Love breaks down the iron bars of thought, shatters the walls of material belief, severs the chain of bondage which thought has imposed, and sets the captive free.

Take Away the Stone

OUR WORD will have Power in such degree as we sense that it is the activity of the Spirit within us, and the Law unto that thing spoken of. We should have a sense of the indwelling Spirit, All-Present and All-Powerful.

If any thought rises which tells us that we do not know, or tells us we cannot accomplish, we must silence this negative argument by using one which is directly opposed to it. We must again reassure our consciousness that there is but One Presence, One Law, and One Power. This Presence, Law, and Power is ours in Its entirety.

A treatment is not complete until it knows that all the Power there is, is flowing through it. There must be no sense of chance about it. When Jesus, standing at the tomb of Lazarus, said, *Take ye away the stone*, he was communing with the Spirit within him and establishing the consciousness that Lazarus was not dead. Then he was able to tell Lazarus to come forth.

The practitioner is continually standing before the grave of some inactive thought, some dead hope, some apparently lost cause whose door is sealed with fear, doubt, despair, and uncertainty. Who shall roll away the stone and who shall tell the dead hope to come forth, to be resurrected, to be born again? That is the work of the practitioner who speaks with assurance and certainty.

There must be no despair or uncertainty, nor even supplication or reverence, for the tomb gives up its dead not to the dead, but to the living.

Do Not Condemn Yourself

KNOWING THE Truth is a spiritual treatment. To know that there is no man external to the likeness of God is a part of this treatment. The treatment must rise higher in consciousness than the condition it expects to heal. If you are treating to heal pain you must come to a conclusion of Peace which is greater than the experience of pain your patient is having. In such degree as you are successful in doing this the pain will cease.

In such a case one should treat until one dissolves fear. Perfect Love casts out fear. Take the thought of Peace, of Love, of Perfection. Work with it from every angle you can imagine until there comes an inner awareness of its meaning. Peace is Perfection, whereas pain is not; pain is an experience which is now eliminated, now completely reversed. Over and over reassure yourself of man's Perfection.

Do not condemn yourself or the self of your patient. The Truth about man is that he is God made manifest—he is the personality of God. Your knowledge of this becomes his freedom. Your knowledge of this is more than the Way-Shower, it is the Way Itself. Jesus said, *I am the way, the truth, and the life; no man cometh unto the Father but by me*, which means that we approach Reality directly through our own spiritual natures. This is the only true and real mediator between God and man—there is no other.

The Real Man and the Real Body are Perfect right now. Your knowledge of this establishes Its manifestation in your patient's experience at the level of your own comprehension of the meaning of the words you use.

Treatment for the Sensitive Person

FEAR AND faith are identical mental attitudes. The energy used in the one is the same energy as that used in the other, since there is but one final Energy in the Universe and this final Energy is the Energy of Spirit. Fear is a positive acceptance that we shall experience that which we dislike. Faith is a positive acceptance that we shall experience that which we do like. But they are identical in their mental content. The difference is in the direction.

We should not fight fear, but should convert fear into faith. If we realize that it is a mental attitude we can do this very easily. Looking at the thing which we fear and examining it carefully, let us convert this fear thought into one of faith, realizing that the energy of fear converted into faith will produce an opposite effect.

By way of illustration we might take a person who is afraid of being misunderstood. He is very sensitive and shuns human contacts. He must convert the energy of this fear into faith. Using the same energy he must declare that people now understand him, that no one misunderstands him, that everyone loves him, everyone desires his presence.

If he will look at the thing he is afraid of until he understands it, it will no longer have any element of fear for him. He can do this in such degree as he is conscious of Perfection, and he must be actively conscious of Perfection. He must state this consciousness of Perfection in a definite manner.

The Family Life

IN TREATING against family confusion, work to know that there is no confusion. The family is a collection of Perfect Ideas.

It may be difficult at times to sense this; but the practitioner is not dealing with the manifestation of discord as though it were a thing of itself, but only as though it were a wrong combination of thoughts operating through persons who are already spiritually unified with each other, desiring each other's Good, and being kindly disposed toward each other.

What the practitioner handles or dissolves is the belief that Good ever can be divided against Itself. The idea of argument and criticism cannot enter into this family life. It certainly cannot upset the equilibrium of the Spirit which indwells every member, joining them together in a community of Spirit. They have a partnership with each other and with the Eternal.

The practitioner must also know that there is no sense of jealousy or any other kindred thought which can operate in the family life. He resolves all of these so-called people into the One Spirit and re-forms them in his own imagination into the image of Perfection. He sees them emerge as unified manifestations of Wholeness. The household of God is a household of peace and happiness, and nothing enters it but love, joy, and understanding.

Group Treatment

WHEN A group of people come together with one accord and with one thought, a greater Power is generated. Not because the Creative Principle responds to a number of people more than It does to one, but because the combined faith of a group reaches a higher level of acceptance. Therefore group treatments should be definitely practiced, with the purpose in mind of arriving at a deeper conviction.

One of the difficulties is to get a group of people to think alike and at the same time. In order to do this in the most effectual manner, the individual needs and desires of the group must be temporarily put aside. For the most effectual treatment is not where each individual member is treating for himself or for some other person. There is not enough fusion of thought. There is not enough coming together in unity of purpose when everyone is treating different individuals.

The best results are gained from group treatment when all members join in treating not for the purpose of acquiring any specific good but for the purpose of reaching a higher state of consciousness. There will be less confusion because of a greater degree of unity.

In such group treatment you would probably meditate on such ideas as Peace, or Joy, or general Wholeness. You would meditate on the concept that there is One Presence which is God, One Perfect Life which is right here, One Divine Intelligence guiding and governing, not for any particular or specific purpose in this case but just to imbibe the Spirit of Wholeness Itself, to enter more largely into a complete acceptance of Peace and Poise and Power.

Another way in which group treatment is effectual is when all agree to work for a specific purpose and, completely forgetting themselves and their personal desires, merge their whole attention for the common good.

We feel certain that in your practice and in dealing with people you will work out a method which will be right for you. If you will watch the performance you will see that a higher degree of consciousness is reached when there is a completely unified concept. For instance, a group of people could work together for an organization, or for a world purpose, or for their country, or for any public good; or they could work together for the purpose of acquiring a deeper consciousness of Reality. And since the greater must include the lesser, no doubt the whole group would be personally benefited during this process.

We are not giving any specific treatment for this purpose because we feel that you should work out the definite method for yourself, following the inclinations of your own heart. Follow your own leadings, but in doing this you will discover that in such group treatment the best results are obtained when each member surrenders every personal desire to the common good.

Much of our field is still in the experimental stage, and you are likely to work out new techniques and perhaps better ways than have been discovered so far. If this were not true, your work would become static and heavy. You must depend upon a certain inspiration rising from your own soul, but always keep this inspiration controlled through purposiveness, because no matter how great a Power is generated it will not produce results unless it is tied to a purpose.

We are now talking about group purposes rather than individual desires. Both are important and should be worked out under the inspiration of your own inward awareness.

God's Bounty

Stand fast therefore in the liberty wherewith Christ hath made us free, and be not entangled again with the yoke of bondage. This is a direct statement that through a right use of the Law we may become free, but through a wrong use of It we may again be entangled in bondage. No plainer statement of the Law of Cause and Effect could be given than this. We may wire the building, turn on the electricity, and have light. But if the wire is short-circuited something will go wrong and we shall again be entangled with darkness.

The darkness was never a thing of itself; it was merely a confused state. The source of our supply was not really cut off; it stopped at our place of confusion and no longer functioned for us. This is a perfect statement of the mental Law of Cause and Effect and it again warns us that we must be aware of the use we are making of the Law; we must keep our thought straight.

It is not always easy to do this, but the Law of Cause and Effect, being no respecter of persons and always working automatically and mechanically and with mathematical precision, must flow through each one of us in the terms of our own acceptance. When we become confused and short-circuit this acceptance we are cutting ourselves off from its supply, but we do not destroy the supply; it is still there.

It is a wonderful thought to realize that the Eternal Bounty can be short-circuited only as far as we are concerned; It cannot be either exhausted or depleted. We shall never be disappointed, for the Law is always operating.

Loose the Consciousness

It is certain that none of us receive as much benefit from this science as we might. We do not permit our consciousness to range in the field of greater possibilities.

A certain time should be taken each day for the enlargement of consciousness. This is done by reminding our imagination that the field with which it deals is Limitless, that Mind is the Creator and the Sustainer, that Mind is Infinite, ever available, and always responsive to us.

There should never be any sense of finality in our self-discovery. No matter how much good we experience today, we should expect more tomorrow. Expectancy always speeds progress; anticipation of better yet to come helps to dissolve the overload of burdens which we now carry with us.

We must learn to loose our consciousness. Nothing is too good to be true. The Kingdom of Harmony is already an ever-present Reality, but as far as we are concerned It waits to be perceived, and only as much good can come to us as we mentally receive.

We must increase our receptivity, continuously extend and expand our comprehension. We should declare a hundred times a day:

Good and more Good is mine. An ever increasing Good is mine. There is no limit to the Good which is mine. Everywhere I go I see this Good, I feel It, I experience It. It crowds itself against me, flows through me, expresses Itself in me, and multiplies Itself around me.

Substance and Supply,
or the Law of Opulence

NATURALLY WE all want what we want when we want it. One of the many criticisms made of the New Thought has been that it is materialistic, since those interested are striving to better themselves materially. This criticism is based on a most materialistic foundation, since it divides Substance from supply, God from man, and Life from living. It makes the Kingdom of Heaven a far-off Divine event, and separates earth from the Eternal Glory. It is just the opposite of the simple but direct statement of Jesus when he said, *What things soever ye desire* and *The kingdom of heaven is at hand.*

The idea that it is wrong for man to pray for or treat to get what we call material good is based on the belief that Reality and actuality are separated by a gulf which can be bridged only through individual suffering, impoverishment, and misery; that man may be redeemed from all this misery in some uncertain future, but not here and now. Yet Jesus stood in the midst of the *here and now* and proclaimed that the Kingdom of Heaven is within and at hand.

We find, then, that the teaching of Jesus is quite at variance with the idea that it is wrong to ask for what we desire, for did he not say, *What things soever ye desire when ye pray, believe that ye receive them, and ye shall have them* (Mark 11:24)? He was announcing a principle, and all principles are universal, changeless, and ever present. All universal principles are available to those who understand them, and they immediately respond to anyone who subjects himself to the way in which they work. For instance, water will reach its own level by its own weight—water will flow downhill. We obey this principle. We use it. We apply it, but we cannot go contrary to that principle and compel water to flow uphill.

It is the same with electricity. The electrician can do anything he wishes to with his principle provided he realizes that it flows from a higher to a lower potential, but he cannot make it act contrary to its own nature. So Jesus was proclaiming the nature of a certain principle, and teaching how to use it.

Jesus announced the Principle of Substance and Supply, or the Law of Opulence. He clearly taught that it is right for us to have what we want provided we subject our desires to the Divine Will and the Divine Necessity. Just what do we mean by Divine Will and Divine Necessity? Divine Will means the nature of God or Spirit, and Divine Necessity means the Law of Cause and Effect.

Jesus announced that when our will complies with the Infinite Harmony, the Law of Cause and Effect has no choice other than to obey our will. We have elsewhere discussed the idea that the Divine Will is toward Life, since being the very Principle of Life It cannot contradict Itself; It must be toward Life. It is toward givingness, since in giving It expresses Itself. Therefore we know that as far as the Divine is concerned, it is always Its Will that we be self-expressed. For God is expressed through the expression of man.

There cannot be the slightest question but that the Divine Will is toward giving us what we want in the way in which we want it, provided we first have complied with the Divine Will, which is Harmony, Peace, Love, Goodness, Truth, and Beauty. If we have complied with the Divine Will, the Law of Cause and Effect, which has no purpose of Its own to execute but is a blind but Intelligent Force, must bring the pattern of our desire to us.

Jesus stated this proposition in its most simple terms when he said, *Seek ye first the kingdom of God, and his righteousness; and all these things shall be added unto you.* He was describing the necessity of our union with the Divine Will, to which all else is added, and the *all else* he included in *what things soever ye desire.* Whether these things be automobiles, undershirts, or sacks of beans makes no difference. Included within the *what things soever* must be all things, past, present, and future. Thus Jesus tells us to comply with the Divine Will.

Next he lays down the way in which the Law will answer us. This is the Divine Necessity, the Law of Cause and Effect. He said: . . . *believe that ye receive them, and ye shall have them* and, again, *For whosoever hath, to him shall be given.* Here he is stating the Law of Cause and Effect as It operates through human consciousness. In no place did this august teacher, this remarkable genius, deny man the right to possess and use the entire gift of God, wholeness of life and its manifestation.

When anyone tells us that it is wrong to use spiritual methods for promoting material well-being, we need not be misled. Such a philosophy contradicts the entire evolution of science, the inspiration of revelation, of Divine insight, and the unfoldment of human personality. It is a philosophy of materialism based upon the superstition that there is God and something else. We do not have to enter into theoretical discussions with anyone, but if we are wise we will remove all barriers from our imagination and come to the Spirit of Truth with a childlike mind, expecting to receive Good.

Let us approach this idea of Substance and Supply and the Law of Opulence with a firm conviction that the Eternal is forever saying to the temporal, that the Father is forever proclaiming to the son: *All that I have is thine*.

Even though manna falls from heaven, we must accept it. The manna is substance, and our receptivity of it is our supply. The Law of Opulence is in us—an ever-increasing mental equivalent of the Good which we desire. The Law of Mental Equivalents says that we can possess any objective thing provided we first have a subjective mental image of it, and provided that this subjective mental image is a real embodiment within our thought.

From what we know about any law in nature, it is safe to say that the more broadly we generalize a principle the more completely shall we be able to specialize such a principle. This means that the more we know about the nature of the principle and the way it works, the more widely shall we be able to use it.

Jesus proclaimed that within the Kingdom of God are contained all gifts. In other words, he generalized that principle which is to be specialized. He announced that the right idea of substance may be applied to everyday needs. So he found money in the fish's mouth, fed the five thousand, brought the boat immediately to the shore, and did many other things which people looked upon as miracles, or Divine interference with universal law, but which Jesus understood to be natural and normal.

It was just as natural for Jesus to turn water into wine as it would be for us to draw a glass of water from the tap. He did not feel that he was concentrating any power or coercing any Divine favors. He did not even petition God; he understood the Law of Cause and Effect. He knew that substance takes form through faith, is shaped by conviction, and projected upon the screen of human experience through the mold of mental equivalents.

We should throw away all doubt, fear, and despair, and enter joyously into our inheritance. But the very Law which we are using should teach us that we shall arrive at the consummation of our desire only by starting from where we are. We are told to despise not the day of small beginnings. Each one must start with the mental equivalent he has today, and by enlarging upon it increase his capacity to receive.

In this connection we must remember that the Law of Cause and Effect, the Universal Subjectivity, has no intention or purpose of Its own relative to any individual. We make up Its mind for It. As far as we are concerned It has no thought for us other than the thought we ourselves entertain about life. It does not know that a million dollars is more money than ten dollars. It does not know that an ocean is larger than a fish pond; that a mountain is more than three foot high. And yet It creates form through idea, for as we have elsewhere stated, there is no big or little in the Law.

This is the crux of the whole matter—not two powers, but ONE. What we need to change is not the Law, but our use of It. We have no power or limitation to contend against, no evil to fight, no hell to cool off. How wonderful! How fortunate! And what a happy outlook! If we can become more in our inner consciousness we shall have more in our external environment.

The Law, having no mind of Its own relative to us, and being compelled by Its very nature to follow the patterns of our thought, is and must remain our obedient servant. But we have affirmed a negation, have declared that there is not Good enough to go around. Hence we lack the experience of that Good which we fail to perceive.

We must not only know that there is Good enough to go around but we must specifically announce this Good. It stands to reason that if the Law knows about us only what we know about ourselves, and that if what we hold to be true about Life Itself furnishes us with our mental patterns, then the Law knows about us only what we believe about Life. Therefore the very belief in the reality of evil creates the evil believed in. Or as Jesus said, *All they that take the sword shall perish with the sword.* The belief that there is not enough Good to go around makes it difficult, if not impossible, for Good to be experienced by the one who entertains such a belief.

We must reverse all these beliefs and accept the simple proposition that God is Good, for this is fundamental to a correct idea of Substance and Supply and the operation of the Law of Opulence. God is Good. This Good is ours now. This should be our permanent and increasing expectancy. We should expect so much Good that we should conceive of It as being more than we even have time to enjoy. We should feel the presence of this Good and appreciate Its meaning and give thanks for Its manifestation. There should be the combination of gratitude, expectancy, and joy. There should be an enthusiastic recognition that we are in partnership with the Divine and that God and Company cannot fail.*

When it comes to actual and specific practice we should definitely know that the particular thing we desire, we already have. In this way we form a mold in our thought, and a definite one around which the Creative Energy of Mind may play. This is our bowl of acceptance, catching, as it were, from the horn of plenty that which we are able to receive.

This Law of Mental Equivalents should never be overlooked,

*See p. 413—*Ed.*

344

for It is the Law which decides how much of this infinite thing we are to experience. We cannot experience more than we can accept, but we can expect more than we have been experiencing. If we are willing to start from where we are today, creating a little bigger, broader, and better mental equivalent than we had yesterday, we shall progressively advance.

Since we are dealing with an Infinite Principle, no possible limitation can be placed upon our use of It, just as there is no number we can conceive of which cannot have a like amount added to it, or which cannot be multiplied by itself. And just as there is no place where this sequence of numbers can stop, there is no place where infinite possibilities can cease to unfold. The only place where they appear to cease unfolding is where our expectancy and understanding inhibit their action through us, for the operation of the Law is always mathematically correct. The Law of Cause and Effect, having no mind of Its own as far as we are concerned, must follow the patterns of our individual thought.

In actual practice we make definite statements, as we have repeatedly emphasized. If you want a home, treat for a home. If you want an automobile, treat definitely for an automobile, and if you want a certain sum of money, treat definitely for that sum of money. There is nothing materialistic about this since all things emanate from pure Spirit and return again to It.

In actual practice, having first complied with the Law and with the Spirit, do not hesitate to work definitely for what you want. Not to do so would be to deny the very Principle which you have affirmed, to inhibit the operation of the very Law which you have come to understand.

Any intelligent perspective of the operation of this Law should cause us to know that when we work we should work definitely for what we want. There is no other way. The Spirit can give us only what we take, and our taking is mental. How can the mind accept what it rejects, entertain what it refuses to listen to, possess what it casts out, or have what it will not take? This is not only unthinkable; it is impossible.

345

Getting and Giving

ONE OF the laws of radiation says that the absorbing power of a substance is equal to its emitting power, which means that the ones that absorb the most must be the ones which emit the most. Or to state the proposition in another way, we can take in only what we give out. Jesus said, *Give, and it shall be given unto you.*

Now here is a law in nature verified by science, and we believe that every law in physical nature is reproduced in the Laws of Mind. This would have to be so if the Universe is one system rather than two, and if Unity is to be maintained throughout the whole.

There is a reason for these things, and the reason is that everything moves in a circle. Everything bends back upon itself. As a man sows so shall he reap, and so must he reap until he sows differently. Whitman said that the gift is most to the giver and comes back most to him, and we all know that since the universe is in balance nothing can leave any point without an equal something returning to it.

Each one of us is a point in the Infinite Mind, a center in the Consciousness of God or the Living Spirit. We do not live because we understand Life or even put Life into our own living; we live because Life lives in us. We could make no greater mistake than to think that we created either Life or Law, but it would be an equal error to suppose that we escape Life or Law. We are subject to it but not in any predetermined sense, for no matter what happened yesterday we can change its sequence today.

If we have given out but little and received only an equal amount, we can begin to give out more, and just as surely as we do this, more will return to us. The giving and receiving are at the center of our own being; the going out from us is but one end of the coming back to us, and the coming back to us is merely the other end of the going out from us.

346

The whole thing is so simple that its very simplicity eludes us, and we look for a more profound reason for the universe being in balance, and why being in balance it automatically proclaims the law of justice.

If the going out and the coming back are equal, then in a certain sense, like the energy and mass of Einstein, they are equal, identical, and interchangeable. To refuse to give is to refuse to live to the fullest extent. To refuse to give love is to refuse to receive love. That which we refuse to give out not only closes the door on the giving but on the receiving as well.

All this sounds like quite a tough proposition until we come to realize that if it were any other way we would not be free, but would be bound by external circumstances. Freedom can exist only on the proposition that it is first of all individual.

If we know that we ourselves are centers of distribution and centers of accumulation and that the two are equally identical and interchangeable, and if we know that nothing interferes with this but ourselves, we are free to act as we would be acted upon. This is why Jesus said, . . . *all things whatsoever ye would that men should do to you, do ye even so to them: for this is the law and the prophets.*

347

Receiving Is as Important as Giving

WE NEED never beseech the Law to operate for us, for if there is but One Mind in the Universe our mind is some part of It, and it is Its nature to respond to Itself. Nothing can hinder the Divine from flowing into us except our own free will.

The sun may be shining even while we persist in standing in a dark basement. The manna may be falling but we refuse to gather it. Now we must come out of our basement of despair into the sunshine of Truth, into the warmth and color of Divine recognition, the instantaneous awareness of the Allness of Good.

God is Life and Life gives Itself to us. It does not give some of Itself; It gives all of Itself. But the gift without a receiver cannot complete itself in individual life. Emerson tells us that we are compelled to perceive that we are beneficiaries; that we stand in the light and the light is all. Then he tells us to get our bloated nothingness out of the way of the Divine Circuit.

This getting out of our own way is what mental treatment does for us, since it declares that there is nothing in us which can keep our good away. Treatment always declares the Presence of Good and the operation of the Law of Love. It is a conscious, active recognition of Spiritual Presence, Spiritual Force, Spiritual Law, and Spiritual Order.

The Servant
May Become an Heir

Wherefore thou art no more a servant, but a son; and if a son, then an heir. How many of us claim our Divine inheritance? How many of us realize that the Will or the Nature of God was written before the foundations of this physical universe were laid, and that in this Will each one of us was endowed with the faculty of True Perception, bequeathed a life of Perfection, and guaranteed immunity from all evil? For surely the Will of God could be no less than this.

The Will of God has been written by the invisible hand of Reality. It is still in probate as far as most of us are concerned; It has never been completely executed. We have not laid hold of our Divine inheritance. Perhaps we have been listening to the wrong counsel. We have accepted the false evidence of the senses. We have been cast into prison for debts which might have been paid had we recognized that Substance already belonged to us. We have been a servant and not a son; hence we have not entered into the heirship.

In another place we are told that it is high time that we should awake from our sleep. Perhaps we have dreamed that we were servants and not heirs. Now we must awake from this mesmeric state. The heir must claim his inheritance; otherwise it is still kept for him and he has not the use of it. He must step forward before the bar of justice, which is the Law of Cause and Effect, and declare that he is no longer a servant, a slave, but a master, a son, an heir. He must announce that all that the Father has is his.

Thus he lays claim to his True estate, laying claim in the name of God through Christ, and the inheritance is at once delivered. That which had been kept in store for him is delivered into his hands.

Man against Himself

NATURE MADE a chemical laboratory within us to take care of our health. In a sense we might say that there are little intelligences within us acting as though they were little people, whose business it is to digest our food and assimilate it, to circulate the blood, and get rid of its impurities. There are millions of these little people inside our bodies whose purpose it is to keep us physically fit. But there also are other little people who are not so kindly minded and they try to tear things down and disrupt the work of the good little people.

Every doctor knows that when he can get the good people inside working with him, things are going to come out all right. We break a bone and when it is set nature gets busy, and all the good little people begin to knit the bone together again, and all the time they are causing the blood to circulate so there will be no infection. But we are learning that we can interfere with these little people inside us because they are subject to a greater intelligence than theirs, which is the person himself.

One of the most popular psychologists in America told me he once suffered from indigestion, and the thought came to him that he could talk to these little people inside him and tell them that it was their business to take care of his digestion. So he talked to them for a few moments every day and told them how wonderful they were and how much he appreciated what they were doing, and that he would not interfere with them any more. He was going to be happy and he knew they would take care of everything for him. He praised them and blessed them and in a few weeks his whole physical condition cleared up.

Well, this is a body-mind relationship. It is reducing psychosomatics to its simplest common denominator. There is an Intelligence hidden at the center of everything, and we are intelligent, and the lower form of intelligence responds to the higher form. The intelligence in the physical body is a subconscious intelligence. It works creatively, but within certain fixed limitations. It is like a man sent on an errand and told what to do and knowing only to do what he is told.

All the little people inside us are supposed to be working for us and with us, but we can so disturb them that we almost hypnotize them and cause them to work destructively instead of constructively.

This can be carried to such an extent that the wrong direction given to these little people produces a large part of our physical diseases. But right direction can reverse this process and produce physical well-being instead of disease. And we now know that while hate, animosity, and confusion can produce discord, love can heal it.

It is from simple but far-reaching facts like these that we learn some of the greatest lessons of life. And the first lesson we should learn is that Life, which is God, intends us to be well, happy, and successful. When it comes to body-mind relationships, it is helpful to imagine and feel that all the little people inside are working for us and with us, and to feel that they are connected with the Divine Intelligence which directs them— the very Power that created them. This brings us back to the need we all have for a faith, a calm assurance, and an inward sense of well-being.

Surely That which had the Intelligence to create has both the will and the ability to sustain. And if in our ignorance we have misused the Creative Power within us, all we have to do is reverse the process and cooperate with It. In doing this one of the first lessons we learn is to bless everything, to be grateful for everything, to gladly acknowledge the Divine Presence—not as something far away but as something close and intimate.

Not only is there an Intelligence directing the activities of our physical bodies, but this same Intelligence is also directing everything we do. Not only does man operate against himself, physically, but he does so in every activity of life. How many of us really expect to be happy tomorrow? How many of us, when we lie down at night, relax and let the bed hold us up? How many of us have confidence enough in God to sleep in peace, wake in joy, and look forward to the coming day with gladness?

What we need is a conscious cooperation, and a glad one, between ourselves and the Power which, if we would let It, would rightly govern everything. But man is so used to operating against himself, so used to thinking of himself as detached and separate, so completely taking the whole burden of life on his own shoulders, that he has almost lost the ability to cooperate with that Divine Presence which seeks to be a partner to all of us. In our ignorance we have not only operated against ourselves, but have contradicted the "Supremacy" of God. We have denied ourselves the privilege of working with the Power that put us here.

You and I know that we did not set the stars in their courses. We did not cause the sun to shine or the rain to come. But we can cooperate with this Power back of and in and through all people.

We cannot unify and cooperate with something we do not believe in. So the starting point, the very beginning of the re-education of our minds, must be a deep conviction, a firm faith. And since, in a sense, life is a stage on which each plays a part, there is no reason why we should not dramatize our relationship with the Infinite.

Just think of all these little people working inside us. God put them there. Why not hook them up in our imagination with the living Spirit, recognize their presence, praise and bless them, and even tell them what we want them to do? Each day we should think how wonderful it is to be cooperating with God. Surely this is the greatest drama of all. We do not strut across the stage of human experience as separated and isolated characters, but rather as actors in the great play of life, the drama of human existence.

But we must not forget the Director of the play, the One who knows how to make each separate line and act become part of the whole piece, until something complete is produced. God is the Great Producer and Director even though He is invisible. We do not see the little people inside us, but they are there, and in our imagination we can feel them. We do not see the law of gravitational force which holds everything in place, and we do not see the Divine Intelligence that causes the rose to bloom or a chicken to come out of an egg.

Let us stop acting against ourselves, each other, and the

world, for we know that our thoughts make impressions on our environments and on the people we meet, and silently mold conditions. Here again the imagination can be combined with the will, and each can think of himself as playing a part in the game of life, and a good one. In the theater, when a man plays a part that convinces us, he must himself first believe in the part he is playing. I recently asked a director what he thought of a certain play which we had both seen, and he replied, "I didn't think much of it. I didn't care for it." And when I asked, "What was the trouble?" he answered, "The people who read the lines didn't believe them."

If our words are of the intellect only, and not spoken from the heart, the audience will not respond. This is the way it is with life. And this is why in all of his teachings Jesus laid such stress on the simple, childlike ability to believe, to feel, to accept, and to act as though the great Giver of Life were still giving; as though the great Creator were still creating in us and through us.

We have wondered so much about the life of Jesus and the wonderful things he did—how he healed the sick and raised the dead and turned water into wine. But has it come to us that perhaps Jesus was the only person in history who never denied the Divine Presence; who always expected It to respond to him? And because we have set Jesus apart, as different from others, we have accepted him without accepting his teaching.

And yet he was the one who said that what he did we could do also. And he told us how to do it—stop acting against yourself; stop acting against anything, and learn to cooperate with what is best, always sensing the Presence of the Divine—and then *let the play go on.*

The Fruit of Good and Evil

EVIL AS a thing of itself never originated unless God created it, for, as our Scripture says, *All things were made by him, and without him was not anything made that was made.*

And yet evil is an experience of the human being, if by evil we mean sickness, want, lack, impoverishment, unhappiness, or physical deterioration. Here we are confronted by the problem of something that is and is not at the same time. How can a thing be and not be? To understand how it could be and yet not be really is a problem.

It seems to us that this problem is solved only in such degree as we realize that evil is never a thing in itself or of itself. It is merely a limited use or perhaps a misuse of a Creative Power which is Complete and Perfect within Itself.

We do not deny that people experience what we call evil, for such a denial would be absurd and would place us in a position of saying that everything we do not like is unreal. This is far from an intelligent position, for everything is as real as it is supposed to be, and people actually do suffer physical and mental pains. But if this suffering were designed by the All-Creative Wisdom, then we could not possibly escape it. Moreover, God Himself would be evil. We read in Habakkuk 1:13: *Thou art of purer eyes than to behold evil, and canst not look upon iniquity.*

The experience of evil is more than imagination. It is actual experience, and it would be useless for us to deny it. If we can feel that it is something the human being has created through ignorance, rather than something that is ordained and predetermined, we shall be in a better position to combat it. We must come to know and sense that certain Something which is Perfect and Complete, and which, being Omnipresent, must be at the center of everything, including ourselves.

The origin of evil is in the human mind, and the belief in devil, hell, purgatory, and limbo has its origin in the human mind, and nowhere else. This belief must be erased from the mind. We must come to know that there can be no ultimate evil. We must have the assurance that evil will disappear from

354

our experience in such degree as we no longer feed it with our imagination, or through our acts create situations that encourage it.

You will remember that, according to the story of the Garden of Eden, God created man and woman and set them in the garden, which was an earthly paradise. The River of Life flowed through the garden, watering it, and it contained every kind of fruit and plant necessary to man's physical well-being.

Adam and Eve were told to enjoy this garden, to live in it and be happy. But they were warned that, while they could eat of all the fruits that grew in the garden, there was one tree from which they should not eat. This was called the Tree of the Knowledge of Good and Evil.

At once we see the meaning of this. We can eat from the tree which bears fruit of love, and the more we eat from it the better off we shall be. But if we begin to mix love with hate we come into confusion. The fruit does not digest because hate is contrary to the nature of love.

It is natural that we should ask: Why did a God who is all-wise, all-powerful, and all-good create a tree that could bear the fruit of hate? The answer is simple: Man has self-choice or he would not be a person, and having choice implies there must be more than one thing from which to choose. The very freedom with which he is endowed makes it possible for him to use that freedom, at least temporarily, in a way that will restrict him; otherwise he would not be free. Therefore, man is given the right to choose, but with the right to choose must come the liability as well as the reward of his choice.

Well, man is a curious creature. He is born with an innate desire to explore everything. He has a great curiosity, and sometimes he wants to know why he cannot do exactly as he pleases and get away with it. This is what he was forbidden to do. He was told he had freedom to do what he wanted to, provided he never used his freedom to destroy himself. And who can doubt the wisdom of this?

And now another symbol appears, the serpent. It is well to look into the original meaning of the word *serpent*. It was used in antiquity to designate the Life Principle and the way It works.

The serpent meant the Life Principle. While it was the serpent that tempted Eve, it was also the serpent that Moses lifted up in the wilderness, upon which the Children of Israel looked and were healed of their physical infirmities. Jesus referred to this when he said, *As Moses lifted up the serpent in the wilderness, even so must the Son of man be lifted up.*

The great principles of nature exist to be used, and the laws of nature become our servants when we use them rightly. But these same laws, wrongly used, impose suffering upon us. We can use our minds to be happy or unhappy; we can think peace or confusion; we can be loving and kind, or disagreeable, because we are free.

If we were so created that we did not have this freedom, we should be eternally bound. Life would have no meaning. Everywhere we look in our own lives and the lives of others we see the use and the abuse of this power. For instance, the atom bomb could destroy civilization, yet atomic energy could run all the machinery in the world. The power that can be used so destructively could be converted into an instrument that would help to bring freedom to everyone on earth.

We are finally discovering that the very power that makes us sick can heal us, the very things that bind us can free us, and that the imagination we use to destroy our happiness, rightly used, could create situations that would make everyone happy. Well, this is the meaning of the serpent and the savior and that great symbol which runs throughout the Bible, depicting the right and the wrong way to use the Power which is within us, the Power that is greater than we are.

But again we must stop and ask ourselves a very important question, one we find to be in almost everyone's mind: Is evil, then, equal to Good? The answer is *No*, for we have already found out that, while we can love to any extent without being hurt, hate finally destroys itself and destroys us with it. But love harms no one. Good protects Itself because God is Good.

We are given the freedom to misuse the Power of Life, but only to a certain point. This is why the symbol goes on to show that, when Adam and Eve finally decided to eat from the fruit of the Tree of the Knowledge of Good and Evil, and after they had done so, they were expelled from the Garden of Eden and compelled to earn their living by the sweat of their brow.

Looking into the story more carefully we discover that it was Eve who first ate the fruit, after which she gave it to Adam. Remembering that the Bible is the story of man and his relationship to life, we must expect to find in the symbol of Adam and Eve a great psychological truth common to all human beings. For Adam and Eve were not really a man and a woman, but represented the two sides of our nature. We can liken Adam to the intellect, to our conscious self-choice, and we can liken Eve to our subconscious reaction, for this is what the story originally meant. And it is only in the last fifty years that we have discovered its importance.

We are all Adam and Eve, and when our intellects become coerced or misdirected they still find a subconscious reaction. When the subconscious reaction becomes powerful enough, it controls the intellect because of the unconscious thought patterns that are laid down in the mind. Finally, when these thought patterns become dominant, they control even the intellect. This is what produces most insanity and the psychosomatic relationships between the body and the mind.

Our present knowledge of the mind tells us exactly how these Laws of Mind work, and we now know that our mental and emotional reactions to life decide what is going to happen to us. Because of man's misuse of the Power within him he is led on the pathway which produces bondage and weakness.

And so we come to the other side of this great story which says, *For as in Adam all die, even so in Christ shall all be made alive.* So the symbol of the savior is presented—the man of God, the Christ within each one of us. And we are told to look unto this Christ, because he is one with God, if we wish salvation.

Of course, we all wish salvation. We all want to be happy; we should like to be well. We have never yet met anyone who did not wish to be successful. We want people to like us. We greatly desire to love and be loved. And above everything else, we want and need an inward sense of security and peace of mind.

It is true that we all long for the Kingdom of God on earth,

357

whether or not we know it. And the great struggle of man is toward freedom, emancipation from want and fear and disease, and from everything that can hurt. We all long to return to our lost paradise. Man is put on earth to enjoy life and he is given the freedom to decide how he is to live; always there is placed before him the possibility of two things: to be, or not to be.

Finally all real Power must rest on the side of Good, and finally evil will be vanquished by Good. This is the whole meaning of the story of the savior, the lifting up of the Life Principle on the Tree of Life—the coming to realize that we are One with God forever.

Just as the Old Testament tells us of the fall of man through his misuse of the Laws of Life, so the New Testament tells us of the redemption of man, the triumph of the Spirit, and the return to that heavenly home from which we all came. This is why Jesus said, *I am the way, the truth and the life*, by which he meant that God in me and God in you is the way, the truth, and the life.

The story of the Garden of Eden is completed through the triumph of the cross, by a man who knew that every man is Divine and that God intends Good to come to everyone. So Jesus exalted the Life Principle rather than debasing It. He discovered the meaning of Life at the center of his own being and showed humanity, for all time, what can happen when someone lives as though God were real to him, as though Love were the final Power, and Good the final arbiter of fate.

What are we going to do with this greatest of all Truths— the relationship that we as individuals have to the Divine Spirit which is already Perfect, and which desires only our good—? We have come to the crossroads of time, and the decision is ours. But, like everything else, this decision has to start with the individual life. If we are weary of our troubles there is something we can do about it. We can begin to exalt the Life Principle within us. We can lift up the serpent until we behold the face of the savior.

The Contagion of Fear

JOHN SMITH was humming a gay tune and seemed to exude great confidence in himself and the world as he boarded the streetcar. He sat down next to a man who was filled with fear and apprehension. By the time John Smith got off the car he was in the grip of a terrible anxiety which he could not explain.

It is possible for us to catch fear from others much as we would catch a cold, for we are all unconscious mental, emotional, and spiritual broadcasting stations. This takes us back to a thought in the Bible which says that a man's enemies shall be those of his own household, for our real enemies are our fears and phobias, our doubts and uncertainties, our anxieties and our inner conflicts.

Many years ago I discovered—and, of course, others had discovered before me—that nervous, fretful, and agitated children, who have nightmares and who cannot retain their food, are affected by the inner agitation of their parents' thoughts and feelings.

But let us broaden this field and say that the whole world is filled with the thoughts of the people who live in it, and that perhaps we are all more or less subject to the passing emotions of the race mind. A leading psychiatrist has told us that fear can render a person completely unconscious as far as his brain is concerned. He tells us that it paralyzes the memory, and, if a person is afraid he will forget something, he is likely to do so. We know that in cases of amnesia people are so frightened by some unconscious thought that they even forget their own names and who they are and where they came from.

Fear produces a mysterious chemical which is released into the blood, but this chemical disappears when the anxiety is over. We all have our little fears and anxieties. And we all wish to get over them. The healing of fear and anxiety is not to be found in any drug or physical manipulation. The cure is to be found only within our own minds. Where fear is the disease, we have to be our own doctors.

The Bible tells us that perfect Love casts out fear, and that where Love is, fear cannot remain. We can apply this Principle of faith and confidence to ourselves as individuals, to our families as the first unit we deal with, and to all the people we contact in the everyday walks of life. Did you ever notice the effect of just being with a person who is calm and poised and unafraid? How different you feel, how buoyed up and confident you become! Why should not each one of us become a broadcasting station for faith?

The world is too largely governed by fear. We are afraid of this and that and something else; we are afraid of what has happened and what is happening and what we think is going to happen. If fear is contagious and does in some mysterious way secrete a germ which acts negatively in the physical body, I think it is not too much to say that it also secretes some kind of mental germ in the whole race mind which affects everyone with a sense of confusion and uncertainty and anxiety.

There is no doubt that this is true, and we should do something about it. Not that we have to become heroic figures who consider themselves the liberators of humanity, for we are probably not in a position to do this. What I mean is that each one of us should analyze his own thinking to determine what is wrong, and replace every fear with faith and confidence.

But where are we going to get this faith and confidence? Certainly not out of the weakness of our previous experience, and perhaps not out of the thoughts that we had yesterday—those thoughts that were so filled with anxiety. It seems to me that we will have to begin all over again. And we must find some reason for having a faith that is stronger than all our fears. So far the world has never found this reason outside what we call a religious or a spiritual idea. And by this I mean a direct faith in God.

There is nothing for God to be afraid of. And if we can, and do, tune in to the thoughts of others, and if they affect us, as they most certainly do, why should we not learn to tune in to the Mind of God, which is free from fear and doubt?

This is what is meant by prayer and meditation. For in the act of prayer and meditation we commune with the invisible

Spirit; we draw Its Strength, Its Peace, and Its Serenity into our own souls. And as a result of this we become strong and self-reliant, because we have built up a confidence in life, a faith and conviction which wards off all fear. Just as a germ of physical disease is less liable to infect a strong body, so the germ of mental fear is resisted by a whole and happy mind.

It would be interesting if some day we should read a headline in the daily newspaper which said, *A germ of fear is now operating in a certain locality*, or *infecting a whole community*. And it would be interesting if the same article were to tell us that a group of people were working to counteract this fear germ by broadcasting faith. And then after a while we would pick up another newspaper which had a headline reading, *We are now inoculated with faith, and the fear germ has disappeared*.

Well, perhaps this sounds a little far-fetched today, but I have complete confidence that the time will come when we shall see such headlines in the papers.

The quickest and most effective method to get rid of fear is to get quiet and lift up the whole thought in confidence and faith to Something bigger than we are. It is like going from a cold, dark room into the sunshine and just sitting there, letting the rays of the sun penetrate the whole being with warmth and color until the darkness and the dampness are gone. So it is with the life of prayer and faith, of affirmative meditation and of communion with that Divine Spirit which is closer to us than our very breath.

Let us not forget that if fear is contagious, faith is doubly so. How wonderful it is to realize that we can so influence our environment that everyone who steps into it will be benefited. If this is what we are doing, the very stars in their courses will conspire to aid us.

And we may be certain of something else—there is at the center of our being a strong fortress of faith, placed there by a Power greater than we are, by an Intelligence that knows everything, and forevermore held in place by a Divine Presence which is God in us. It is to this indwelling God that we must turn. So how would it be if we worked out a method for doing this?

To begin with you might follow a few simple rules. First of all, if you are filled with fears do not harbor them as a great secret in your life, but find some close friend or confidant to whom you may unburden your whole soul. This will release the tension which your fears have built up in your body. Just to talk with a calm, confident person, who can point out the reason why you need not entertain these fears, is a great relief.

This is, however, but a temporary thing, for next you must learn to face the fears. You should not be afraid to analyze them and you should explain to yourself just why you know there is nothing to be afraid of. Whenever you find yourself brooding over some fear or entertaining some anxiety, begin at once to do something about it.

And the next thing to do is convince yourself that you would not be here were there not a Power greater than you are that put you here. And learn to have confidence in this Power. Never be afraid to say to this Power and this Divine Presence: ''I now lay down all my fears and doubts and anxieties. I pass them back into the great and perfect Life of which I know I am a part.'' Confess your fears to yourself before this Power, and then reach just a little higher in faith than you were in fear and you will discover a miracle is taking place—fears will begin to recede, until finally they appear as a speck on the horizon of your mind, and then they seem to walk over that horizon and disappear entirely, like darkness running away from light.

This is not as difficult as it sounds, if you just become as a little child. We all need to resurrect this little child within us, who unfortunately has been so buried in our unhappy experiences that we have almost forgotten that he was ever there. But we have not quite forgotten, have we? We all need to resurrect the confidence in life which we had in our youth.

To recapture this dream of youth is the wisest and the most intelligent thing any person can do. Fear has brought confusion. Faith will give birth to confidence. Anxiety has brought days filled with conflict and nights full of dread. Faith alone can heal this confusion and drive from our minds all thoughts of fear, and dissipate all anxiety. Love alone can bring harmony into our lives. So say to yourself:

I lay all fear aside, and in confidence and complete faith I turn to the one perfect Divine Presence, knowing that the light of Truth shines upon my path even as Divine Love guides me into the Secret Place of the Most High, where I dwell under the shadow of the Almighty.

I know that there is nothing to be afraid of in God's world. Fear cannot operate in me, nor can it go forth from me. At the very center of my being there is complete confidence, complete faith. At the very center of my being there is a consciousness of the protection of Divine Love, the guidance of Divine Wisdom, and the strength of Divine Power.

And so I turn in thought to the whole world and know that my word is bringing light and life and a feeling of strength and confidence to everyone. I turn in thought to the leaders of the world everywhere, and know that Love and Intelligent Guidance is directing their thoughts and actions.

I turn in thought to all the nations of the earth and awaken in them the realization that there is Good enough to go around; that there is a Divine Government under which they all may be protected from the fear of each other.

I turn in thought to the great creative imagination of the human race and assure it that there is a feeling and a Presence at the center of everything waiting to make Itself known.

And I turn to the great God, who knows all things and who can do all things, and say: "Lead, kindly light, amid the encircling gloom; lead Thou me on."

Fear and Punishment

WE ALL know what fear can do; how it can shrivel up hope and dampen the ardor of living, and how finally it can close up the avenues of self-expression. When carried to an extreme it leaves one a wreck, physically and mentally. And we have observed what faith can do. We have seen people so filled with fear that nothing in life seemed worthwhile to them, and we have seen them learn to have faith in life, and have watched the transformation that has taken place in their lives.

The psychologist might say that such a person has a phobia—an inferiority complex—which means that he feels unable to cope with life. Or the psychiatrist might say that he is neurotic. But we must look at him and say, "Here is a spiritually complete man who is doing nothing that he has not been trained to do. He has had the intelligence and the emotional capacity to learn these lessons of fear, and to learn them well."

If it is possible for us to learn to be afraid, we can reverse the process and learn to have faith.

In the study of mental suggestion it has been discovered that if a mother fears that her child's food will not digest, it will affect his digestive processes. If she is afraid that he will not sleep well at night, his sleep will be disturbed. If he is surrounded with thoughts of irritation and emotions of anger, they will all register in him. Times without number he has listened to such warnings as "Keep away from that dog, he may bite!" or "Don't go too close to the edge, you may fall!" or "Be sure to wash your hands, there are germs on them."

The signposts on the road to fear are too numerous to mention, but each leaves its imprint upon the growing mind and plastic memory of the child. It is little wonder that he arrives at maturity in a state of perpetual fear. He has learned it in his home, in his school, and unfortunately, in his religious instruction. We sometimes wonder whether God is not feared more than He is loved and trusted.

It is unfortunate that the idea of a future state of punishment should have been so emphasized in our religious training. For out of it have come the most morbid fears the human mind has ever entertained. How can we believe that a *Good* God, a God of Love as well as Wisdom, would seek to destroy His own creation?

This does not mean that we are not responsible for our acts. We cannot escape the logical result of our thoughts and acts. The punishment for any act flows out of the act itself. Jesus said, *Forgive, and ye shall be forgiven.* In this masterful statement we find a teaching of justice but not retribution. The moment we forgive we are forgiven. God is the eternal Forgiver.

You will remember that in Jesus' parable of the laborers, some came early in the morning to work in the vineyard, some at noon, some in the afternoon, and some did not come until the eleventh hour. But the lord of the vineyard gave them all equal pay. This parable portrays a message of great significance. What Jesus was really saying is this: No matter what happened during the day, no matter how wrong we might have been in our previous experience, when the time comes that we actually do enter into the vineyard—which means life as we live it—then the lord of the vineyard—who represents God—receives us. There is no condemnation, no judgment. We are not sent into eternal perdition or future punishment. Jesus taught that there is no sin but a mistake, and no punishment but a consequence.

Again we find Jesus forgiving the thief who was crucified with him, and saying, *Today shalt thou be with me in paradise.* He told people that when they go into the temple to pray, forgiveness should be their first act. Can we ignore that this forgiveness means forgiving ourselves, just as certainly as it means forgiving everyone else? Jesus clearly taught that God is the great Giver, and because He is the great Giver, He is also the great Forgiver.

Here is another illustration: Suppose a room has been in darkness for years and we bring in a light. What becomes of the darkness? It just is not there. It would make no difference how long the room may have been dark; when the light appears, the darkness disappears.

Perhaps our ideas of being good and doing good have been based on the expectation of reward or the fear of punishment instead of on common sense. Goodness should be natural and spontaneous. Goodness is normal; evil is abnormal. We should live by faith and not by fear. But because we have had so many fears and because we have built up such an unconscious sense of guilt, we seek a release from the emotional tension of this guilt feeling by projecting the thought that we need to be punished for our mistakes. This, no doubt, is the orgin of the belief in hell.

Many believe that the Bible teaches that there is a literal hell. Nothing could be further from the truth. What the Bible teaches is the Law of Cause and Effect. It teaches It over and over again, in many different places and in many different ways.

The Bible teaches that all unkind and negative reactions must be purged from the mind. This is where we get the idea of purgatory—it means a purging of the mind. It tells us that the pain of this mental purging can be likened to the fires of Gehennah, which was a place outside the city of Jerusalem where they burned the garbage. This teaching we can accept because it is logical. If our minds are filled with hatred toward others, we really hate ourselves. If we lack confidence in life, it is because we first lack confidence in the self. And if we are afraid of God and of the future, it is because we are not acquainted with Love and confidence.

Unfortunate as it may be, there is no question but that one of the great fundamental fears of the whole human race is the belief in hell and in future punishment. And probably more sorrow, human suffering, and morbidity have come from this one belief than all others combined. It is time for us to clarify the situation and realize that the God of Love cannot hate, the God of Life cannot destroy, the God of Good cannot desire evil.

It is on this basis that we should create a great hope and faith. We should be willing to admit that we are punished by our mistakes, and in common sense recognize that while we continue our mistakes we must of necessity continue to suffer; but always with the certainty in mind that when light comes darkness disappears, when forgiveness comes to our own mind we are forgiven, when we are willing to give we shall receive, when we learn how to enter into heaven we shall leave everything unlike heaven behind us.

The Divine Peace is not disturbed by any hymn of hate, nor is the majesty and might of the Eternal Presence disturbed by our thoughts of discord.

There is another thought that Jesus gave us which we should not overlook. He said that the Kingdom of Heaven is at hand; It is here and now. It is not something to wait for, something that is going to happen by and by. It is at hand. The question is, are we seeing It? Are we actually beholding It as he did in the here and now?

The reason that Jesus forgave people their sins was that he recognized the fear and morbidity that had been built up throughout the ages because people were afraid of God. They feared Him rather than loved Him. And so Jesus forgave them all these mistakes and told them to think the whole thing over again until they finally realized that God is Love, God is Life, God is Peace, God is Joy, God is Givingness, God is Forgivingness.

But at the same time he warned them that there is a Law of Life which reacts to a person in the way he uses It, and that while he refuses to forgive he cannot be forgiven; while he refuses to see in every person he meets the Divine image he hopes is within himself, he cannot find the Son of God at the center of his own being. Jesus taught justice without judgment, liberty without license, and showed that there is a perfect balance between our thoughts, our acts, and what is going to happen to us. And it is upon this that we should base all our beliefs and acts.

Again let us remember the story of the Prodigal Son who had lost in a far country everything he possessed. And when, sick and discouraged, he returned to his Father's house, his Father did not condemn him, but welcomed him with open arms. He did not even ask where he had been or what he had been doing, but said, ''Let us rejoice together.''

367

How wonderful is this idea of being enfolded in the Everlasting Arms of Peace and Love on the very day that we forsake our distrust, our hate, our fears and doubts. And how simple should be our salvation. All that it means is turning from wrong to right, from darkness to light, from fear to faith, from hate to love, from hell to heaven. How satisfying to know that no one can hinder us but ourselves, and except for the help of the Great and the Good God, no one can help us but ourselves.

Some day, as surely as we live, this is the God that will be presented to humanity—one Universal Divine Presence forevermore blessing Its creation; one infinite ocean of Love in which all are immersed; our Father which art in heaven, the One and only God, who is not a God of wrath or retribution but a God of Peace and Joy and Wholeness. The day will come when the other God will be forgotten, and humanity will learn to live as though this earth were the Kingdom of Heaven, with God Himself the host.

Overcoming Fear and the Inferiority Complex

Fear not, little flock; for it is your Father's good pleasure to give you the kingdom. Here is the implication that some kingdom over which we should have complete dominion has already been given, and if there is such a kingdom, and if we should have dominion over it, then we should act as kings, not as vassals, not as slaves, and not as those who cringe before an inexorable fate.

If all people are made in the image and likeness of the Divine Being, then surely one person should not be afraid of another. And if Life Itself is a Unity of Good, then why should we be afraid of life?

Experience has proved to us that some people are afraid of life; they are afraid of each other, and seldom do we find anything which even resembles a kingly attitude. Moreover, in those rather rare instances where we do find a kingly attitude it is too often attended with arrogance. It is of the utmost importance to solve this perplexing problem which every priest, physician, metaphysician, and psychologist meets in his daily contact with people.

Under analysis it has been found that an inferiority complex is based on the fear of life. The basic fear is an inability to properly adjust to everyday living.

An oversensitive person is always handicapped and too often assumes an attitude of arrogance or blustering bravado to cover up his inward hurt. Generally speaking he will not admit that such a hurt is there. And even though he trains his will and studies every psychological method known with which to combat life, unless he has overcome the fundamental fears of life he has only covered them that much deeper by his mental maneuvering.

Anyone who is familiar with mental reactions knows that a man who goes blustering around saying he has no fear, asserting loudly that he is just as good as anyone, and who always demands the attention of others, is sick inwardly. He is attempting to cover up some part of himself, although this is impossible to do. The Chinese sage said, *How can a man conceal himself?*

Though we crowd all of our emotions back into the unconscious, they always come up in another form. It is impossible to bury a living spring. We can merely change its course. It is just as impossible to destroy that dynamic urge which some call the libido, some the will to power, and others—more rightly perhaps—designate as the Life Force seeking Self-Expression.

If we would heal the inferiority complex we must arrive at conclusions more basic than merely teaching our student or patient to shout that he is self-sufficient. For the louder he screams the more frightened he becomes, until finally his scream is a shriek and his attitude toward life becomes hysterical.

We are told that inferiority complexes often arise from youthful frustration and early childhood repressions, or from emotional reactions which have shocked the finer sensibilities when they first come in contact with the hard realities of life.

This may be true, and proceeding upon this theory it becomes necessary to uncover the psychic stream of previous experiences and unconscious memories. In this process of uncovering, this analysis of the soul or psyche, if the incident which started the stream of consciousness in the wrong direction (which turned it back upon itself) is brought to the surface and self-seen, it is generally dissipated.

To analyze every person psychologically is out of the question, and it seems just as impossible to convince everyone of the truth of certain religious dogmas. All people do not wish to become orthodox religionists, nor do they wish to believe in some particular form of spiritual philosophy. What, then, are we going to do? The answer is so simple that it seems surprising when we arrive at its correct conclusion.

We should not overlook the fact that there are innumerable persons who have been what we call twice born. Through religious convictions their whole lives have been instantly transformed and the entire psychic stream of previous experiences reversed. Fear has been overcome through faith and through spiritual conviction, and morbid neuroses have given way before some spiritual force which we cannot completely analyze but which no person who has investigated the facts would think of denying.

All religions which have helped people have helped them because of one common denominator running through each, and that is faith in something greater than the isolated self. Equally, all psychological processes which have been beneficial in removing fear and the inferiority complex have been able to do so because of one common denominator running through the process, namely, the giving back of the self to the self followed by the re-education of the self and the readjustment of the self to life, in confidence, in faith, and in self-assurance.

This should teach us that there is one basic negation, which is a denial of the Life Principle, and one basic affirmation, which is an acceptance of the Life Principle; and that the affirmation reduces the negation to its native nothingness.

It would be impossible for a man to remain filled with fear if his confidence in the indwelling Spirit were greater than his fear. For such confidence would automatically neutralize fear. This is what has taken place in that particular type of religious conversion which has caused an individual to become "twice born." What his religious convictions were is of no consequence if by them he arrived at the Truth and the salutary effect took place.

In recognizing this we do not dishonor his religious conviction. Rather we affirm it. But in such degree as we understand the working of any principle we need no longer approach it along the spasmodic and more or less uncertain avenue of some peculiar form of conversion. The same may be said of the different schools of applied psychology. They all arrive at practical results, and these results generally depend upon the practitioner more than upon the methods involved, since the principle underlying all of these methods must be one of faith.

However, the religious faith has a certain superiority over the psychological, for it naturally follows that if a man can be brought to have faith in God, his faith in God will be greater than any faith he could have in an individual or a group of individuals.

It is not only important, but necessary, to discover what kind of belief we must have. In what way shall we use faith to overcome fear and to heal the inferiority complex? The answer is obvious—faith in God, faith in each other, faith in Life, faith in destiny, and above all, faith in the eternality of our own souls.

The uninformed may indulge in a smile when we speak of having faith in the eternality of the soul. Nevertheless, if they care to investigate the matter with thoroughness they will discover that without this faith in the eternality of the soul the other types of faith of which we speak are weakened. The reason, I think, is apparent. We could have no real faith in God or in the integrity of the Universe unless such faith included a definite relationship on the part of the individual soul to the Universe.

Now if that relationship is only a temporary one, the relationship of a candle to its flame, then it bears no weight whatsoever. Such a conviction would lead most people to despair, for they would exclaim, *For what shall it profit a man, if he shall gain the whole world, and lose his own soul?* (Mark 8:36). Faith in immortality is necessary to a real healing of the inferiority complex and fear. Our faith in Life must be so great that in our imagination it bridges the gulf which we call death.

A careful analysis of the great characters of history who have had this faith would soon prove to us that with its advent the sense of inferiority and fear has lessened. The chapters of religious history are filled with the accounts of those who have passed from weakness into strength, from timidity into courage as a result of the transforming power of faith. Whether or not we choose to call this a psychological reaction makes no difference, since all mental reactions are psychological.

If, on the other hand, we wish to call such experiences spiritual we are equally right. The spiritual experience has come to the mind, has convinced the intellect, and has penetrated the emotions. When such experiences have sunk deeply enough they have become subjective, which means they have become permanent.

The thing we wish to do, then, is to find a faith greater than our fears, whether they are fears of people, of conditions, of life, or of death. Such faith is born out of a complete conviction of the eternal destiny of one's own soul and of all other souls.

We cannot fail to realize that fear and the inferiority complex are always a turning of thought back upon the self. This is why it has so often been called a form of selfishness, but it is more than this. It is a self-centeredness rather than selfishness in the ordinary sense of the term. We have all known many unselfish persons who have made a complete sacrifice of themselves to good causes but who have felt martyred in so doing, persons who have devoted their entire lives to others but who have been very conscious of doing so.

This self-centeredness often accompanies the inferiority complex and it too must be healed. It is healed by realizing that there is but one final Self in which all selves converge. The Infinite desires neither martyrs nor those who sacrifice anything of their true nature. The Law of the Infinite is toward Self-Expression, and self-expression in the individual means the expansion of the individual, the evolution of the individual, and eternal on-goingness. Hence the self-centered person must be given a goal or an ideal greater than his individualized self. He must surrender the smaller self to the greater Self.

This is the sacrifice which he is called on to make. He must die to his concept of the limited self and become resurrected to the consciousness of that Self which is one with all persons, places, and things, one with all ages, one with God. He must give up his fears and his hurts. After he has learned to look upon all other persons as he looks upon himself, then he will know that the True Self cannot be hurt, nor does it wish to hurt. His soul will have entered that mental atmosphere where hurt is no longer possible.

In such degree as all vindictiveness, hate, and animosity disappear, he will find himself merging with the spiritual atmosphere of others. He learns to respect and admire others, and expects that others will respect and admire him. He overcomes his fear of life by understanding life, not by fighting it. He overcomes his fear of people by coming to understand rather than shun them.

This type of understanding is beyond the ordinary concept

of tolerance. He does not learn to tolerate people; he learns to understand them. There is a vast difference. He sees through the weakness and frailty and inconsistency of human life, even its fears and morbidities. He no longer cringes. With calm placidity he faces his inevitable exit from this world, knowing that as glorious as this life has been, he is certain to go to a better.

If we would eliminate fear and morbidity this is what we must realize. Human experience has never found a better way. Indeed, it is the only way which is certain to produce the desired results.

In actual experience this work is done somewhat after this manner, with the understanding that if you are treating yourself you say, "I am thus and so," or if you are treating someone else you say, "He is (or she is) thus and so." This is the method of procedure for all treatment:

I know that I am one with Life. I now understand that Life Itself is perfect, complete; that there is a Spiritual Presence and a Divine Unity running through everything. I understand how it is that this Divine Unity personifies Itself through all people. I see clearly how it is that this Divine Unity operates every form and animates every event. I am conscious of this Divine Presence at the very center of my own soul. It is the Reality of myself. This Reality is strong, positive, certain, confident, and whole.

I see that the Reality within me is the same as the Reality in all people whom I shall ever meet, and that the Reality within them responds to the Reality within me; therefore in our human greeting there is a Divine Unity. All my human relationships are established in this Divine Unity. All of my relationships flow from It. There is no fear, no sense of inferiority. I am conscious of my ability to meet every situation. I am conscious of my ability to meet every person with perfect frankness, perfect openness, and in complete understanding.

Moreover, I know that every person wishes me well. Every situation which I experience tends to promote my

374

well-being, to increase my happiness and self-expression, and all the good that there is, is my good today.

My faith in Good is complete, my union with Life is Perfect, and I shall always meet appreciation, helpfulness, encouragement, and certainty. This is the Law manifesting Itself in my experience today, tomorrow, and always.

Living without Fear

FEAR IS the great enemy of man. It is impossible for a person to do his best if he is filled with anxiety. We are speaking about morbid fear, the type of fear that devitalizes us mentally, emotionally, and physically.

It is these morbid fears that we wish to rid ourselves of, and not the ordinary caution that is necessary to intelligent living. For instance, a person standing on top of a high cliff would naturally exercise the caution of not getting too close to the edge. But if one has a dread of high places for fear he might fall or be seized with an irresistible impulse to jump, then he has a morbid fear of altitudes. And if we could trace this fear back to its original cause we might possibly find that sometime in a previous experience he has been threatened by someone who may have suggested that he would be thrown off the cliff.

Or take the case of a child shut in a dark closet for discipline. It might be that later in life, after the child has become an adult, he would have a morbid fear of being in closed places. This is called claustrophobia, which means a morbid dread of being shut away alone. In adult life the one who had been punished by being shut in a dark closet might find it emotionally impossible for him to be alone even in an ordinary room where there are plenty of exits.

They tell us that an infant has only two fears—the fear of loud noises and of falling; that all other fears must be acquired. It was never intended that we should go through life filled with fear, doubt, and uncertainty.

Perhaps this is why Jesus laid such great stress on our need for faith and why he told his followers that they should not be afraid of what was going to happen tomorrow. But rather, that they should live today in a sense of confidence and peace and joyful expectancy. When tomorrow comes it will take care of itself. Today is the only day in which we can live. For when tomorrow comes it will be another today, and so on through all eternity.

But unless we do live without fear today we shall dread tomorrow. Those who live in the dread of tomorrow generally live in the morbid thoughts of what happened yesterday. Their minds are filled with things that were unpleasant in their previous experience and the unhappy events that they fear will transpire in the future. The present day in which they live is robbed of all peace and joy, and becomes a torture chamber sandwiched between yesterday and tomorrow. This so disturbs the mind that restful sleep is impossible. Such people seldom rise in the morning filled with buoyant hope, joyful expectation, and the natural enthusiasm and zest for living which we all need if we are to get the most out of life.

Yesterday is forever past. We cannot relive it. No matter how we may regret what happened yesterday, it is impossible actually to live it over again; but too often in imagination we do live it over again and again, and in so doing bring all the misery of yesterday into today. Learn to forget yesterday. After we have gone over it and learned by our mistakes, the thing to do is to correct those mistakes and forgive ourselves for anything that we have done.

And we must learn to forgive others. This is not always the easiest thing to do, but it can be done. If a person can be made to see that he must forgive in order to be healed of unhappiness, he generally will make an effort to do so.

We usually give people some affirmations or affirmative prayers that will help them to do this. And particularly we encourage them to affirm that tonight they will sleep in peace and wake in joy and live in a consciousness of Good. We try to get them to feel that there is nothing in the Universe seeking to harm them; that while we all have made mistakes there is no God of vengeance, no Divine Power that could will or wish harm toward anyone. We are the product of the Universe; we are the offspring of the Divine Spirit; we are some part of Its life shaped and formed and acting as man, as an individual, as a person. And how could the great Divine Cause of our being seek to destroy or in any way harm that life which is the offspring of Its own being?

This whole morbid thought that there is some deific power that is always testing us to see how much we can stand, or always restricting us lest we fail to recognize its overlordship, is one of the great psychological crimes of the ages. It really is man against himself. But we have come to interpret it as though it were God operating against man; as though it were the Creator seeking to blot out His own creation.

The person who has learned to forgive himself, simply and directly, and who has come to believe that God eternally forgives, and who has learned to forgive all others, finally comes to a place where he knows that the Divine is for him and not against him. He reaches a place where he knows that Love is the great Reality.

If you want to get rid of fear you need not take the time to consider each separate fear you may have—the fear of people, the fear of things, the fear of conditions, the fear of yesterday, today, and tomorrow. For all these varying forms of fear are rooted in one fundamental negation: We do not know that we belong to the Universe in which we live. We do not realize that God needs us or He would not have put us here.

While it is true that we can trace specific fears to certain incidents that transpired early in life, and while it is true that if we do this we can remove them, most fears finally resolve themselves into a very few attitudes of mind, most of which are based on the belief "no one wants me, needs me, or loves me; probably I am unworthy, unnecessary, and useless; I am inadequate to meet life, I have not the strength or the power or the will to overcome obstructions, and I do not fit anywhere."

Most of our fears can be traced to these unconscious attitudes of mind which rise from our repressed desires to live more abundantly, and our inward sense of inferiority because we are uncertain of the future.

Well, the way to get rid of fear is through the cultivation of faith; a faith founded on the thought that God is all there is. If we learn to see God in people, in circumstances and situations, we shall find Him—*Seek, and ye shall find.* When we turn in complete confidence, with a simple, childlike trust and faith, to Life Itself, It will always respond to us.

It does not matter what the history of any evil experience may have been, or how long we may have harbored fear or resentment or doubt. In the very moment when we turn from it, it will depart from us. You see, Eternity is *here* and *now*. God is everywhere. The Divine Spirit is in every person. And the movement of the Law of Good is in all human events. We alone block our good, and we alone reaffirm it. We alone can readjust our lives to a new way of thinking until all our patterns of thought are changed.

In doing this we shall be making the best bargain we have ever made, for we shall be swapping fear for faith, doubt for certainty, hell for heaven. It is destined that we shall all do this, sooner or later, so why delay the day of our freedom from fear? This is the day that we should accept that Kingdom which is forever given. This is the day that we should get complete clearance from all of our yesterdays. This is the day God has made. Let us be glad in it.

MEDITATION

Today shall contain joy and happiness; shall be filled with peace; and through it all there will be running the silent Power of spiritual force, that which harmoniously and happily governs our thoughts and decisions and acceptances, so that everything will be done without effort.

So we lay all weariness aside and accept the life-giving, invigorating, dynamic Power of the Spirit, knowing that It vitalizes every organ of our body, It flows with strength and purpose through everything we do, even as It leads us gently down the pathway of life.

Today is the day that God has made, and we are glad in it. And when the evening time comes, the cool shadows of peace shall fall across our pathway and the quiet of the night shall enter into our souls, the beatitude of the Spirit shall flow through us as a river of life. We shall sleep in peace, and wake in joy, and live in a consciousness of Good, for God is over all, in all, and through all.

Insecurity

IT IS believed that there are four different subjective or unconscious components underlying the insecurity and anxiety complex. In order to understand this let us go back to the idea that the ego must not be rejected.

When the infant or the adult suffers from an unconscious sense of being rejected, not wanted, needed, or loved, he unconsciously receives the impression that there must be something wrong with him. Without the objective faculties being aware of it, he argues with himself somewhat after this manner: "Nobody likes me, no one wants me around; I am in everyone's way. There must be something wrong with me or this wouldn't happen." Thereafter he develops an unconscious sense of guilt and self-condemnation.

But nature has provided that certain processes of the mind, which seek to protect the ego, keep this inward feeling covered so that it never gets to the surface. For most of our inner conflicts are never brought to the light of day. If they were they would cease to exist. From this sense of not being wanted, needed, or loved, and this unconscious sense of guilt and self-condemnation which is not permitted to come to the surface because the ego must not reject itself, there comes a sense of insecurity, a feeling that "I am not safe anywhere; I don't fit anywhere; everything about me is wrong." And out of this sense of rejection, guilt, and insecurity, a feeling of anxiety is generated.

You can easily prove this for yourself by talking with people who have a continuous anxiety complex. There never seems to be any specific reason for this feeling. They cannot put their finger on some point of experience and say, "This is it." Rather, the inward conflict, seeking release from its tensions, projects the anxiety first into one situation and then another, as though it were a searchlight seeking out an object for itself.

It does this to get rid of tensions, for inward conflicts are a result of the outpush of the desire for self-expression which has been crowded back upon itself through repression. Since the ego must not be rejected because it would lose its self-esteem if it were, a certain mechanism of the mind pushes the stream of desire back into the mind. The conflict is between the desire for self-expression and the repression which shoves it back into the unconscious where the conflict silently goes on.

This is a simple and altogether too brief explanation of the nature of our inner conflicts, yet, as simple as it is, it is fundamental. You will notice in any book you may read on the subject, that some reference is made to these few simple facts. In psychiatry and analysis, and in most psychological counseling, the purpose is to uncover these inner conflicts and cause them to come to the light of day where they will be self-seen and understood, on the theory that when they are self-seen they will disappear. That is, we shall understand why we feel as we do and why we need not feel that way.

This process is cumbersome, time-consuming, and therefore expensive. However, it is scientific and the techniques for exposing the inner conflicts, when successfully used, should and often do completely relieve the pressure and thus rehabilitate the individual, causing him to be a normal, happy, and spontaneous person.

But we believe there is more to it than this. Man is rooted in pure Spirit, he is some part of Life; he is an incarnation of God, and no matter what his inward conflicts may be or what may have occasioned them, there is a way for him to get a complete clearance from them without the elaborate process of analysis. If he could forgive himself for all the mistakes he may have made, if he could get a clearance in his mind from the fear that there is some God condemning him, that some terrific evil awaits him hereafter, he would get complete relief.

This is one of the salutary purposes of the confessional, and perhaps this is why Jesus so frequently told people that their sins were forgiven them.

If it is true that at the core of every neurosis there is a sense of being rejected, attended by a consciousness of guilt from which arises a feeling of insecurity and an attitude of anxiety, why could not we with our method get a complete clearance by attacking these four fundamental native attitudes and silently assuring ourselves that there is nothing in the Universe that holds anything against us? We have not done anything so terribly bad after all. Why should we feel insecure in the Universe in which we live, or have any anxiety, if our whole confidence is placed in God or Good?

This brings us right back to the fundamental proposition upon which our whole thought is based: God is One, God is Good, God wills only Good, God is right where we are, God is within us and around us.

If self-condemnation is an unconscious thing, and as a result of it we protect ourselves from inward conflicts by projecting condemnation to others, then it would follow that if we could relieve the tension of the burden of guilt and condemnation from our own unconscious thinking we should no longer project it toward others.

Perhaps this seems too simple to be true, but great truths *are* simple, and the most effective methods are the most direct ones. The starting point for a clearance of the inward burdens that are too heavy to bear and the conflicts that tear so many people apart is to get a clearance in our own mind about ourselves and our relationship with God.

Some might think that this is a way whereby one excuses oneself for wrong-doing. Nothing could be further from the truth, for while the sense of condemnation for others remains, one has not reached a clearance in one's own mind. A consciousness of Love would be the basis for the assurance we need, a feeling that Divine Love gives of Itself, that we give of ourselves, and that there is nothing in us that can project anything but love and peace and joy to others.

It has been my experience that whenever any individual arrives at complete self-forgiveness while also understanding that any cause he sets in motion toward others will react upon himself, he has reached a place where his judgments are no longer harsh. He becomes a kind and lovable person and he has peace within his own mind. There can be no peace until this clearance is made. In one of the great books of wisdom of the East it says that the self must raise the self by the self. There is no other way, for the blind cannot lead the blind. There must be a seeing eye.

Not only can you do this for yourself, but you can do it for others by using the same method. The only difference between treating yourself and others is that when treating yourself you say, "This is the truth about me," while in treating others you say, "This is the truth about him (or her)." Forgiving and being forgiven, loving and being loved, living and letting live, is the simple basis for it all. Just to be yourself in God. Just to be simple and spontaneous. Just to live as though today is God's day and you may rejoice in it.

I would like to make this further suggestion for your careful consideration: Is it not possible that the belief in a devil or devils and in a future state of judgment from which one must shrink in horror are themselves a result of projecting our own unredeemed lives into the Universe, judging God by our own misfortunes, our own lacks, our own fears, doubts, and uncertainties? It is my belief that the unconscious imagination of man has made this projection, for there can be nothing to fear from God. Man's problems are within himself alone, and to himself alone, and from himself alone. Suffering is not designed by the All-Creative Wisdom.

There is still another reflection that must be made. Jesus said, *judge not, that ye be not judged. For with what judgment ye judge, ye shall be judged; and with what measure ye mete, it shall be measured to you again* (Matthew 7:1,2). Is this not a veiled statement of an immutable Law of Cause and Effect from which we cannot hope to escape?

This is not an easy philosophy. It is the toughest that ever confronted the mind and imagination of man. Many people may be under the mistaken concept that the metaphysical philosophy is attractive to people because it says God is Good and everything is all right; therefore there is nothing to fear. This is far form the truth. What it says is this: Do you wish to be loved? Then stop hating. Do you want to be happy? Then be sure that you are never the occasion for unhappiness in others. Do you wish to stop shedding tears? Then be sure that you are never the instrument which causes others to shed them.

Am I certain there is nothing in me which can hurt anyone? Then as surely as God is God and justice is justice nothing can harm me, but the harm I would do to another I myself must suffer. Only from a cleansing of the self comes redemption.

Regression

FROM THE Science of Mind viewpoint, emotional regression means withdrawing to a place of safety and security. When a thing regresses it goes backward. Often there is a tendency in the mind to get away from meeting objective situations which are unpleasant by withdrawing from all objective activity, and in imagination reverting to a chronologically earlier or less adapted pattern of behavior and feeling.

It is easy enough to see how one who is surrounded by confusing situations might feel inadequate to cope with them, and unconsciously might seek some place of peace or retirement where nothing could bother him.

A completely integrated person is one who has learned to meet everything as it comes along and to make the best of it. In our science this is not a hopeless situation. When we say one should make the best of things, we do not mean that one should grin and bear it, or even suffer it to be so, for we know there is a way to meet every situation through the use of the Power greater than we are.

However, we should not close our eyes to reality if there is a tendency toward regression in ourselves or in those we seek to help. We must recognize it just as we would any other error, and meet it with quiet but positive determination.

If a person finds himself apparently unable to cope with objective situations, and consequently finds his mind reverting with a certain morbid longing to the thought of getting away from it all, he is in a bad emotional state and should be helped. This is done by knowing that there is nothing to be afraid of, that we are One with an Infinite Partner, that there is nothing in the Universe designed to harm us. Confidence and faith in a Power greater than we are must be generated.

Often, even in poems which make a great appeal to us, we find this unconscious sense of regression creeping in. For instance the words of Elizabeth Allen, *Backward, turn backward, O Time, in your flight, Make me a child again just for tonight!*

show that in writing these beautiful lines she had an unconscious desire to get away from it all. Note the first verse of "The Cry of a Dreamer," by John O'Reilly:

I am tired of planning and toiling
In the crowded hives of men;
Heart-weary of building and spoiling,
And spoiling and building again.
And I long for the dear old river
Where I dreamed my youth away;
For a dreamer lives forever,
And a toiler dies in a day.

In both instances you will note an unconscious desire to get away from objective reality. Something has happened to the individual that causes him to desire to revert to some former existence where there were no cares or burdens or obligations.

How wonderful to accept the thought of Jesus when he said, *Come unto me, all ye that labour and are heavy laden, and I will give you rest. Take my yoke upon you, and learn of me; for I am meek and lowly in heart; and ye shall find rest unto your souls. For my yoke is easy, and my burden is light* (Matthew 11: 28–30).

This is not resignation; it is just the opposite. It is a proclamation that the mind finds sanctuary in the Spirit, and that there are no burdens when we unify ourselves with Life.

In a certain sense, amnesia, or suddenly forgetting one's identity, is a form of regression because it is a means of getting away from reality. But at the base of amnesia there is fear, a sense of separation, a disunion which faith alone can heal.

The psychological approach, while scientifically correct, will never completely solve the problem of regression. For while it can uncover the cause of regression, generally speaking it lacks the spiritual faith to supply what is needed to make one more completely whole.

There is nothing to be afraid of in the past, the present, or the future. Our faith should be based on the only rock of salvation there is, which is that God is all there is, there is nothing else. *In him we live, and move, and have our being.* There is nothing to be afraid of. *Underneath are the everlasting arms.* We are cradled in love.

Statements like these will clear the track of the mind straight back to the eternal Source of Life, where there are no fears, doubts, or uncertainties: *The Lord is my shepherd, I shall not want; He that dwelleth in the secret place of the most High shall abide in the shadow of the Almighty.* These statements are wonderful in helping to establish faith and stability, without which life is but a shambles of frustrated hopes and unsatisfied yearnings.

You might wonder why we mention these negative emotional states. The reason is that in the Science of Mind we never seek to avoid an issue, because any condition which is psychologically avoided becomes buried in the unconscious. And unfortunately it is buried alive. Thus the conflict goes on beneath the surface of consciousness, where it does more damage than it would if left objective. We must meet every situation as it comes with faith and trust, thereby avoiding regressions, escapes, and frustrations.

If the Blind Lead the Blind

JESUS MUST have been the wisest man who ever lived. Today we can connect many of his sayings with our new outlook on the mental and emotional life.

For instance, in psychological analysis it is believed that if a physician, in analyzing a patient, uncovers in the patient an unconscious hatred for his father, and if the physician had the same aversion for his own father, then the analysis might as well stop right there. This is because the physician is not able to see with clarity a block in another if he has the same type of block in himself.

In psychological terms this is expressed by saying that wherever there is an emotional bias there will be an intellectual blind spot. This means that we cannot think with truthful clarity about things that we are too emotionally affected by. Jesus understood this, and that is why he said that if the blind lead the blind they will both fall into the ditch.

We all have such emotional biases, and this is why we think it strange when someone whom we hold to be highly intelligent seems to be irrational on certain points. We often say, "How can he believe as he does when such belief contradicts common sense or reason?" But could we uncover his whole mental life we should discover the emotional bias deep down there in his unconscious, where he has a block which makes it impossible for him to think straight on that particular subject.

This is where many of our theological conflicts come from. This is why people are prone to say that they alone are right, or their system of thought alone is right. They have not yet gotten a clearance back to the fundamental proposition that God is One, and that every man is an incarnation of the same God. Therefore, intolerance and harshness, unkindness and criticism, coldness and indifference are projected. This is one of those tricks which the mind plays on us.

When we understand these things we shall become more

tolerant, more kind, more compassionate, because we shall realize that we are all on the pathway of evolution, not of the Spirit, which is already Perfect, but of the mind which so often is blindly groping in the dark.

We will be helped over many a difficulty if we realize that an emotional bias does create a mental blind spot. Then if we learn to overlook the differences because we understand them, we shall no longer bring condemnation to add to condemnation, or judgment to add to judgment, and our own lives will become enriched as they always must with new knowledge.

Living is an art as well as a science. It is a thing of beauty as well as form; a thing of the heart as well as of the intellect. It is a combination of all these that makes up the factors of a well-rounded life.

And again we come right back to the fundamental proposition that the problems we face are not external; they are within. They are not some other person's fault; neither are they necessarily our own fault. They are the fault of ignorance, from which enlightenment alone can free us.

No, the blind cannot lead the blind, and we all are blind in spots. Therefore no person should set himself up as the great example, but humbly following the pathway of Truth as he sees it, with a good-natured and flexible tolerance for himself and others, learn to overlook all mistakes and feel his way through confusion back to the central flame from which every man's life is lighted.

Transference

THE MENTAL and emotional analysis of the mind as practiced in psychology, particularly in the analytical field, is supposed to carry the patient from where he is back through his entire life history, even to the place of birth; some have already advanced the theory to the period of conception.

In the process of clearing the passageway of the mind from the present, straight back through all experiences to the place of beginning of the individual experience, a point is reached in the analysis where the feeling that the patient once had toward his own parents becomes transferred to the one conducting the analysis. In other words, the patient reacts to the analyst as he did to his own parents, since the analyst by substitution or by proxy takes the place of the parents.

If the original feeling of the patient toward his parents was one of hostility, there may be what is called a negative transference; indeed, he could even come to despise the analyst and wish to do him harm. It is evident that this could become a difficult situation. Unless this feeling could be overcome, the analysis would become futile.

On the other hand, if the original feeling of the patient toward his parents was one of confidence and trust, the transference is what is called positive, and the patient might even fall in love with the analyst. This is why it has been suggested that men should be analyzed by women, and women by men.

Generally speaking, the patient is apt to have either a sense of hate toward the analyst or one of warm affection. The theory is that the patient will now feel as he did earlier in life toward his parents; therefore the emotions he felt toward them will more quickly come to the surface to be self-seen.

It is believed that this transference of the emotional reaction of earlier life to the analyst is necessary, but at once we are faced with another proposition, and a difficult one. The patient could not go through life with the feeling that he must depend on the analyst, so there comes a time when the transference must be broken.

This means that the patient's possibility of happiness must return to himself and not be imposed on the analyst, for where the treasure is, there will the heart be also. Consequently the transference must be broken in order that the patient may be made whole psychologically, which in this instance means emotionally. He must find within himself the stability and security he needs. This is called *breaking the transference*, and the analysis is not complete without it.

Now we have no doubt that this theory in the main is true, but from it we should draw a broader generalization, which is this: No matter what the external object may be in which we place our security or possibility of happiness, we shall never become whole until we have separated all negative reactions from that object, because wholeness is within the self and no where else.

Even the idea of salvation through some particular religion constitutes in a certain sense a kind of unbroken transference. People believe they can be saved or healed only through certain formulas, certain methods of procedure, through certain prayers or incantations. This is not wholeness; rather it is just the opposite, for it is a complete dependence on a form, or a word, or a person, or even an institution, rather than upon the self.

There are people who depend upon certain books, perhaps even the Bible, for their happiness. Without in any way discrediting the value of these books or the supreme value of the great bibles of the world, or of those great teachers who have brought to us the highest and the best the world knows, even these transferences must be broken if we are to become whole, for nothing should stand between us and the Universe.

It is not necessary that someone else do this for us. We merely have to go back through our entire lives and say:

Bless my father and my mother, my brothers and my sisters; everyone whom I have ever depended on. I love and appreciate them. I recognize the good I received from them at the time when it was necessary that I receive that good. But now, without thinking any less of them, I know I am whole within myself. There is finally only

One Father and One Mother, which is God, and in this One we are all brothers and sisters.

I love everyone but depend upon no one. Nothing can rob me of this love I have for others. It cannot be rejected, because I am Love and That which never rejects Its own creation.

People, things, institutions, methods, sciences, philosophies, all are good. From each I shall learn everything that I can, and with deep gratitude acknowledge the good I am receiving from whatever source, but I am still whole within myself, dependent upon nothing, and yet always interdependent with all things.

Breaking the transference does not mean isolation from Life. Quite the opposite. It means being whole in Life, so that we may discover the love and the friendship of all people without seeking to destroy them or permitting them to destroy us.

The individual security is within the self. Recognizing the same security within others, we work and play with them in gladness. We are whole and they are whole, because God in us is whole.

The Divine Givingness

It is the nature of Spirit to give. Spirit is the Essence of Life as well as the Intelligence back of everything. It is Complete and Perfect within Itself. It is All-Power and All-Presence. We have nothing to offer nature other than a willingness to cooperate with her laws. If we are to demonstrate that the Divine Givingness is a Principle in the Universe, then we must set up a receiving center; for no matter how abundantly the Horn of Plenty may pour out Its universal gifts, there must be a bowl of acceptance, a chalice of expectancy, or the gift cannot be complete.

The Divine Givingness is from eternity to eternity. Our receivingness may be spasmodic, but many great souls have, through faith, reached back of the appearance to the cause of things and received directly and constantly from the Divine Bounty. The reason we do not all do this is because we do not *believe* that there *is* a Divine Givingness.

The Spirit not only gives but It also creates the channel through which this giving may become our receiving. In other words, the bowl of acceptance which we hold beneath the outpouring Horn of Plenty is Itself a part of the Divine Givingness, for how could there be a givingness unless there were an equal receivingness? It is receivingness which fulfills the givingness, and the interaction is complete only when our bowl of acceptance is full.

We need have no sense of unworthiness, nor should we fall under the illusion that it is spiritual to be poor, or the equally wrong thought that people who happen to possess enough of this world's goods to make life comfortable are thereby unholy.

It is the Divine Will that we should receive, but since we are individuals, even the Divine Will cannot compel us to receive that which we refuse to accept. Therefore our part in the Divine Givingness is to have faith and to cooperate with the Law of Abundance. *In the beginning* means before any particular creation takes place. Before our request was made—in the beginning, before the treatment was given—the state of being already

393

existed which made possible the fulfillment of our desires. There were no prior conditions to impose themselves upon the creation of our desire.

The Spirit is absolutely without limit; nothing has ever imposed any restriction upon It; It knows no limitation, no limiting circumstances. We impose the bondage of our belief upon the Law. This is why it is written: *So we see that they could not enter in because of unbelief*, and because they *limited the Holy One of Israel.* In this way our unbelief becomes our acceptance. Our fear becomes a misplaced faith. We are bound by the very Power which alone could free us.

We should likewise remember that the Creative Law is one of reciprocity, of reciprocal action, and that It responds by reflection. Since our imaging in It restricts our use of It to the things we image, or to our expectation, it follows that to secure better results we must re-image, create a new faith, increase our receptivity, enlarge our mental concept, and maintain a more enthusiastic expectation. When we do this we are starting a new chain of cause and effect.

Believe in Divine Givingness; believe that It is the Divine Will that you should receive this Divine Givingness, and then consciously accept It. This sounds simple, but the meaning is profound and describes a perfect method of procedure. Frequently, when we reduce an abstract thought to a simple statement, we feel that we have lost its significance. Such is not the case. The wisest man who ever lived said, *As thou hast believed, so be it done unto thee.*

Thus Jesus laid down a law of faith for those who could not understand the working of the Law, knowing that all who complied with the Law would receive a direct benefit even though they did not completely understand Its intricate mechanics. Not every person who drives an automobile is an electrician or a mechanical engineer, but it has been planned for him that he can do certain simple things and get certain results—he can drive a car and he can get somewhere in it. So Jesus understood that even blind faith based more or less on superstition was still an affirmative attitude in the Law. He knew that the Law, which is Perfect, is Freedom, Givingness, and must reply to faith. However, it is better when faith becomes understanding, for it is then that faith becomes perfect.

This is the secret of the answer to prayer throughout the ages. Few people have any conscious knowledge of what must take place as the result of their prayer. They have faith in God; hence their receivingness fulfills the Divine Givingness. Law and faith come together. The bowl of acceptance is held up and the outpouring of the Spirit is measured into the individual experience according to the Law of Mental Equivalents, which says that whatever we inwardly conceive, we outwardly experience. This is because the external is merely a reflection of the internal.

Faith is not trying to compel the mind to accept something which it denies. It is merely causing the mind to see why it may believe in that which it affirms. All we have to do is to look about on nature to reassure ourselves that there is a Creative Power at work and that the entire physical universe proceeds from an Invisible Source.

It is evident that the seen comes out of the Unseen in accord with Law, and it is equally evident that the Creative Principle can express Itself only in terms of the instrument through which It flows. In our case the instrument is our faith, belief, acceptance, mental equivalent, spiritual embodiment, understanding of the meaning of the words we use in treatment.

Our mental attitude toward the Divine Givingness should be simple and direct. We are to *accept the gift*. We are to look forward to it with anticipation and with enthusiastic attention. We are to maintain an inner joy. And why not—if we are to realize that the Divine Givingness is the gift of a perfect Law of Liberty, forever made, and if the Divine Will is the outpouring of the Spirit into Self-Expression through us—? Let us, then, receive the gift!

The Divine Forgivingness

JUST AS there is a Principle of Divine Givingness in the Universe, so there is a Principle of Divine Forgivingness. It is self-evident that if such were not the case we should never be able to transcend the limitation of previous mistakes. It is this ability to transcend previous mistakes which may be described as *forgivingness* from the standpoint of a spiritual system of thought. Sin belongs to no one; it is merely a *mistake operating through someone.* Evil of itself is not person, place, or thing.

Jesus forgave people their sins in order to demonstrate that the Creative Principle within us is greater than any use we have ever made of It, and also to demonstrate that when we reverse our position in the Law, It simultaneously reverses Its position toward us. The very nature of the Law of Cause and Effect, and the reality of personal volition, compel us to see that Divine Forgivingness is a Principle in nature and that this Principle is the essence of Love. That is the reason those who have sensed the Love of God have also experienced Divine Forgivingness and, through the alchemy of thought, have transmuted the energy of despair into the energy of hope. Thus they have been reborn. We could make no greater mistake than to suppose this rebirth to have been an illusion.

We should not think of God as conceiving sin or arguing over mistakes. To think of the Creative Spirit as conceiving sin and mistakes is to think of It as both evil and limited, and if evil and limited, then self-destructive; if self-destructive, then you and I could not exist. This is so evident that we do not need to argue the point. It is written: *Thou art of purer eyes than to behold evil, and canst not look on iniquity.*

Sin is a mistake and punishment is a consequence. Nothing ever happens to the Law of Cause and Effect. We use It and we abuse It, but even when we abuse It, we are still using It. As long as we abuse It we find undesirable consequences coming to us and may feel that a vindictive spirit is punishing us because of our mistakes. But the Laws of the Universe are not vindictive. When we wish to escape from the wheel of the Law which seems ready to crush us, we must deliberately turn away from the mistake.

To all who feel that they are surrounded by a Law which must grind them to powder for endless time, this should come as a spiritual shock thundering at the door of their minds. For they suffer only as deluded men suffer. How can we doubt that the same Law which creates can recreate? Do we believe that the artist has stepped into his canvas or that the clay replies to the potter?

Because we believe that the Spirit holds something against us we seek propitiation through burnt offerings, sacrifices, petitions, prayers for redemption from the vast hosts of fears and doubts which have beset the pathway of most religious systems. We feel that our previous mistakes must be punished in order that God may be happy and that our souls may be saved. We may well know this right now: The spirit of man is some part of God and cannot be lost. What needs to be saved is a *situation* and not a *Principle*.

The nature of the Divine Forgivingness is written into the very constitution of Being Itself, and the Forgiving is simultaneous with our new use of the Law. When we stop making the mistake, we are automatically forgiven; but, of course, we will be punished by a mistake while we continue in it. However, let no intelligent person say that, because the Spirit knows no sin, there is no mistake made by the human or the individual mind.

The act of enlightenment becomes our part in the Divine Forgivingness. For the Divine Forgivingness cannot be complete until we have received the offering of Its Love, not with fear or morbidity but in joy. And when we have transcended previous mistakes they no longer exist, nor is there any effect of them. This means a complete salvation from the *sin* which was the *mistake*, and the *punishment* which was the *consequence*. This particular sequence of cause and effect is now transmuted into something else. This should happen every time a scientific treatment is given.

The whole thing is summed up in the thought that, in such

degree as we embody the spirit of Love, Truth, Givingness, etc., we transcend hate and ugliness. We cannot continue in the mistake without continuing in punishment, but the moment the mistake ceases the punishment stops. Thus, the Apostle tells us that the Law of the Spirit of Love makes us free from the law of sin and death.

Jesus clearly stated that the son of man has power to forgive sins, and to prove his position he said to the one who was palsied, *Arise, take up thy bed, and go unto thine house.* He proved his ability to transcend, not the Law Itself, but some particular use, some limited use of the Law. He must have been conscious that the man was suffering from ignorance and that in some way this ignorance was connected with the belief in condemnation. He removed the sense of condemnation which bound the physical body; then the physical body could get up and walk. He knew it was an *outpicturing of thought.* He relieved the tension at its source—removed the sense of separation—for this was the man's sin.

All limitation is sin, but of course some mistakes are more vicious than others. Some affect the individual personally, while others affect larger groups, and the Law of Cause and Effect says that every man must suffer while he imposes suffering. Only in the concept of the Infinite Love transcendent over all human error does the world find a mental equivalent, a spiritual perception adequate to meet its need. In our system of thought we in no way belittle this concept.

In this thought we explain it more rationally when we announce that *the Nature of God is Givingness and Forgivingness;* that the Universe holds nothing against us and that Its whole desire is for our well-being. Ignorance of the Law excuses no one. The race labors under the sense of condemnation, handed down from generation to generation and operating through the consciousness of most people. Thus, the sense of sin is both individual and collective.

Many individuals have been burdened with the sense of race condemnation. Some of them have been fanatics, some have been fine, outstanding, intelligent people. Many of them have done much good, some have done great harm. It is not for us to judge, nor should we permit ourselves to be judged. Our judgment must be the criterion of reason, the evidence of intelligence, the logic of sequence built upon the knowledge that we are living in a Universe of Law and Order, a Universe which makes sense, and a Universe out of which we can make sense.

Each of us exists in direct relationship to this Cosmic Whole. In the long run there is no law but that set by one's own soul, since each one individualizes the Universal Law of Cause and Effect. If we have been sinners we can become saviors, and the first thing we should save is our own thought. We should elevate our lives upon the Cross of Divine Unity, and there, where the winds of God blow free, we should permit the soul to be purified.

The Divine Givingness and the Divine Forgivingness, which are eternal in the nature of Reality, should be accepted. Thus the action of the Law, as it has stood, will be transmuted from bondage into freedom. This should be done consciously, definitely, and scientifically through the direct reversal of thought, and it should be considered a definite part of every treatment which we give.

Our Need for Forgiveness

WE ALL are human beings and we all have made mistakes. We all carry an unconscious burden of guilt and we all need a sense of being forgiven. One of the most revealing things in the new Science of Mind is our need to feel that we are right with God, with life, and with each other.

We know that a continuous state of resentment can produce many types of physical disease. This does not mean just diseases of the imagination. It means diseases that the imagination creates in the body through psychosomatic relations between the mind and the body. A continuous state of resentment against others can badly affect the digestive system. It can produce many forms of physical irritation. It can cramp our whole style of living and block the spontaneous flow of enthusiasm, without which there is very little joy in life.

Much of our inability to forgive others comes from a deep-seated inferiority complex. Often our antagonistic attitude toward others rises from a need within our own minds to be relieved of our unconscious sense of self-condemnation, as though we have such a burden of guilt within our minds that we can hardly bear it. And so we project it to others just for the relief it gives ourselves.

This brings us back to one of the fundamental thoughts of Jesus: *Forgive, and ye shall be forgiven.* Of course Jesus knew that we do not make bargains with God, but the more carefully we study his method the more clearly we see that he often removed emotional blocks before he healed people. On one occasion he forgave a paralyzed man, much to the dismay of some of those around him who told him that he had no right to forgive others. Jesus' only answer was to ask them whether they thought it was easier to forgive the man or to tell him to get up and walk; but, he said, to show that the Son of Man does have power to forgive, I will tell the man to get up and walk.

There is a definite tension which accompanies the emotional state of condemnation, and so Jesus forgave the man and removed this tension. In view of what we know today, he was

400

practicing a perfect spiritual science. He must have been able to look inside people, mentally, and he probably knew exactly how people thought, and why, and of course he knew that anything that stops the flow of Life, anything that blocks our God-given right to live happily and with faith in the Universe, must affect the physical body.

Probably Jesus knew more about spiritual psychosomatics than anyone else who ever lived. He also knew something that most of us have yet to discover: we cannot give what we do not possess. And certainly he knew that we all have a need for a feeling of being one with God.

No one can feel one with God who hates anyone or anything. You will remember that in the Lord's Prayer Jesus said, *Forgive us our debts as we forgive our debtors.* For he knew that it is only as we forgive that we can be forgiven.

At first thought this looks as though we were bargaining with God, but such is not the case. God is Life and Love, and how can Life and Love flow through us if we stop them at any point? It is not because we bargain with the Almighty that Jesus said, *Forgive us our debts as we forgive our debtors.* The real reason is that it is impossible for us to have a sense of being forgiven while we condemn others.

And now we are putting the proposition in the only place where it can be handled   within ourselves. For when there is nothing in us that would condemn others, then there will be no condemnation left, toward either the self or others. It is then and only then that we unblock the stream of Life which so freely flows to all and through all, when we permit it.

Jesus also said, *Give, and it shall be given unto you.* Life intends and wants to give us every good thing, but when the circuit is stopped at any point it is retarded at every point. A good enough illustration is the circulation of blood in our physical bodies. Stop the circulation anywhere and it is retarded everywhere, and wherever the circulation is stopped stagnation sets in, and infection is likely to follow. We never drink from stagnant pools because we know they are poisonous. We seek the free-flowing water which purifies itself as it flows.

Our minds are mental pools through which flow the thoughts

of Good, which are thoughts of love and generosity, good will and peace, poise and power. Wherever there is stagnation in our mental lives we shall discover that the reason is because we have not permitted this flow.

Everything moves in circles. This is the way of life, and what we refuse to give we refuse to accept. Nothing is more important than that we learn how to forgive both ourselves and others. Jesus carried this proposition to a complete finality when he forgave the man who died on another cross beside him. It seems to me that this forgiveness was one of the greatest lessons of the cross.

There is another instance in history which shows the same sublime attitude as that of Jesus. When Mahatma Gandhi was assassinated his last act after receiving the mortal wound was to make the sign of forgiveness with his hands. Jesus and Gandhi—two of the greatest spiritual geniuses of history. Each knew the necessity of the human mind to relieve itself of the burden of condemnation, and each made the supreme sacrifice as an object lesson to all humanity that even God cannot give us what we refuse to accept.

The great lesson we learn from this is that it is impossible for us to feel relief and release from self-condemnation while we bear condemnation toward others.

We long to be free from burdens. How we yearn for a sense of release from fear and doubt and uncertainty. How greatly we long for a security which takes fear from our lives. We pray for a certainty and a faith that will make us whole.

The physician and the surgeon can patch up this physical body of ours, and the psychologist or psychiatrist can help us to straighten out our emotional tensions, for all of which we should be grateful. But only Life can give life. Beyond this body and deeper than this mind there is a perennial Wellspring of Life which can flow through us to Eternal Givingness and to Everlasting Forgivingness.

Who would not be in Paradise? If we felt that someone beside us had the power to say to us, *Today shalt thou be with me in paradise*, in the Garden of Eden of the soul, in the fields that bloom forever, beside the still waters—if we knew that there was someone who could do this for us, would we not exchange everything we have for this gift? Of course we would.

Emerson said that the Universe remains to the heart unhurt, and Jesus said, *It is your Father's good pleasure to give you the kingdom.* This Kingdom is something we do not earn; it is the gift of heaven. This heart that is unhurt is the heart that God gave us. We alone have refused to receive the gift; it has never been withheld. From the day we are first ushered into this world, until that last moment when the soul takes its silent flight into the unseen, our life is drawn from an Invisible Source.

It is intended that we should be happy. It is meant that we should live to the full; that we should sing and dance and be glad; that we should love and be loved in return. But in our ignorance we have inhibited the action of God in our lives, and so we have cut ourselves off from the only Power that can help us.

The only sensible thing to do is retrace our steps and start all over again. We should not do this with any sense of morbidity or fear, but rather with the feeling of an explorer who knows that there is an undiscovered country, and who is willing to take time to find it. There is an undiscovered country in our own minds. It is the world the way God made it. There is a humanity that we have not yet met. It is the Divinity hidden within each one of us. There is a God who exists everywhere. We shall never see this God until we look through the eyes of our own Divinity.

Let us start with this simple proposition in mind:

God is all there is. God is Love. Love is the motivating Power of the whole Universe. God is in everything; God is in everyone.

Realizing that Love is the great motivating Power of Life, and knowing that God must be at the center of everything, today I am meeting this God in everyone, and seeing the manifestation of His Life in everything.

If there is any condemnation or animosity in me, I

gladly loose it. I loose it and let it go as I turn to that silent Presence within me which gives all and withholds nothing.

I enter into the harmony of Eternal Peace, into the joy of knowing that I am now in the Kingdom of God, from which no person is excluded. My yesterdays are gone forever, my tomorrows stretch forth into an endless future of pure delight. And from out of the Invisible there come to me these words: TODAY THOU ART WITH ME IN PARADISE.

The Will to Live

WE ARE told that we are born with a will to live and an almost equal will to die; that when we look forward to more pain and unhappiness than to peace and joy in living, the mind begins to destroy the body so we shall not have to suffer the pain we unconsciously anticipate.

The will to live and to be happy is necessary to our physical well-being. The more we study the way the mind works the more we realize that most of our physical ills, and perhaps all of our unhappiness, come from certain deep-rooted reactions to life that generally are built around the idea that we are not wanted or needed or loved. We feel some deep sense of guilt, and this gives rise to a feeling of insecurity and anxiety. Thus we reject ourself, and suffer because of this self-imposed condemnation.

So the morbid race goes on in the inner conflicts of the mind, until finally the frustration is so great that the mind begins to destroy the body because the impressions it has received are destructive. When this reaches a point where there is no longer a will to resist it, we say the person does not have the will to live and so even nature cannot restore him, and generally in such cases he passes on.

What we need is a deep, underlying faith or conviction about life that will remove this inner conflict and frustration and let the original Divine Pattern come to the surface, for we all are rooted in God, the Living Spirit. There would have to be Perfection at the center of our being or we should not be here. This is what Jesus meant when he said, *Be ye therefore perfect, even as your Father which is in heaven is perfect.*

Our roots run deep into the creative soil of the Infinite Mind, and if we had not stopped drawing straight from the roots of our being we should be all right.

The Science of Mind, under different names and schools and methods, recognizes this, and its endeavor is to find out where and when and how we started on the wrong path—the pathway that leads to destruction rather than life, the pathway that leads to unhappiness and frustration rather than joy through self-expression. Man is born to be happy, to live creatively, to love, to sing, to dance, and to express himself to the full. When he does not do this he feels unhappy, sad, and alone, and wishes he were dead—he no longer has the will to live.

We must find a method that can easily and quickly reach the seat of our trouble. Instead of probing the mind to see just where, when, and how this whole negative chain of destructive thoughts started, we can go back to that which is more fundamental. We can go back to God, the Creative Spirit, and say:

> *I was born of God. There is One Life, that Life is God, that Life is Perfect, that Life is my Life now. Nothing has interfered with that Life, nothing can interfere with it.*

And then:

> *I know that there is nothing in the Universe that holds anything against me.*

And following the thought of the Great Teacher, *Forgive, and ye shall be forgiven*, we can say:

> *I forgive myself. I forgive everyone else. The past is gone. It need no longer affect me. I know that God holds nothing against me, and if I have done anything to hurt others, or they have done anything to hurt me, I now forgive myself and them. Therefore I am conscious that I have complete clearance. There is no judgment, no condemnation.*

We must also know there is no fear. Perfect Love casts out all fear. Therefore we can say:

> *I have confidence in Life. I have a deep faith and a complete conviction that God is all there is and that I am wanted and needed and loved, not only by the Divine Spirit but by everyone I meet. I belong to Life, It belongs to me, and I am going to enter into It with joy. Life is ready to give me everything that is good, and I am ready to pass it on to others. I am a channel through which*

Good flows in every direction. Giving and receiving, and receiving and giving, the channel is never stopped.

We can say to ourselves:

I have no sense of insecurity or anxiety. I feel secure in God. I know that I will be guided and guarded and loved into fulfillment. I have no anxious thought for tomorrow, for I shall know what to do when tomorrow comes. I shall be guided to know what to do. Having no morbid regrets over the past and no anxiety over the future, I live today as though God were all there is, because God is all there is. There is no other Power, no other Presence, and no other life.

Jesus knew what was in people's minds. He knew about what today we call the blocks and conflicts, the repressions, the inhibitions, which go under the names of inferiority complex, or superiority complex, or a sense of rejection or guilt. And he took people's minds straight back to Life and told them that it did not matter so much what had happened in the past because they could get a complete clearance from it. What mattered was that they should forgive themselves and others, know that they are forgiven, and that, no longer indulging in what is wrong, they would feel a new will to live surging up within them.

You remember how frequently Jesus spoke of the joy that was his and how he said that he had come that they might have life and have it more abundantly. He placed great emphasis on the will to live creatively and to enjoy life.

Jesus did not say that Life held anything against us, or condemned us, or judged us. He said that at any hour of the day we can get a complete clearance. This is what he meant in the parable of the laborers, where the man who came in at the eleventh hour received the same compensation as the ones who had labored all day, as though he were saying: ''What if you have been lurking in the dark or damp shadows of previous experience until you are so depressed that you don't know what to do because you are surrounded by darkness? The very moment you

step out into the sunshine you are in the light. Just place yourself in the position so that all shadows will be cast behind you,
so there will be nothing between you and the sun, and let its
warmth and energy fill you with a new will to live.''

No person has the will to live unless he feels that life is
worth living. And he cannot have a deep sense of the will to live
unless he feels that he is going to live forever somewhere. It is
impossible to divorce this will to live eternally, this belief that
we are immortal beings, from the best possible mental hygiene.
This is why Jesus laid so much emphasis on Eternal Life—that
there is always something worthwhile to look forward to. The
play has just begun and it will never end.

It has been my opportunity to consult with thousands of
people over a period of years, and my experience has taught me
that Carl Jung was right when he said he had never yet seen one
single permanent healing from neurosis without a restoration of
spiritual faith, and that it is impossible to get the most out of
life while we are here unless we believe in immortality.

There is nothing complicated about this. We should stop
thinking it is so difficult to get our thought straightened out, and
begin to realize how easy it must be, for there is no mystery
about it. We know that thoughts are things, and we know that
our inward emotional reactions to our ways of thinking do produce inward psychic or mental diseases, which in turn give rise
to most of our physical afflictions. And we know that the reason
this happens is because our thoughts are based on the negative
rather than the positive, on fear rather than faith, on disappointment rather than fulfillment, and on all the other negative attitudes we could name.

We know that the battle for the right to live happily through
the will to live rightly is half won when we have correctly diag-
nosed the trouble. And if we have been walking down a road
that leads nowhere, where the trail runs out and stops, all we
have to do is reverse our steps and remember that the Power
which took us down the wrong road can just as easily lead us
back on the right one.

It takes less energy to live constructively than it does to live destructively. It takes no energy to have faith, while fear devastates such energy as we have. It takes no energy to love; it is hate that is destructive. It does not take mental or physical energy to be happy, but unhappiness and morbidity consume so much energy that it devitalizes us mentally and physically. It does not take mental or physical energy to build up hope; it is despair that blocks us. All it takes is faith.

It sometimes seems strange that Life should have delivered such Power into our keeping, such a will and imagination, and then let us alone to make the great discovery for ourselves. Sometimes we wonder why It did this, as though we were questioning the providence of God. But a little thought will show us that God never made any mistakes, and never can. This is the only way we could have been created as free people, for the very idea of freedom carries with it the obligations of ignorance and the rewards of understanding.

And now it is high time that we awake from our sleep and come back to a direct and intimate relationship to the Power greater than we are and to a Law of Good acting creatively on our prayers of affirmation, our meditations of faith, and our hymns of praise. The Science of Mind conspires with us because it has led us back through the dim and dark caverns of our own thinking to the original Source of our being, which it has hesitated to call God but which it knows is a Power greater than we are.

No one can travel the new road for us but ourselves. Science may put up a sign: *This is the way; walk in it.* But even as the Prodigal of old remembered who he was and resolutely turned his steps homeward, so must we decide that Life is for us and not against us and, turning from everything that denies this, take our journey into the Promised Land.

Spiritual Conviction
Is Essential

A MAN without a spiritual conviction cannot hope to make the same use of the Creative Power of his thought as the one who has it. We must deliberately play with the idea that the Kingdom of Heaven is at hand, that the Kingdom of God is within.

We must reorganize our thought on this basis, taking as our central theme the conviction that pure Spirit is ever at the center of our being. We should keep the door of our thought open to the Invisible Guest who would enter and sup with us; to that *I AM* which is the Resurrection and the Life.

Jesus intimated that one may pass from death into life even while in the flesh. One may die from one experience and be born into another in this world. We are learning how to do this by mentally letting go of the old and taking hold of the new.

Our mental vision must be guided by the star of hope and not the illusion of despair. We are to know that the Spirit triumphs over everything, Love is all-conquering, Joy becomes supreme.

We could not have a more definite statement or a more direct teaching. Wherever the mental vision is set, there at the end of that vision is either freedom or bondage, joy or grief. If our concept of Love and our belief in Its beneficent presence is greater than our fear of Its opposite, we shall win.

The mental argument is within our own minds. We alone are the arbiters of our fate. Fate becomes not a thing of itself but a certain use of the Law, and we are to use this Law in Love, in faith, with confidence. The Spirit is Love, Joy, Peace!

The awakening of our thought to the Divinity within us should not be a dreary process but a joyous one. There should be great spontaneity in it, a sense of exhilaration and jubilation. Thus alone can Life more abundant enter into us.

The Principle
of Divine Guidance

NOTHING IS more important than the realization that
since we are surrounded by Infinite Intelligence we are immersed
in Limitless Wisdom. Emerson tells us that human history is
the working of the Infinite Mind on this planet.

We are, of necessity, inlets to the Divine Mind, but since we
are individuals we become outlets to the degree that we permit
ourselves to become. We are surrounded by Divine Wisdom,
Love, and Intelligence, and still lack Divine Guidance. Not that
we lack the Principle of Divine Guidance, for that is the gift of
God forever made and forever delivered, but that we lack the
perception of this Guidance and Its operation through us.

Principles of themselves do nothing in particular for the individual until they are specialized or used. The desert is made to
blossom as the rose when man cooperates with the principle of
productivity latent in the desert. Experience has taught us that
this cooperation must be conscious and definite. Moreover, it
has taught us that we must understand the Law with which we
are going to cooperate before we can draw upon It for special
results.

We are surrounded by a Principle of Mind and Intelligence
which will become Divine Guidance to us provided we permit
It to do so. Our part is to realize that Divine Guidance is a Principle, and to accept this Principle as operating in our everyday
life. The answer to every problem is in the problem itself. It is
usually so self-evident that its very obviousness conceals it.

So Divine Guidance is ours for the asking, and no matter
how crude that asking may be, or may have been in the history
of religious evolution, there has always been an answer. God has
answered every request at the level of the mentality from which
the request was made. When the scientist listens, the artist
imagines, the mathematician calculates, or the poet waits for

411

the muse to guide his fancy into word pictures, all are praying for Divine Guidance. Each in his own sphere of action receives as much Guidance as he is capable of perceiving.

Why not, then, consciously specialize this Law of Divine Guidance, for surely this would be a practical thing to do. It is not enough to believe that Divine Guidance can guide; we must know that Divine Intelligence is guiding. We must know that there are no mistakes in the Divine Plan, and we must know that we are some part of the Universal scheme of things.

According to our theory it is not enough merely to know this. For while we understand that Law is Mind in Action and that there is a Universal Law of Cause and Effect, we know that this same Law, working for us, is inhibited or accelerated in Its action through our faith and acceptance of It. Indeed this is one of the secrets of this science, and it is really no secret at all, for experience has taught us that this is true of every law of nature. We must understand a law before we can make conscious use of it.

We must specialize any law which we wish consciously to use, and the Principle of Divine Guidance is no exception to this general rule. We must believe that there is a Divine Guidance, we must affirm that there is a Divine Guidance, and we must deny every tendency to disbelieve in Divine Guidance. If Law is Mind in Action, and if we specialize this Law through the activity of our thought, which we most certainly do, then we must consciously know that we are daily guided and directed into right action. We must know that there is an Intelligence which goes before us and makes our way plain and immediate.

Whenever any problem confronts you, take it into the silence of your own contemplation and declare that there is no problem; that you already know the answer. Dissolve the belief in the problem and announce the belief in the answer. Mentally act as though the problem were an argument trying to convince you that you do not know the answer, and then through the conscious activity of your thought destroy the argument either by picking it apart a bit at a time until there is nothing left, or by the complete realization that dissipates it as the sun dissipates the mist.

When you dissolve the problem and seek Divine Guidance you are announcing that there is no problem. Announce that there is a complete answer and that this answer is made known to your mind right now, today. In this way you wait upon your Indwelling Lord, the Supreme One, the Creator and the Sustainer of your destiny.

Divine Guidance is just as definite a Principle in the Universe as is the Law of Attraction and Repulsion. Your use of Divine Guidance must be just as conscious as an architect drawing a plan; just as certain as a mathematician solving a problem; and the answer is just as definite.

GOD AND COMPANY

It is evident from the foregoing conclusion, relative to the Principle of Divine Guidance and our use of It, that we are in partnership with the Infinite Mind, and the name of this partnership is *God and Company*—God standing for the Supreme Intelligence, the Universal Creative Order, the Dynamic Law, and the All-Perfect Presence. This is God, the senior partner. We are the company. This partnership cannot be dissolved, although it may appear to be dissolved.

We must feel that we are in league with the Universe, and that this company with which we do business, having its center everywhere and its circumference nowhere, that is, being Omnipresent, is localized wherever *thought* and *consciousness* function. Wherever we place our attention, there this company is doing business.

Wherever this company does business there is activity. We must learn that the activity of right ideas is not only the Father's business, but likewise the business of the Son. The individual mind and the Parent Mind are "One," and to whatever point we turn our mental attention, at that point the firm of God and Company establishes a branch which is certain to be successful.

Since there is no competition God and Company has no competitors. There are no other goods so perfect as those they manufacture, there are no other patterns so attractive, there is no

413

other machinery so perfect and efficient. God and Company, therefore, never deals with competition but always with completeness, and wherever our thought is, there this Company establishes its branch. In each branch it carries an entire stock of the Divine Goods, and we need have no fear that any one person has a monopoly on any of these Divine Goods.

What mathematician would deny us the privilege of using the principle that two and two make four? Or what musician would claim that some note which he struck used up all harmony? The mathematician uses the principle of mathematics and the musician uses the principle of harmony. A principle is that which, no matter how much it is used, is neither less nor more than it was. It always refuses to be anything except that which it is, and it is what it was, and it was what it is, and when tomorrow comes it will still be that which it is. Hence, what it was it is, and what it is it will remain.

Wherever our attention is set, there God and Company is doing business, and at that point business is good because God is Good. To know this is to know the Truth about one's business, to understand what is really true about one's profession, and to know what activity really means.

Who would attempt to dissolve such a Divine Partnership as this? Surely no sane person. If we have a business which has no competitors and over which there is no monopoly, and if we have a business that is always good because it is always active, and if we have the intelligence to run this business, and if this business is really the business of living, then we are indeed successful.

In actual practice we must claim this Divine Partnership; we must claim that we are members of this firm of God and Company, and we must never deny it. We must learn to counsel with this silent Partner of ours and we must state that business is good, that the business of life is active, it is happy, it is whole. Therefore we come to the other proposition, which is that of transferring the burden of life—lifting the load.

LIFTING THE LOAD

THE BURDEN of life arises from the belief that we have neither the power nor the intelligence to solve our problems. But if we realize that our Partner, the Law, makes things of Itself by Itself becoming the thing It makes, we shall know that no matter what undesirable facts may be manifesting themselves in our present experience, the Law can dissolve them for us.

We transfer the problem into the Divine Ideal. If anyone should ask us how the Divine Intelligence is going to recognize our small problem, our answer would be that the Divine works through the Universal Law of Cause and Effect.

Whoever specializes this Law will find that he can transfer the burden of personal responsibility to the Law, and that the Law will work for him as an individual on the pattern of his thought, just as It works in the rest of the Cosmos. It does not do this because It likes one person better than another, but because it is Its nature to do so.

Again we must remember that the Law knows neither big nor little. It knows only to do. Because the Word sets the Law in motion, and because we can speak the Word, we know we can use the Law. For as Universal as this Law is, It is also particularized through us; It specializes Itself at our request and flows through our thought into performance.

In making practical use of this we must realize that our word is Law. Hence our word of expansion means expansion, and our word of contraction means contraction. If we use the Law as limitation it is not the fault of the Law; it is the way in which we have used It. If we get a clear idea of how the Law of Cause and Effect works we shall see that our word specializes the Law in a unique and individual way—in a personal manner.

We transfer the burden, passing it over, as it were, to the Law governing our Divine Partnership, and we rely upon Divine Guidance to speak the right Word into the Law. The Word of Trust executes Itself. Our acknowledgment of Good becomes the Good which we acknowledge. We are told that the Word of God is faithful and true. Paul speaks of "the sword of the Spirit, which is the Word of God.'' Or we may think of the Word as protection—*His truth shall be thy shield and buckler.*

The Word of Truth is based upon the changeless Principle of Reality. We are told in Psalm 33:6: *By the word of the Lord were the heavens made.* This means the passing of the Word, through action, into form. Naturally, then, we transfer the burden of individual responsibility into the Law of Right Action.

We start with the proposition that the Word is the Power back of the thing; that words actually produce conditions, and that the Law flows from the Word. And if the Law flows from the Word, and if Divine Guidance compels us to speak the right word, and if our Divine Partnership can never be dissolved, then surely the load of life is lifted, and we may pursue our way in quietness and in confidence.

However, we must always be sure that this word is in harmony with Eternal Reality, for when we transfer our burden into the Law we are setting Cause and Effect in motion. And if we wish to experience only that which is Good, our use of the Law must be Good. This is but another way of saying that the Universe is foolproof.

But how are we to know when we are speaking the Word of God? There is only one way of knowing: Is our word harmonious? If we are sure there is nothing in it which has an element of hurt, hate, fear, limitation, or destructiveness of any nature, then it is self-evident that we are speaking the Word of God, and we may rest in absolute reliance upon the outcome.

The more we study the nature of these Principles the more convinced we are that they are true; that they are the statements of the great Law of Cause and Effect which the illumined of the ages have proclaimed. They are not true because the illumined have announced them, but, because they were true, the spiritually minded have perceived them.

Thus our Divine Partnership with Its Divine Guidance transfers the burden and lifts the load of life. Our part is to plant the right seed; to know that the Law flows from the Word; to know that the Word is the starting point of every creation; to know that ideas are things; to know that the entire physical universe is a thing of thought. And when we have transferred the burden into the Law, and when we have consigned our own soul to Peace, we shall have a new interest and a fresh outlook, for we shall be entering into the spirit of Life, into the livingness of Life, and into the Joy of that livingness.

In our individual world we have the power and the knowledge to create these individual experiences which make life worthwhile. And there is no limit to the evolution of these experiences, for one conclusion will lead to another. This is the symbolism of the octave, which means that the end of any particular creative series is but the beginning of a new creative series.

There is in each one of us the will to live, to enjoy, to express and to unfold; this will is Divine, and our will is in partnership with this Divine Will, and our mind with this Divine Mind. Thus we expect and believe that all Good shall come to us.

As we transfer the load, a new meaning comes into life, a more spontaneous self-expression; sadness gives place to joy, and confusion surrenders itself to peace. Action robbed of friction moves without fatigue, and the endless drama of life presents us with inspiring scenes and ever-moving experiences. This is the New Heaven and the New Earth. And when that final transference shall take place from this world into the next, we shall exclaim, "Into Thy hands I commend my spirit."

What Do We Mean by *The Silence?*

IN THE metaphysical world you frequently hear people speak of going into *the silence.* Naturally, one wonders what is meant by *the silence*, and if there is one thing we must avoid it is confusion. To make plain the few simple facts of the Science of Mind, to deliver a simple and definite technique for its practice, and at the same time to give proper spiritual value to such practice, is your whole aim and purpose in studying one of the finest of all arts—the art of spiritual mind healing.

Very frequently people will say to you, "What is meant by the silence?" Or they might say, "I have been reading how to go into the silence," and you will need to explain to them that the very idea that it is necessary to go into some place called *the silence* is itself confusing. With great patience you will find it necessary to point to the simple and direct approach to Principle, and particularly to the necessity of maintaining a self-conscious state at all times.

All life is in motion, or at least all manifest life is in a state of vibration. But at the very center of this vibration there appears to be something which is motionless, something which itself does not move and yet from which all motion must come. We can liken this to the Creator and His Creation, to the artist and his art, or to the thinker and his thought.

The thinker exists before his thought, the Creator exists before any particular creation, and within all action there evidently is a Principle which does not move. We might state it this way: God does not move, but movement takes place within God. Spirit does not move anywhere, but all particular *wheres* exist in Spirit.

Going into *the silence* does not mean that either our mental or our physical reactions are obliterated, for if they were we should pass into oblivion. We are not trying to discover how to be less ourselves, but how to be more ourselves.

418

Jesus gave a good example of going into *the silence* when he told us that in prayer we should enter the closet and close the door. It is evident that he was not referring to any real objective closet. He could not have been referring to any particular phys ical space, walled in like a small room. His language was sym bolic. Entering the closet means withdrawing into one's own mind. For it is from one's own mind that the creativeness which one possesses emanates.

The closet has been referred to as the Secret Place of the Most High, the Holy of Holies, and the Tabernacle of the Al mighty, and typifies the silent processes of nature. The creative principle in plant life is silent; all processes of nature are silent. The Invisible Cause is always silent. Expansion and self-expres sion are always the loosing of an energy which already exists at the center of the evolving or expressing medium or vehicle.

To enter one's closet is to put aside the external confusion, the clash of will and intention, to judge not from outward appear ances but from inward tranquillity. The Chinese sage said that all things are possible to him who can perfectly practice inac tion, which is but another way of saying, *Be still and know that I am God.* We are told that God is not in the wind nor in the earthquake, but in the Still, Small Voice.

It is evident that the closet is not a place of mental and spiritual oblivion, for a movement of consciousness still takes place. He who practices this movement of consciousness in *the silence* is practicing the inaction from which action flows. To *Be still and know that I am God* is to enter the sanctuary of one's own consciousness. From this center the issues of life pro ceed. *Keep thy heart [mind] with all diligence; for out of it are the issues of life.*

Here in our Secret Place of the Most High, the inner cham ber of our own soul, are written the sacred words: *I AM.* It is from this consciousness, this *I AM*, conceived in silent recog nition, that Power flows.

It was said that only the high priest could enter the sacred precinct. The high priest symbolizes our own Divine Self. That which belongs to external causation must be left outside, for we shall never discover the true Creative Cause while we are limiting It to any existing effect. We do not judge righteously when we judge according to appearances only. We must enter the closet and close the door. Our mental gaze is to be upward and inward and not external, for this is the secret of the Secret Place of the Most High.

Next we are told that having entered this Secret Place, and having closed the door, and having temporarily shut out external appearances, which means all created facts and every circumstance whatsoever (and do not forget that this shutting out includes both sin and sinner, all erroneous cause and effect and any and every idea which denies the Unity of Good)—having entered this Secret Place, and having closed the door, we have entered into *the silence*. This is what *the silence* means. We are still alive, awake, and aware. We are still conscious, and consciously conscious. We are not less but more ourselves. We have more consciously entered that place of inaction from which action proceeds. It is certain that we enter the Absolute in such degree as we withdraw from the relative, and vice versa.

The next step, we are told, is to *make known our requests in secret.* It is evident, then, that this Secret Place of the Most High, this Tabernacle of the Almighty, this inner chamber, is not a place where we pass into unconsciousness. Nor is it a place where our consciousness ceases to operate as an individual entity.

We are told that whatsoever things we desire, we are to make known, implying as it certainly does the highest possible degree of specialization and conscious use of the Law. We are to make known our requests in secret to *the Father which seeth in secret.* This Father, of course, represents the eternal Principle of the ever-present Mind, the Parent Mind, the Originating Creative Intelligence in the Universe.

We are to bring our petitions, our thoughts, and our desires to some place in our consciousness symbolized as the closet and as the Secret Place of the Most High, where Absolute Causation exists, unconditioned by any existing fact or circumstance. Good and bad have disappeared; big and little have melted into Unity. The Creative Cause receives our desire at first hand, directly, completely.

We have brought no contradictions, no denials, no fears, no sense of lack or limitation into this silence. The unconditioned Cause receives the imprint of our thought exactly as we formulate it. This is the Father which seeth in secret, the secret process of nature, the silent Power projecting Itself through nature, the invisible Presence, the unseen Host whose guests we are.

Jesus nowhere implied that the Father is likely to refuse our request. In the parable of the Prodigal Son we are told that the Father saw the son afar off and advanced to meet him. So we have this beautiful symbolism of the Father turning to us as we turn to Him. The Creative Principle, which sees and receives in secret, rewards us openly. What is this but a statement of the invisible Law of Cause and Effect, the silent process of nature honoring our requests?

This does not constitute the entire teaching of Jesus, for he also said that it is useless to bring our gifts to the altar while we have anything in our consciousness against our brother. This we could interpret to mean while we have any pettiness, animosity, hate, fear, or any other attitude which tends to draw the veil before the face of Reality. It is but another way of saying that Love alone can beget Love, that if we wish to have joy we must give it; it is a subtle pronouncement of the Law of Cause and Effect.

When we have complied with the conditions of Love, Harmony, and Unity, whatsoever requests we make are to be honored, even the requests for happiness, health, success, and friendship. The Great Teacher never denied man the privilege of enjoying the life he lives. He affirmed that he would always enjoy it if he were always in tune with Reality. Therefore, whatsoever things we desire, the Father which seeth in secret does give us openly. That is, the silent creative process of nature, which we employ in giving a mental treatment, projects actual, tangible, visible effects, gives birth to form, and creates after the pattern and the type of the thought we entertain.

It is good for us to have these thoughts clearly in mind, and it is good for us to teach those who come to us that *the silence* is not some peculiar, strange place which we arrive at either by

421

fasting or by feasting. It is any moment in our experience, day or night, when the mind realizes its Unity with Good, its Oneness with *the Father which seeth in secret.*

Sometimes we enter this silence in a momentary flash of consciousness. Sometimes we travel laboriously toward it. Sometimes we seem to miss it. But at all times we should be conscious of its existence. Nor should we ever fall into the mistaken idea that there is any secret way to Reality. All ways are good ways. But our way must be our way and not the way of someone else. The approach is direct and conscious. We need not hesitate to bring our requests, to make them known, to enumerate them.

Good is not withheld from anyone, but ignorance of the Law excuses no one from Its use or Its abuse. Anything is good to have provided it harms no other person but helps our own self-expression. Whatsoever things we desire we are to receive.

Suppose we had a friend who never refused our petitions, who always had the power to grant our requests; someone strong, affluent, and self-sufficient, who had at his disposal infinite resources so that he could honor our requests. And suppose his greatest desire was to benefit us. Should we not feel fortunate indeed?

Further, let us suppose that the only condition this friend imposes on us is that everything he gives us is to be used for constructive purposes. And suppose he promises us that if we use all these gifts for constructive purposes alone no harm should ever come to us—suppose he guarantees us absolute protection. Should we not feel him the most wonderful of all friends?

This is exactly the principle which Jesus laid before us when he said to enter into the closet of our own consciousness and make known our requests in secret to that Father which seeing in secret rewards us openly. Should we not consider this the greatest of all gifts, and should we not consider our approach to it the most fascinating of all experiments?

On the other hand, suppose our friend laid down the condition that we must come and take the gift. And that we could not take it unless we first believed that he fully intended to give it to us, and that he already had made the gift but we must receive it. Even this would not be difficult for us to understand, for we should immediately say to ourselves, "Why, of course, if my friend has made the gift I must receive it. He cannot force me to take it. The gift cannot be complete without a receiver. Someone must receive the gift." We should not hesitate to receive the gift, and this is exactly the position we are in relative to the Universal Creative Mind and Intelligence. The gift awaits our taking.

Certain natural and necessary restrictions are laid upon us. They are merely those restrictions that keep us from using the gift destructively. They are not restrictions of limitation or of bondage. They are merely such restrictions as must necessarily be consistent with a Universe of Law, of Order, of Harmony, of Unity, and of Love. We cannot consider them as being restrictions, since we know that Peace, Joy, and Happiness go with the gift. Surely, if we had a friend who was such a giver we should think of him as being no less than Divine.

Now suppose we take a closer and more intimate viewpoint of this Friend and think of Him as being at the center of our own life, at the very center of our own thought and consciousness; think of Him as being the very Presence and Intelligence by which we think, so that we do not have to go out to find Him; He is always at home and His home is within our own souls. Should we not feel that we have the most wonderful Companion imaginable? Should we not spend some time in daily communion with this Companion? Leaving all external confusion and fear outside, should we not enter this Holy of Holies and, meditating before the Ark of the Covenant, should we not reach in, unroll the scroll, and read from it the Divine message: *Before they call, I will answer; and while they are yet speaking, I will hear* (Isaiah 65:24)—?

The Great Surrender

EVERY MAN'S search is for something that will make him whole and happy, something that will cause him to feel safe and secure, and, we believe, something that will make him certain that he is going to live forever somewhere. We cannot believe that the Divine Intelligence which created everything, including ourselves, could possibly have done so without at the same time providing a way for us to live as happy and whole human and Divine beings.

Jesus said that he was the Way, the Truth, and the Life. He had discovered the secret which delivered to him all Life, Love, and Power. This Life, this Love, and this Power is what he taught. Since he so completely proved his Power, it is wise for us to follow the rules he laid down for us. He stated one of these rules when he said, *he that loseth his life for my sake, shall find it.*

At first this seems like a hard and strange thing to do. None of us wishes to lose his life. It cannot be possible that Jesus meant that we should literally lose our lives, but rather that there must be things in our lives that we should let go of. There must be something that is attached to us that does not belong to the Real Man. And so we should seek to find the fundamental Truth that he taught.

If we do this we shall find that the thing Jesus laid the greatest emphasis on was the idea that we are Spiritual Beings living in a Spiritual Universe, right *now*; that God, the Supreme Spirit and Intelligence in the Universe, and the Power that governs everything, is not some far-off Presence; It is something that is immediate, a Presence that is here with us *now*. He said that this Presence is not only with us but *within* us; we live in It and It moves through us.

When Jesus said that we must lose our lives he must have been referring to that part of us which denies this Supreme Presence, that part of us which lives contrary to It, that part of us which is out of harmony with It. He was telling us that there

424

are certain things we have to surrender before we can find our true center, the Real Spirit or the Perfect Man which he always assumed to be there.

Jesus said, *Blessed are the meek: for they shall inherit the earth.* This sounds as though he were telling us that we cannot inherit the Kingdom of God until we renounce the kingdom of man. Yet we find him multiplying the loaves and fishes when the multitude was hungry. He turned water into wine at the wedding feast, and in every way seemed to meet human needs whenever they arose.

So, even in teaching us that we must surrender something, he was not telling us that we should live in poverty or limitation. What he was saying is that when we put our trust in external things alone we are certain to become disillusioned, for a person may have a fortune one day and lose it the next; he may have a position of high power and suddenly lose all public acclaim.

Jesus was telling us something more real than this, but something which contained everything necessary to living in this world. For he knew that we need food and clothing and shelter. He was not saying that the Divine Will imposes suffering upon us, but rather that when we fail to live in accord with the Divine we bring suffering on ourselves.

So we see that losing our lives, or making the great surrender to the Spirit, does not mean losing anything worthwhile, but getting rid of those things which deny the Presence and the Power of the Spirit right here on earth. It is the great negations of life that we have to surrender, the doubts and fears and uncertainties, the coldness and unkindness, the lack of love.

All of these negative things Jesus called sins. But the word *sin* has been misinterpreted and misconstrued, for the original meaning of sin was to miss the mark, to make a mistake, to err in judgment, or to do something that separates us from the conscious daily realization that we already are One with the Supreme Giver of life.

God is Love and we cannot get close to the nature of Love while we hate. It is the hate we have to surrender and not the

Love. When Jesus said you have to lose your life to find it he was saying: You have to lose your hate if you wish to find Love; you have to let go of everything that is unkind if you wish to discover kindness; you even have to surrender fear if you wish to discover faith. Everything that denies faith and Love and Life and Truth and Beauty Jesus called a sin, a mistake, missing the mark.

It is not easy to make this surrender, because we are in the habit of thinking of ourselves as being such strong, self-reliant personalities that we can sweep everything before us. It is not easy to be meek.

But again we should examine the meaning of meekness. While we do not find any arrogance in the life of Jesus, we find a terrific strength of character, a will to accomplish what he set out to do, a determination to fulfill his mission. When he said that the meek shall inherit the earth, he was not saying that we have to be wishy-washy or willy-nilly, but that in true meekness we should recognize that all Power finally rests in the Spirit.

To be meek is to be humble before the Truth. A person is truly meek or humble when he looks upon the grandeur of a mountain or considers the vastness of the ocean or thinks about the bigness of things. He does not become lost in this bigness or this grandeur, but he does stand in awe before it. When he does this something deep within him responds, something within him embraces the ocean, something within him melts into the mountain, and he becomes one with them. This is true meekness.

Jesus said, *Blessed are they that do hunger and thirst after righteousness: for they shall be filled.* Everyone longs to be made whole; everyone hungers and thirsts after peace and joy. Jesus used the expression *hunger and thirst* because everyone knows how it feels to be hungry and thirsty. When we are hungry we go in search of food. When we are thirsty we look for water. There is a deep hunger in everyone, a deep thirst after another kind of food and another kind of drink, which Jesus said is not only natural but necessary to man. For he said that man does not live by bread alone, but by every word that proceedeth from the mouth of God.

Consider how the scientific mind hungers after knowledge. The scientist feels incomplete until he has wrested the secrets of nature from the invisible and brought them forth into realities. But in his search he has to surrender all personal opinion, all arrogant attitudes of mind, and in true meekness follow the scientific pathway which leads to the discovery of a principle in nature that he inherits after he has first surrendered himself to it.

No one makes a greater surrender than the scientist, for he is always willing to be led by the Truth no matter what path It seems to take. Truth and science in many ways mean the same thing, for all scientific research is a process of seeking out the laws of nature, discovering how they work, and then subjecting the individual will to the way they work. It is in this way alone that science makes progress. This is always the path that it follows.

We all hunger and thirst after Love because we feel incomplete without It. But have we looked into the nature of Love? Have we followed the method that science, which is a search after Truth, finds necessary? We hunger and thirst after Love, but how often do we follow another thought of Jesus when he said, *Greater love hath no man than this, that a man lay down his life for his friends—?*

We cannot suppose that Jesus meant that we should give up our lives, because this would serve no good purpose. He must have meant that we lay down everything that constitutes the great unreality, the great lie, the great separation. Love is kind, and we must lay down all unkindness before we can discover Love.

We want peace of mind and an inward sense of security, but are we willing to follow another teaching of Jesus in which he said, *But I say unto you, That ye resist not evil. . .?* We are full of resistance and combativeness and antagonism. And the reason we are over-aggressive is because we feel insecure. We put up a great big bluff and make a big noise and throw ourselves around because of this feeling of insecurity.

Resist not evil. We wonder if Jesus knew what he was talking about until we discover the secret, which is simplicity itself.

When we resist we make that thing real in our imagination which we are sincerely trying to get rid of. We become a house divided against itself, which Jesus said cannot stand. True non-resistance is the surrender of every arrogant attitude of mind to Good, and Good alone. Those who have made this surrender have found real peace of mind, happiness, and wholeness in the only place where it can be found, which is within themselves.

Perhaps Jesus was teaching the greatest surrender of all when he said, *Fear not, little flock, for it is your Father's good pleasure to give you the kingdom.* We have thought that we must work so hard to attain this Kingdom; there is so much we have to do about it. This has become such a burden on our minds, and we have gotten our little human selves so completely in the way, that the Kingdom which was given cannot be accepted. Life is the gift of God and not of man. That is why Jesus said that no man has the Power to give it or to take it away. Are we willing to let go of this inflated ego of ours, this gigantic make-believe, this mask we wear, this camouflage, and in simplicity accept Life?

Jesus taught another thing that has to do with the great surrender. He said we must become as little children. How difficult it is for us to become as a child! Yet every searcher after scientific truths knows that he must become as a little child if he wishes to unlock the secrets of nature and find the true cause of things.

The intellect is apt to get in the way of faith, for while the logic of faith may be of the intellect, its essence and meaning are in the childlike heart. We must be born into the Kingdom of God, in a certain sense, just as we were born into the human kingdom from the great mother heart of Love and Life.

Jesus taught that the great Reality of Life is Love, but the way this Reality works is through Law, and every man must reap as he sows. So he put before us the two great possibilities of life and asked this question: Wilt thou be made whole? If so, follow the Divine Light that I have revealed to you and you will discover It within yourself. There in the Secret Place of the Most High you shall abide under the shadow of the Almighty.

Self-Awareness Is Not Enough

LET'S TALK about the need for meeting situations as they come along, without fear and without in any way trying to avoid them. For every issue of life must be met right where it is, and what is wrong must be made right.

This coming to understand our psychological difficulties, and how to clear the passageway in order that the original Source of Life may flow through us unobstructed, in its broadest sense is called *self-awareness*. It means a clearing-up in the mind of the unconscious repressions and conflicts which are so deeply buried that we are aware of them only because they re-echo in everything we do, say, and think. Coming to one's self, coming to awareness, coming to understand why and how we started on the wrong path emotionally, explaining this to the self—this is what is meant by self-awareness.

But self-awareness alone is not enough, for this reason: There is an incessant urge back of everything to create, to express life, to come to the gratification of happiness, peace, joy, and self-expression. Self-awareness is not enough. It is merely clearing the track for right action. Something has to be done with self-awareness. We are not seeking a way to escape from life or living, for this would be the exact opposite of the whole purpose of existence, which is to express the self.

We have hands and feet as well as a mind, and, unless the hands and feet are employed, together with all our other faculties, we shall not come into complete self-expression. This is why physical therapeutics is used. People are told to do something with their hands and feet, to paint pictures or write poems or songs, to learn to dance, to have a hobby, to play golf, to enjoy life; all of which means entering into the spirit of living and being some part of it.

Self-awareness without self-expression can almost as readily produce emotional disturbances as can the lack of self-awareness. It can easily become another frustration, causing the mind to continually revert to itself and become self-centered.

Life must be expansive and expressive. One is not happy unless one has a purpose in living.

Too frequently older people become frustrated because there is no longer anything to engage their attention. They must find something to take up their time, whether it be gardening or calling on the sick or helping to take care of someone's children. Any activity that engages the attention and produces the gratification of outward self-expression is not only good, but necessary.

We do not teach people to sit still and monotonously repeat "God is all there is," for, while it is true that God is all there is, it is also true that God is everything that is. The Creative Genius of the Universe goes forth into action everywhere. There is no monotony in nature. The individual life must avoid monotony and self-centeredness through self-expression.

Consequently, after we have come to self-awareness we must start expressing again, no matter what our age. Engage in the joy of living, and do it with others. The well-integrated person gets along with other people, not by tolerance but through cooperation. This is the game of life and it must be played.

Happiness

Do you wish to be happy? This is a foolish question, for who would not be happy? Someone has said that we used to think we had to be well in order to be happy, but now we know that we must be happy if we wish to be well.

Happiness must be based on an inward sense of security, a sense of belonging to life and to each other; a desire to give, to be kind and compassionate, and to be able to put ourselves in the other person's position.

Most of our unhappiness comes from our relationships with others. If we cannot be happy unless some other individual or some group of individuals admires and loves us, we have not yet realized that every person is complete within himself. For when we reach back to the true Self, which is God in us, we shall have penetrated to the innermost depths of all people.

Happiness is never external. All the money in the world will not make a person happy. The highest position of dignity or trust cannot make one happy. Jesus stated it this way: *For what shall it profit a man, if he shall gain the whole world, and lose his own soul?* (Mark 8:36). Of course he was not referring to any actual loss of the soul, because the soul is the incarnation of the Spirit within. *Hid with Christ in God* means that we trace the human back to its Divine Source, which is God, and rest in the security of being enfolded in Infinite Love and Wisdom, and kept by an Infinite Law of Good.

It is true that we cannot be well unless we are mentally and emotionally happy. To a much greater extent than we realize, the physical body reflects our mental attitude. Our food neither digests nor assimilates properly when we are filled with unhappiness and fear. The stream of Life flows fully and freely from the innermost recesses of our being only when we are happy.

Children are happy because they have not learned to be afraid; there can be no happiness where fear is.

Blest the children playing on the shore,
To them belongs the Pipe of Pan;
The song of surf, the waves' uproar,
The fog, the wind, and freckled tan.

No thought of care, no gain to reap,
No fear of darkness, dread of night;
No dream of turmoil in their sleep,
Their evening star shines clear and bright.

With hearts o'erfilled with happy zest
And joy for what the new day will bring,
They lay them down in peace to rest;
At morn for them the lark will sing.

They hail the day with wild delight—
Their feet in naked gladness shod,
Their eyes with wonder gleaming bright.
"For of such is the kingdom of God."

Well did Jesus say that we must become as a little child if we would discover the kingdom of happiness. The child expects its parents to meet its needs, to provide for its comfort, and to give it love.

We are all children, not so much of a larger size as of a broader experience. There is a little boy or a little girl inside each one of us, a child just emerging from the unknown, meeting experiences, learning how to live. But too often the spontaneous joy is pressed back into the unconscious, where it still seeks the self-expression which it has been denied.

Why should we have to be so cold and indifferent, harsh and critical, or so troubled over living? It is because the child has been crucified on the cross of negative experience. And now we must retrace our steps, because the child in us will not be denied. The spontaneous joy of the child playing on the shore, the gladness of meeting the new day with the expectation of pleasure, and the quiet peace of rest at night, untroubled by inward conflicts—these are what we all long for. We must regain this lost ground if we are to have happiness, security, and peace.

This is what faith does for us. It makes no difference what form it takes as long as it is sincere. But even here the clearance will not be complete if we continue to worry over the question of salvation and the ultimate well-being of the soul. This, too, must have a clearance, a redemption, and a new birth. This is why Jesus told us that we must be born again, that we must become as little children.

Is it so hard, then, for the intellect to give up its vast accumulation of false knowledge based on a concept of separation from the original Source of its being? Somewhere along the line we shall be called on to make this surrender and again become as children. Our attempt to become happy will be futile without this. It matters not what we possess or what ambitions we entertain; we are so constituted that we are incomplete until we consciously unite ourselves with That which is Whole and Perfect.

Can we learn to surrender all our doubts and fears, our uncertainties and forebodings, and live our lives with enthusiasm, expectancy, and confidence? I venture to say that, could we learn to do this, our inner conflicts would dissipate themselves. Our prophetic feelings of evil would vanish, and we should be at peace with God, with ourselves, and with others.

Meditation

I KNOW there is a Power for Good which is responding to me and bringing into my experience everything that is necessary to my unfoldment, to my happiness, to my peace, to my health, and to my success. I know there is a Power for Good that enables me to help others and to bless the whole world.

So I say quietly to myself: There is one Life, that Life is God, that Life is perfect, that Life is my life now. It is flowing through me, circulating in me. I am one with Its rhythm. My heart beats with the pulsation of the Universe, in serenity, in peace, and in joy. My whole physical being is animated by the Divine Spirit, and if there is anything in it that does not belong, it is cast out because there is One Perfect Life in me now.

And I say to myself: I am daily guided so that I shall know what to do under every circumstance, in every situation. Divine Intelligence guides me in love, in joy, and in complete self-expression. Desiring that the Law of Good alone shall control me, I bless and prosper everything I am doing; I multiply every activity; I accept and expect happiness and complete success.

Realizing that I am one with all people, I affirm that there is a silent Power flowing through me and them, which blesses and heals and prospers, makes happy and glad their pathway.

And realizing that the world is made up of people like myself, I bless the world and affirm that it shall come under the Divine government of Good, under the Divine providence of Love, and under the Divine leadership of the Supreme Intelligence. *For thine is the kingdom, and the power, and the glory, for ever. Amen.*